"All medievalists will rejoice to see the publication of this final volume
of the English translation of the sermons of Aelred, abbot of Rievaulx
in Yorkshire (1110–1167), a project that has been years in the making.
As in the rest of the series, we meet Aelred at home, delivering these
talks in the chapter room, surrounded by the monks in his care. Most
of these talks were given on the major feast days of the church, of the
Blessed Virgin Mary, and of well-known saints. A few exceptions—two
sermons for abbots, two for nuns, three on Edward the Confessor, and
one on the martyred St. Katherine—may have been delivered outside
the monastery. The inclusion of the recently discovered sermon that
Aelred preached for the translation of the relics of St. Edward the
Confessor in Westminster Abbey in 1163 is particularly welcome."

— Jean Truax

CISTERCIAN FATHERS SERIES: NUMBER EIGHTY-SEVEN

Aelred of Rievaulx

The Liturgical Sermons
The Reading-Cluny Collection, 2 of 2
Sermons 134–182

Translated by
Daniel Griggs

and
A Sermon Upon the Translation of Saint Edward, Confessor
Translated by Tom Licence

Introduction by
Marjory Lange

Cistercian Publications
www.cistercianpublications.org

LITURGICAL PRESS
Collegeville, Minnesota
www.litpress.org

A Cistercian Publications title published by Liturgical Press

Cistercian Publications
Editorial Offices
161 Grosvenor Street
Athens, Ohio 45701
www.cistercianpublications.org

A translation of the critical edition by Aelredus Rievallensis, ed. Gaetano Raciti, *Corpus Christianorum, Continuatio Mediaevalis* (CCCM) 2C (Sermons LXXXV–CXXXIII). © Brepols Publishers, Turnhout, Belgium. All rights reserved. Used with permission.

The translation of the Sermon Upon the Translation of Saint Edward, Confessor is printed with the permission of *Cistercian Studies Quarterly*.

Biblical quotations are translated by Daniel Griggs. All rights reserved.

1   2   3   4   5   6   7   8   9

Library of Congress Cataloging-in-Publication Data

Names: Aelred, of Rievaulx, Saint, 1110–1167, author. | Griggs, Daniel K., translator. | Lange, Marjory E., writer of introduction. | Dutton, Marsha L., writer of introduction.
Title: The liturgical sermons : the Reading-Cluny Collection / Aelred of Rievaulx ; translated by Daniel Griggs ; introduction by Marjory Lange and Marsha L. Dutton.
Other titles: Sermons. Selections. English.
Description: Collegeville, Minnesota : Cistercian Publications, [2021] | Series: Cistercian Fathers series ; number eighty-one | Includes indexes. | Summary: "These volumes contain Aelred's ninety-eight liturgical sermons from the Reading-Cluny collection. For the most part, the collection follows the liturgical year. Volume 1 begins with three sermons for Advent and ends with five for Pentecost and three for the Solemnity of the Holy Trinity. Volume 2 begins with the Nativity of John the Baptist (June 24) and concludes with the Feast of All Saints"—Provided by publisher.
Identifiers: LCCN 2020032643 (print) | LCCN 2020032644 (ebook) | ISBN 9780879071813 (v. 1 ; paperback) | ISBN 9780879071875 (v. 2 ; paperback) | ISBN 9780879076795 (v. 1 ; epub) | ISBN 9780879076795 (v. 1 ; mobi) | ISBN 9780879076795 (v. 1 ; pdf) | ISBN 9780879073879 (v. 2 ; epub) | ISBN 9780879073879 (v. 2 ; mobi) | ISBN 9780879073879 (v. 2 ; pdf)
Subjects: LCSH: Catholic Church—Sermons. | Church year sermons. | Sermons, Latin—Translations into English.
Classification: LCC BX1756.A448 L59313 (print) | LCC BX1756.A448 (ebook) | DDC 252/.6—dc23
LC record available at https://lccn.loc.gov/2020032643
LC ebook record available at https://lccn.loc.gov/2020032644

Contents

Abbreviations

Acta SS	*Acta Sanctorum*
Ant	Antiphonae
CCCM	Corpus Christianorum, Continuatio Mediaevalis. Turnhout: Brepols.
CCSL	Corpus Christianorum, Series Latina. Turnhout: Brepols.
CF	Cistercian Fathers series
CO	Corpus Orationum. CCSL 160AH. Turnhout: Brepols, 1993–1994.
CP	Corpus Praefationum. CCSL 161D. Turnhout: Brepols, 1980.
CS	Cistercian Studies series
CSEL	Corpus Scriptorum Ecclesiasticorum Latinorum. Turnhout: Brepols.
CSQ	*Cistercian Studies Quarterly*
Ep(p)	Epistola(e)
GCS	*Griechische Christliche Schriftsteller*
Hesbert	René-Jean Hesbert, ed. *Antiphonale Missarum Sextuplux*. Rome: Herder, 1935.
Hom	Homilia
Hymn	Hymnus
Lit	*Litaniae*. Enzo Lodi, ed. *Enchiridion euchologicum fontium liturgicorum*. Rome: C.L.V.-Edizioni liturgiche, 1979.
Orat	Oratio

Orat div	*Orationes divinae ad repellendas malas cogitationes.* Placide Bruylants. *Les Oraisons du Missel Romain* 2. Louvain: Centre de documentation et d'information liturgiques, Abbaye du Mont César, 1952.
OS	Festivitate Omnium Sanctorum
PL	Patrologia Latina. Ed. J.-P. Migne. Paris, 1841–1855.
PLS	Patrologia Latina Supplement
Proverbia	Hans Walther. *Proverbia sententiaeque Latinitatis Medii ac Recensioris Aevi.* Göttingen: Vandenhoeck & Ruprecht, 1964, 1982.
Resp	Responsoria
Rhetorica	*Rhetorica ad Herennium*
SBOp	Sancti Bernardi Opera. Ed. J. Leclercq, H. M. Rochais, C. H. Talbot. Rome: Cistercienses, 1957–1977.
S(S)	Sermon(es)
SCh	Sources Chrétiennes. Paris: Les Éditions du Cerf.
Seq	Sequentiae
Tract	Tractatus

Works by Authors and Collections

Ambrose

Exp Ev Luc	*Expositio Euangelii Lucae*
Ex Ps	*Expositio psalmi*
H	*Hymnes.* Trans. and ed. Jacques Fontaine, et al. Paris: Cerf, 1992.

Augustine

Doc	*De Doctrina Christiana*
En in Ps	*Enarrationes in Psalmos*
Gen ad litt	*De Genesi ad litteram*
In Ep Ioh	*In Epistulam Iohannis ad Parthos*
Ioann	*Tractatus in Evangelium Ioannis*
Trin	*De Trinitate*

PsAugustine
Tract Ass   *Tractatus de Assumptione Beatae Mariae Virginis*

Gaufridus Babion
Sanc   Ad Sanctimoniales

Bede
Hom II   Homiliarum lib. II
Luc   In Luci Evangelium expositio
Marc   In Marci Evangelium expositio

Bernard of Clairvaux
Circ   Sermo in circumcisione Domini
Epi   Sermon in Epiphania Domini
Miss   Homiliae super "Missus est" in Laudibus Virginis Matris
PP   Sermo in festo SS apostolorum Petri et Pauli
SC   Sermons on the Song of Songs

Boethius
Cons   *Philosophiae consolatio*

PsBruno
Exp Heb   *Expositio in epistolam ad Hebraeos*

Cicero
Inv   *De Inventione*

Clemens Romanus
Ep ad Iac   Epistola ad Iacobum, ex Rufini interpretatione

Corpus Orationum
Def   Pro defunctis
Nat Dom   In Nativitate Domini
Pro pace   Postcommunio pro pace
Vig Nat JB   Vigilia Nativitatis Sancti Ioannis Baptistae

Corpus Praefationum (CP)
Pref Asc   Praefatio Ascensionis
Pref S Maria   Praefatio de S. Maria

Eusebius – Rufinus
Eccl hist   *Ecclesiastica Historia*

Glossa Ordinaria
Gal   In Galatas

Gregory I
Dial II   *Dialogues* libri II
In Ev   *Homilia in Evangelia*
In Ez   *Homilia in Ezechielem*
Mor   *Moralia in Iob*

René-Jean Hesbert
Ant
Agnes   Festo S. Agnetae
And   Festo S. Andreae
Anima   "Anima Mea"
Ass   Assumptione Sanctae Mariae
Ave   "Ave Regina"
Beata   "Beata Dei Genetrix"
Cath P   Festo cathedrae Beati Petri
Com apos   Communi apostolorum
Com conf   Communi unius Confessoris
Com mar   Communi unius martyris
Com virg   Communi virginum
Ded eccl   Dedicatione ecclesiae
Domus   "Haec est domus"
Epi   Epiphania Domini
Exal   "Exaltata es"
Felix   "Felix namque es"
Gen   "Genuit puerpera"
Glor   "Gloriosi principes"
Hod   "Hodie Maria Virgo"

Ioan	"Ioannes Apostolus"
Ioh	Festo St. Iohannes
Iste	"Iste sanctus"
Maior adv	Maior adventu
M Vir	"Maria virgo"
Nat Dom	Nativitate Domini
Nat gl	"Nativitas gloriosae"
Nat JB	In Nativitate et in Decollatione Sancti Ioannis Baptistae
Nat SM	Nativitate Sanctae Mariae
Nat tua	"Nativitas tua"
Oct apos	Octava apostolorum Petri et Pauli
OS	Festo Omnium Sanctorum
Pastor	"Tu es Pastor"
Paul	Fest Sancti Pauli
Pur	Purificatione Sanctae Mariae
Sab	Sabbato sancto
Senex	"Senex puerum"
Mart	Festo Sancti Martini
Mich	Festo Sancti Michaelis
Tota	"Tota pulchra"
Vas	"Tu es Vas"
Vig Mich	Vigiliarum in festivitate Sancti Michaelis die 29 septembre

Resp   *Responsoria*

Adduxi	"Adduxi vos"
Adorna	"Adorna thalamum"
Adv	Adventu Domini, Dominica IIIa
Ann	Annuntiatione Sanctae Mariae
Ass	Assumptione Sanctae Mariae
Beata	"Beata es Virgo"
Beata M	"Beata Mater"
Cath P	Festo Cathedra Beati Petri
Com con	Communi confessoris
Com virg	Communi virginum
Dere in Quad	"Derelinquit" in Quadragesima
Dom IV Quad	Dominica IV Quadragesimae

Dom in P	Dominica in Palmis
Exal	"Exaltata es"
Heb I Quad	Hebdomada 1a Quadragesimae
Hod	"Hodie Maria Virgo"
Hod nata	"Hodie nata est"
Iste	"Iste sanctus"
Nat Dom	Nativitate Domini
Nat SM	Nativitate Sanctae Mariae
Nut	"Ad nutum"
Orn	"Ornatam"
Pastor	"Tu es Pastor"
Paul	Fest Sancti Pauli
Plat	Plateae
Praecursor	Praecursor Domini
Quae de Sap	"Quae sunt in corde" de Sapientia
S Mart	Festo Sancti Martini
S Mich	Festo Sancti Michaelis
Spec	"Ista est speciosa"
Stirps	"Stirps Iesse"
Vas	"Tu es Vas"
Vidi	"Vidi speciosam"
Vig Cath	Officio vigiliarum in festo Sanctae Catharinae
Vig nat S Ed	Officio vigiliarum in festo Sancti Edwardi die 13 October

Hugh of Saint Victor

Ass	*Pro Assumptione Virginis.* In *L'œuvre.*
BMV	*De Beatae Mariae Virginitate.* In *L'œuvre.*
De sac	*De Sacramentis Christianae Fidei*
Egred	*Egredietur virga.* In *L'œuvre.*
L'œuvre	*L'oeuvre de Hugues de Saint-Victor.* Turnhout: Brepols, 2000.

Isidore of Seville

Ety	*Etymologiarum sive Originum.* Ed. Wallace Martin Lindsay.
Sent	*Sententiae*

Ivo of Chartres
Ann   *In Annuntiatione Beatae Mariae*

Jerome
Ep ad Aug   *Epistolae ad Augustinum* = Augustine, Ep 75.4
In Eccl   *In Ecclesiasten*
In Hab   *In Habacuc*
In Isa   *In Isaiam (Epitome explanationum in Isaiam Beati Hieronymi presbyteri).* Ed. Roger Gryson. Turnhout: Brepols, 2018.
In Matt   *In Mattheum*
Int nom   *Interpretatio Hebraicorum nominum.* CCSL 72.
Tract Ps   *Tractatus in Psalmos*

PsJerome
Brev in Pss   *Breviarium in Psalmos*

Johannes Diaconus
Vita S Greg   *Sancti Gregorii Magni vita*

Josephus
Bello   *De bello Iudaico*

Origen
Hom Exod   Homiliae in Exodum
Hom Gen   Homeliae in Genesim
Hom Ier   Homeliae in Ieremiam
Hom Lev   Homeliae in Leviticum
Hom Luc   Homeliae super Lucam
Hom Nave   Homeliae in Iesu Nave

PsOrigen
Hom Gen   Homeliae in Genesim

Paschasius Radbertus
De Ass   *De Assumptione Sanctae Mariae*

Sedulius
Pasc   *Paschalis Carmen*

Sulpicius Severus
Vita S Mart   *Vita Sancti Martini*

William of Saint-Thierry
Brev Com   *Brevis commentatio in Cantica*

Introduction

Marjory Lange

This volume completes the English translation of Aelred of Rievaulx's liturgical sermons. The first 182 were edited by Gaetano Raciti and published between 1983 and 2012 in three volumes of Brepols Publishers' Corpus Christianorum, Continuatio Mediaevalis series (CCCM).[1] The 49 sermons translated below (SS 134–82), comprise the second half of the 98 sermons in the Reading-Cluny Collection of Aelred's sermons,[2] the first half of which (SS 85–133) appeared in 2021 in Aelred of Rievaulx, *The Liturgical Sermons: The Reading-Cluny Collection*, Volume 4.1. The last sermon translated in the current volume was edited by Peter Jackson from the only manuscript in the Peterborough General Collection (UK), translated by Tom Licence, and published in *Cistercian Studies Quarterly* in 2005. Jackson has persuasively argued that it was the sermon Aelred

---

[1] Gaetano Raciti's critical editions of the 182 sermons in 5 collections of Aelred's liturgical sermons are published in 3 CCCM volumes: CCCM 2ABC (Turnhout: Brepols, 1983, 2001, 2012). Their English translations appear in 5 volumes: CF 58, 77, 80, 81, 87 (Kalamazoo, MI, and Collegeville, MN: Cistercian Publications, 2001, 2016, 2018, 2021, 2022).

[2] For a discussion of the origin and contents of the Reading-Cluny collection, see Gaetano Raciti, Introduction to *Sermones LXXXV–CLXXXII*, ed. Gaetano Raciti, CCCM 2C (Turnhout: Brepols, 2012), VII–XIV; Marjory Lange and Marsha Dutton, introduction to *Aelred of Rievaulx, The Liturgical Sermons: The Reading-Cluny Collection*, trans. Daniel Griggs, CF 81 (Collegeville, MN: Cistercian Publications, 2021), xxiii–xxvii.

wrote and preached at the 1163 Westminster translation of Saint Edward the Confessor.[3]

In all of these sermons Aelred renews the familiar by new ways of interpreting it and by presenting refreshed symbols, metaphoric connections, and clear language. At the same time, from time to time he judiciously recycles particularly powerful or beautiful material.[4] It seems safe to say that even someone familiar with the rest of Aelred's sermons may be surprised by what is to be found here.

Aelred's Audience

When Aelred preached, his usual audience was the members of his community, gathered in the familiar setting of the monastery's chapter room. For that reason, his liturgical sermons are better referred to as *chapter discourses*, to avoid the implication that they were preached from a pulpit during the liturgy. For the most part, they address Aelred's concerns for his monastic community, rather than those of an audience of secular priests or laypeople.[5]

Basil Pennington explains the setting for these discourses:

In those early days of the Cistercian Order, abbots were expected to speak to their monks in chapter every morning, commenting on the passage of Saint Benedict's *Rule for Monasteries* that had just been read in the chapter house in which the monks assembled immediately after the celebration of the office of Prime in church. In addition, they were required to preach to the whole community, including the lay brothers, on fifteen principal days of the

---

[3] Peter Jackson, "*In translacione sancti Edwardi confessoris*: The Lost Sermon by Aelred of Rievaulx Found?" CSQ 40, no. 1 (2005): 45–83; sermon ed. Peter Jackson, trans. Tom Licence, 65–83. The translation of this sermon is reprinted here by permission from *Cistercian Studies Quarterly* and from Peter Jackson.

[4] For a tabulation of the occasions of Aelred's known sermons, see Domenico Pezzini, "The Sermons of Aelred of Rievaulx," in *A Companion to Aelred of Rievaulx (1110–1167)*, ed. Marsha L. Dutton, Brill's Companions to the Christian Tradition 76 (Leiden: Brill Academic Publishers, 2017), 74–76.

[5] Michael Casey, "An Introduction to Ælred's Chapter Discourses," CSQ 45, no. 3 (2010): 280–81.

liturgical year as well as on the anniversary of the dedication of the monastery's church.[6]

Aelred himself alludes to the chapter room setting of his preaching in one of his late sermons: "We are all fed by a similar corporeal bread in the refectory, and by spiritual bread at the altar, but we shall be separated as we go out from the present chapter" (S 150.9).

Chapter-room preaching offered an intimacy that Fr. Chrysogonus Waddell has explained as intrinsic to much of medieval monastic preaching, intimacy created by both the shared monastic life of the audience and the setting:

> Their preaching took place within a closely knit family of brethren who shared the same ideals and enthusiasms and struggles. . . . Chapter room preaching was accordingly conditioned by the immediate milieu, so that even the "loftiest" discourse bore the marks of familiarity and intimacy. The special *cachet* of Cistercian preaching was perhaps encouraged, too, by the fact that, though based on texts drawn from the liturgy of the day, the preaching took place . . . in the chapter room, with the brethren seated shoulder to shoulder in a kind of circle of which the preacher formed a part.[7]

Shoulder to shoulder with the preacher part of the circle—so these discourses can also be referred to as "conferences." As Aelred addresses his community and asks questions of them, he can look around to see how well he is being heard. He can temper his words to the changing conditions of each day.

Aelred speaks often of his solicitude for his brothers' needs. In his *Pastoral Prayer*, he calls on God to assist him in his relationship with his monks: "Grant me a true and upright way of speaking

---

[6] Basil Pennington, Introduction to *The Liturgical Sermons: The First Clairvaux Collection, Advent–All Saints*, trans. Theodore Berkeley and Basil Pennington, CF 58 (Kalamazoo, MI: Cistercian Publications, 2001), 13–14 (hereafter CF 58).

[7] Chrysogonus Waddell, "The Liturgical Dimension of Twelfth-Century Cistercian Preaching," in *Medieval Monastic Preaching*, ed. Carolyn Muessig, Brill's Studies in Intellectual History, 90 (Leiden: Brill Academic Publishers, 1998), 339.

and an eloquence of mouth to build them up in *faith, hope, and love*, in chastity and humility, in patience and obedience, in fervor of spirit and devotion of mind."[8] He makes that concern specific to preaching in one sermon: "the one who speaks ought not to reflect so much on what he feels in himself as on what others may feel in themselves. For people listen willingly when what they hear from another they also feel in themselves" (S 33.5).[9] He opens another sermon by explaining how the preacher prepares for his task and giving some reasons for his occasional failures:

> It is no wonder, dear brothers, if today our prayer [*oratio*] does not proceed with the usual sweetness. For, as you know, the usual repose did not come before this sermon [*sermonem*]: prayer did not enliven it, reading did not strengthen it, and meditation did not adorn it. For a sermon to renew the speaker and build up the listener, it is necessary for repose to prepare, reading to build up, meditation to strengthen, and prayer to enlighten the mind of the speaker. You perceive, then, that I am particularly unprepared for this subject today. (S 73.1)[10]

He goes on to ask, "Can I raise my eyes, weary and stinging from the care and dust of outer things, to that bright heaven to which the blessed Mother of God climbed in such great splendor today?" (S 73.2). He continues with a powerful and beautifully crafted conference on Mary's Assumption.

Aelred's sermon-commentary on the *Prophetic Burdens of Isaiah* contains a thoughtful passage about the preacher's awareness

---

[8] *Oratio pastoralis* 7; *For Your Own People: Aelred's* Pastoral Prayer, ed. Marsha L. Dutton, trans. Mark DelCogliano, CF 73 (Kalamazoo, MI: Cistercian Publications, 2008), 50–51.

[9] Aelred of Rievaulx, *Liturgical Sermons: The Second Clairvaux Collection, Sermons 29–46, Christmas to All Saints*, trans. Marie Anne Mayeski, CF 77 (Kalamazoo, MI: Cistercian Publications, 2016), 37 (hereafter CF 77).

[10] Aelred of Rievaulx, *The Liturgical Sermons: The Durham and Lincoln Collections, Sermons 47–83*, trans. Kathryn Krug, Lewis White, and the *Catena Scholarium*, CF 80 (Collegeville, MN: Cistercian Publications, 2018), 302 (hereafter CF 80).

of the interaction between himself and his audience, their familiarity with his regular return to the same sermon topics and the same scriptural texts, and his need to respond to some of the consequences of that familiarity:

> Because many of you grow bored with the same sermon and the same reading repeated again and again, we need to renew what seems old and familiar, either by adding certain ideas or at least by changing the words. In this way we can rouse the attentiveness that we seek and call the heart back from its useless and vain digressions to what is useful. So the mind that in its boredom had fled the familiar can, after being renewed by the sweetness of a reading or sermon, beneficially return to that from which it had been unconsciously distracted. (Hom 1.6)[11]

A little later Aelred acknowledges his larger responsibility to his community: "I recognize my obligation to your progress in all respects, because of my office, of course, but mostly because of my affection for you. But necessity also compels me. Woe to me if I do not preach the gospel, especially since I do not doubt that whatever progress I make in spiritual teaching or in understanding of the Scriptures is not so much for me as it is for you, given through me" (Hom 1.10).[12]

The Sermons in This Volume

As a Cistercian abbot, Aelred was required to address his community on defined occasions: "the great liturgical feasts: . . . the First Sunday of Advent, Christmas, Epiphany, Palm Sunday, Easter, Ascension, Pentecost, all the solemnities of the Virgin Mary (Purification, Annunciation, Nativity, Assumption), John the Baptist,

---

[11] *Homeliae de Oneribus Propheticis Isaiae*, ed. Gaetano Raciti, CCCM 2D (Turnhout: Brepols, 2005), 25; Aelred of Rievaulx, *Homilies on the Prophetic Burdens of Isaiah*, trans. Lewis White, CF 83 (Collegeville, MN: Cistercian Publications, 2018), 24 (hereafter CF 83).
[12] CCCM 2D:26–27; CF 83:25.

Peter and Paul, All Saints, and the Dedication of the local church."[13]
The previous volumes of Aelred's sermons in English translation
present almost exclusively discourses designed for these obligatory
occasions.[14] The Reading-Cluny Collection, however, is more a
homiletic miscellany than are the previous volumes, with a wider
range of topics, an array of more fluid techniques, and a greater
grace of voice. The collection still follows the liturgical calendar,
beginning with the First Sunday of Advent and concluding with
three sermons for the Feast of All Saints. But the second half of the
collection, which begins with the Nativity of John the Baptist (June
24) contains a surprising number of sermons intended for days
other than those requiring abbatial preaching. Two sermons are
titled "To Abbots," one concerns the Feast of Holy Relics, and one,
"To Nuns," is identified as being for the Thursday after the resurrection.

This volume also contains a number of sermons commemorating individual saints ancillary to the calendrical scheme of the core
of the book: Saint Gregory the Great (3/12), Saint Martin (11/11),
Saint Katherine of Alexandria (11/25), Saint Andrew (11/30),
two each on Saint Vincent (1/22) and Saint Mary Magdalene (7/22),
and four on Saint Edward the Confessor (1/6; 10/13). Regarding
such sermons, Pennington suggests, "We could well imagine a
popular abbot being called to preach at popular celebrations in
honor of these saints" (CF 58:20, n. 33). Aelred's style in these
sermons, sometimes amounting to exuberance, indicates that he
found unusual pleasure in them. None of the earlier collections has
such variety or such a large proportion of non-obligatory subject
matter.

---

[13] See Michael Casey, "An Introduction," 279. See Danièle Choisselet and Placide
Vernet, eds., *Les* Ecclesiastica Officia *Cisterciens du XIIe siècle*, La Documentation
Cistercienne 22 (Reiningue, 1989), 190.

[14] All the collections contain some exceptions, however; for example, three
sermons address Priests or Clerics of the Synod, and one is designated for the First
Sunday in November (SS 28, 63, 64).

Sermons in this collection incorporate substantial passages from other preachers and church fathers, often without attribution but frequently emended by Aelred, thus making them more characteristic of his own style. Sometimes all or almost all of a sermon is borrowed from another writer; for example, except for the final paragraph, Sermon 164 in this volume is entirely the work of Geoffrey Babion. More often, however, Aelred adopts appropriate or flavorful passages from his sources, inserting them at logical points within his own sermons. Sermon 150 on the Feast of Mary Magdalene, for example, contains examples from Augustine, Gregory the Great, and Bernard of Clairvaux, all inserted without comment. Aelred often claimed to be unlearned,[15] but he was clearly a voracious reader with a good memory—and a good library.[16] He quotes his sources accurately enough that Raciti has been able to identify hundreds of them, so smoothly interwoven with Aelred's own prose that had Raciti not identified them in his edition (many cited marginally in this translation), most could pass unnoticed.

Life as a Battle: Aelred's Use of Job 7:1

Aelred frequently reveals the development of his thinking in his exposition of a particular scriptural text from sermon to sermon. One such passage is Job 7:1, to which he returns ten times in six sermons (13, 26, 123, 140, 177, 178).[17] The verse encapsulates one aspect of Christian experience: life as a battle. In the Vulgate, it reads *Militia est vita hominis super terram et sicut dies mercennarii dies eius*, translated in the Douay-Rheims version as, "The life of man upon earth is a warfare, and his days are like the days of a

---

[15] See, e.g., *Homilies*, Hom 1.10 (CF 83:25).

[16] For the thirteenth-century catalogue of the Rievaulx library, see David N. Bell, ed., *The Libraries of the Cistercians, Gilbertines and Premonstratensians*, Corpus of British Medieval Library Catalogues 3 (London: The British Library, 1992), 87–140.

[17] Sermons 13 and 123 are essentially identical, with Sermon 13 for the Feast of the Ascension in the First Clairvaux Collection reworked as Sermon 123 in the Reading-Cluny Collection.

hireling." Aelred always focuses on the first half of the verse, ignoring the comparison of a person's days to those of a paid laborer. He writes of the nature of life, not the status of the one living it, treating all the members of his community—lay brothers as well as choir monks—as participants in the struggle.

Aelred's use of this passage demonstrates the ease with which he adapts Scripture to the argument of his sermons, in all but one case citing Job 7:1 to explain human life as a battle. So while in three of the six sermons—140, 177, and 178—he retains the scriptural term *militia*, in the other three—13, 26, and 123—he alters it to *temptatio*, "temptation" or "trial," explaining that for the monks whom he addresses, resisting temptation or facing a trial is the same as battle or warfare for a soldier, with enemies always present in both cases. Monks' enemies are internal rather than external, but their battle is as real as the soldier's, with the stakes even higher because the soul is at risk. Human life on earth is a trial, a warfare, or a temptation, and Aelred suggests that these various experiences are intimately related. Thus although he distinguishes between being at war and being tempted, depending on the topic of the sermon, his citations of Job indicate that the connection between the ideas is stronger than the difference.

The three sermons in which Aelred retains *militia* from Job 7:1 insist that all Christians must engage in battle against evil. The motif appears once in Sermon 176, the first of two sermons for the Feast of Saint Vincent of Saragossa, the protomartyr of Spain, who was tortured and put to death during Roman persecutions of Christians in 304. In this sermon Aelred cites the Job verse only once while explaining to his monks that in the world they fight on behalf of God against the devil: "Our Lord and God has placed us all in the field so we might bravely do battle for him against his adversary. The field is this world, in which we are never safe; we are never without misfortune, without misery, without battle. So it is written, *The life of a man upon earth is warfare.* We all serve in combat for one king. Each one of us has entered into combat for God against a strong athlete, a cruel combatant, a wicked and grievous fighter: against the devil" (S 176.9).

The second sermon for the Feast of Saint Vincent continues the idea of Christian life as warfare, but now taking that conflict as its central theme. It begins by citing Job 7:1, then repeats the phrase five more times while also twenty-three times repeating the word *militia*. It hammers relentlessly on the call for all Christians to fight against the devil. The tone is martial, the language thuds like drumbeats, and the life of the Christian is presented as uncompromisingly militant. Alluding to the feast of the day, Aelred exhorts the community to recognize the nature of their life, spelling out the metaphor at the head of the sermon: "On the illustrious solemnity of this particular soldier of Christ the subject teaches and the reward persuades to take up spiritual warfare. . . . But please do not understand these things in a carnal way, but rather spiritually. Rank is profession, skill is instruction, fortitude is steadfastness, weapons are virtues, the enemy is the foe of virtues" (S 177.1). Although life on earth is warfare, he explains, every element in that warfare is essential for Christians' victory.

The third sermon in which Aelred retains *militia* is Sermon 178, for the Feast of Saint Gregory the Great. Unlike the two sermons for the Feast of Saint Vincent, Aelred here speaks less of the warfare of Christians against evil than of the necessity of monks' combining prayer and contemplation with action, a favorite Aelredian concern.[18] So he exhorts his hearers to imitate Gregory in calling on God: "Any feeling of piety is a voice acceptable to him, but more acceptable is a voice crying out when the fervor of love, when the vehemence of desire, when the power of love is more ardent. Who thus cried out, who loved so affectionately, who prayed so piously, who so delighted heaven's attention as this blessed Gregory?" (S 178.5). He goes on to urge the monks to complement prayer with service: "No one can persist in the pursuit of contemplation without the training of action, just as action itself without contemplation is less valued, less wise, less useful, less pure. So you have, *Be not*

---

[18] See for example, "On Jesus at the Age of Twelve," trans. Theodore Berkeley, in Aelred of Rievaulx, *Treatises, The Pastoral Prayer*, CF 2 (Kalamazoo, MI: Cistercian Publications, 1971), 37–39.

over just, and be not excessively wise, lest you be stupefied. Justice dwells in service; wisdom dwells in contemplation" (S 178.6).

Only toward the end of this sermon does Aelred summon up the memory of human life as a battle. In this case again his concern is the life of monks, of himself and his community: "us whose *life upon earth* in this interim especially professes warfare, us for whom the conflict ought to be a continual clash and continual *struggle,* not *against flesh and blood, but against the spirits of wickedness*. . . . Finally, contending *in the struggle* . . ., let us tremble and refrain *from all* sins as much as we can" (S 178.15–16).

The sermons in which Aelred replaces *militia* with *temptatio* in his citation of Job 7:1 each use the phrase only once, again in passages focusing on the battle Christians fight against the devil. In Sermons 13 and 123, about Christ's ascension, he addresses the community's fear of having been left alone when Christ withdrew his physical presence, speaking reassuringly: "And lest we be too downcast that he left us physically, let us hear what he told them [the disciples] according to another evangelist: *Behold,* he said, *I am with you for all days, unto the end of the ages.* . . . In his divinity, he is always with us. By his loving providence he always surrounds us" (S 123.15). He complements this assurance by recalling Moses' holding up his hands to conquer the Amalekites, explaining that "the raising of Moses' hands signified the passion of our Lord Jesus Christ" (S 123.18).

That promise is Aelred's transition to all the struggles inherent in human life after the ascension, as Christians and specifically the monks of his community understand that even after Christ's ascension, even as they continue to battle against evil, they may be sure of Christ's presence: "And we, as long as we are in this wretched life, which is *a trial* [temptatio] *upon earth,* as long as *our fight is against the principalities and powers, against the rulers of the dark things of the world, and against the spiritual forces of evil in the heavens,* we need our Lord to have his hands lifted up within us— that is, that the remembrance of his passion be continually present in our minds" (S 123.19). Christ's presence within each monk through the memory of the passion means that despite his physical absence, Christ remains always present with them.

In Sermon 26, for the Feast of All Saints, Aelred again uses Job's plaint to recall the ongoing struggle of human life while contrasting it with the joy of the life to come, the one already experienced by the saints. So Aelred defines the church on earth in scriptural words: "This is the family of Christ, the Bride of Christ, who says in the Song of Songs, *I am black but comely*" (Song 1:5). He goes on, completing the contrast, "Blackness belongs to this life, comeliness to that in which we shall—God willing—be after this" (S 26.13). After considering the range of blackness experienced in human life, from the suffering of the martyrs and saints to the pain of responsibility for others when they fail, he declares, "blessed is someone who suffers this blackness for Christ" (S 26.19). Then he arrives at the blackness of temptation:

> There is still another blackness which you have often experienced. It is one that none of the saints has ever been able to avoid. This blackness, brothers, is temptation, whether from the enemy or from the flesh or from this world. . . . This blackness the whole company of God's saints has experienced, so it is able to say: *I am black but comely.* . . . For what saint is free from temptation, when Job says: *Human life on earth is temptation. I am black but comely.* Is not the soul of each and every one of us able to say this? (S 26.20–21)

Once again in this passage he points to the inevitability of struggle in human life, experienced in the resistance to the forces that try and tempt and torment men and women.

Aelred does not often cite Job 7:1, but often enough to make it clear that he hears the verse as characterizing the nature of human life, whether understood as warfare against evil or as temptation. Whereas he insists on that idea in the second sermon for the Feast of Saint Vincent, in other sermons he only touches on it, introducing it briefly as a verse that speaks for itself. This life is full of pain and struggle, he says, quoting Job, but Christ is present with his people in his divinity just as he was when he walked among them, and if they cry out to God and continue to fight the good fight, after the blackness of human life the beauty of beatitude awaits.

Some Unexpected Sermons

The second half of the Reading-Cluny collection addresses seventeen topics and/or audiences not recorded elsewhere, with some sermons apparently intended to be preached outside of Rievaulx. So Sermon 148, On the Feast of Holy Relics, is clearly designed to be preached at Westminster, as it calls attention to the presence among the relics being celebrated of the ring and "virgin body" of "the Blessed King Edward [the Confessor]," and to the church's dedication to Saint Peter: "The prince of apostles and shepherd of the church, our principal patron, blessed apostle Peter, in whose honor the present church is dedicated and its precious relics are abundantly enriched" (S 148.14). In these sermons, like those on more familiar topics, Aelred guides his hearers to recognize how the suffering of life—Christ's and their own—leads at last to joy.

Another Consideration of Life as a Battle: A Sermon to Nuns

Sermon 179, "To Nuns: On the Thursday of the Week after the Resurrection," is the only one of Aelred's surviving sermons identified as being intended for nuns.[19] In it Aelred again treats the enduring conflict between humankind and the devil, but not now quoting Job. What's more, he speaks not of generalized warfare but of its origin in the garden of Eden, and its reason: the devil's jealousy of Adam and Eve. The sermon begins with a celebration of the natural world, associating the monastery garden with those of Eden, of the Song of Songs, and of the place of Jesus' entombment and resurrection. The sermon lacks a formal exordium. After the initial text from Song 4:16, Aelred addresses his audience familiarly, almost *in medias res*, linking the first and last of these gardens: "That holy woman, O daughters, who believed the Lord to be a gardener was not much mistaken. For *from the beginning* he planted *a garden of pleasure*, and in the end times he willed to be buried *in a garden*, like *the tree of life* planted *in the middle of Paradise*. He loves gardens and the splendor of gardens; he delights in lilies and roses" (S 179.1).

---

[19] Marie Anne Mayeski, " 'The Right Occasion for the Words': Situating Aelred's Homily on Saint Katherine," CSQ 33, no. 1 (1998): 45.

Having celebrated gardens' beauty and God's love of gardens as shown by his setting creation in such a place, Aelred turns to human conflict with evil, represented by the story of Satan's seduction of Adam and Eve. A core aspect of this sermon is thus the explanation of the Fall in that first garden, and the way it necessitated Christ's incarnation, passion, and resurrection in another garden. Aelred points to the enduring conflict between humankind and the devil, tracing it back to its beginning in the beauty of the world God made and the human exile from that paradisal garden.

The conclusion of the sermon, though, returns to the joy of the opening: "*Exult and praise, O dwelling of Zion*, singing psalms and saying, *Mercy and judgment I shall sing to you, O Lord. . . .* How you ought to be loved, you who so love souls that you chose to die rather than not pardon the sinner" (S 179.22–23). Although the heart of the sermon is its extended consideration of Satan's achievement in exiling men and women from Paradise, the sermon's Christian comedy of light emerging from darkness, beauty from despair, fulfills God's plan for his creatures.

The Sermon for the Feast of Blessed Mary Magdalene

Aelred's Sermon 150, the second of two for the Feast of Mary Magdalene, begins with a declaration that the community is celebrating "the festive assumption of Christ's lover [*Christi dilectricis*] into heaven." As the converted sinner—the one both loved by Christ and loving Christ—is now with her beloved, Aelred invites those who listen to join with those in heaven as they rejoice at Christ's love for the undeserving: "Let us also rejoice with a twin feeling of joy, two [things] that prove the evidence of the inborn gentleness in the Lord Jesus: that he patiently awaits a wrongdoer and that he mercifully accepts a penitent" (S 150.1). Christ's loving, patient longsuffering thus becomes the fulcrum for the sermon, Mary the example of the fruit of that longsuffering, and the monks the beneficiaries.

In this sermon Aelred accepts and explores the traditional medieval conflation of Mary Magdalene with the unnamed woman in Luke 7:36-45 who prostrates herself before Jesus' feet and pours

ointment over them, and with the similar (or same) woman who anoints his head in Matthew 26:6-7 (S 150.4). For the time being, though, he delays the connection of the Magdalene with the woman or women who anoint Jesus. Then, a little later, he recounts her coming to the tomb with ointment for Christ's body:

> Therefore Mary is blessed and happy, she who deserved to anoint not only Jesus' feet, but also his head and whole body. *Mary Magdalene*, the evangelist says, *and Mary the mother of James, and Salome, bought aromatic spices to come and anoint Jesus.* There are three ointments with which blessed Mary anointed Jesus. With the first ointment she anointed his feet, with the second his head, with the third his whole body. The first is ointment of contrition, the second of devotion, the third of love. The first ointment expresses grief, the second mitigates grief, the third repels distress. (S 150.13)

Aelred repeatedly weaves his celebration of Mary's love of Jesus shown in the gospels with exhortation to the listening monks. As in many of his sermons for the feasts of saints, he allegorizes her story, urging the community to learn from it and to imitate her: "One who has not yet renounced his own sins . . . can at least come to [Jesus'] feet. . . . Mary brings ointment with her. You, after sin, offer also repentance!" He then develops this image in words from Saint Ambrose's commentary on Luke:

> Wherever you might hear the name of Christ, run to him. You might have learned that Jesus has entered into the interior of someone's house: hurry also to enter! When you have discovered wisdom or justice reclining in someone's inner chambers, rush to the feet, that is, seek the extreme part of wisdom. . . . Confess your offenses with tears, so that the heavenly justice may say about you, *With her tears she has rinsed my feet, and wiped them with her hair.* . . . Good tears <can>[20] not only wash our sin, but also rinse the footprints of the heavenly Word, so that his

---

[20] Words included in angle brackets signal Raciti's insertions in his editions of the sermons, followed in the translations.

steps are fruitful in us—good tears, in which are not only redemption of sins, but also refreshment of the just. (S 150.11)[21]

In this sermon, then, Aelred offers Mary Magdalene and the women who anointed Jesus' feet and head as models for all who hear him, declaring that by uniting penitence and love for Jesus, they too may be his lovers.

The Sermon for the Feast of Saint Katherine

Sermon 174, commemorating Saint Katherine of Alexandria, is not only Aelred's single surviving sermon devoted to a non-scriptural female saint but also, as Marie Anne Mayeski notes, "one of the very few homilies given by a twelfth-century Cistercian on a woman saint other than the Virgin."[22] According to tradition, Katherine was a heroic virgin martyr, one of the most popular saints of the early and high Middle Ages, particularly acclaimed for her wisdom. After debating successfully with fifty pagan philosophers and converting many of them to Christianity, she was tortured by being broken on a wheel (now known as a Katherine wheel), then put to death through decapitation, reportedly in AD 305.

Aelred shows Katherine as the bride of the Song of Songs, summoned by her bridegroom and then seeking him through the city. In addition to defining her in the words of the Song, he creates a new narrative reliant on the words of the Song:

> It is as if her bridegroom were to say to her, "In vain do you seek me *in your bed*. For there you will not find me. But *arise and make haste, my love, my dove, and come.* Follow the way on which I have gone before, if you wish to come to me." So as she was advised and invited by her friend, she joins in, saying, *I will rise and go about the city, through the streets and the broad ways, seeking him whom my soul loves.* (S 174.16)

---

[21] Ambrose, *Expositio Euangelii Lucae* 6.17–18 (CSEL 32/4:238). This sermon seamlessly blends Aelred's own words with passages from not only Ambrose, but also William of Saint-Thierry and Bernard of Clairvaux.

[22] Mayeski, "'The Right Occasion,'" 45.

Aelred then explains how this biblical narrative underpins Katherine's own life: "afire with the fervor of Christian religion, inflamed with love of the bridegroom, having left the throne of her father, she prostrated herself amid a sinful nation and fearlessly presented herself to a cruel tyrant who sacrificed to idols" (S 174.17).

The happy outcome of the story as Aelred tells it, of course, is that after Katherine's death, "she found her beloved, whom she had sought through so many and such great dangers . . . having secured the reward of her labors, she erupts into an expression of confidence, saying, *I hold him and I will not let go.* She truly holds him, now joined and united to her bridegroom, and she does not let him go" (S 174.21). So in this sermon Aelred presents Katherine, like Mary Magdalene, as a worthy model for his hearers in loving Jesus, now not through penitence but through passionate love—through contemplation. And once again, he concludes this sermon with words of encouragement: "imitate, brothers, this glorious virgin and, if we cannot do so by that wonderful way by which the Lord her God led her, then at least let us seek our beloved *in* our *bed*, according to her example; that is, let us through a pure conscience and the quiet of contemplation and holy living, seek God, so that *when the Lord comes* to us, he may find us *keeping watch*" (S 174.22).

Sermons on Saint Edward the Confessor

In addition to his sermons on women saints, Aelred surprises the readers of this collection with three sermons on a recently canonized saint and former English king: Edward, known as the Confessor (r. 1042–1066). Edward, who died without an heir of the body, was canonized by Pope Alexander III not quite a hundred years later, in October 1161, in acknowledgment of the significant support given Alexander by King Henry II in the recently concluded papal schism. Thus Henry received a familial saint who was both his predecessor on the throne and a relative, however distant.

Aelred had good reason to be aware of Edward in that period, and unusual access to information about him useful for writing sermons for his feast day. Before the canonization Aelred had

showed no particular interest in Edward,[23] but afterward, Abbot Lawrence of Westminster asked him to write a new Life for the translation of Saint Edward's relics into a shrine at Westminster. Aelred must have set about this task quickly, since while Henry was in France at the time of the canonization, once he returned, the translation would surely take place at once.

To assist Aelred in his work, Abbot Lawrence had provided him with the previous *Life* of Edward, written in 1138 by Osbert of Clare, himself a monk of Westminster. According to Marc Bloch, the editor of Osbert's *Life*, only two manuscripts of this work survive today, one probably copied in the late twelfth or thirteenth century for a monastery in the diocese of Trier, and another in England from the middle of the thirteenth century.[24] Apparently, then, the mid-twelfth-century manuscript that Lawrence provided to Aelred no longer exists—did Aelred fail to return it to Westminster after he used it?

Although the new *Life of Saint Edward, King and Confessor* of course focuses on Edward's sanctity, Aelred manages to make Henry not only its principal audience but also in some ways its hero, beginning with a letter to Henry addressing him as "most glorious King Henry" (CF 56:126) and urging him at beginning and end to imitate Edward. Aelred partly justifies this emphasis on Henry by implying Edward to have been Henry's ancestor. But Edward was in fact only the half-great uncle of Henry's great grandmother, Queen Margaret of Scotland, a connection so remote that English lacks even a word to define it. But in the letter to Henry that serves as the prologue to the *Life*, Aelred speciously declares,

[23] See "The Genealogy of the Kings of the English," in Aelred of Rievaulx, *The Historical Works*, trans. Jane Patricia Freeland, CF 56 (Kalamazoo, MI: Cistercian Publications, 2005). In this work Aelred devotes 7 1/2 pages (106–13) to Edward's older half-brother, King Edmund Ironside (r. 1016), and a little less than 2 pages to Edward (113–15).

[24] "La Vie de S. Édouard le Confesseur par Osbert de Clare," ed. Marc Bloch, *Analecta Bollandiana* 41 (1923): 56–58. For more detail on Osbert's *Life*, see Marsha L. Dutton, "The Staff in the Stone: Finding Arthur's Sword in the *Vita Sancti Edwardi* of Aelred of Rievaulx," *Arthuriana* 17, no. 3 (2007): 26.

"The special pride of our Henry is that his physical descent is from such a holy line. . . . Now, most illustrious king, you have assumed the kingdom of your great ancestor by a twofold right, having merited the kingdom and your aristocratic blood from both your father and your mother."[25] So he suggests that Henry has inherited not only the throne of England but his character from the new saint.[26]

After the canonization Aelred wrote the three sermons on Edward found in the Reading-Cluny collection—Sermons 170, 171, and 172.[27] These are distinctive for several reasons. First, few such sermons exist, and surely no others written by a Cistercian abbot. Further, unlike most of Aelred's known sermons, these may be easily dated, certainly to between October 1161 (the date of the canonization) and January 1167 (Aelred's death), and probably in fact between January 1162 and October 1166. As Sermon 170 is intended for the Feast of Edward's Deposition on January 5, Aelred may have written it not long before that date in December 1161 or in the first week of 1162.[28] He must have been writing the *Life* at about the same time.

[25] Aelredi Rievallensis, *Vita Sancti Edwardi Regis et Confessoris*, ed. Francesco Marzella, CCCM 3A (Turnhout: Brepols, 2017), 88–89; "The Life of Saint Edward, King and Confessor," in Aelred of Rievaulx, *The Historical Works*, trans. Jane Patricia Freeland, CF 56 (Kalamazoo, MI: Cistercian Publications, 2005), 127. For a chart of Henry's English ancestry (omitting Edward but including Edmund Ironside), see Marsha L. Dutton, "Aelred, Historian: Two Portraits in Plantagenet Myth," CSQ 28, no. 2 (1993): 143.

[26] Mayeski has considered the influence of Anselm's early twelfth-century treatise *On the Virgin Conception and Original Sin* on Aelred's suggestion in *Genealogy* that Henry had inherited virtue from his ancestors (Marie Anne Mayeski, "Secundum Naturam: The Inheritance of Virtue in Aelred's Genealogy of the English Kings," CSQ 37, no. 3 [2002]: 221–28). Aelred seems to make the same point in *The Life of Saint Edward*.

[27] Jackson provides a helpful overview of Aelred's three recognized sermons on Edward (51–54) and points out the repeated references in the first two to Edward as "our patron" (*"In translacione,"* 51). He suggests that the third sermon may not actually be by Aelred but perhaps by a Westminster scribe.

[28] Jackson calls attention to the words, "Today he moved from death to life, ascending from earth into heaven" (*hodie de morte migrauit ad uitam*) (§20; Jackson, *In translacione*, 52).

In the three sermons on Edward in this collection, Aelred focuses on two aspects of Edward's life. The first is Edward's devotion to God since infancy, exemplified in his humility, simplicity, mercy, justice, willed poverty, and chastity—monastic virtues, offered to his hearers for imitation—but unusual in the case of a wealthy king. The second aspect that Aelred emphasizes is Edward's kingship, its origins and effectiveness, especially in putting down the Danish invaders and bringing peace to England. These two themes inevitably intertwine during the sermons.

Repeatedly Aelred contrasts the luxury and pride that is expected of a king with the devout, humble, and generous nature of Edward's life. In the first of the three sermons he insists on his virtues:

> So, by all means, *he scorned all things that give service to the flesh*. The pomp of the world, suggestion of the enemy, pleasure of desires, enticement of temporal delights all serve the flesh. . . . Still it is astonishing and extraordinary how the glorious king could scorn these, he who was exalted in royal power, eminent in authority, great in glory, glorious in power. . . . he preserved not only <chastity> but even virginity in marriage, humility in his reign, uprightness and truth in judgment. (S 170.8–9)

Aelred regularly praises Edward's chastity, bringing virtue from necessity and avoiding any mention of its devastating consequences: Edward's failure to father a successor to the throne of England, leading to the Norman Conquest of England in October 1066 and the coronation of William of Normandy in Westminster Abbey in December of that year. Further, none of the sermons remarks the irony of Edward's being canonized as a mark of favor to the great-grandson of the founder of the dynasty that had replaced the ancient Anglo-Saxon line of England's kings (which in *Genealogy of the Kings of the English* Aelred traces back to Adam).[29]

[29] See *Genealogy of the Kings of the English* (CCCM 3:23–24; CF 56:72–73). In both the *Genealogy* and the *Life of Edward* Aelred does consider those consequences, however, explaining how by God's will everything turned out for the best:

Aelred not only emphasizes Edward's devotion and virtue as a king, but in the first and third sermons he also explains Edward's kingship as God's choice, seen in Edward's election by the people to be their king even before he was born: "before his days in the cradle, as the Lord appointed and sanctified his boy [*puerum suum*], still enclosed within his mother's body, he had been chosen as king equally by clergy and the people" (S 170.4; see also S 172.20–25). It is not surprising, then, that Aelred shows Edward as blessed by God and a bringer of peace to England: "After the Danish battles, . . . like the great Solomon himself, Edward restored times of peace for us, times of calm, times of tranquility, enriching his people and kingdom with gold and silver, peace and justice, riches and glory, because *God was with him and set in order all his works*" (S 170.6).

The Sermon for the Translation of Saint Edward the Confessor

In translacione sancti Edwardi confessoris, the fourth sermon on Edward the Confessor included in this volume, was almost surely the first written. It is not in the Reading-Cluny collection, and it is not certain that it was by Aelred. But Peter Jackson has explained the probability that it was written by Aelred and is the one he is said to have preached at Edward's Westminster translation, showing how its text corresponds to the medieval description of Aelred's sermon for the translation and identifying numerous stylistic similarities between this sermon and Aelred's other works.[30] Cistercian Publications has thus included it here for scholars' convenience.[31]

In the *Life of Aelred of Rievaulx*, Walter Daniel records Aelred's writing of both the *Life* of Edward and a sermon for Edward's translation:

Genealogy (CCCM 3:52–56; CF 56:115–16), and the *Life of Edward* (CCCM 3A:150–55; CF 56:202–9).

[30] Jackson, "*In translacione*," 50–64.

[31] Jackson provides a helpful analysis of the sermon and compares it with the three Reading-Cluny sermons for Edward.

he published the life of the most holy King Edward, a work whose pages shine with the great glory and splendor of the miracles. Next he expounded in honor of the same saint and to be read with the passage at his solemn vigils the gospel lesson which begins, "No man, when he has lighted a candle, puts it under a bushel but on a candlestick." He wrote [these] at the request of his kinsman Laurence, the abbot of Westminster, and to please the brethren serving God in that place.[32]

An anonymous set of annals ending in 1369 goes further, crediting Aelred with having preached the sermon at the translation: "Saint Aelred, the abbot, was present at this translation, presenting a life of the king and a wonderfully expressed homily on 'No one lights a candle' in honor of the same saint."[33] Two known early manuscripts of this sermon apparently no longer exist.

In translacione begins by addressing the monks of Westminster in words celebrating Edward, declaring the connection between him and those present. It refers to him as their patron (as in the first two of the other Edwardian sermons) and recalls him as the founder of the church of Westminster, consecrated just before his death. The sermon calls particular attention to Edward's lifelong virtue and his working of miracles:

> Brothers, rejoice and give thanks to God, the bountiful giver of all good things, for a holy day has begun to dawn upon us, a solemn day, the feastday of Edward, glorious king of the English,

---

[32] Walter Daniel, *The Life of Aelred of Rievaulx*, trans. Maurice Powicke, CF 57 (Kalamazoo, MI: Cistercian Publications, 1984), 121, chap. 32. The last sentence begins "Hec scripsit," that is, "He wrote these things." Powicke inaccurately translated the plural neuter accusative (*hec* = *haec*) as the singular neuter accusative (*hoc*). (Walteri Danielis, *Vita Ailredi Abbatis Rievall'*, ed. and trans. Maurice Powicke [Oxford: Clarendon Press, 1950], 41). I am grateful to Marsha Dutton for calling this error to my attention.

[33] Jackson, "*In translacione*," 46, citing *Chronicon Angliæ Petriburgense*, ed. J. A. Giles (London, 1845), 98, AD 1163. Jackson also notes (pp. 46–47) that N. R. Ker published the discovery of the Peterborough manuscript in 1992 (N. R. Ker and A. J. Piper, *Medieval Manuscripts in British Libraries* 4: *Paisley York* [Oxford: Clarendon, 1992], 170).

your patron,[34] your protector, your defender, the intercessor for
your sins, and the founder of your church. This is the day, I
declare, of that most holy confessor of Christ, whose whole
illustrious life from boyhood to old age shone brightly with virtues and miracles. (§1)

As this sermon was intended for presentation before King
Henry II, it is more explicitly concerned with the excellence of
Edward's kingship than are the three in the Reading-Cluny collection, and it is full of language familiar from Aelred's other works
celebrating Henry's kingship. Repeatedly it refers to Edward as
"the lofty king" (§2), "this blessed king" (§3), "O great king" (§8),
and it associates him with both the lawgiver Moses ("this our
Moses" [§9]) and the peacemaker Solomon (§12). It particularly
celebrates Edward's wise rule:

> England rejoices, I say, which this holy king endowed with laws,
> with customs adorned, tamed at his command, educated by his
> sagacity, strengthened by his faith, molded by his example, raised
> up by his authority, ornamented with his sanctity, and, leveling
> superiors and inferiors to a certain equality, ordered throughout
> its realm with judgment and justice (for justice and judgment
> prepared his throne). (§11)

This sermon also recounts more of Edward's miracles than do
Aelred's other Edwardian sermons, repeatedly linking his humility
to his kingship and his ties to Westminster. So he tells of Edward's
healing a cripple by carrying him on his back, as the man's "ulcerous pus flowed over the royal purple" (§4), and of two visions
granted him at Westminster: on Easter, of the Seven Sleepers on
Mount Celion (§6), and on Pentecost, during Mass, of the drowning of the king of the Danes (§7).[35]

By the time of the 1161 canonization Aelred was an obvious
candidate to celebrate Edward in writing and in person, and

---

[34] *patroni uestri*; but in SS 170 and 171 Aelred writes *our patron* (e.g. S 170.10:
patrono nostro).

[35] When Aelred tells this story in *Genealogy* (CF 56:89–90), he assigns it to King
Edward the Elder (r. 899–924); in the *Life of Edward*, he assigns it to Edward,
specifying Edward's presence at Westminster Abbey at the time (CF 56:149–51).

through him to acclaim Henry II. Having written two works in the 1150s to introduce Henry of Anjou, the newly named heir to the English throne, to his ancestors and to advise him on how he might by imitating them achieve similar peace and prosperity in his own reign, Aelred now had the opportunity to write a new work containing much the same advice and to present it before King Henry, now seven years into his reign.[36] It is no wonder that Aelred's *Life of Saint Edward* is the most important of his historical works and indeed through the centuries the most popular of all his works.[37] The likelihood that the Peterborough manuscript sermon is the one described as preached at Edward's translation is one of the great Aelredian discoveries of recent years.

As Walter Daniel states that the abbot of Westminster commissioned Aelred to write a new Life of Edward the Confessor for the translation of his relics and a sermon for the translation, surely he also invited him to preach it. While only circumstantial detail allows for assessing the likelihood that Aelred wrote *In translacione sancti Edwardi confessoris* and preached it at Westminster, the case Peter Jackson has made seems solid—and readers of this last volume of Aelred's sermons are fortunate to have this singular sermon included.

A Retrospective Look at the Translations of Aelred's Sermons

The publication of this final volume of Aelred's liturgical sermons, twenty-one years after the publication of their first translation into English, provides a fitting occasion to look back over the translations of the five collections that Gaetano Raciti has identified

---

[36] See Marsha Dutton, "This Ministry of Letters: Aelred of Rievaulx's Attempt to Anglicize England's King Henry II," in *Monasticism between Culture and Cultures, Acts of the Third International Symposium, Rome, June 8–11, 2011*, ed. Philippe Nouzille and Michaela Pfeifer, *Analecta Monastica* 14, *Studia Anselmiana* 159 (Rome, 2013), 169–93.

[37] Marzella lists twenty-nine known manuscripts of the *Life* that survive and three now lost (CCCM 3A:13–26). It has also been translated numerous times into prose and poetry in both Latin and vernacular languages; see Domenico Pezzini, "Aelred of Rievaulx's *Vita Sancti Edwardi Regis et Confessoris*: Its Genesis and Radiation," *Cîteaux* 60 (2009): 27–77.

and edited—the First Clairvaux, Second Clairvaux, Lincoln, Durham, and Cluny-Reading[38]—and the additional sermon edited by Peter Jackson. These sermons constitute a substantial portion of Aelred's oeuvre, spanning much of his abbatial career. The wide range of expertise and life experience of the sixteen translators involved in the project has brought benefits and challenges. Translators have needed to respond to changes in various aspects of monastic life and Cistercian practice through the years as well as in readers' liturgical and scriptural knowledge.

Various practical aspects of the apparatus in these books have required the two editors of the books, E. Rozanne Elder and then Marsha Dutton, to rethink various decisions. From volume to volume the abbreviations for biblical books and Aelred's sources have changed, as have decisions about which sources to cite and how to abbreviate their titles, and different indices have been included from volume to volume. All this variation also means that the cumulative indices in this final volume are somewhat inconsistent in reflecting differences among the five volumes. Nevertheless, the presence of indices in each volume, however inconsistent, and especially of the cumulative ones in this final volume, is of enormous value.

The First Clairvaux Collection:
Advent to All Saints (2001) (CF 58) (SS 1–28)

Theodore Berkeley, OCSO, and M. Basil Pennington, OCSO, translated this first volume, with their shared monastic perspective shaping the volume. Pennington's Introduction deals primarily with large thematic issues suitable for the initial foray into this realm, including Aelred's role as a man of the church, Christ as the center, Mary, the saints, all aspects of monastic life, and Aelred's preaching style. Pennington is apposite in his characterization of the value of

---

[38] Some of these have been duplications or near duplications of others, suggesting, not surprisingly, that Aelred sometimes preached variations of sermons he had given earlier. See Gaetano Raciti, Introduction to Aelredi Rievallensis, *Sermones I–XLVI*, ed. Gaetano Raciti, CCCM 2A (Turnhout: Brepols, 1989), V.

Aelred's sermons for his community: "Aelred's sermons gave monks what they were familiar with, what they were looking for. They correspond to daily life, to experience. They clarify basic monastic themes, they comfort the struggling, they stimulate and ward off *acedia*. The teaching is rich, not pedestrian; it is elevated but neither abstract nor theoretical" (CF 58:32).

Pennington's introduction is particularly valuable in explaining the monastic context of Aelred's sermons. He explains, for example, that in some manuscripts of the First Clairvaux collection an Advent sermon became identified as intended for Palm Sunday because at one time a portion of the gospel for the first Sunday in Advent had recounted Jesus' entry into Jerusalem. He even expresses a slight criticism of the scribe responsible for moving that sermon and commends Raciti for correcting it: "One would think, however, that a cistercian scribe, being fully aware of this, would not have misplaced the sermon. . . . If the scribe had attended to the internal evidence he would not have made this mistake. . . . Father Raciti in this critical edition has restored the sermons to their proper places" (CF 58:14).[39] He also explains Raciti's decision to keep the published collections distinct on the basis that "Each of the different collections has its own particular selection of sermons with its own particular coherence and homogeneity" (CF 58:19).

The editor and translators of this first volume helpfully explain some of their textual decisions, allowing current readers to consider how those early decisions helped to establish the pattern for what would follow. So Elder, editor of the first volume, includes a list of significant Latin terms found in the sermons and explains the effort to regularize their translation:

---

[39] See Raciti, Introduction to CCCM 2A:vi, xiii. Because of Raciti's rearrangement of the sermons to correct this error and others, CF 58 includes a concordance showing the relationship between the sermon numbering in J.-P. Migne's Patrologia Latina series, vol. 195, and the corrected numbering in CCCM 2A and CF 58. The concordance also shows the absence of SS 15, 16, and 28 from PL 195 (CF 58:51–52).

We have tried to use only a single english word to represent a single latin word. The polyvalent and nuanced meanings of words in both languages has in some passages forced us to abandon this attempt in the hope of avoiding incomprehensible sentences or precious artificiality. The specifically theological meanings that certain words have taken on over the centuries has meant that the most variation occurs with terms which have both a general and a specific meaning.[40]

This note represents an example of a significant feature of the translation of the First Clairvaux collection, the explicit intention to reproduce Aelred's style by controlling the diction. Subsequent translators have not employed the lexicon in a similarly systematic way, or at least have not explained their decision to do so.

Pennington explains some of his decisions as a translator as guided by his lived experience of Cistercian life. For instance, in Sermon 8, *For the Feast of St. Benedict*, he explains the translators' choice to keep the word *lectio*:

> *Lectio* has been retained here, rather than "reading" or "sacred reading." *Lectio*, as understood in monastic tradition, is not simply what we moderns mean by reading. It may range from serious study to little more than holding an open book while conversing with God. It is directly ordered to and wholly permeated by the quest for God and aims at the experience of God's indwelling. (CF 58:150, n. 2)

The reader of this introduction and of these sermons thus receives expert insights into medieval Cistercian life and experience.

The Second Clairvaux Collection:
Christmas—All Saints (2016) (CF 77) (SS 29–46)

Marie Anne Mayeski, Professor Emerita of Theological Studies at Loyola Marymount University, translated the sermons in this collection, and Domenico Pezzini, Professor Emeritus of English

---

[40] [E. Rozanne Elder], "A Note on the Translation by the Editor," in Aelred of Rievaulx, *The Liturgical Sermons*, CF 58:54.

Language at the University of Verona (Italy), introduced the volume. Pezzini argues—quoting Psalm 34:8—that Aelred's sermons ask one to "taste and see," explaining that the sequence of these verbs "means something, since it seems that taste comes before sight, the eyes of the heart being excited and led by taste!"[41] His introduction provides a sensitive, detailed "reader's guide," identifying particular aspects of each of the eighteen sermons in the volume, "highlighting the way the argument is developed . . . to mark the 'movement' of the discourse" (CF 77:xi).

Pezzini calls particular attention to the characteristics of Aelred's language found in these texts: "What is original in Aelred's discourses . . . are certain preferences and above all the language he uses. Attention to nouns and verbs, adjectives and adverbs, figures and metaphors is essential to take the most profit from reading Aelred's writings." He also calls attention to his intention "to stress some characteristically Aelredian points or accents and occasionally to indicate such linguistic features . . . that are meant to underline Aelred's probable intended emphasis on specific topics, attitudes or figures" (CF 77:xi). His concern with these details balances the approach of Berkeley and Pennington as monastic insiders, so that the two collections, each arranged to follow a liturgical year, can be read in two different, equally satisfying ways.

The Durham and Lincoln Collections (2018) (CF 80) (SS 47–79)

The thirty-eight sermons in these two collections have several translators. Of the thirty-two sermons of the Durham collection, Kathryn Krug translated the first twenty-one (47–67) and Lewis White the remaining twelve (68–79); nine scholars composing the *Catena Scholarium* at Notre Dame University translated the five sermons of the Lincoln collection.[42] Ann W. Astell, Professor of

---

[41] Domenico Pezzini, "An Introduction to *The Second Clairvaux Collection*," CF 77 (Collegeville, MN: Cistercian Publications, 2016), viii–ix (hereafter CF 77).

[42] The members of the *Catena Scholarium* were Margaret Blume, Thomas Clemmons, Breanna Nickel, Benjamin Wright, Elisabeth Kincaid, Emily Ransom, Gregory Cruess, and Gilbert Stockson.

Theology at Notre Dame, worked with the *Catena* in preparing those translations and wrote the introduction for the volume. Her introduction highlights what she has identified as "an important Aelredian theme with both theological and rhetorical valence, namely, that of *varietas*."[43] Her approach thus combines what she refers to as the "broad thematic and stylistic overview" of Pennington's introduction to the First Clairvaux collection with Pezzini's "close attention to individual sermons" in his introduction (CF 80:ix).

Astell begins her discussion by considering the significance of *varietas* for Aelred and his audiences. She suggests that Aelred's familiarity with the diversity of the fellow monks with whom he lived and to whom he spoke allowed him to serve their individual needs through his sermons' diversity "in content and style . . . even as it opposed the generally destructive fault of *taedium animi*" (CF 80:xii), and she notes that Aelred's variation in content and style "befits the Sacred Scriptures themselves and the created and redemptive orders signified by them. Indeed, the proper experience of *varietas* necessitates a beholding from a divine perspective, from a position of Sabbath rest toward which the preacher hopes to move his audience" (CF 80:xii–xiii).

To demonstrate the way in which Aelred approached these goals, Astell carries out a close reading of three sermons to examine Aelred's use of *varietas*. She shows the treatment of Joseph's tunic of many colors in Sermon 59 to be one "emblem of *varietas*" through which Aelred offers "a threefold interpretation of God's self-revelation . . . using a wondrous vocabulary that requires his listeners to see the variety of things anew" (CF 80:xvi). In Sermon 74 she notes that Aelred describes Mary herself as *"clothed in variety* [Ps 44:14]" (CF 80:xxviii). And in Sermon 50 she directs attention to Aelred's initial words, which declare "his decision to

---

[43] Ann Astell, Introduction to the Durham and Lincoln Collections, in Aelred of Rievaulx, *The Liturgical Sermons*, vol. 3: *The Durham and Lincoln Collections, Sermons 47–83*, CF 80 (Collegeville, MN: Cistercian Publications, 2018), ix–xxii, here ix (hereafter CF 80).

vary the choice of topics appropriate to a sermon for Epiphany" by preaching on the wedding at Cana rather than the more usual topics of the visit of the Magi and Jesus' baptism (CF 80:xix).

Astell's introduction thus offers a particularly close look at Aelred's rhetorical approach, signaling his purposefulness as a writer and speaker, his careful choice of which text to use for each sermon and the development of his argument, and his images and diction, always considering the individuals who constitute his audience. As she asserts, "The rhetorical colors he employs in stylistic *varietas* are meant to confirm his sons in the variety of their different gifts and virtues within the monastic community" (CF 80:xxii).

The Reading-Cluny Collection (2021–2022) (CF 81, 87) *(SS 85–182)*

The fifth collection of Aelred's sermons, the ninety-eight sermons of the Reading-Cluny collection, is by far the largest of the five, as witnessed by the Cistercian Publications decision to divide it into two volumes. Its translator, Daniel Griggs, has done yeoman's service in translating all of these over the past several years, bringing to the work his own experience as a former Cistercian monk and as the holder of a doctorate in Byzantine theology from the University of Leeds. The first volume, with Sermons 85 through 133 introduced jointly by me and by Marsha Dutton, provides an overview of the manuscript history of the collection, explains the five categories into which Raciti placed the sermons, and examines several of the sermons contained in that volume, juxtaposing them with others on the same topics, with three sermons on the Feast of the Purification and three on the solemnity of Christ's circumcision.

Because in this collection Aelred so frequently includes extensive passages from other writers in his sermons, our introduction to this last volume of Aelred's sermons pays particular attention to some of the sermons in which such borrowing predominates. So for example it considers Aelred's smooth incorporation of two sermons by Geoffrey Babion, a popular early twelfth-century preacher, into two of Aelred's own sermons, demonstrating both Aelred's appreciation for Babion's insights and his ability to adapt

Babion's words to his own homiletic purpose. This final collection not only invites readers into Aelred's own thought and words but also reveals his appreciation and use of some of his predecessors and contemporaries.

Conclusion

Since the late nineteenth century Aelred's treatises have been the center of interest for scholars of his writing, who have long shown a particular interest in his ascetic or spiritual works, especially *Mirror of Charity* and *Spiritual Friendship*. In the last fifty years interest has grown in his historical and hagiographical works, with a concurrent recognition of his deep engagement with the history of England and desire to help shape England's present and future by advising King Henry II to achieve peace and prosperity in his reign. But through all the time that Aelred was writing his spiritual, hagiographic, and historical treatises, he was also writing and delivering sermons, mostly to the Cistercian monks of Revesby and then Rievaulx, but also to other groups of people gathered to hear his words: abbots, nuns, church synods, and parishes celebrating special events, such as the installation of a new bishop or even the translation of the relics of a newly canonized saint.

Throughout a thirty-three-year career as monk, teacher, reader, administrator, diplomat, and historian, Aelred was continually, regularly, speaking to his monks, on occasions both obligatory and voluntary, observing his listeners in all their variety of needs and strengths, attempting to guide them with passion, compassion, wit, vulnerability, honesty, and faith. In the chapter room as at the altar, he ministered to them and served them, offering himself to them as he had always sought to do. Now, nine hundred-some years later, we are fortunate to join their company.

Bibliography

Aelred's Works

For Your Own People: Aelred's Pastoral Prayer. Ed. Marsha L. Dutton. Trans. Mark DelCogliano. CF 73. Kalamazoo, MI: Cistercian Publications, 2008.

"The Genealogy of the Kings of the English." In Aelred of Rievaulx, *The Historical Works*, translated by Jane Patricia Freeland, edited by Marsha L. Dutton. CF 56. Kalamazoo, MI: Cistercian Publications, 2005. 71–122.

Homeliae de Oneribus Propheticis Isaiae. Ed. Gaetano Raciti. CCCM 2D. Turnhout: Brepols, 2005.

Homilies on the Prophetic Burdens of Isaiah. Trans. Lewis White. CF 83. Collegeville, MN: Cistercian Publications, 2018.

In translacione sancti Edwardi confessoris. Ed. Peter Jackson, trans. Tom Licence. In "The Lost Sermon by Aelred of Rievaulx Found?" CSQ 40, no. 1 (2005): 65–83.

"Jesus at the Age of Twelve." Trans. Theodore Berkeley. In Aelred of Rievaulx, *Treatises; The Pastoral Prayer*. CF 2. Kalamazoo, MI: Cistercian Publications, 1971. 1–39.

"The Life of Saint Edward, King and Confessor." In Aelred of Rievaulx, *The Historical Works,* translated by Jane Patricia Freeland. CF 56. Kalamazoo, MI: Cistercian Publications, 2005. 123–243.

The Liturgical Sermons: The Durham and Lincoln Collections, Sermons 47–83. Trans. Kathryn Krug, Lewis White, and the *Catena Scholarium*. CF 80. Collegeville, MN: Cistercian Publications, 2018.

The Liturgical Sermons: The First Clairvaux Collection, Sermons One – Twenty-Eight, Advent–All Saints. Trans. Theodore Berkeley and Basil Pennington. CF 58. Kalamazoo, MI: Cistercian Publications, 2001.

The Liturgical Sermons: The Reading-Cluny Collection. Trans. Daniel Griggs. Intro. Marjory Lange and (vol. 4.1) Marsha Dutton. 2 vols. CF 81, 87. Collegeville, MN: Cistercian Publications, 2021, 2022.

The Liturgical Sermons: The Second Clairvaux Collection, Sermons 29–46, Christmas to All Saints. Trans. Marie Anne Mayeski. CF 77. Kalamazoo, MI: Cistercian Publications, 2016.

Sermones. Ed. Gaetano Raciti. 3 vols. CCCM 2AB. Turnhout: Brepols Publishers, 1983, 2001, 2012.

Vita Sancti Edwardi Regis et Confessoris. Ed. Francesco Marzella. CCCM 3A. Turnhout: Brepols, 2017. 85–181.

Other Primary Sources

Chronicon Angliæ Petriburgense. Ed. J. A. Giles. London, 1845.

La Vie de S. Édouard le Confesseur par Osbert de Clare. Ed. Marc Bloch. *Analecta Bollandiana* 41 (1923): 6–131.

Les Ecclesiastica Officia Cisterciens du XIIe siècle. Ed. Danièle Choisselet and Placide Vernet. La Documentation Cistercienne 22. Reiningue, 1989.

The Libraries of the Cistercians, Gilbertines and Premonstratensians. Ed. David N. Bell. Corpus of British Medieval Library Catalogues 3. London: The British Library, in Association with the British Academy, 1992.

Walter Daniel. *The Life of Aelred of Rievaulx and The Letter to Maurice.* Trans. Maurice Powicke. CF 57. Kalamazoo, MI: Cistercian Publications, 1984.

Walter Daniel. *Vita Ailredi Abbatis Rievall'.* Ed. and trans. Maurice Powicke. Oxford: Clarendon Press, 1950.

Studies

Astell, Anne. "Introduction to the Durham and Lincoln Collections." In Aelred of Rievaulx, *The Liturgical Sermons: The Durham and Lincoln Collections, Sermons 47–83*, translated by Kathryn Krug, Lewis White, and the *Catena Scholarium.* CF 80. Collegeville, MN: Cistercian Publications, 2018. ix–xxii.

Casey, Michael. "An Introduction to Aelred's Chapter Discourses." CSQ 45, no. 3 (2010): 279–314.

Dutton, Marsha L. "Aelred, Historian: Two Portraits in Plantagenet Myth." CSQ 28, no. 2 (1993): 112–43.

Dutton, Marsha L. "The Staff in the Stone: Finding Arthur's Sword in the *Vita Sancti Edwardi* of Aelred of Rievaulx." *Arthuriana* 17, no. 3 (2007): 3–28.

Dutton, Marsha L. "This Ministry of Letters: Aelred of Rievaulx's Attempt to Anglicize England's King Henry II." In *Monasticism between Culture and Cultures, Acts of the Third International Symposium, Rome, June 8–11, 2011*, edited by Philippe Nouzille and Michaela Pfeifer. *Analecta Monastica* 14. *Studia Anselmiana* 159. Rome, 2013. 169–93.

[Elder, E. Rozanne]. "A Note on the Translation by the Editor." In Aelred of Rievaulx, *The Liturgical Sermons*, translated by Theodore Berkeley and Basil Pennington. CF 58. Kalamazoo, MI: Cistercian Publications, 2001. 53–55.

Jackson, Peter. "*In translacione sancti Edwardi confessoris*: The Lost Sermon by Aelred of Rievaulx Found?" CSQ 40, no. 1 (2005): 45–83.

Ker, N. R., and A. J. Piper. *Medieval Manuscripts in British Libraries* 4: *Paisley–York*. Oxford: Clarendon, 1992.

Lange, Marjory, and Marsha L. Dutton. Introduction to Aelred of Rievaulx, *The Liturgical Sermons: The Reading-Cluny Collection*, Vol. 4.1. Trans. Daniel Griggs. CF 81. Collegeville, MN: Cistercian Publications, 2021. xxiii–xlvii.

Mayeski, Marie Anne. "'The Right Occasion for the Words': Situating Aelred's Homily on Saint Katherine." CSQ 33, no. 1 (1998): 45–60.

Mayeski, Marie Anne. "*Secundum Naturam*: The Inheritance of Virtue in Aelred's Genealogy of the English Kings." CSQ 37, no. 3 (2002): 221–28.

Pennington, Basil. Introduction to *The Liturgical Sermons: The First Clairvaux Collection*. Trans. Theodore Berkeley and Basil Pennington. CF 58. Kalamazoo, MI: Cistercian Publications, 2001. 9–49.

Pezzini, Domenico. "Aelred of Rievaulx's *Vita Sancti Edwardi Regis et Confessoris*: Its Genesis and Radiation." *Cîteaux* 60 (2009): 27–77.

Pezzini, Domenico. "An Introduction to *The Second Clairvaux Collection*." Trans. Marie Anne Mayeski. CF 77. Collegeville, MN: Cistercian Publications, 2016. vii–lxxvi.

Pezzini, Domenico. "The Sermons of Aelred of Rievaulx." In *A Companion to Aelred of Rievaulx (1110–1167)*, edited by Marsha L. Dutton. Brill's Companions to the Christian Tradition 76. Leiden: Brill Academic Publishers, 2017. 73–97.

Raciti, Gaetano. Introduction to Aelredi Rievallensis, *Sermones I–XLVI*. Ed. Gaetano Raciti. CCCM 2A. Turnhout: Brepols, 1989. V–XVII.

Raciti, Gaetano. Introduction to Aelredi Rievallensis, *Sermones LXXXV–CLXXXII*. Ed. Gaetano Raciti. CCCM 2C. Turnhout: Brepols, 2012. VII–XX.

Waddell, Chrysogonus. "The Liturgical Dimension of Twelfth-Century Cistercian Preaching." In *Medieval Monastic Preaching*, edited by Carolyn Muessig. Brill's Studies in Intellectual History, 90. Leiden: Brill Academic Publishers, 1998. 335–49.

The Reading-Cluny Collection

Sermons 134-182

Sermon 134

On the Nativity of Saint John the Baptist

1. *You shall go to all to which I shall send you; be not afraid!** *Who* among us *can boast†* that he himself has accomplished these things! And who among us cannot fear that he himself has promised these things? It was not written about me, *You shall go to all to which I shall send you.** But it was written by me and promised by me that I should go to all things to which my Lord shall send me. These things are *my* own *vows, which my lips* have specifically pronounced and *uttered.** So I, so each and every one of us, committed himself to every obedience. What is a profession of obedience, if not a certain solemn promise that I shall go to all to which the Lord sends me? So it is, Lord, my God, *before many witnesses*:* I have obliged myself by these words, I have pledged myself into these vows.

2. *If I should choose* to refuse, *then my mouth shall condemn me,** because *I have spoken with my tongue*:* "I shall go to all to which you shall send me."* If I have confessed, then my hand will help me, because I have extended it to my mouth. In fact, *the slothful person hides his hand under his armpit and will not extend it to his mouth** to accomplish in action what he promised with his mouth. *May you not enter into judgment with* your servants* concerning this imperfection. Why do I say, "concerning imperfection"? Transgression is *to vow* and *not give.** I know that you enter into judgment with your

*Ant in Nat JB
(Hesbert 3:1249);
Jer 1:7, 8
†see Sir 48:4

*Ant in Nat JB
(Hesbert 3:1249);
Jer 1:7

*Ps 65:13-14

*see 1 Tim 6:12

*see Job 9:20

*Ps 38:5

*Ant in Nat JB
(Hesbert 3:1249);
Jer 1:7

*Prov 19:24

*see Ps 142:2

*see Eccl 5:3-4

servants reluctantly, Lord, insofar as you might be compelled. I know that you do not enter if we ourselves, at any rate, do not enter. Let us lift his judgment against us by a certain precedent from the Lord.

3. Let us see what we have promised to the Lord, let us see what we may have overlooked, if our hand has completed *what* our *lips have uttered.** And why have your lips uttered, if not because you will go to all to which the Lord shall send you?* See if we do go to all. See if harshness and cheapness do not call you back from executing a command. You have removed nothing in your profession. Investigate whether anything fell out in the execution of your vows! How many today have apostatized from their order because they did not hold this obedience that the Lord recommends when he says, *You shall go to all to which I shall send you.** Therefore *grief and misfortune in their ways, because they have not learned the way of peace* and obedience.†

4. *They eat*, it says, according to Solomon, *the fruit of their own way, and are satiated with their own devices.** Well does it say, *They are satiated.* For such as these, after they break out from the Order, become wanderers and unstable and wavering in their own devices,* and they feel disgust of sadness concerning them, not the fruit of joy. And they suffer all these disadvantages, because they walk in ways that are not good and go where they wish,* not to where they are sent. But even certain people who do not apostatize from the order of their profession with an obvious separation but persist in it as far as appearances, when they are required to do what they wish, then they comply; when however what they do not wish is required, they refuse. This only is the form of true obedience, that you go to all to which you are sent.*

*see Ps 65:14

*Ant in Nat JB (Hesbert 3:1249); Jer 1:7

*Ant in Nat JB (Hesbert 3:1249); Jer 1:7 †Rom 3:16-17; Ps 13:3

*Prov 1:31

*see RB 1.11

*see Isa 65:2

*Ant in Nat JB (Hesbert 3:1249); Jer 1:7

5. What is "all"? <To> hardships and adversities, to harsh and mean circumstances. To all things that you shall be sent to, not to what you are sent to by your own will. To all things that you are sent to, not to what you come to by yourself. Actually, *all, as many as have come, are thieves and robbers.** As *many as have come by themselves*, he says, not who were sent by me. Listen, brothers, and understand the virtue of obedience, or, more correctly, of truth. Work does not measure obedience, but the mind.* For the authority of the one who orders must be attended to more than the nature of the work. If you choose useful things to be done, then it is foresight; if you comply with the one who orders, then it is obedience. Therefore Jeremiah, thus John. See how they were sent to insults, how each suffered persecution from an unjust king. The former is tortured, <the latter> is decapitated in prison.* Why, if not because they proceeded to all things to which they were sent, and they spoke what was commanded to them?

6. *You shall go to all to which I shall send you; be not afraid*!* He expressed the form of obedience, and he added the purpose. It is the form of obedience if you omit nothing; it is for the sake of effectiveness if you love. Therefore he says, *Be not afraid*. When he has cast out fear, he induces love. Fear is lazy and icy, love is swift and fervent. And what does blessed Benedict say about obedience? "Then it will be pleasing to God and welcome to human beings, if what is ordered is done not tepidly, not slowly, not with trepidation."* Therefore tepidness, slowness, trepidation refer to fear; fervor, haste, trust to love. Still, from where, Lord, comes the strength of this flame-bearing love to your prophets, if you do not send *fire from heaven in* their *bones*,* fire that instructs them, that dissipates the cold of fear? Jeremiah had said

*John 10:8

animus

*Jer 38:4-13; see Mark 6:25-28

*Ant in Nat JB (Hesbert 3:1249); Jer 1:7, 8

*RB 5.14

*Lam 1:13

this concerning himself, and our other Elijah was also able <to say> the same thing as Jeremiah concerning himself.

7. In fact, insofar as it was *the law of* his *God in* his *heart*,* the fiery law, if you do not believe me, then *believe the works*,* although John himself is *a greater testimony** than works. For the Lord Jesus, who knew what he sent into John's heart, said, *John was a burning and a shining light.** And because he was the forerunner of the Lord, we ourselves can use that verse of the psalm in his commendation: *A fire shall go before him, and a mighty tempest around him*,* a tempest of unfaithful, common people and a crowd of a wicked generation, that preferred only *to rejoice for the hour*, not in fervor, but *in his light.** The Holy <Spirit>'s light of knowledge delights with the fervor of charity but also inflames. Therefore, to teach the knowledge that does not puff up but rather edifies in John,* he says that indeed he was a shining light, but he sent him ahead burning.*

8. The good ardor of charity dissipates fear and swollen pride at the same time. Good ardor of charity was in him that melted and removed from him all stubbornness, carnal concupiscence, avarice, anger, envy, jealousy, slander. And, so that I might conclude the remainder briefly, all depravity and perversity. Good ardor of charity was in him that inflamed and ignited him. For how would a faithless and empty person not fear when sent to such harsh suffering, and how would he not swell with pride, intending to proclaim such a lofty gospel? Others also had the *gift* of prophecy,* but John was *more than a prophet.†*

9. For he was called both *voice* and *prophet*. He *prepared the way for the* coming *Lord. He pointed out* his presence.‡ He immersed the sacred head in

*see Ps 36:31
*see John 10:38
*see John 5:36

*John 5:35

*Ps 96:3; Ps 49:3

*see John 5:35

*see 1 Cor 8:1
*John 5:35

*see 1 Cor 7:7;
12:10-11
†see Luke 7:26;
see Matt 3:3; see
Resp "Praecursor"
in Nat JB
(Hesbert 4:7420)
‡see John 1:29-
36; see Resp "Hic
Praecursor" in
Nat JB (Hesbert
4:6837)

the waters of the Jordan River.* He performed the office of baptizer with the Lord; him whom, baptizing *in Spirit and fire*,* the Lord had made a burning and shining light.* Burning and shining indeed, not for himself but for the bridegroom, whose friend and best man he was.* Shining also not for himself but for the bride. For he knew that he had not received the Spirit to display his own boasting and vanity, but for usefulness to his brother.

10. Everyone receives a manifestation *of the Spirit for usefulness*.* Otherwise, how will one be *a friend of the bridegroom*,* if one loves <to shine> not for the bridegroom but rather for oneself? Also, how would one be a friend of the bride, when one does not strive for her to succeed through him, but for himself to excel through her? He is not a friend of the bridegroom or the bride who *seeks his own glory*.* He seeks not freely who seeks secretly; afterward he will be one *who seeks and judges*.* Heal us, Lord, from this flying and returning passion,* and send *fire from above*.* into our marrow; may that blazing fire purge the smoke of this insolence.

11. Happy John, who among sublime gifts seemed unpretentious* and felt not high-minded,† merited to be called *a burning and shining light*.‡ Outwardly he was shining confidently in his word, inwardly anticipated by the flame of love. It is a bad substitution if anyone shines outwardly and yet inwardly just makes smoke. He presents well, but shares badly. He presents well, but he takes away, causing his own soul to shine among others, taking away from God. How often are we extolled concerning the smallest things, and for what good? John, *friend of the bridegroom*,* zealous for the bridegroom, *faithful* to him *in all his house*,* among sublime dignities and privileges of merits, when strengthened he was unwilling

*see Matt 3:13-17

*see Matt 3:11

*see John 5:35

*see John 3:29

*see 1 Cor 12:7

*see John 3:29

*John 7:18

*John 8:50

*see Ps 90:6

*see Lam 1:13

*see 1 Tim 6:17
†*nil sublime videns, nil sapiens altum*
‡see Rom 11:20;
see John 5:35

*see John 3:29

*see Heb 3:5;
see Num 12:7

to be extolled; he did not think to be puffed up or to fear.

12. He did not fear the course of his whole life, nor a humble death, a wrongful death, a death given with mockery. For on account of honest and useful rebukes, he provoked the hatred of princes against himself, and he was beheaded in prison. Thus indeed your saint, Lord, did not fear the words of the executioners, but keeping your precepts, he went to all to which you had sent him,* and he said everything that you had entrusted to him. He did not fear the threats of humans, but much more his *heart trembled at your words,** or rather, it was inflamed.

13. You gave him, Lord, a fiery tongue, *an educated tongue that he might teach* and know whom to support *by word,** whom to strike with harsh rebukes, whom to call *brood of vipers,** to whom he should say, *It is not lawful for you to have your brother's wife,** whom to teach <to be> content with their own pay,* whom to call to *fruits worthy of repentance*, whom to restrain from the swelling pride of Abraham's tribe,* and, from the hardness of stones, to raise some to the good hope of God's children. *God is able*, John says, *to raise up children of Abraham from these stones.** Therefore rightly *a burning and shining light,** by vow, by life, by word, thus reforming, thus directing, thus restraining, thus warming the souls of a variety of individual listeners.

14. Let us rejoice, brothers, and let us exult *in his light,** and in imitation of his obedience, <let us go> not just to some things but *to all,** not just to pleasant things but to harsh, not *for the hour* in the manner of the Jews but *even to death.** And if you have not been charged to speak about doctrine in sermons to others, if you have not been sent for the word, but for silence, then do what you were sent for. May you

*see Jer 1:7-8

*see Ps 118:161

*see Isa 50:4;
see Ps 104:22
*Luke 3:7

*Mark 6:18

*see Luke 3:14

*see Luke 3:8

*Luke 3:8

*see John 5:35

*see John 5:35
*see Jer 1:7

*see John 5:35;
see Phil 2:8

not exceed the boundaries of your mandate, because you were also thus sent to speak. Others are sent to speak by word; you are sent to speak by silence. How does a modest silence not speak through you, through whom holy worship is entrusted and speaks in you? Silence, processions, habits, gestures, all parts of a disciplined way of life, commend God in you and you in God, and yet you think that you are silent?

15. David says, *All my bones say: Lord, who is like to you?** Because he says "bones," then accept   *Ps 34:10 mighty works, distinguished works, yet suitably composed to complete one unbroken body of a holy way of life. Speak and exhort in this way, and you shall be efficaciously equipped. In this way, all things that the Lord has commanded you, you shall speak effectively. And if you have been sent, then you may not be silent. Consider that you were likewise <sent> to listen. It is said to you, "may you <not> be silent," and at the same time, "hear!" Therefore listen and hear what he who for you was made by God into a god* said in you,† what contrary to you, what against   *see Exod 7:1 your customs. *Be in agreement with your adversary*   †see Ps 84:9 *on the way** so he does not condemn you but rather   *see Matt 5:25 commend you to the judge—so that he does not *hand* you *over* like the guilty party, but rather delivers *the kingdom to God the Father.**   *see 1 Cor 15:24

16. No fear restrains you from imitation of all this obedience and listening, but by avid desire for obedience, *when you shall have done all these things, then say, We are useless servants; we have done only that which we ought to do.** Therefore may the Lord   *Luke 17:10 Jesus Christ, who went eagerly to all things to which he had been sent,* *made* for us *obedient to the Father*   *see Jer 1:7 *unto death*,* by the merits and prayers of his blessed   *Phil 2:8 precursor lead us by the way of obedience to the kingdom of life. Amen.

Sermon 135

On the Solemnity of the Apostles Peter and Paul

*2 Sam 1:23

1. **S**aul and Jonathan, lovable and handsome in their life: even in death <they were> not divided, swifter than eagles, stronger than lions.* It is not within our ability, nor even within our possibilities, to explain how great is the solemnity of this day. In fact, this solemnity is immense and illustrious, because they whose feast this is are great and illustrious. If, moreover, we were to celebrate individual solemnities for each one of these, one for Peter and one for Paul, you see, we would not be qualified to praise even one. Therefore what shall we say when we celebrate solemnities of such great apostles? We are not at all qualified. Nevertheless, rather like the devout woman who offered *two farthings*,* and like someone else who gave *a cup of cold water*,* let us do what we can; let us offer what we know.

*see Mark 12:42
*see Matt 10:42

2. What shall we say? Whom shall we put before whom? I am not sure. For great is the apostle Peter; Paul is also great, and Paul not less <than Peter>; perhaps Paul is <even greater> than Peter. Peter, teacher *of circumcision*; Paul, teacher *of un-circumcision*.* Peter, shepherd of the church, and Paul, shepherd of the church. Peter filled Judea with the Gospel <of Christ>.† Paul filled *the whole world from Jerusalem to Illyricum* with the Gospel <of Christ>.‡ This is greater: Peter <is> *prince of the apostle*s.# Paul *is a vessel of election*.§ Nevertheless,

*see Gal 2:7
†see Acts 10:37
‡see Mark 16:15;
see Rom 15:19
#see Ant et Resp
Pastor in Cath P
(Hesbert 3:5207;
4:7787)
§Acts 9:15; see
Ant et Resp Vas
in Paul (Hesbert
3:5211; 4:7789)

10

Peter <seems> to be superior* in three things: in firmness of faith, in authority of power, in strength or
doing of miracles.

  3. Peter's firmness of faith is preached everywhere,
everywhere put first. For when the Lord asked, as
though to others who doubt and stay silent, *Who do
people say that I am,** as a minister and teacher of
true faith, Peter said, *You are Christ, the Son of the
living God.*† And what did he receive from the Lord?
You are Peter, he said, *and upon this rock I shall
build my church:** that is, on the firmness of the faith
that you confessed, the whole church shall be established. Peter's faith is everywhere present. If at any
time it wavered, then it was aroused to be stronger.*
By faith he walked upon the waves.* By faith he did
many other things.

  4. Peter is superior in authority of power. For
when he himself was not present, he learned in Spirit
about the deceit of Ananias and Saphira, and by his
prerogative of power he declared the punishment of
death with just a word.* In order to assign this power,
the Lord gave to him *the keys of the kingdom of
heaven* and bestowed the power *of binding and loos-
ing.** He excels in the strength of miracles. For who
has worked as many mighty deeds as Peter? He is
the one whose shadow cured the sick,† whose prayer
healed a paralytic,‡ whose word raised the dead,#
whose power closes and opens heaven.§ Who therefore is like him? Paul, as I judge.

  5. In fact Peter's faith was Paul's faith, Peter's
power Paul's power, Peter's miracles Paul's miracles.
In fact, the Lord says not to Peter alone, *The works
that I do, you also shall do, and the greater of these
you shall do.** Therefore all things that were assigned
to Peter were granted to Paul. We find that Peter said
and did many things within the view of Paul, and Paul

praecellere

*Percunctanti enim
Domino quem eum
dicerent homines*
†Matt 16:13-16

*Matt 16:18

*see Luke 22:31-32
*see Matt 14:29

*see Acts 5:1-11

*see Matt 16:19;
see Resp Pastor
(Hesbert 4:7787)
†see Acts 5:15
‡see Acts 9:33-34
#see Acts 9:40
§see Matt 16:19

*John 14:12

was silent and did nothing. Why? Paul's humility and discretion were so great that [as] the younger, he supposed that he should defer to the elder, *the vessel of election** to the leader. Nevertheless what Peter did within Paul's view, Paul also did with Peter in faith. Just as we said that Peter seems to be superior* to Paul in three ways, so also Paul seems to surpass* Peter in three ways: in knowledge, in labors, in lifestyle.

6. In knowledge, as he says in the epistle, *I speak as one less wise; I am more. Although I am unskilled in speech, nevertheless not in knowledge.** Paul, while he was not yet old but in his very youth, *was caught up to third heaven.** Therefore let no one despise young people! Look, Solomon obtained a kingdom when twelve years of age.* For God is able to work for a young person as well as an older person. The youth Daniel, or rather the boy, adjudicated between two senior elders.* Joseph as a youth solved a riddle for a king and freed Egypt from plague and famine.* Paul had not yet come to his fifty-third year, in which he was allowed to watch over the Lord's vessels. He had not yet served from his twenty-fifth year to his fifty-third. But in the beginning of his apostleship, still in his very youth, he was made a guardian of the vessels of Christ, that is, of holy souls.* Paul was still a young man *caught up to third heaven.**

7. He calls three heavens the heaven of angels, the heaven of archangels, the heaven of the Trinity. Or, three types of vision are received through three heavens, as Augustine says: corporeal vision, spiritual vision, intellectual vision. Moreover, there is a corporeal vision by which material bodies are observed by corporeal means. Spiritual vision [is that] by which a soul or enraptured spirit sees corporeal images of material bodies by dreams or visions. Intel-

*see Acts 9:15

**excellere*
**praecellere*

*2 Cor 11:23, 6

*2 Cor 12:2, 4

*see 1 Kgs 1:28-30

*see Dan 13:45-62
*see Gen 41:25-57

*see Num 8:24-26
*see 2 Cor 12:2, 4

lectual vision is strength of mind by which it understands those realities that are seen by spiritual vision. Or, historical, mystical, and moral intelligence are received through three heavens. Paul *was snatched up* to the perfection and sublimity of these heavens. And *he was* snatched up *into Paradise, and* there *he heard words that a human being is not allowed to speak.** To no one has so much ever been revealed as to Paul, not to Peter and not to Andrew. So he says in another place, *Lest the greatness of the revelation should exalt me,* <etc.>.*

*2 Cor 12:4

*see 2 Cor 12:7

8. Paul is superior in sufferings, as he himself testifies: *In many more labors, in prisons more frequently, in lashings above measure, often in danger of death. Five times I have received forty lashings minus one from the Jews.** It had been established that each transgressor of the law should be judged; he was to be struck with forty blows, so the flogger might spare him if he wished.* However, the jealousy of the Jews so raged against Paul that when five times <he was> judged a transgressor, five times he received forty lashes,* yet never did the flogger spare him except by one lash. The mercy was small and the punishment great.

*see 2 Cor 11:23-24

*see Deut 25:2-3

*2 Cor 11:24

9. And still the apostle added more about his sufferings, saying, *Thrice was I beaten with sticks, once I was stoned, thrice I was shipwrecked. I was in the depth of the sea for a night and a day, in dangers of rivers, in dangers of robbers, in dangers from my own nation, in dangers from the Gentiles, in dangers in the wilderness, in dangers in the city, in dangers from false brethren,* and in many others.* Who has been found similar to this apostle in sufferings? He therefore surpassed Peter and all others in labors, as he himself says: *I have labored more than all.** And, *I suppose that I have done nothing less than the*

*2 Cor 11:25-26

*1 Cor 15:10

*2 Cor 11:5
*great apostles.** And likewise, *I ought to have been
commended by you. I have done nothing less than
those who are apostles above measure. For although
I am nothing, nevertheless the signs of my apostleship
have been done among you in all patience and signs*
*2 Cor 12:11-12
*and wonders and mighty deeds.**

10. Therefore he is a match for Peter, similar to
Andrew, equal to John. Because if he labored *more*
*see 1 Cor 15:10
*than all,** as he testifies, and to each is rendered ac-
*see Matt 16:27;
see Prov 12:14
†*Agrapha*, logion
38 (Resch 315–16);
see Isa 62:11 (LXX)
cording to his labor*—when what is written shall
happen, "Behold the person and his works"†—then
Paul, who labored more than others, will not receive
less than others. Therefore what shall we say? Can
it be that Paul is of greater merit, of greater glory
than Peter? Far be it from me to say this! Although
perhaps he was of greater knowledge, this is not an
increase of merit or glory, because sometimes an ignorant simpleton is of more [merit] in the sight of
God than a versatile philosopher. For knowledge
does not always increase merit, but oftentimes it di-
minishes it. So Solomon says, *One who adds knowl-*
*Eccl 1:18
*edge adds also sorrow.** And the apostle: *Knowledge*
*1 Cor 8:1
*puffs up; charity edifies.**

11. Peter knew as much as he required. Paul knew
<more> (if only more) because he required more, for
he was to be heard by many more people. This was
not for an increase of merit, but according to the
Lord's command, which Peter would have undertaken if he had been so charged. Likewise if it is a
question concerning worldly knowledge, then there
is nothing. If however it concerns heavenly knowledge, then Peter had that knowledge than which
there is none better, none greater, he whose wisdom
was Christ, he whose knowledge was God's Son.
Furthermore, Paul does not even profess something
else, saying, *I judge myself to know nothing among*

*you except Christ, and him crucified.** If Paul knew nothing besides Christ and not anything more than Christ, since Peter also knew the same Christ, then Paul did not know more than Peter. Peter and Paul are therefore equals in knowledge, because they are equals in Christ, who is their knowledge.

12. In sufferings, Peter and Paul are equally significant. Although in fact Peter suffered not so many lashings or riots in his body, nevertheless he suffered <mentally>, because he suffered compassion for one who had suffered; this suffering is sometimes greater or more severe. He who has suffered in mind and will is truly said to have suffered. So it is said about blessed Peter that he left behind things that he never had, because he abandoned a will for having. *Behold,* he says, *we have left behind everything and have followed you.** It is said concerning Mary, having suffered with her son on the cross, *And a sword shall pierce your own soul.** For there are two kinds of martyrdom and suffering, one of mind, the other of body. [That] of mind is not less than that of body. Therefore Peter and Paul are equals in sufferings. Similarly equal significance can be inferred from their labor.

13. In way of life, however, Paul seems to be superior, because he calls Peter blameworthy. For it is greater to be one who blames than the one blamed, if the latter is justly blamed and the former bothered to correct himself justly, as he should.* Still, that for which Peter is blamed had not tainted his way of life, nor had it caused sin. For it was not so much what was not permitted, but what was not expedient. For that reason blessed Jerome <says> that Paul did not blame Peter in fact, but rather by "applying a pretense."* Therefore Peter and Paul are equals in lifestyle. For Paul's rebuke did not pre-judge Peter's way

*1 Cor 2:2

*Matt 19:27

*Luke 2:35

*et ille iuste hoc
corrigere satagit
ut debeat;
see Gal 2:11

*see Jerome,
Ep ad Aug =
Augustine,
Ep 75.4 (CCSL
31A:56–57)

of life: "In fact it is uncertain who is put above whom. Moreover I believe them to be equal in merits" and glory, those whom "the same day, the same place, one persecutor" honored with the glory of martyrdom, as it is written, "The day is kept for merit, the place for glory, the persecutor for virtue."* By their prayers and merits may we join them in heaven, those whose triumphs on this present day we celebrate on earth. Amen.

*Maximus of Turin, SS 1.2 (CCSL 23:2–3)

Sermon 136

On the Solemnity of the Apostles Peter and Paul

1. *S**aul and Jonathan, lovable and handsome in their life: even in death they were not divided.** Many things in the Old Testament, in the law clearly, in the psalms and prophets,† in the books of Kings and Judges, are not only about Christ, but in truth are also interpreted [as being] about the apostles. Therefore, by the elder—Saul—Peter is understood; by the younger—Jonathan—Paul. By the father Peter, by the son Paul. Paul in fact, although not by carnal begetting, was Peter's son by spiritual rebirth, because he was baptized by the church, whose pastor and leader was Peter.

2. Moreover, Saul sometimes bears the character of Christ, sometimes of the devil, sometimes of the apostles, sometimes of the Jews. Saul is interpreted as "requested"* and signifies anyone chosen whom the Son asks from the Father, just as the psalmist says, *Ask of me, and I will give to you the Gentiles for your inheritance.** Peter was more specifically requested not only by the Lord, but even by the devil, as Truth himself says: *Behold Satan has requested you so that he may sift you like wheat.**

3. Paul is understood through Jonathan, interpreted as "dove's gift."* For the gift was a dove's, because when [Paul] had received letters for binding and killing all who were invoking the Lord's name,* Christ appeared to him on the road, and after the light of wickedness was removed from him, [Christ]

*2 Sam 1:23; see Ant "Glor" in Oct apos (Hesbert 3:2960)
†see Luke 24:44

*Jerome, Int nom 14 (CCSL 72:77)

*Ps 2:8

*Luke 22:31

*Jerome, Int nom 33 (CCSL 72:100)
*see Acts 9:2, 14

17

gave to him the light of knowledge and gifts of the Spirit:* wisdom and understanding, counsel and fortitude, knowledge and piety and a spirit of fear of the Lord.* He struck down Saul and raised up Paul. Behold the dove's gift.

4. *Saul,* therefore, *and Jonathan, lovable and handsome.** Five virtues are assigned here in which the holy apostles Peter and Paul are strongly commended. Charity when he says *lovable*; chastity when he says *handsome*; patience when he says *in death they were not divided*; contemplation when he adds *swifter than eagles*; perseverance when he inserts *stronger than lions.** Although we would be able to speak about each of these at greater length, let us run through them briefly.

5. Charity therefore is divided into two: into love of God and love of neighbor.* Charity begins some things, accomplishes some things, perfects others. In the <first place> God ought to be loved more than ourselves. In the second place we ought to love ourselves more than parents and relatives. In the third place, parents and relatives more than the rest of our friends. In the fourth place, friends more than outsiders who are neither friends nor enemies. In the fifth place, outsiders more than enemies. In the sixth place, enemies. It is better to love friends than enemies, but it is more virtuous and perfect to love enemies than friends. The latter belongs to few, the former to many. But how must this order in charity be observed, when we are commanded to love all neighbors as ourselves?*

6. Therefore the aforementioned order must be observed in charity, and anyone is to be loved *as* ourselves.* Yet we should love ourselves more than enemies or friends, but [love] them also *as* ourselves. *As* is an adverb of similarity, not quantity. In fact, we

*see Acts 9:8, 17-18

*see Isa 11:2-3

*2 Sam 1:23

*2 Sam 1:23

*see Matt 22:37-39

*see Mark 12:31

*see Matt 22:39

love all as ourselves when we aspire to the good for everyone that we desire for ourselves. Nevertheless, we can aspire to the same good things both for ourselves and for others, although more for ourselves than for others. In fact, nothing prevents the same good things from happening to various people by various means. But because there are many who put carnal love before spiritual, he removes this from Peter and Paul, saying *lovable and handsome in their life,** that is, in Christ, who was their life, as Paul says: *For me to live is Christ, and to die is gain.** And the Lord himself: *I am the way, the truth, and the life.**

    *2 Sam 1:23
    *Phil 1:21
    *John 14:6

7. Therefore because he says *handsome*, purity is understood. This consists in two aspects, that we be chaste in body and in spirit. In fact, one who has a soiled spirit has a chaste body to no purpose. This virtue is therefore necessary for all, because without it one benefits in no other way. For if anyone were to put a good drink in an unclean vessel, then an invited guest would turn up his nose and throw away the drink or tray. So as our Lord wants to be satisfied by good works from us, if we offer them in unclean bodies, then he will spurn our tables and trays. In fact, without cleanness, all good works that seem to be good are dirty, as it is written, *All things are clean to the clean, but to the unclean*, etc.** Moreover, there is a cleanness not only in chastity, but also in hands, in tongue, in eyes, and in caring for all members. So Scripture says, *At all times let your garments be white.** *Garments* it says, not "garment." But how great was the purity of the apostles Peter and Paul is not within our ability to explain. They always observed purity, preached incessantly, ceaselessly renounced those who were morally defiled, zealously commended virgins. Read their writings and you will find these things.

    *Titus 1:15

    *Eccl 9:8

*2 Sam 1:23

8. It follows, *In death they were not divided.**
Behold patience. This is a royal virtue that is signified
by purple. It is ordered to be offered in the Lord's
tabernacle, that is, in our body, which is his tabernacle that must be guarded.* Regarding how great
is the fruit of patience, Scripture is not silent. In the
psalm one reads, *The patience of the poor shall not
perish in the end.** And the Lord in the gospel, *In
your patience you shall possess your souls.** And
James, *Patience has a perfect work.** So also Solomon, *The patient man is better than the valiant man.**
Likewise, *Woe to those who have lost patience!**
What shall we say about the patience of these
apostles who freely embraced death for Christ, desiring *to be dissolved and to be with Christ?** Also, after
very many torments, one triumphed on a cross, the
other under a sword.

*see Exod 26:1,
31, 36

*Ps 9:19
*Luke 21:19
*Jas 1:4
*Prov 16:32
*Sir 2:16

*Phil 1:23

*2 Sam 1:23

*see Ezek 1:5

*Job 28:7

*Matt 24:28

*Job 39:27

*Exod 19:4

9. They are called *swifter than eagles* and *stronger than lions.** Here contemplation and perseverance are expressed. An eagle is sometimes taken to
mean Christ, just as by those four spiritual animals.*
By a bird also, as in that saying of Job, *The bird has
not known the path, nor has the eye of the vulture
beheld it.** By eagles any spiritual men might be designated. So Truth says, *Where the body shall be, there
the eagles shall also be brought together.** So blessed
Job: *The eagle shall lift up your command, and put
her nest in high places.** And the Lord in the Law:
*You have seen what I have done to the Egyptians
and how I have led you away on the wings of eagles
and have taken you to myself.** He says Moses and
Aaron are eagles who ascended to higher realities by
contemplation, or he calls the doctrines of the two
testaments eagles.

10. Rightly is a spiritual man taken to be an eagle.
For one who has recognized the qualities of an eagle

will be able to pay attention to these things. In fact, an eagle flies faster than all flying creatures and higher than all. After she has grown old, an eagle approaches the sun to the point that her old feathers are forced out by the heat of the sun. Once the feathers have been cast off, new ones begin to grow, and thus the eagle regains her youth. Also, after one restoration, she is able to abstain from food for a long time and is [so] accustomed. She hunts and catches and eats a hawk. With her unblinking eyes, she focuses on the light in the sun's rays. What are these if not qualities of a spiritual man? One who flies faster by obedience, higher by prayer and holy meditation. He approaches the sun and casts off old age by confession. He abstains <from> food by frugality. He pursues a hawk, that is, the devil, by alms. He gazes upon the rays of the true sun by contemplation.

11. Therefore one who does obedience unwillingly, or slowly, or lazily, or with murmuring* does not fly swiftly, is not an eagle. One who is not attentive to prayer or reading (by one of which he ought to speak with God, by the other God with him) does not fly high, is not an eagle. One who disregards the smallest sins (which Solomon warns against, saying, "Son, you have avoided large [boulders]; may you not be buried by sand")¹* and thus neglects confession does not cast off old feathers, is not an eagle. Similarly, in another place Scripture says, *One who disdains small things shall fall by little and little.*† One who eats "before the established hour"‡ or more often than others, or prepares food in a different way

*see RB 5:14

*see Augustine, En in Ps 39.22 (CCSL 38:441); Ioann 12.14 (CCSL 36:129) †Sir 19:1 ‡see RB 43.18

---

¹ The edition adds to this citation, *sententia deprompta, ut videtur, ex Augustino et saepe adhibita saec[ulo] XII*, i.e., "This sentence is drawn from Augustine, as it seems, and often applied in the twelfth century."

from the rest, is not an eagle. One who does not hunt the devil through alms, who does not catch the hawk, is not an eagle. One who does not love contemplation, but wandering, who does not focus his eyes on the rays of the sun, is not an eagle.

12. Truly how great are these prerogatives guarded by the holy apostles Peter and Paul, their works bear witness more than our words will suffice to declare. In fact, we do not suffice to say with what great perseverance they embraced not only these but also many other virtues. So it adds *stronger than lions,** for perseverance is the consummation of all good works. For there is no profit in beginning if there will not be enough to also finish.* There are many good beginners who are not steadfast. Perseverance reaps and collects whatever good each has accomplished, according to the judgment of the Lord, who says, *One who reaps receives wages.** And, *One who shall persevere unto the end shall be saved.** This is the strength of the saints, about which the psalmist says, *I will guard my strength to you.** This belonged to the holy apostles whom we called *stronger than lions.**

13. The lion is of such a nature that when he has eaten more flesh than he needs, and then a hunter has chased him, even with a pack of dogs, he habitually extracts the eaten flesh from his mouth with his claws.* His mercy is great. He spares people when they lie prostrate; he rages against men who resist but is touched by mercy on women and children.† He has courage in his heart, strength in his head.‡ He fears the crowing of chickens and the noise of wheels, but he fears fires even more. When he hunts prey, he makes a trap in the method of a circle with his tail flat upon the ground. And then, so that he does not fear any wild animal, he strikes himself with

*2 Sam 1:23

*see Luke 14:30

*John 4:36
*Matt 10:22

*Ps 58:10
*2 Sam 1:23

*see Pliny Sec., *Naturalis historia* 8.18
†see Pliny Sec., *Naturalis historia* 8.19
‡see Isidore, *Etymologiae* 12.2; see Pliny Sec., *Naturalis historia* 8.19

his own tail;[2] afterward he lets out a terrible roar, and so, feeling secure, he seizes the prey.* *Pliny Sec., Naturalis historia 8.19

14. Whenever Christ is represented by a lion, or whenever the devil, whenever any accomplished saint, whenever irreverent people, we recognize them as examples. These are the qualities of a spiritual and brave man. When he has eaten flesh more than is proper, he extracts it from his mouth with his own claws; that is, when he has fallen into some carnal conversation, he tries to eject it by his own rebuke and abstinence in every way, lest he be captured by the spiteful enemies who pursue him.

15. The lion is said to be of great mercy, and so should a spiritual man be. For this is the virtue that made God's Son descend from heaven to earth. So the Lord himself said to Peter, who asked if he should forgive a guilty person seven times when he asks <pardon>, *I say not seven times, but till seventy times seven.** He spares those who lie prostrate, he rages *Matt 18:21-22 fiercely against those who resist, according to that saying, *God resists the proud, but gives grace to the humble.** And he says about the humbled Ahab, *Jas 4:6; *Have you not seen Ahab humbled before me?* There- 1 Pet 5:5 fore *I will not bring evils in his days.** He says about *1 Kgs 21:29 Sennacherib, who resisted and rebelled, *Whom have you reproached, and against whom have you raised your neck: was it not against the holy one of Israel?** *2 Kgs 19:22 On which account *I will put a loop in your nose and a bit between your lips, and I will lead you back by the way that you came.** *2 Kgs 19:28

16. He shows mercy to the weak and innocent, according to that saying, *Blessed are the merciful, for they shall obtain mercy.** And again, <I wish> *Matt 5:7

---

[2] According to Pliny, lions beat their sides with their tail to make themselves ferocious.

*Matt 9:13

*mercy and not sacrifice.** One has courage in his heart who always has that courage that is from God,

*see 1 Cor 1:24

and God's wisdom in his mind and will.* So the heart

*see Exod
29:27-28;
see Lev 10:15

is ordered to be a sacrifice *by perpetual right** for the use of a priest. He has strength in his head, that is, he has a firm faith with hope and love in Christ, who is the head of all who believe, as the apostle says: *The head of the woman is the man, the head of*

*1 Cor 11:3

*a man is Christ, the head of Christ is God.**

17. He fears the crowing of roosters. Christ is the good rooster, as Ambrose says: "Hope returns at the crowing of the cock." And: "The rooster <awakens>

*Ambrose, H 1
"Aeterna rerum
conditor," 151,
vv. 21, 18, 20
*Prov 10:29
LXX

those who recline, <it> rebukes <those who deny>."* The good lion fears him, according to that saying of the prophet: *The defense of the saints is fear of the Lord.** Priests are the good roosters. The spiritual person fears and respects and honors them. He does not toss aside their reproof but receives it with fear and satisfaction. Demons are the bad roosters, who do not cease whispering evil things in the ears of saints, and these must be feared, lest they plant wicked seeds in us. Evil roosters, detractors, adulterers, murmurers. These are the servants of demons. The spiritual lion pursues all these, that is, lords and servants, with a relentless hate.

18. The noises of wheels are the ways of the unjust. The spiritual man fears to go by these ways, and to hear and to see them. But [he fears] fire even more. Infernal punishment is understood by fire, as in blessed Job: *they shall pass from the heat of fire to*

*see Job 24:19

the cold of snow.[3]* The advance of the wicked is designated by the turning of wheels, according to the

---

[3] *Transibunt a caloribus ignium ad frigora nivium.* Vulg: *Ad nimium calorem transeat ab aquis nivium, et usque ad inferos peccatum illius.*

psalm: *The wicked walk around in a circle.** But
other wheels are taken in a good sense.

    19. When a lion strives to hunt prey, he makes a
trap with his tail flat on the ground; thus enclosed
wild animals dare not go out, and excluded animals
do not go in. By wild animals is meant perverse suggestions or thoughts, which when a spiritual lion tries
to kill, he sets a trap in the manner of a circle with
his tail. The tail is the posterior part of the body, and
it signifies later works, by which the devil always sets
traps. For he does not care what sort of person you
were before, if you are going to be within his law.* As
it is written, *He shall lie in wait for her heel.** Therefore with our tail, that is, by our last works, we should
make a circle and catch the worst wild animals in it.

    20. The circle is the life of a just person and a
good lifestyle, not having a haughty eyebrow or an
angle of duplicity. We ought to make this circle among
ourselves with interdependent virtues, according to
that saying of Gregory: "One virtue without another
is little or nothing." "For what does proud virginity
or soiled humility profit?"* Finally the circle is rightly
taken to mean a good lifestyle, because a circle lacks
beginning and end, but anywhere you wish, you can
place a beginning or end. Thus a good lifestyle has
no limit to good service, but wherever you look at
it, you shall find the beginning of behaving well and
of achieving an end. Wild animals remain enclosed
in this circle, not going out, but thoughts are caught
and die within, if they are admitted.

    21. If some pride creeps into a thought, it does
not go out into a work. For humility resists in the
circle and says, "You shall not go out through me;
you shall die within." If avarice steals into a thought,
it does not progress into action.* For magnanimity
makes a stand in the circle of virtues and says, "You

*Ps 11:9

sui iuris
*Gen 3:15

*Gregory I, Mor
21.III.6 (CCSL
143A:1068)

*see RB 57.7

shall not go out; you shall die within." If lust stains
the mind by some suggestion, it is held in check by
service. For chastity is present in the circle and says,
"In vain do you struggle, enemy temptation. I resist.
I am stronger. I have superior power. You shall not
go out through me; you shall be held firmly within."
And so think carefully about other things. In the
same manner, vices, which are the worst wild animals, if they are not admitted previously into thought,
then they are not able to force themselves through
the circle of virtues. For the virtues resist, not allowing the passage of vices through themselves.

22. After he has made a trap with his tail, the lion
strikes himself with his tail so that he might fear no
wild animal. Thereupon the spiritual lion strikes himself with his tail when the spiritual person considers
his works less perfect, less holy; he judges himself,
condemns himself, accuses himself in view of the
supreme judge; he declares himself a sinner; he testifies that he is wretched and unfortunate. One who
thus accuses himself in contrition of heart, in true
and pure confession of his mouth before God and his
vicar, will utterly extinguish suggestions of demons
and the harmful deceptions of thoughts. By which
fact, after the joining of virtues, after interrogation
and accusation of himself, whatever thought or
whatever temptation has emerged shall at once be
dissipated, annihilated, and dissolved. [Temptations]
enclosed [within the circle] shall not go out, and
those excluded shall not be admitted, but *a thousand*
*Ps 90:7   *shall fall at his side, and ten thousand at* his *right.**
One shall pursue a thousand, and two chase ten
*Deut 32:30   *thousand.** And thus the spiritual man, like the lion,
strongest of beasts, shall not fear to meet anything.

23. Therefore, brothers, we extol the proclamations of the apostles, each of whom is not only com-

pared to eagles and lions, but truly called *swifter than eagles* and *stronger than lions** as well. Considering their doctrine, frequently reading their life, let us be conformed to them according to our small measure, let us imitate their examples, let us embrace their virtues. For in fact one who imitates their works truly venerates their feasts. The glorious leaders Peter and Paul, joined in firmness of faith and sincerity of charity, *even in death were not divided.** Therefore so that we might live with them eternally, in true charity let us persevere. May our Lord Jesus Christ deign to grant this to us, who lives and reigns through all ages forever. Amen.

*see 2 Sam 1:23

*2 Sam 1:23

Sermon 137[1]

On the Nativity of
Saint John the Baptist

1. We ought to celebrate all the feast days of the saints as they are established in the church with joy and devotion, but especially those feast days that have authority from the Gospel, not only by the institution of the fathers. The feast of the blessed John the Baptist has Gospel authority. Thus the angel: *And many,* he said, *will rejoice in his birth.** These are the many about whom the Lord said, *Many will come from the east and the west and will recline with Abraham, Isaac, and Jacob in the kingdom of God.** Accordingly, because we are among those many, let us rejoice in the birth of Saint John.

2. However, let our joy not be in such things as those that are customarily the joys of worldly people, <that is,> in precious clothes, in delicate foods, and in many meaningless things. All of these are outside, and they go out of themselves; they care for the body that is outside, and they neglect the soul that is within. Our glory and joy ought to be within, because our greater care is for the soul rather than the body. Thus says the apostle, *<This is our glory, the testimony of our conscience.** For it is necessary that our joy be mixed, as the same apostle says:> As if sad, always however rejoicing.** Who can have perfect

*Luke 1:14

*Matt 8:11;
Luke 13:29

*2 Cor 1:12

*2 Cor 5:6, 10

---

[1] This sermon is in close agreement with S 44 (CCCM 2A:345–51; CF 77:136–44).

joy in this life? The body weighs us down, the devil troubles us, temptation attacks us. Nevertheless, we have great joy in the hope we have in the Lord, through whom we will be freed from these evils and come to perfect joy.

3. The Lord gives us a certain analogy about this sadness and this joy: *A woman,* he says, *when she is in childbirth, has sadness.** This woman signifies the soul that is bearing spiritual children, of whom the prophet says, *Your children shall be like olive branches,* etc.* Children are good works. Therefore, as a *woman giving birth has sadness* about the pain she feels and yet has joy <of her hope for> what she bears, so also we have sadness in this spiritual childbirth because of labors and temptations, because without those we cannot do good works. But we ought also to have joy because of the hope for that blessedness we will have because of good works, which we do with a certain measure of sadness.

4. Therefore we ought to rejoice not only because of the reward we expect for these tribulations, but also because we are worthy to suffer some trouble for our Lord and to return something to him for the trouble that he suffered for us, as it is written about the apostles: *The disciples went rejoicing to face the council,* etc.* And truly, brothers, I do not know if anyone can have this joy of which we speak in his conscience if he does not know that he suffered something for the Lord. Therefore we can rejoice in these festivals of the saints insofar as we see that we follow their faith, their manner of life, and the suffering they endured for the Lord.

5. Accordingly, let us now observe the conduct and life of that man whose feast we celebrate today, and insofar as our life is in accord with his, let us rejoice. He fled into the desert because he did not

*John 16:21

*Ps 127:3

*Acts 5:41

wish to live among the worldly. His clothing was
camel skins, because he did not care for precious and
comfortable garments. He ate *locusts and wild honey*

*Matt 3:4;
Mark 1:6

because he did not seek rich and refined foods.* Regarding his way of life, pay attention to his with-
drawal from the world, the roughness of his clothing,
the meanness of his food and drink. I believe that
you see and rejoice that our life greatly harmonizes
with his life. For you are similarly withdrawn from
the world, you are dressed in cheap clothing, you are
nourished on rough foods. Is it not therefore just that
you who imitate his life share in his joy?

6. But where did his joy come from? His joy
could not be from external things, of which he had
nothing but labors and severity. Everyone wondered
and praised because he so lived. Did he perhaps rejoice about that? Many do this. They do not rejoice
because they do well but because they are much
praised. Such was not Blessed John. For had he been
like that, could he not have accepted that praise from
people showing that they believed that he himself
was Christ, as many did? But he dissuaded them from
believing this when he said, *I am not the one whom*

*Acts 13:5 Vulg

*you believe me to be.** Do you see how clear it is that
he had no joy in human praise? Therefore where did
his joy come from? Let him tell us, let him show us
what we ought to desire.

7. *The one,* he says, *who has the bride is the bridegroom; the friend of the bridegroom however stands
and listens to him and rejoices with joy because of*

*John 3:29

*the voice of the bridegroom.** He called Christ the
bridegroom. But of whom is he the bridegroom? Un-
doubtedly of the soul! Who can make the human
soul his bride, except our Lord? Who can unite a
human soul to himself and make himself one with
her and make her a sharer in his joy and his sweet-

ness except the Christ? Therefore he says, *the one who has the bride is the bridegroom.* And what was Saint John? Hear what he was: *The friend of the bridegroom.* Great is this John, who is the friend of Jesus Christ. Who can be greater than the friend of Christ? He has servants; he has friends. What more could he have? Without a doubt he had neither lord nor father. No one at all can be greater than his friend. Therefore *among those born of women <there arose none greater than John the Baptist>.** *Matt 11:11

8. *The friend of the bridegroom stands.** He is *John 3:29 not moved, he does not waver, he does not fall, but he stands. Therefore a certain friend of the bridegroom [says], *The Lord lives, in whose sight I stand.** Blessed *1 Kgs 17:1 the one who stands in the sight of the Lord. There are many who stand in the sight of people but who fall* in the sight of the Lord. But the friend stands. *iacent The one sinks* who passes from a good life to an *cadit evil one. The one falls* who hangs onto his vices and *iacet sins and carnal desires. But the friend of the bridegroom stands, the one who holds *straight his way, who does not* turn *toward either the right or the left,** who does not bend toward the earth. Such was *Isa 30:31; 31:21 this *blessed man.** He did not fly upward, he did not *Ps 1:1 bend himself down; therefore he stood.

9. The one who wished to fly upward said, *I will place my seat in the north, and I will be like the Most High.** People incited John to fly when they said, *Are* *Isa 14:14 *you the Christ?** But he did not wish to fly, but to *John 1:19;
Luke 3:15 stand in the position in which the Lord had placed him. *I am not the Christ,* he said.* Oh, how unhappy *John 1:20; 3:28 was Adam, who did not wish to remain in the position in which the Lord had placed him but wanted to fly and be like God. He did not wish to be a friend, but an equal. Therefore from a friend he was made a wretched slave. [John] could have been supposed

to be Christ, and he didn't want to. Therefore from a slave he was made a friend.

10. *The friend, however, stands and listens to him.** Happy the one who can listen to the bridegroom.** The soul who is the bride† can do so. Some people listen to him as a king, others as a judge, others as a teacher. But the friend of the bridegroom, whose soul is <the friend>* of the bridegroom and the bride of Christ, listens to him as a bridegroom. Adam heard him when he was walking in Paradise; he heard him as his judge. Therefore he feared and *hid himself.** The one heard him as his king who said, *You yourself are my king.** Moses heard him as a teacher when he said to him, *Go, <do> all things according to the example that I showed you on the mountain.** The soul that can say, *I will listen to what the Lord God speaks within me** hears him as a bridegroom. There the friend of the bridegroom stands, there *he listens to him and rejoices with joy because of the voice of the bridegroom.** Oh, how interior is that joy! *All his glory is from within.** There within, there he rejoices because of the voice of the bridegroom.

11. Just as you have heard that you share the rigors that Saint John endured, also understand how you share those joys that are interior, not outside— you who are accustomed inwardly to hear *the voice of the bridegroom* and to rejoice *because of his voice.* Where do your frequent tears and your sighs come from, except because you hear inwardly something I know not how sweet, I know not how delightful? As you read in Ezekiel, sometimes a hidden voice came to his soul, which sometimes came from below the firmament, sometimes from the firmament itself, sometimes from above the firmament.*

12. Sometimes the Lord makes the soul feel <something> of his sweetness, by which he makes

*John 3:29
*sponsum
†sponsa

*amica

*see Gen 3:8, 10

*Ps 43:5

*Exod 25:40;
Heb 8:5; Num 8:4

*Ps 84:9

*John 3:29

*Ps 44:14

*Ezek 1:22-25

him consider the beauty of his creation and so consider how beautiful is the one who created such beautiful things.* But this is the voice from under the firmament. The spiritual creation† that the Lord made, that is the firmament, and it is called *heaven* because of unity, and sometimes *the heavens* because of multiplicity. Consider what great joy the soul conceives when she* can see how marvelously, how mercifully, how sweetly our Lord works in these heavens, in this firmament!

13. How much the soul has of joy within herself when she considers those fishermen becoming rulers of the whole world, when she sees publicans become evangelists, thieves changed into preachers! What [joy] when the Lord places before her eyes the greatness of the mercy at work in herself when she sees herself, formerly given to luxury, become chaste; formerly drunk, become sober; formerly wrathful, become patient; formerly proud, become humble! What person to whom the Lord says this in her heart and shows his great mercy does not rejoice *because of the voice of the bridegroom?* But these things are the voice from the firmament.

14. But when the Lord illuminates the soul with his presence and in some marvelous way reveals his secrets—now of Scripture, now of heavenly joy, of his sweetness, of the mysteries,* of his divine plan— then the soul hears the voice from above the firmament, because it is not through the creation of the world, not through a human being, not through an angel, but through his own proper presence that he makes that soul hear what he is pleased [to say]. In that way, Paul heard the mystery* of the Gospel, he who said, *Not from men nor through a man.** And again: *My Gospel which <is announced is not from me, nor did I receive it from any human being,> etc.**

*for §§12–14 see Gregory I, In Ez 8:12–16 (CCSL 142:108–19)
†*creatura*

*i.e., the soul

sacramentis

sacramenta
*Gal 1:1

*Gal 1:11-12

15. The *friend of the bridegroom* certainly heard this <voice>. And he heard it very early. In the womb of his mother he heard the *voice of the bridegroom*. Therefore he rejoiced, as his mother said to blessed Mary: *As soon as <the voice of your salutation* *sounded in my ears, the infant in my womb exulted>.** Think, brothers, what joy he had in his heart when he saw him, when he touched him with his hands, when he saw the Holy *Spirit descending like a dove* upon him, when he heard the voice of the Father *from heaven,* he who had had such joy in that narrow space of his mother's womb! What kind of joy he had when he saw and experienced all those things outwardly and heard the causes of all those things within!

16. Would that we might experience this inward joy! We worthily and rightly rejoice in his birth if we imitate his way of life. Therefore praise him. How? Let your life be his praise. Then we may well show how much he is to be praised if we choose to live as he lived. And rightly so. Without a doubt and with great security we can follow him whom our Lord calls his angel. *Behold*, he says, *I am sending my angel, who will prepare my way before your face.** The Lord said this about him through the prophet a long time before he was born. For the Lord says in the Gospel that this was *written* about [John].* He was sent before our Lord as the dawn before the sun. This is that dawn before which Jacob could not receive the blessing of the Lord.

17. You have heard how Jacob wrestled the whole night with an angel. When the dawn arose, the angel wished to depart from him. And Jacob said to him, *I will not let you go until you have blessed me.** *And immediately he blessed him.*† The whole human race was under a curse. Jacob stands for the

*Luke 1:44

*Mal 3:1;
Matt 11:10;
Luke 7:27

*Matt 11:10;
Luke 7:27

*Gen 32:26
†Mal 3:1;
Gen 32:29

holy fathers who were before the incarnation of the
Lord, who with tears and prayers and a good life
wished to constrain our Lord to take flesh, he who
would remove this curse and give a blessing. Because
of the great desire that they had, they were impatient.
But he was waiting for the time that he with the
Father had foreseen. That wrestling match perhaps
signified that. And what did the Lord say? *Behold, I
am sending my angel, who will prepare your way
before you.** It is as if the angel had said to Jacob,
*He is coming at once.** "Why do you constrain me
to bless you? First the dawn must arise, and at once
I will bless [you]."

18. When that battle took place, it was night. <It
was night> as long as that curse lasted, as long as the
devil, who truly is the night, dominated the world.
However, the dawn rose before the sun, that prophet
before our Lord prepared the way for the sun, as the
Gospel says: *He was not the light,** that is, the full
shining of the sun. But just as the dawn is not the
sun but somehow a witness that the rising of the sun
is coming soon, so blessed John was *not the light but
came forth as a witness to the light.**

19. And it seems to me that not only then, but
even now that angel *prepares the way of the Lord,**
because as you follow his example, mortifying *your
members* and being eager for the renunciations and
austerities of this life,* without a doubt the way is
prepared by which our Lord wills to come to our
hearts so that we, like true friends of *the bridegroom,*
may be able inwardly to hear his voice and, on account of his voice, rejoice.*

20. And therefore, brothers, let us hold with all
fervor to this way that this friend of Jesus has prepared by his example, so that when we have shared
in the austerities he himself endured, we may share

*Mal 3:1;
Matt 11:10;
Luke 2:27
*Mal 3:1

*John 1:8

*John 1:8

*Matt 3:1;
Isa 40:3;
Mal 3:1

*Origen,
Super Luc 4.6
(SCh 87:134)

*John 3:29

the interior joy that he experienced. And so may we come to that perfect and eternal happiness to which he arrived through the mercy of our Lord Jesus Christ, *to whom* is *honor and glory* through infinite ages of ages. Amen.

Sermon 138[1]

On the Nativity of
Saint John the Baptist

1.   Someone who speaks the word of God to others ought to aim not at how he can vaunt his own knowledge but at how he can build up his hearers. Therefore he ought to moderate his speech for the ability of his audience and, with a motherly compassion for weaker intellects, as I might say, should prattle, descend to baby talk. However, I consider Zacharias, the father of this holy man whose feast we celebrate today. When he wanted to express the name of John, while expressing the name itself he who had previously been mute became extremely eloquent.* And perhaps we, if we begin to speak about John, will not be altogether mute.

    *Luke 1:63-64

2. But what shall we say about him or what in his praise, he who before he was born was praised by angelic authority, and who in the womb was by an inexpressible grace made a most worthy dwelling place of the Holy Spirit?* And it should also not be overlooked that a priest was chosen, from whom he was to be born; a temple, in which his birth was foretold; a name, which was to be conferred on him; and an angel, who conferred it.* And indeed the hour should not be overlooked: indeed it is *the hour of incense.**

    *Luke 1:15-17

    *Luke 1:8-13

    *see Luke 1:10

---

[1] This sermon is in close agreement with Aelred's S 14 (CCCM 1A:114–20; CF 58:218–26).

3. Would that, brothers, we also might be among those priests to whom the apostle Peter <said>, *You also are a chosen race, a royal priesthood.** Would that our hearts might become *the temple of God*, as the apostle says: *The temple of God is holy, and you are that temple!** Perhaps the hour of the incense offering is the hour of salutary compunction, when our *prayer rises like incense in the sight* of the Lord,* and an angel, a messenger of divine grace, will appear to us. For John means "the grace of God."*

4. And this name is aptly conferred at the command of an angel on him who while still in his mother's womb recognized that inexpressible grace by which *the Word was made flesh,** and with his finger he pointed out that same Word in flesh. He was the wonderful preacher of God's grace, and by his words he opened the doors of the kingdom of heaven to publicans and harlots,* doing violence, as it were, to heaven's purity by their conversion. So the Lord says in the Gospel, *Since the days of John, the kingdom of heaven has suffered force.** It surely did not suffer before the days of John. For till then the cherubim with the whirling sword kept wretched Adam, hiding beneath the leaves of a fig tree, away from the entrance of Paradise* and to some degree frustrated his efforts to do it violence.

5. Until then those *seven women* who ate their own bread and dressed in their own clothes suffered *reproach** as they went about looking for some one man upon whom they could all lay hold, and they did not find him. Individually they indeed laid hold of various men and women, but there was no one person they could all lay hold of together who would take away their reproach until that one man <came>, because he was unique, because he was singular. For he was singular until he came over. He, I say, was the one man whom a woman encompassed.* His wife is

*1 Pet 2:9

*1 Cor 3:17

*Ps 140:2

*Jerome,
Int nom 69
(CCSL 72:146)

*John 1:14

*Matt 21:31

*Matt 11:12

*Gen 3:7, 24

*Isa 4:1

*Jer 31:22

human flesh, which in the virginal womb by a <marvelous> dispensation divinity took [the flesh] that in the other children of Adam was long sterile. In this lordly man it has borne sevenfold, because the Lord himself dwelled wondrously, because physically.* *Col 2:9

6. This is the one man all those seven women had hold of together, that is, the seven graces,* which do not need bread or clothing. What is the food of the Holy Spirit? The Lord says in the Gospel, *My food is to do the will of my Father.* The Holy Spirit delights to breathe in this food. His clothes are the saints, in whose hearts this divine fire is accustomed to be nurtured and, as it were, warmed. Thus it says, *And with all of these you shall be clothed as with garments.* Even before the coming of John they were clothed with these garments, and with this bread they were delightfully fed. They shone with the aid of the grace of the Holy Spirit: some with the spirit of wisdom, others with that of understanding, others of counsel, others of fortitude, others of piety, others of knowledge, and others of fear.* *Isa 4:1 *John 4:34 *Isa 49:18 *Isa 11:2-3

7. What *reproach* then did the Holy Spirit suffer in these seven women? He conferred justice on men and women, and they did not return the recompense of justice. For what is the recompense of justice? The kingdom of heaven. Therefore the force of justice demanded the kingdom of heaven for itself, but the kingdom of heaven did not admit this force until the one who took away the reproach came and, with the cherub and the whirling sword taken away, opened the portal of Paradise to those who with force, crucifying *their flesh with its vices and passions,* claim justice for themselves. *Gal 5:24

8. But what does it mean: *Let us bear your name?* Let this man Jesus be wisdom, let him be understanding, let him be counsel, fortitude, knowledge, piety, fear. For it is also written, *You are our fear.* Let *Isa 4:1 *see Gen 31:42

wisdom set aside the cherubim and the whirling sword. The cherubim seem to me to be divine justice, which excluded the proud and disobedient from Paradise until they were released from their pride by humility, from their disobedience by obedience. <Because> they were released by our Jesus, the justice that excludes was taken away, and the justice that admits took its place.

9. But what was that whirling sword? I hear the Lord mention a sword in the Gospel: *I have come to bring not peace but a sword.** By the sword, therefore, he wanted to signify something that is contrary to peace. And what is so contrary to peace as discord? Here indeed, as it seems to me, the sword signifies that discord that by the sin of the first man was brought about between God and humankind, between the angelic and the human nature, between heavenly and earthly creation. Therefore this sword is said to be whirling because eventually by God's grace it was to be taken away. For he came, the true Solomon, the true peacemaker* by name and by the blood of his cross, *restoring peace to all things that are in heaven and on earth.*† And because this amazing grace began to be *preached from the days of John, from the days of John the kingdom of heaven has suffered violence, and the violent have rapt it away.**

10. The kingdom of heaven can also be understood as purity of heart,* to which we can attain only by subjecting ourselves to use violence. Of this kingdom the Lord says, *The kingdom of God is within you.** And the apostle: *The kingdom of God is not food and drink but justice and peace and* spiritual *joy.** It was by means of certain force that the same apostle strove to carry off this kingdom. So he says, *I chastise my body and bring it into subjection, lest after I preach to others I myself should be cast away.**

*Matt 10:34

*Jerome,
Int nom 63
(CCSL 72:138)
†Col 1:20

*Matt 11:12

*see Cassian,
Conferences 1.6

*Luke 17:21

*Rom 14:17;
Vulg *in Spiritu
sancto*

*1 Cor 9:27

The first to teach this violence in the gospel was John, first by the example of his way of life and then by the word of preaching, saying, *Produce fruits worthy of repentance.** *Luke 3:8

11. We *produce fruits worthy of repentance* if in the same way that we use our members to serve injustice and evil, we use them to serve justice and holiness,* so *that sin shall not reign in* our *mortal body,*† but *justice and peace and* spiritual *joy,*‡ that is, *the kingdom of God.* We produce *fruits worthy of repentance* if, renouncing the works of the flesh by which the devil reigns in men and women, we violently tear open the earth of our heart with the plow of compunction, so that *the fruits of the Spirit—charity, joy, peace,* and the others listed by the apostle*—spring up in it. In the next verse the same apostle shows by what force we truly come to these fruits, saying, *Those who belong to Christ have crucified their flesh with its vices and obsessions.**

*Rom 6:19
†Rom 6:12
‡Rom 14:17;
Vulg: *gaudium in Spiritu Sancto*

*Gal 5:22

*Gal 5:24

12. Does John not show this by his example, he who from his very infancy was fearful of being contaminated by the sordidness of the crowds that milled around him? Like that most chaste of birds, the turtledove, borrowing wings of purity and innocence, he took flight into the hidden places of the desert,* there showing that the first step toward this heavenly kingdom is contempt of the world. For *anyone who loves the world does not have the love of the Father in him.** Where there is no love, however, the kingdom of God cannot exist. It is then aptly said of John, *And he was in the desert until the day when he appeared publicly.**

*Ps 54:7-8

*1 John 2:19

*Luke 1:80

13. And we, brothers, if we desire *the kingdom of God to be in us,** must fly away to a spiritual desert. May our hearts be *a trackless and waterless wasteland,** so that in it the Lord may appear and

*Luke 17:21

*Ps 62:3;
Exod 3:1-2;
Acts 7:30

his kingdom be established there. May it be a *waste-land* from the occupations of this world, so that <*the world> may be crucified to us and we to the world.**
May it be *trackless* to spiritual beasts—unclean spirits—lest they say to our soul, *Lie down, so that we may walk over you.** May it be *waterless,* lacking any rivulet of harmful pleasure, so that *our soul* may have nothing to do with *the water that lacks substance.**

14. Now, about contempt of one's own flesh, what shall I say? The Gospel says, *He had clothing of the hair of camels.** Behold what kind of garments adorn Christ's soldier. It seems to me that this man even by his habit cried out, *Woe is me, because the time of my sojourn is lengthened.** And this: *I am an inhabitant in the earth; I am a stranger among you and an exile like all my fathers.** Sackcloth, which is the habit of penitents, is made from the hair of camels. What [John] later preached by his word, he therefore first showed by his example: *Do penance,* he said, *for the kingdom of heaven has drawn near.** Now let us also hear about his amazing abstinence. His food was *locusts and wild honey.** By his habit, therefore, he trampled on the delicacy of the body; by this food, on gluttony.

15. This is the violence by which *the kingdom of heaven* is carried off. *This is the force it has suffered since the days of John.** For from now on it is not against Canaanites and Perizzites* that we have to fight, so that we might secure their earthly kingdom by force, but against those most savage enemies, our physical passions, so by driving them out of the recesses of our hearts, we may prepare the temple and kingdom of the true Solomon in the land of the heart *by crucifying our flesh with its vices and desires.**

16. This force to possess the kingdom of heaven had been neglected by those of whom Paul said, *As*

*Gal 6:14

*Isa 51:23

*Ps 123:5;
Ps 68:3

*Matt 3:4

*Ps 119:5

*Ps 38:13

*Matt 3:4

*Matt 3:2

*Matt 11:12
*see Gen 13:7

*Gal 5:24

*I have often told <you>, and now say with tears, many walk as enemies of the cross of Christ.** He makes these clear when he adds, *Their stomach is their god, and they glory in their private parts.** This is to be an enemy of the cross of Christ: to ally oneself with the greed of the stomach and the sensuality of the body. By these words he expresses those two vices to which nearly the whole world surrenders: gluttony and lust. Add to them pride and avarice, and you have the four wheels on which the devil infiltrates nearly the whole universe.

17. As for the heavenly flights of the locusts and the sweetness of spiritual honey,* since this sermon has already been long, we leave those to your own meditations. <We have skipped over> the *leather belt,** which symbolizes the virtue of chastity. In its excellence, purity of heart consists above all. Although it is of little or no use without the other virtues, just as they are of little or no use without it, still the absence of any other is easier to bear for a time than its absence.

18. Indeed, it has a prerogative that gives it a special luster among the other virtues: not only is it, like them, concerned with a quality of the soul, but it invests the corruptible flesh itself with a certain real incorruptibility. It gives it a foretaste of some of the delights of the future resurrection, when people *will not marry or be given in marriage, but they will be like the angels of God.** Among all the other virtues this is the one that merits the company of the angels, the approach of the Holy Spirit, and, even more intimately, the embrace of *the fairest among the sons of men.**

19. *John had a leather belt around his waist.** He thus became an extremely energetic practitioner of evangelical perfection before he heard of it. May almighty God grant that we may travel along the

*Phil 3:18

*Phil 3:19

*see Matt 3:4

*Matt 3:4;
Mark 1:6

*Matt 22:30;
Luke 20:35

*Ps 44:3

*Matt 3:4

way he showed, that by following the exhortations of so great a prophet we may come safely to him whom he foretold, our Lord Jesus Christ,* who lives and reigns with God the Father in unity with the Holy Spirit, through all ages of ages. Amen.

*see Gregory I, Orat in Vig Nat JB (CO 7:4492; CCSL 160F:89)

Sermon 139[1]

On the Feast of the
Holy Apostles Peter and Paul

1.   mong all the martyrs and apostles of
  A   our Lord Jesus Christ, these two whose
      feast we are celebrating today seem to
have a special dignity. Indeed, to them the Lord especially commended the holy church, to the one saying, *You are Peter, and upon this rock I will build my church,* <and> *to you will I give the keys of the kingdom of heaven.** The Lord also made Paul [Peter's] *Matt 16:18-19
equal, as he himself said: He *who made Peter an apostle also made me one,* etc.* *Gal 2:8

2. These are those whom the Lord promised to holy church through the prophet, saying, *In the place of your fathers sons have been born to you.** The *Ps 44:17
fathers of the holy church are the holy patriarchs and prophets who first taught God's law and prophesied the coming of the Lord. But before the Lord's coming prophets ceased to be because of the sins of the people. The Lord came anyway, and in place of the prophets he chose the holy apostles; this fulfilled what the prophet had said: *In the place of your fathers,* etc. And notice how he shows that the dignity of the apostles is greater than that of the prophets. The prophets were princes of one people, in one nation, in one part of the earth. Of the apostles he

---

[1] This sermon is in close agreement with S 18 (CCCM 2A:140–46; CF 58:254–62).

*Ps 44:17

however says, *You will make them princes over the whole earth*, etc.*

3. What land is there in which their dignity and power are not found? Kings, earls, rich and poor—all today praise and glorify these friends of God, our fathers and princes. Let us also praise them and prepare ourselves that we may be able to praise them worthily. We will be able to praise them worthily if we strive to imitate their life. Let us imitate their fortitude, their holy life, and their good lifestyle. They had great fortitude: they are those pillars that the Lord made firm. Of them the prophet said, *The earth has melted, and all who live in it. <I> have made its pillars firm.**

*Ps 74:4

4. Before our Lord came upon earth, the whole earth was frozen and hard. It was frozen because it had no warmth of charity* but was in the cold grip of iniquity, hard when it had none of the suppleness of love or kindness. Our Lord came, however, and set *fire on the earth* to counteract the cold, as he himself says: *I have come to set fire on the earth, and what do I desire but that it burn?** This fire thawed the cold, and the earth began to melt and to stream with tears.

*Matt 24:12

*Luke 12:49

5. But what does it mean when he says, *all who live in it?** All were melted, brothers. Yet there are some like her who says in the Song of Songs, *My soul was melted.** Others, however, are as the prophet says: *Like wax melting before the fire*, etc.* Some were melted by repentance; others by envy. By this earth we can understand the holy church. She *was melted** in the presence of our Lord, *and all who live in it** ought to live in the church in that way—that is, in true faith and charity. These were indeed all melted by the fire of divine love.

*Ps 74:4

*Song 5:6
*Ps 67:3

*Song 5:6
*Ps 74:4

6. *I have made its pillars firm.** The pillars of this earth are the holy apostles, especially those two

*Ps 74:4

whose feast we are celebrating today. They are the pillars that uphold the church by their prayers, by their teaching, and by the example of their patience. These are the pillars that our Lord made firm. For at first they were very weak, quite unable to hold up either themselves or anyone else. And this was our Lord's great way of working. For if they had always been strong, someone could think that they had this strength from themselves. Therefore our Lord willed first to show what they were like of themselves, and then to make them firm so that everyone might know that all their strength was from God. Again, because they were to be the fathers of the church and doctors to cure the sick, in order to know how to *have compassion on the infirmities** of others, they first experienced infirmity in themselves. The Lord therefore made firm the pillars of the earth—that is, of the holy church.

*see Heb 4:15

7. The one pillar, Saint Peter, was very infirm when the comment of a single maidservant cast him down.* Afterward the Lord made this pillar firm. First, when he asked him three times, *Peter, do you love me?** For it was as if by denying him three times he had somehow lessened within himself the love of our Lord, and therefore this pillar collapsed and cracked. So by professing his love three times, this pillar was made firm. So with Peter answering, *I love you*, the Lord immediately said to him, *Feed my sheep.** It was as if he said, "In this way show the love that you have for me: that you feed my sheep." Someone who says he loves God without wanting to feed his sheep speaks falsely.

*Matt 26:69-70 and par.

*John 21:15

*John 21:17

8. But someone will say, "What has this to do with us? This pertains to bishops, to abbots, and to priests, who have the care of souls." It pertains to them, and to us. For Christ's sheep are fed in two ways: by word and by example. Many prelates in the church feed

Christ's sheep by word, but because they live badly
they would feed them better if they kept silent or
withdrew physically from them, or if they provided
them an example of humility, poverty, abstinence,
chastity, and the other virtues. However, the one does
better who does both. Someone who cannot do both
does better to feed by example than by word. The
one who can feed only by word profits hearers, but
less himself; the one [who feeds] by example profits
both himself and his hearers. If therefore you love
the Lord, so live that Christ's sheep may be fed by
your example. As the Lord says, *Let your works so*
shine before men and women, etc.*

    9. In each and every holy soul our Lord possesses
certain sheep—that is, virtues—that should be fed
by anyone who loves Christ. We feed these sheep
when we do the kinds of works that make these
virtues grow in us. Each of us ought also to feed these
virtues in the other. This we do if we behave before
our brothers in such a way that our example increases their charity, joy, humility, and patience.

    10. For how do I feed humility in my brother if
I am proud in his presence, if I speak proudly, if I
answer proudly, if I walk proudly? How do I feed
obedience in my brother if he sees me contrary and
disobedient? How do I feed his patience if I murmur
or lose my temper or speak harshly? Someone who
behaves like this in his brother's presence does not
feed Christ's sheep in him, but as much as is in him
he destroys and slaughters them because he scandalizes them. Someone who scandalizes his brother,
however, sins against him. Yet someone who sins
against his brother sins *against Christ*.* Therefore,
if you love Christ, feed Christ's sheep, giving a good
example to your brothers, and you will belong to
this pillar, which was made firm by the love of Christ.

*Matt 5:16

*1 Cor 8:12

11. After this firming up, when the Holy Spirit was sent, then this pillar was made so strong that strokes and stones and threats and in the end death itself could not move it from its place. That other pillar, that is, the blessed Paul, was at first infirm. For sins are an infirmity of the soul. Hear how infirm he was: *Who was at first a blasphemer*, etc.* Again, when he was hurled to the ground and blinded and in that state led into the city, when Ananias came to him and instructed him, then he was infirm.* But hear how strong he was afterward: *I am convinced,* he said, *that neither death nor life, neither angels nor any other creature can separate me <from the love> of God.**

12. Therefore, brothers, all strength is in love,* as it is written, *Love is as strong as death.** What does death do to a person? It extinguishes all his vices and all his evil passions; it closes the eyes and renders the body senseless, so that only the spirit lives. Love* too does this. It extinguishes lust, takes away anger, overpowers pride, and drives out all vices. It closes the eyes so that they may not be curious, and it extinguishes all the physical senses so that people can say with Paul, *I live, yet not I, but Christ lives in me.** He himself does not live, because love* puts to death in him whatever was his own. But Christ lives in him, because only the love* of Christ has any force in him. Therefore, let us imitate this fortitude of these pillars.

13. But now, concerning the holiness of these fathers, what can we say? All holiness is in purity of heart and the testimony of a good conscience. Contempt of the world* brings about purity of heart. For all impurity of heart comes from love† of the world. Love of the world contaminates the heart. Therefore the one who perfectly despises the world has no

*1 Tim 1:13

*Acts 9:10-19

*Rom 8:38-39

*caritate

*dilectio;
Song 8:6

*caritas

*Gal 2:20

*caritas

*amor

*contemptus
mundi
†amore

contamination in his heart. The good *testimony of a conscience* is born of two things: good action and a right intention. A person who does not act well cannot have a good conscience. A person who does praiseworthy deeds out of love of praise, or in order to acquire some temporal advantage, cannot have a good conscience.

14. Who more perfectly despised the world than the one who said to the Lord, *Behold, we have left everything and are following you?** What *a testimony* of his own *conscience* he had who confidently said, *You know, Lord, that I love you.** Paul similarly despised the world perfectly, he who judged all carnal things *as dung.** Of his own deeds, he said, *I have worked harder than everyone. I have fought the good fight,* etc.* Concerning the testimony of a good conscience, he says, *This is* my *glory, the testimony of* my *conscience.**

15. Therefore let us imitate these holy fathers. Let us strive to do good, to despise the world, to have a good conscience, so that we may come to share their company. Let us imitate good perseverance. For although people may begin speedily to serve God, it is of no advantage to them if just a little while before death they abandon the good they began. And although a person may live long in evil, if for a little while he perseveres in a good way of life, he is saved.* To persevere is nothing else than to end one's life praiseworthily. All praise is sung in the end. Our salvation* consists only in perseverance. Of this perseverance, no one ought to be confident before death. Therefore, *work out your salvation in fear and trembling.**

16. The more tribulations and sorrows a person suffers in the service of the Lord, the more praiseworthy is that person's perseverance. Accordingly,

*Matt 19:27

*John 21:15-17

*Phil 3:8

*1 Cor 15:19;
2 Tim 4:7

*2 Cor 1:12

*salus

*salus

*Phil 2:12;
Eph 6:5

these saints, who endured so much for Christ and nevertheless persevered, are preeminently to be praised. It is no great thing to persevere with Christ in joy, in prosperity, in peace. But it is a great thing indeed to be scourged, stoned, and buffeted for Christ and through it all to persevere—to be blasphemed and to pray, to be cursed and to bless, to suffer persecution and to hold up, to be *as it were the rubbish of <this> world* and to glory in that.*

17. How praiseworthy is the perseverance of Paul, persevering in such things? He was nearly always either *in prisons* or *in chains*, or *hungry or cold or naked*:* he did not murmur but was content when he endured such trials. Thus he says, *I am content in insults, in tribulations, in hardships for Christ.*† To the end, today, he perfectly commended his perseverance, freely accepting *for Christ* the cutting off of his head.

18. What shall I say of Peter's perseverance? If he had borne nothing else for Christ, it would be enough that today he was crucified for him, leaving an example of patient and blessed perseverance for all. Great is his discretion, that he did not want to be crucified in the same way as our Lord, but so that his feet were higher and his head lower. He knew where he whom he loved was, him for whom he longed, for whom he sighed. Where if not in heaven? He made it so that his feet were upwards, so that he might show that by his passion he would go to the Lord. That cross was as it were a way.

19. Truly, brothers, the cross of Christ is the way to heaven, and there is no other. Therefore let us place before our eyes the life and death of these and of their reward. So may we imitate their passion and way of life that we may come to share their company, that through their merits our Lord Jesus may grant

*1 Cor 4:12-13

*2 Cor 6:5;
11:23–27; Phil
1:7; Phlm 10:13
†2 Cor 12:10

us this, he who lives and reigns with the Father and the Holy Spirit, God through all the ages of ages. Amen.

Sermon 140

On the Feast of Saint Benedict

1. T*he path of the just is right; the trail of the just is right to walk on.** A path and a trail are the same, and thus it seems that the same thing is said twice by these words. Nevertheless, not without great purpose is this repetition made, as in many other examples. In fact, emphasizing words is customary at times for expressing some matter, either to designate joy or to express some sorrow or anger or refutation or praise or reproach. Concerning all these, if we had the leisure, we could suggest examples. Besides, one might emphasize words to aid in understanding something difficult or remembering something useful. So it is said, "The reading, having been read, pleases; repeated ten times, it will continue to please."* This same reason can also be applied here.

2. Besides, authorities and teachers are often accustomed to say the same thing by way of some addition, as here. For when it said previously, *The path of the just is right,* and afterward, *the trail* is *right—* which seems to be the same thing—he adds, *to walk on.** Actually it is called another thing for this reason and for that, because this word *just* signifies one thing here and another there. For in one case it signifies *the just person,* who is naturally and specifically *just,* and in the other case the just person who is made just by grace.* Therefore, so that I may say something properly, there is the just one and the other, and the path of the just and the other, although they

*Isa 26:7

*Proverbia 2:708, #13614; Horace, *Ars poetica* 365

*see Isa 26:7

*see Rom 3:24

who were thus designated differently are not properly called "the one" and "the other."[1] But who might be the just one by nature and who by grace, and what is the path of the latter and what is the trail of the former, and how should anyone walk on each? Let us first say according to previous definitions who might be just and what is justice.

3. "The just one," as Augustine says, "is one who in word and deed, in knowledge and habits, assigns to each its due."* As Anselm says, "Any justice, great or small, is righteousness of will preserved for its own sake."† Or it can be defined thus: "Justice is fairness, duty bestowing to each according to its worth."‡ It is defined by various writers in many ways. And although justice might be defined in so many different ways by many writers, nevertheless our justice, which is perfect, is indefinable and indescribable. For although a definition might be a complete proof of the matter, no one ever happens to demonstrate it perfectly or wholly, because no one ever happens to know perfectly. For our justice, according to the apostle, is Christ.* About him Job says, *He is higher than heaven and deeper than the abyss.** And the Lord says, *Heaven is my throne and the earth my footstool.** For he it is who, *standing on the earth* and reaching *all the way to heaven,* fills *all things.**

4. Therefore Christ is naturally just. However, many others are just, or rather, if any are just, they are just by his grace. For there is *not one born of a woman clean in his sight,* as Job says.* Also, *Behold, those who serve him are not steadfast, and among his angels he found wickedness.** When however God

*Augustine, Trin 8.6.9 (CCSL 50:382)
†Anselm, *De concordia* 1.6 (*Opera Omnia* 2:256)
‡Rhetorica 3.2.3

*see 1 Cor 1:30
*Job 11:8

*Isa 66:1
*Wis 18:16; see Eph 4:10

*see Job 25:4-5

*Job 4:18

---

[1] *Est itaque, ut quiddam proprie dicam, iustus alius et alius, et semita iusti alia et alia, quamvis non proprie dicantur alia et alia quae ita diverso modo sunt significata.*

is called justice or virtue or something of this sort, not some feeling or quality is understood, but the very essence of divinity, majesty, greatness.* So when Christ is called virtue, not a certain one of the virtues is understood, but the essence of the Son, by which the Father *works all things,** and when he is called wisdom, not one quality is meant, but the substance of the Son,* by which he arranges all things.† For in heaven indeed, as Augustine says, "no virtues are laborious," if not "the one and supreme virtue, to love what you see, and the supreme happiness, to have what you love."*

5. And so Christ is called intrinsically and specifically just, because he himself is his own justice, the Father is justice, and the Holy Spirit is justice, yet not three justices, but one justice. Similarly wisdom, power, goodness, majesty, and so on concerning the rest. Although these might be common to the whole Trinity, nevertheless sometimes certain things are said specifically about the Son, some things about the Father, other things about the Holy Spirit. For the Father is specifically called power, the Son wisdom, the Holy Spirit goodness. So to sin against the Father is said [to be] by fragility, as if against power; against the Son through ignorance, as if against wisdom; against the Holy Spirit by malice, as if against goodness. The first two, fragility and ignorance, of course, need an easy remedy. The third, that is, malice, is not forgiven here *and not in the future.**

6. Fragility is divided in two, as is ignorance. In the case of fragility, one is from feebleness of nature, the other from debilitation of the mind: the former is excusable, the latter subject to condemnation. So too with ignorance: one is from accident, the other from negligence. What is from accident is pardonable; what is from negligence is punishable. "For accident

*see 1 Cor 1:24

*see 1 Cor 12:6

*see 1 Cor 1:30
†see Wis 8:1

*Augustine,
Gen ad litt
12.26 (CSEL
28/1:419)

*see Matt 12:32

is an unexpected event from a confluence of causes in these matters that are managed for the sake of something else."* Concerning negligence, however, it is said, *Cursed be one who does the work of God negligently.*† But the third, that is, malice, is an incurable sickness, a deadly pestilence, an unnatural venom, that makes the whole soul swell and decay. This is the very worst demon, that *is not cast out except by prayer and fasting.** And it seems amazing that none are so malicious that they do not consider themselves to be honorable, and they use the name of him whose works they despise.

*Boethius, Cons 5.1.18 (CCSL 94:89) †Jer 48:10

*Mark 9:28; see Matt 17:20

7. Let us flee, dearest brothers, from fellowship with these people, just as the Lord says about the rebellion of Core, Dathan, and Abiron: *Flee from the tents of wicked people.** Why? Because according to the psalmist, *with the chosen you will be chosen, and with the perverse you will be perverted.** For *one who has touched pitch shall be stained by it.** And the psalmist says about their retribution, *The earth opened up and swallowed up Dathan, and covered over the congregation of Abiron.** What happened to them in the body happens to all the malicious in soul. So in the book of Kings, *If you persist in wickedness,** both you and your king shall perish together.** So again the psalmist, *The Lord will return their iniquity to them and will destroy them in their wickedness.**

*Num 16:26; see Jer 51:6

*Ps 17:27
*Sir 13:1

*Ps 105:17

*malitia
*1 Sam 12:25

*Ps 93:23

8. But our just one can also transform evil into goodness, because he it is *who justifies the ungodly.** For he is the *just justifying*; some just people are only *justified.** Still no one is just in his sight. So Job says, *If I wish to justify myself, then my own mouth shall condemn me.** Therefore let us see what is the path of this just one [who is just] by nature, or what is the trail of him who [is just] according to grace.

*see Rom 4:5

*see Rom 3:26; 3:24

*Job 9:20

9. Christ is *the path of the just.** He is the path, he is the way. The way among laity, the path among religious. None advances by the path except one. Many can advance at the same time through the way. Wagons are driven through the way. There is also a spacious and wide way that leads to death,* the devil's way, of course. But the way of Christ is the good lifestyle of laity, his path the high lifestyle of the religious. And so both the latter and the former lead to eternal life, because both the way and path tend to the same objective. But the path arrives at that place more quickly than the way, because the path leads through a shortcut and across steep places, but the way is directed through the plains and skirts the mountains.

*see Isa 26:7; see John 14:6

*see Matt 7:13

10. And so two who advance at the same time by this way are those faithful who are in the love of God and of neighbor. The three who advance equally are the three orders in the church. Four: those who imitate the Gospel doctrine. Five are penitents, six are actives, seven are followers of the grace of the Spirit by baptism, eight are gainers of beatitude, nine (who are contained in a squared number) are long-suffering, and ten are those who keep the ten commandments of the law. Wagons and baggage advancing along the way signify those who are burdened by secular cares and business of the world. Going around the mountains is an expense of the laity. But the path on which none except one advances pertains to men and women of contemplation, who seek none except God alone: those who take the highest road.

11. There are, however, certain people far outside the way, such as the unfaithful, and certain people alongside the way, such as those who have faith without understanding. So it is said, *A blind man sat alongside the way.** However, some are on the way,

*Luke 18:35

but certain others withdraw from the way and cross the way. Others lie down on the way, others sit, others stand, others walk, others run. Christ is the way, as he himself says: *I am the way, and the truth, and the life.** He is the means by which one advances, he is where one advances to. He is the way by means of himself and to himself. He is the way leading, the truth teaching, the life justifying. He is the beginning through which all things, from which all things, in which all things. He is the unmediated medium, he is the consummate end. He is the beginning of conversion, the end not of consuming but of consummation. "If you wish to come to truth," as Augustine says, "keep to the way."* If you wish to have life, keep to the way and do truth. "You wish to walk: *I am the way*, he says. You wish not to be deceived: *I am the truth*. You wish not to die: *I am the life*."*

*John 14:6

*Augustine, Ioann 13.4 (CCSL 36:132)

*Augustine, Ioann 22.8 (CCSL 36:3–6); see John 14:6

12. Certain people enter into this way, as we said, but exit quickly and cross into another part. Beware of them, because they are perverse and *plot evil.** These are the heretics, about whom it is written, *Avoid a person who is a heretic after the first and second admonition, knowing that the person has been perverted.** Certain people lie down on this way. One who lies down presses his whole body downward. These are people who devote their mind and intention and will to earthly pleasures and carnal desires at the same time with their body; they are on the way insofar as they have faith, but they do not arrive at the goal. On the other hand, other people sit. One who sits is partly upright, partly pressed downward. These are people who do many good works, but because they similarly do many bad things and seek worldly goods, they do not arrive at the goal.

*see Prov 6:12, 14

*Titus 3:10-11

13. Therefore let both the former and the latter arise. So the psalmist says, *Rise after you have sat, you who eat the bread of sorrow.** And in another

*Ps 126:2

place, *Arise, you who sleep, and get up from the dead.** Likewise in Judges: *Arise, arise, O Deborah, arise, arise, and utter a canticle. Arise, Barak, and take hold of your enemies, O son of Achitob.** Lazarus lay in the tomb *four days* and was stinking;† so also someone lies here in hardness of heart as in a tomb, *four days,* in thought and pleasure, of course, in action and habit, stinking in desperation. *Lazarus! Come out,* says the Lord.* And afterward to the disciples, *Unbind him and let him go.** After one who lies down or sits has arisen, he ought to go. So again the Lord in the Gospel: *Arise, take up your bed and walk.** That is, arise from your sins and carry your neighbor and confess to your Lord God.

14. On the other hand, some stand who leave behind all wicked works, but they do not confess the sins that they have done, and therefore they do not arrive. In many places, to stand is also taken to mean persistence, as in that place: *You who stand in the house of the Lord, in the courts of the house of our God.** And as the Lord says to Ezekiel, *Son of man, arise and stand upon your feet.** And David: *He has set my feet upon a rock.** And the Lord to Moses: *Let the people return to the camp, but you stand here with me.** And in another place, *Arise, O Jerusalem, and stand on high, and look.** And so it is good to stand, but it does not suffice unless one will also walk, that is, renunciation of sins does not suffice if confession of past sins does not follow. So it is that Paul says, *With the heart one believes unto justice, but with the mouth one makes confession unto salvation.** Others walk—I mean those who make a worthy confession by recognizing sins and praising God. So the Lord says in the Gospel, *Walk while you have the light, lest the darkness overtake you.**

15. Some others run: those who vigorously seek the apex of monastic life. And these ought to hurry,

*Eph 5:14

*Judg 5:12; see 1 Sam 22:12 †see John 11:39

*John 11:43 *John 11:44

*John 5:8

*Ps 133:1; Ps 134:2 *Ezek 2:1 *Ps 39:3

*Deut 5:30-31 *Bar 5:5

*Rom 10:10

*John 12:35

lest through delay they be hindered and dragged back. So a wise person says, "To delay when ready always does harm."* The apostle says about this running, *So run that you may obtain.*† One who must run is required to go empty and unburdened. So the same apostle says, *One who competes in a contest is abstemious in all things.** What is it to abstain from all things, if not to love voluntary poverty? But such a one is rarely found, who has nothing and does not want to have. The converted must run to the Lord. So blessed Jerome says, "Make haste, I beg you, and cut rather than untie the rope [that keeps] your vessel stuck in the open sea."* Let one who is converted to God not delay because of some worldly obstacle or restraint of cupidity. An unfaithful person is held back and soiled *by wallowing in the mud.** The journey of conversion must be run by those who take it up. Those who walk or run sometimes stumble with their feet and fall. Some of these will die by their fall, although others arise injured and by habit take up the journey more swiftly. Of those who come to conversion, certain ones fall into temptation and succumb; certain others become stronger after a fall.

16. Therefore *the path of the just*, that is, Christ, who is naturally and specifically just, *is right.* Also, the *trail of the just is right* by grace,* like blessed Benedict's. On his trail no crookedness is found, as is shown in his Rule by his brilliant words. He took up the Lord's way by running swiftly, as he abandoned his inheritance and all the things in the world that he was able to have, taking refuge in a desert. Thereby he succeeded in so much that he not only gained his \<own\> soul for the Lord, but he also joined to the Lord many who had been deceived by the devil's error. And may he unite us and our souls to the same our Lord Jesus Christ. Amen.

*Lucan,
Pharsalia 1.281
†1 Cor 9:24

*1 Cor 9:25

*Jerome,
Ep 53.11.2
(CSEL 54:464)

*2 Pet 2:22

*see Isa 26:7

Sermon 141

On the Feast of Saint Benedict

1. **W**ith all watchfulness guard your heart, because life proceeds from it.* The counsel or teaching of the wise is that the heart be guarded with all watchfulness. And he shows the reason that it is to be guarded with such great zeal, such great diligence, and such great watchfulness, saying, *Because life proceeds from it.** There is a *corrupt heart* and a pious heart,† a heart contemplating God and a heart regarding the devil, a heart from which proceed honorable and holy thoughts and a heart from which arise corrupt and *perverse thoughts.** How does life proceed from a corrupt and perverse heart, which does not contemplate anything but deceitful, mendacious, and false testimony? Life does not proceed from the heart about which the Lord speaks in the Gospel: *From the heart go out evil thoughts, murders, adulteries, fornications, thefts, false testimonies, blasphemies.** From the heart, from which these things go out, good things do not proceed, but rather bad things; *life* does not *proceed*, but *death and* eternal *ruin.**

2. What therefore does this mean: *with all watchfulness guard your heart, because life proceeds from it?** Do not understand from this that *life proceeds* from the heart, as if a heart could bring a person to life if it were corrupt. But *with all watchfulness guard your heart, because from it*—that is, out of this—insofar as you guard your heart with all watchfulness, you prepare life for yourself. In fact, life proceeds

*Prov 4:23

*Prov 4:23
†Prov 11:20

*see Wis 1:3

*Matt 15:19

*see Job 28:22

*Prov 4:23

from this watchfulness. If therefore you desire eternal life, then *with all watchfulness guard your heart,* *so that no entrance might be opened through which an adversary can enter your heart. In fact, *If the head of the household* were to know at what hour the thief would come, then he would surely keep watch and not allow his house to be broken into.* *

*Prov 4:23

*paterfamilias

*Luke 12:39

3. This paterfamilias can be understood as our soul, whose family is thoughts, movements of the soul, and also senses and interior actions. This family will be exceedingly wanton if the paterfamilias is not rigorously restrained. For if this paterfamilias, that is, the soul, grows slothful in care for his own, who will explain how thoughts, eyes, tongue, ears, and all the rest grow haughty! The house is the conscience in which this paterfamilias gathers the treasure of virtues. There is not one thief but many, because individual vices set traps for individual virtues. However, the thief is understood primarily as the devil, against whom the paterfamilias, if he should be concerned, safeguarding his house with brave watchfulness, sets up prudence at the first entrance, to discern what is to be avoided, what to be sought, what to be expelled from the house, what to be retained in the house. Next to this should be courage, so that he may bravely drive back the approaching enemies. In the middle, let justice be stationed so that he may assign to each his own. And because the hour at which the thief is going to come is not known,* let every hour be feared. Lest therefore the sleep of sin creep in, *with all watchfulness guard your heart.* *

*see Luke 12:39

*Prov 4:23

4. Therefore let us place a guard for our heart before, behind, to the right and to the left, beneath and above. Then on every side guard your heart, surrounded with a palisade and on all sides, fortified with virtues, so that it may nowhere be able to devi-

ate toward illicit behavior. Place a guard in front lest you desire to have things contrary to God. Place one behind, lest you return to things thrown away for the sake of God. Place one on the right, lest you be lifted up by prosperity. Place one on the left, lest you be broken by adversities.

5. Place a guard on the right, lest in virtues granted to you from God you incur the vice of boasting. In fact, the vice of boasting is serious and exceedingly dangerous, because it throws down a soul from the very peak of perfection. This evil has two types. One type happens at once among these beginners in monastic life, when <those who> have practiced some little bit of abstinence, or have given among the poor, place themselves before others and thus perceive themselves as though more distinguished than anyone who abstains less, or more than those who have donated a little bit. Another type of boasting is when anyone who arrives at the peak of virtue assigns it not wholly to God but to his own efforts and zeal,* and while he seeks *glory from human beings,** he loses that which is from God.

6. Therefore we place a guard on the right side, so that we might avoid the vice of boasting, lest perhaps we slip and fall as did the devil. We place a guard on the left, lest we be enveloped by vices and sins by the danger of despair. Death and ruin proceed from despair, as it is written, *When a sinner comes into the depth of evil, he is given over to contempt.** Place a guard above, lest you place your hopes too high; beneath, lest you succumb in fear. You guard in front in order to act if you provide for goods that are in the future. Behind, in order to punish, if you call to mind bad things that you have done. On the right, if you turn to works of mercy; on the left, if you flee from human praise, according to that saying,

*RB Prol. 30–32

*see 1 Thess 2:6; see John 5:44; 12:43

*Prov 18:3

*Matt 6:2-3

When you give alms, let your left hand not know what your right hand is doing. * Therefore in good deeds that you do, may you not seek human favor. Above so that you hope for eternal realities, below lest you fear hell. And lest some crack be opened to ambushing pride, may you build a circle of humility around yourself.

7. This is what one reads in Ezekiel: *<The whole body> was full of eyes on the circumference of these* *Ezek 1:18 *four.* * *<That is>, The whole body of these four was full of eyes on the circumference.* For it is necessary for holy people to be circumspect in every direction, lest they be deceived <in> evils that they flee or seduced by good things that they strive to do. Often in fact, vice feigns the face of virtue, and because it is corrupt, it seeks to please under the name of righteousness, so if pride is called freedom, then meticulousness is referred to as humility, doggedness as frugality, extravagance named magnanimity. Therefore true humility, as though a circular guard, guards the heart on every side. This ought to be four: in place, in countenance, in heart, and in mouth. All of these can be noted in that publican who went up into *see Luke 18:10 the temple with the Pharisee to pray.*

*see Luke 18:13

8. *The publican*, in fact, was standing *afar off.* * Behold, humility is noted by the place, as elsewhere *Luke 14:10 it says, *Sit down in the lowest place.* * *He would not* *Luke 18:13 *even raise his eyes towards heaven.* * Behold the humility in his countenance. Obviously exaltation is usually noted more in the eyes, as it reads: *And you* *Ps 17:28 *will bring down the eyes of the proud.* * And that other saying: *Lord, my heart is not exalted, nor are* *Ps 130:1 *my eyes raised up.* * But humility of place or countenance has little influence unless it is also in the heart. *Luke 18:13 Therefore it follows, *He was striking his breast.* * For this is true humility of heart, compunction and con-

trition for past evils with upright faith, which is noted by beating of his breast. But as *with the heart one believes unto justice*, so *with the mouth confession is made unto salvation.** Therefore humility should be in one's mouth; humility was in the mouth of the one who said, *O God, be merciful to me a sinner.** There should be two things in confession of one's mouth: a plea for pardon and a supplication. For a plea for pardon is hollow if not accompanied by supplication. The publican makes a supplication when he says, *O God, be merciful to me.* He concedes when he adds *a sinner.*

*Rom 10:10

*Luke 18:13

9. Humility suffices when it is shown to superiors, abundant [when shown] to equals, superabundant to subordinates. Jesus had this when he went down to baptism by his servant.* Therefore *with all watchfulness guard your heart,** so that you can imitate him who said, *Learn from me, because I am meek and humble of heart.**

*Matt 3:13-15
*Prov 4:23

*Matt 11:29

10. Indeed, let us enter *through the narrow gate, because wide and spacious is the way that leads to death*, but *narrow and strict that which leads to life.** Lavish is the way of the soul when she would satisfy every one of her desires; the way is truly narrow when she opposes her own wishes.* If any therefore think they have rejected the world and the works of the devil, it does not suffice to forsake possessions and estates and the rest of the world's business, unless they have also renounced their own vices and thrown out useless and empty wishes. For these are the things about which the apostle says, *Empty and harmful are the desires that plunge people into destruction.**

*Matt 7:13-14;
see Prov 12:28

*see RB 5.11-12

*1 Tim 6:9

11. Therefore, *with all watchfulness guard your heart,** because the devil, through vices and corrupt wishes, finds entrance to a heart that is not secured

*Prov 4:23

by virtues. For vices are from the devil, just as virtues
are from God. If then there are vices in the heart

see John 14:30 when their leader the devil comes, as if by their own
authority they make room and introduce him, as if
to their own property. This is why hearts of this type
can never have peace and quiet but are always confounded, always frightened, and sometimes weighed
down by empty joy, sometimes by useless sadness.
For they have within themselves the worst resident,
to whom the vices gave access to themselves through
their passions.

12. On the other hand, a heart that truly re-
nounces the world, that cuts off and removes from
itself every vice and is safeguarded on all sides, neglects no entrance to itself for the devil, but restrains
irascibility, represses rage, flees mendacity, and detests jealousy, and not only does it not permit itself
to disparage a neighbor, but it does not even let itself
feel bad or be suspicious; it considers a brother's joy
as its own and regards another's sadness as its own.
A heart that observes these things and the like opens
a place for the Holy Spirit to enter unto itself. When
[the Holy Spirit] has entered and illuminated it, always in that place arise joy, always happiness, *charity, patience, goodness*, and all that are *fruits of the*
*see Gal 5:22-23 *Spirit.**

13. This is what the Lord says in the Gospel: *A
good tree cannot produce bad fruit, nor can a bad*
*Matt 7:18 *tree produce good fruit.** For *a tree is known by its*
*see Matt 7:20;
12:33
†Prov 4:23 *fruit.** However, a heart is attested by its works.
Therefore *with all watchfulness guard your heart.*†
And so that no access to your heart may be opened
for a cunning enemy, when you have done good
deeds, do not bring them up in public with boasting
as hypocrites do, so they will be praised *by humans,*
but rather strive to keep them secret, lest because of

approval from humans you lose the *reward* promised by God.*

14. "Scripture reports that a certain person from the tribe of Levi gave birth to a male child and saw that the infant was *well-favored* and so hid him three months."* *Intelligibly*, Solomon says, *understand what is put before you.*† *Pharaoh*, the king of Egypt, had ordered *his people, "Throw into the river each and every male child that is born to the Hebrews, and let every female child live."*‡

15. "In sacred Scripture, flesh or affections of the flesh are designated by the female, but rational senses and intellectual <spirit> are represented by the male. Pharaoh hates this rational sense that is able to sense heavenly realities, that is, able to understand God and to seek *things that are above.** The king of Egypt (the devil, *prince <of this>* world,* who is designated by Pharaoh) wants to kill and put an end to this rational sense."* So he orders, *Throw into the river each and every male child that is born to the Hebrews, and let every female child live.*† "For the devil wants everything whatsoever of the flesh to live, and he wants whatever pertains to corporeal matter not only to live, but to be developed and increased. For he wants everyone to taste carnal realities, to desire temporal things, to seek what is upon the earth."* This is to let *every female* live.

16. But the devil wants *every male child* to die, because he desires "that no one raise his eyes to heaven, no one ask how he came here, no one recall his homeland of Paradise. When therefore you see humans leading lives of pleasure and delights, flowing with sumptuousness, feasts, wine, dinner parties, giving their attention to wantonness and shameless eroticism, in these you know that the king of Egypt kills the male children and gives life to the females.

*see Matt 6:2

*Origen, Hom Exod 2.3 (SCh 321:80); see Exod 2:1-2
†Prov 23:1 (as cited by Origen)
‡Exod 1:22 (as cited by Origen)

*see Col 3:1-2
*see John 16:11

*Origen, Hom Exod 2.1 (SCh 321:70)
†Exod 1:22 (as cited by Origen)

*Origen, Hom Exod 2.1 (SCh 321:70–72); see Col 3:2

But when you see someone turning to God, raising eyes upward, seeking what is everlasting and eternal, contemplating heavenly realities, hating pleasure, loving self-control, fleeing luxury, avoiding vices, and cultivating virtues, as though Pharaoh wants to kill this man and male child,* he pursues him, hounds him, fights against him with a thousand schemes. The king of Egypt hates such people; he does not allow them to live in Egypt. Because of this, God's servants in the world, and all who seek God, *suffer persecution,** are exposed to contempt and insults, filled with taunts, and shaken by many and various annoyances, because Pharaoh hates them."*

17. "Egyptians, to whom Pharaoh gave the orders, let females live, because they nourish only vices and pleasures; they hate males because they pursue and assail virtues. Even now the Egyptians set ambushes, that is spiteful spirits, if perhaps any male is born to the Hebrews, so that at once they persecute and kill, unless they take precautions, unless they keep watch and hide the masculine shoot."* That we are the Hebrews who daily make the death of Christ a Passover† for the Lord,‡ through which he crossed *from the world to the Father,*# let us faithfully preach. The Egyptians set an ambush for us by the order of the Pharaoh (that is, evil spirits): if by chance some male is born to us, that is, if some good work should come forth from us, immediately they tear it to pieces and bury it under the waves. Therefore when the father of Moses begat a *male* and saw that he was *a well-favored infant, [he] hid him for three months.**

18. Therefore let us not bring forth a male shoot for the Egyptians, because divine Scripture urges us "not to wear our good deeds in public, *lest* we do our *justice in the presence of humans,** so that we might

*see Exod 1:22

*see 2 Tim 3:12;
see Matt 5:10

*Origen,
Hom Exod 2.1
(SCh 321:72)

*Origen,
Hom Exod 2.3
(SCh 321:80)
†Lat. *phase* [*of the moon*]
‡see Num 9:4;
see Exod 12:11
#John 13:1

*Exod 2:1-2 (as
cited by Origen)

*Matt 6:1

pray *to the Father in secret with the door closed,* ⃰
and what *our right hand* does, let *our left hand* know
not.⃰ For if it were not in secret, then it would be
ripped apart by Egyptians, seized, thrown into the
river, plunged in the waves and current. If I give alms
because it is God's work, then I beget a male. But if
I do it to be noticed by people, and I seek praise from
human beings and do not keep it secret, then my
donation is snatched away by Egyptians and plunged
in the river."⃰ "Therefore, you who hear these things,"
<take heed> *that you do not your justice before*
human beings so as to be seen by them,† "but that
you recognize the order of life, the principles of morals, the struggles of faith and virtue."⃰

19. Let each one do what we proposed in the
beginning of this sermon: *With all watchfulness guard*
your heart, because life proceeds from it.⃰ Benedict,
the glorious confessor of the Lord, did this strenuously, he to whose praises today we devote ourselves.
For when he overflowed in works of perfection, wishing to please not humans but rather God, he left
behind his homeland and relatives, he turned away
from well-known and hectic places, he lived solitary
for a long time in a wilderness, wearing down his
flesh with fasts and vigils, not only resisting vice and
sin, but vigorously and bravely defeating their originator, the devil and all his accomplices.

20. Suitably therefore is he called Benedict, whom
the Lord *blessed with every* heavenly *blessing,*[1]⃰ into
whom the Lord gathered every fullness of spiritual
graces. If you consider the grace of charity in him,
you will not be able to express its abundance in a
few words. If you turn your attention to his humility,

Marginalia:

⃰Matt 6:6

⃰see Matt 6:3

⃰Origen,
Hom Exod 2.3
(SCh 321:80)
†Matt 6:1

⃰Origen,
Hom Exod 2.3
(SCh 321:80)

⃰Prov 4:23

⃰see Eph 1:3

---

[1] *Benedictus vocatur, cui Dominus benedixit omni benedictione*
caelesti (*Benedict* = blessed).

you will admit that he excels in this gift far beyond the rest. In turn, if you consider how he surpasses everyone in patience, kindness, and gentleness, you will be utterly at a loss as to whom he can be compared. Truly the Lord conveyed the gift of wisdom and knowledge so much to him that one might believe that almost no one from among the preceding fathers had entered so deeply into the halls of all knowledge.[2]

21. Finally, received within the chamber of God's wisdom, he illuminated with much knowledge and adorned with the honor of morals all to whom was given enjoyment of his fellowship on earth, as he established the life of monks and left his Rule for us. If we live according to his Rule, without doubt we shall arrive at eternal life, to which, by the merits and prayers of our glorious patron, may all-powerful God deign to lead us, Father and Son and Holy Spirit. Amen.

---

[2] Aelred paraphrased the previous four sentences from Tyrannius Rufinus, *Historia monachorum sive de vita Sanctorum Patrum*, Caput 23 "De Ammonio," ed. Eva Schulz-Flügel (Berlin: Walter de Gruyter, 1990), 360.

Sermon 142

On the Octave of the Holy Apostles Peter and Paul

1. ***T**hese are men of mercy, whose justice has not been forgotten.** A proof may some-   *Sir 44:10 (LXX) times be made for the eye of the heart, sometimes for the eye of the body. A proof might be made for the eye of the heart when the matter about which one makes the proof is proposed not for the exterior eye but for the intellect, and one speaks about an absent matter as if it were present. But a proof might be made for the eye of the body when material things are put before corporeal eyes. And a proof might not be made for the eye of the body if it is done about a matter that is not present. But it is not thus in sacred Scripture.

2. Obviously divine Scripture frequently speaks about absent things as if present. And when the proof is given without any context, then it is tacked on as if from a spontaneous lesson and not from preceding arguments. As in this place, *Its foundations in the holy mountains,** even though before that place nothing   *Ps 86:1 was said about mountains. And in the prophets, *And it came to pass,** even though nothing preceding   *Ezek 1:1 shows what happened. And here concerning the men whose solemnities today we venerate, it is said, *These are men of mercy*, even though nothing was said concerning men of mercy in preceding passages. And so saints, before they speak, first discuss and frequently turn over in mind what they speak about. And thus from forethought, as if from preceding remarks

71

they connect a reason, just as we have demonstrated in aforesaid examples.

*Sir 44:10 (LXX)

3. *These are men of mercy.** *Men* is sometimes taken in a bad sense, sometimes in a good sense. In a bad sense as in, *Deliver me from those who work*

*Ps 58:3

*iniquity, and save me from men of blood.** And: *Men*

*Ps 54:24

*of blood and deceit shall not live out half their days.** And that saying of Solomon: *Wicked men have said:*

*Resp Dom in P
(Hesbert 4:7905;
see 4:6464);
see Wis 2:1, 10;
Wis 12:20
†see Acts 1:11
‡Acts 1:10
#Sir 44:10

*Let us kill the just.** However, *men* is taken in a good sense when it says, *Men of Galilee, why are you astonished at his going into heaven?*† And, *Behold two men stood near them in white garments.*‡ And here, about the men whom we extol today, *These are men of mercy.*# Therefore they are called men of mercy because they were dealt with mercifully, or because they acted mercifully toward others.

4. They were mercifully dealt with because they deserved the whole of mercy, because the manifest saints despised the world's glory, and they inherited the glory of the kingdom of heaven. For who can become holy if not through the grace of the Holy Spirit? *The sufferings of this life are not worthy [to*

*Rom 8:18

be compared] to that *future* incorruptibility,* to that ineffable beatitude and indescribable *glory* that the

*see Sir 44:7

saints, whom today we glorify, already *inherited.** Therefore they are well called men of mercy who were dealt with so mercifully by the Lord, so that they might forever be living *heirs of God* and, *more-*

*Rom 8:17

*over, coheirs of Christ.**

5. Or indeed they are called men of mercy because they showed mercy to others in nourishing the poor, in giving alms, in rebuking and correcting sins of neighbors and saving souls of brothers. Obviously true mercy not only fosters and nourishes the body with corporeal foods, but also restores and saves the soul with spiritual lessons. *These*, therefore, *are men*

*of mercy,** calling to mind the Lord's precept, *Be merciful as your Father also is merciful.** Just as they were dealt with mercifully, so they acted mercifully with others; from their means they expended corporeal goods for bodies and diligently supplied spiritual goods for spirits. *Blessed are the merciful, for they shall obtain mercy.** Indeed our holy patrons already achieved that, happily reigning in heaven, and on earth gloriously triumphant.

6. *These are men of mercy.** This name *man* signifies a certain vigor of soul and good zeal that *men of mercy* have, by which they punish their own sins within themselves and the sins of others in them. The saints trample earthly things by this vigor of soul and good zeal, aspire to heavenly realities, are not broken by adversities, not extolled in prosperity. This good zeal in certain people is bad zeal and mean-spirited vigor—certainly, in those of whom Scripture says, *They have the zeal of God, but not according to knowledge.** Zeal that is not according to knowledge is bad zeal because it is used indiscriminately. But this bad zeal is sometimes hidden, sometimes manifest.

7. It is hidden in those who deceitfully pursue their brothers, secretly disparaging neighbors. All of these, as if under the persona of one, the psalmist refutes, saying, *One who disparaged his neighbor in secret, this one I persecuted.** Those who in hiding and in secret disparage their neighbors imitate the son of perdition,* about whom it says in the psalm, *He waits in ambush, in hiding with the rich to murder the innocent.** Mean-spirited zeal is manifest in these who manifestly rage against the chosen, afflicting God's servants with controversies, quarrels, and many injustices, following the enemy of the human race, about whom blessed Peter says, *Your adversary the devil, as a roaring lion, goes about seeking whom to devour.**

*Sir 44:10 (LXX)
*Luke 6:36

*Matt 5:7

*Sir 44:10 (LXX)

*Rom 10:2
(as cited by Augustine *passim*)

*Ps 100:5

*see 2 Thess 2:3

*Ps 10:8

*1 Pet 5:8

8. When a lion roars, he wishes not to be hidden but manifest. Therefore, in fact, he roars so to terrify those whom he wants to attack. Similarly, *the kings and princes of the earth*, in whom was the mean-spirited zeal when *they met together against the Lord and against his Christ,** like roaring lions with fury and a great assault, with quarrels and threats, attacked God's servants, so to divert them from [the Lord's] service and subjugate them to idols. Among these was a perverse vigor and an obvious, mean-spirited zeal, which obviously raged against the innocent. Therefore vigor of soul among the saints is a virtue and a good zeal; however, among the reprobate it is discerned to be a vice and bad zeal.

9. *Men of mercy** have vigor of soul and a good zeal. So they are rightly called men, because they are truly just and stand out as merciful. "True justice has compassion,"* because those who are truly just stand out as merciful. "In fact, although they reject sinners, nevertheless, as they reject them they do not raise persecution against them, but they are loving, because even if outwardly they heap up criticisms through discipline, inwardly they still preserve sweetness through charity. They do not put themselves before those whom they reproach, but they frequently judge those whom they rebuke as better than themselves. And so they mercifully guide subordinates through discipline, and they guard themselves by humility,"* because they do not have a mean-spirited vigor, but holy zeal and good vigor.

10. "But on the other hand, those who are proud of false justice look down upon all the rest; with no compassion they condescend to weak brothers,"* because "false justice has contempt; true [justice has] compassion."* Among these, vigor of soul is not a virtue, but rather a vice and mean-spirited zeal. There-

*see Ps 2:2

*see Sir 44:10
(LXX)

*Gregory I,
Hom in Ev 34.2
(CCSL 141:300)

*Gregory I,
Hom in Ev 34.2
(CCSL 141:300)

*Gregory I,
Hom in Ev 34.2
(CCSL 141:300)
*Gregory I,
Hom in Ev 34.2
(CCSL 141:300)

fore, these look down on the rest because they are able to fast, to keep vigil, and to pray more than the rest. These follow Uzzah, who, when the ox was disobedient* and the Lord's ark tilted, extended his hand to raise the ark, and the Lord struck him there and he died at once.*

11. One reads in the book of Samuel that when David wanted to take the Lord's ark into Jerusalem, and he and those who were with him approached Chidon, *Uzzah, who with his brothers drove the wagon, extended his hand to hold up the ark. For the ox were wanton* and had made it lean a little bit. And so the Lord was angry at Uzzah; he struck him because he had touched the ark, and he died there before the Lord.*

12. The ark of the Testament, *in which* were *manna, a staff, and tablets of the Testament,** signifies prelates and pastors of the church, among whom ought to be manna of refreshment, a staff of rebuke, and <tablets> of teaching, so that they may be experts in both testaments and have *new things and old** to offer. The oxen signify subjects and subordinates who sometimes march along the strait path, not deviating *to the right or to the left;** sometimes they go off the track, and, being disobedient,* tilt the ark. Uzzah signifies those who, boasting about their strength, look down without compassion on others and condescend to the weak.

13. The ark was tilted by the disobedient oxen, because a discreet pastor mercifully has compassion on those who fall short out of weakness of the flesh, adapting himself to all as he knows "is best for each individual."* For not <all> should be restrained by the same rigor of discipline. Because just as we have various faces, so also we have manifold and various habits. This one is corrected with threats, that one

recalcitrantibus

*1 Chr 13:9-10; see 2 Sam 6:1-7

lascivians

*1 Chr 13:9-10; see 2 Sam 6:1-7

*see Heb 9:4

*see Matt 13:52

*see Prov 4:27
recalcitrantes

*RB 64.14, see 2.32

with coaxing. That one is chastened with words, this one with lashings. This one must be humbled with discipline, that one worn down with fasting. This one must be frightened with the punishments of Gehenna, that one relieved by coaxing with promises of eternal life.

14. And so a discreet pastor does not constrain all with just one rigor, but as "a wise physician"* he heals the feebleness of all, placing before all what they need. So rightly does it say that *the wanton ox tilted* the ark *a little bit.** The wanton ox is an undisciplined and straying brother, who is oppressed by weakness of the flesh and does not endure the rigor of regular discipline. For this one, the ark* tilted a little bit, because the prelate and merciful pastor mercifully condescended to that one who failed out of weakness of the flesh, knowing that he owed to that one, *for whom Christ has suffered,** the compassion of fraternal piety.

15. But *Uzzah extended his hand to hold up the ark,** because the one who lacks fraternal piety and is vigorous *in fasting, in vigils, in labors,*† presuming on his own strengths and despising the wanton ox (that is, a weak and straying brother), condescends to a weak brother with no regard for fraternal piety and does not allow the ark to tilt on account of the wanton ox, but restrains it as much as he can (lest the kind pastor condescend to the weak brother), and *he extends his hand to hold up the ark,** because he tries with zeal and sagacity to make the prelate restrain all the stumbling and straying ones who fall short by infirmity of the flesh, not only with reproofs, but with abuse, threats, and lashings without mercy.

16. So Uzzah is interpreted as *vigorous*, because those who lack the vital organs of loving-kindness and are strong in the rigor of discipline do not have

*RB 27.2; 28.2

*see 1 Chr 13:9

*i.e., the pastor

*see Rom 14:15; see 1 Cor 8:11

*1 Chr 13:9; see 2 Sam 6:6 †see 2 Cor 6:5

*1 Chr 13:9; see 2 Sam 6:6

a kindly vigor of soul, but a vicious and mean-spirited zeal by which indiscreetly and without mercy they rage against weak brothers. And therefore what Uzzah has suffered in body, they suffer in soul. What did Uzzah suffer? When he held up the ark, he was struck by the Lord and died at once there in his presence.* The Lord strikes him who neglects fraternal piety. Certainly the Lord strikes this one with the sentence by which he says, *The mighty shall be mightily tormented.* *Judgment without mercy for one who has not done mercy.* If, in God's Judgment, no one is saved except through mercy, then it is evident that one shall perish in the future Judgment who in the present life lives without mercy.

*see 1 Chr 13:10

*Wis 6:7

*Jas 2:13

17. But *men of mercy*, whom today we on earth extol, lived justly and mercifully; therefore in heaven they reign truly and happily, *whose justice has not been forgotten.* There is a justice that is erased by forgetfulness, and there is a justice that remains in memory. Unhappy and worthy of every misery [the one] whose justice is erased by forgetfulness. But the former is blessed, whose justice remains in memory. *The just one shall be in everlasting memory; he shall have no fear from the evil report.* Evil the report that the reprobate are destined to hear: *Go, you cursed ones, into everlasting fire!*

*Sir 44:10 (LXX)

*Ps 111:7

*Matt 25:41

18. *From* this *report the just one shall have no fear*, because as he is placed by God's right side, he will be secure from every punishment and attack of his enemies. Blessed Job says, *Set me beside you, and then let anyone fight against me.* [When I am] set beside you, I shall fear no adversary if I have you well-disposed. Therefore *the just one shall have no fear from the evil report,*　but with immense desire and no little affection he will await the good report that the chosen are destined to hear: *Come, blessed*

*Job 17:3

*Ps 11:7

*Matt 25:34
of my Father, possess the kingdom that was prepared for you from the foundation of the world. *

19. Therefore let us imitate the men of mercy so that, with the chosen, we may hear this sweet invitation of the Lord. Let us be careful lest our justice be forgotten, but rather let it remain in memory. May our justice not be sold or short-lived or tepid. The first belongs to hypocrites, the second belongs to beginners and those who do not persevere, and the third belongs to the negligent. Justice that is sold is ignored, short-lived justice is forgotten, tepid justice is purged.

20. Sold justice, which belongs to hypocrites, is ignored, because hypocrites (who shine outside and are like whitewashed tombs that *are full of dead* *see Matt 23:27 *people's bones inside,* * who desire more to be considered holy and not to be, rather than to be [holy] and not considered so, who aspire to *greetings in the* *Matt 23:6-7 *market place and the first seats in the synagogues,* * who put the whole of their worth in the mouth of humans) are ignored by the Lord as though alienated from him. To these in the end, as they shout with the foolish virgins, *Lord, Lord, open to us,* the Lord shall *see Matt 25:11-12 say, *Amen I say to you, I do not know you.* * Their justice is sold, because they sell every good deed that they do for a worthless price. For they do not do their own good deeds so that God is glorified, but so *see Matt 6:2 that they are praised more by human beings.* So the Lord says about them, *They have received their re-* *Matt 6:2, 5, 16 *ward.* * Vanity of the vain. So certainly sold [justice] is ignored.

21. Short-lived or momentary justice is forgotten. *No one putting his hand to the plow and looking* *Luke 9:62 *back is fit for the kingdom of God.* * In fact, a crown is promised not for beginners, but for those who *see Matt 10:22 persevere.* Those who withdraw from evil and after

a little while look back to it imitate Lot's wife, who,
as she withdrew from Sodom, as the Sodomites were
crying out, looked back and did not go out from the
borders of Sodom, but remained on the way, changed
into a statue of salt.* If anyone therefore goes out
from Sodom or Gomorrah, let him not look back to
Sodom or Gomorrah, but let him desire the land of
promise. One who begins well and afterward withdraws from the good way is like *a dog returning to
his vomit,* or *a washed pig to her wallow.** Their
justice has no reward, but punishment. Because
short-term justice is forgotten, the Lord says through
the prophet, *If the just person turns away from his
justice, and does iniquity according to all the inven-
tions that the wicked man is accustomed to work, all
\<his\> righteousness that he had done shall not be
remembered. In the transgression by which he has
transgressed, and in his sin that he has committed,
in them he shall die.**

22. Tepid justice is purged, because one who is
tepid and negligent, who keeps himself with laxity
and comfort, is despised by the Lord. So in Revelation it says, *If only you were hot or cold! But because
you are tepid, I will begin to vomit you out of my
mouth.** The mouth of the Lord signifies the chosen
in whom and through whom the Lord speaks. Thus
the Lord says in the Gospel, *It is not you who speak,
but the Spirit of your Father who speaks in you.**
From this mouth the Lord begins to vomit the tepid,
because, in the present, he deprives those who are
remiss and complaisant, and who conduct themselves
tepidly, of his gifts and charisma by which he enriches the chosen. And in the future, he will exclude
them from the fellowship of the saints, when in the
end, through the holy angels, he will separate the
goats from the sheep.*

*see Gen 19:26;
see Luke 17:32

*2 Pet 2:22;
see Prov 26:11

*Ezek 18:24

*Rev 3:15-16

*Matt 10:20

*see Matt 25:32

23. Therefore let our justice not be bartered, because bartered righteousness, which belongs to hypocrites, is ignored. So that it not be bartered and ignored, let our justice be true and in good works; let us seek not our glory, but God's. Let it not be short-term or momentary, but let us steadfastly see through good deeds that we begin with the Holy Spirit's inspiration. Let our justice not be tepid but fervent, so that, fervent with charity, we may be joined to those in heaven whose triumphs today we glorify on earth. With the merits and prayers of all the saints whose justice is not forgotten,* may the all-powerful God deign to bring that to pass for us, Father and Son and Holy Spirit. Amen.

*see Sir 44:10 (LXX)

Sermon 143

To Abbots

1. **D**avid *said to Amasa: Assemble for me all the men of Judah on the third day, and you also be present. He went to call Judah, and he delayed beyond the time that the king had set for him. And David said to Abishai: Take your lord's servants and pursue Sheba son of Bochri, lest perhaps he find fortified cities and escape us. Joab's men went out with Abishai, and all the valiant men went out of Jerusalem to pursue Sheba the son of Bochri. And when they were near the great stone that is in Gabaon, Amasa came to meet them. Now Joab had on a tight coat of equal length with his habit, and over it he was girded with a sword hanging down to his hip in a scabbard that was made in such manner that it could come out with the least motion and strike. And Joab said to Amasa: Greetings, my brother. And he took Amasa by the chin with his right hand as if intending to kiss him. But Amasa did not take notice of the sword that Joab held; he struck him in the side and poured out his intestines onto the ground.** ^(*2 Sam 20:4-10)

2. Divine Scripture commands that when we are invited *to a meal with a rich person*, we put our *hand to the dishes* with care.* The meal of this rich person is a sacred series of Scriptures. In this meal various and precious trays are put before us, not for refreshment of the flesh but of the spirit. With care let us put a hand to the dishes, so that out of the previous words, which are divine and mystical, we might take

*2 Sam 20:4-10

*see Prov 23:1

something for understanding and refreshment of
souls.

3. David, who is interpreted as *strong hand,**
signifies Christ. Amasa, who delays *beyond the time
that the king had set for him,** signifies a tepid and
negligent prelate, who follows his Lord's order in a
fussy and resentful manner. The king, that is, Christ
the King of kings and Lord of lords,** commands him
to call together *all the men of Judah on the third day**
and to be ready himself. Judah, who is interpreted
as *confessing,** signifies the faithful who confess and
worship the one and true God. Christ orders them
to be called together, that is, to be called into one, so
that they come together in one, remain in one, and
happily arrive at him who is one and supreme.

*The Lord will revive us after two days, and on the
third day he will raise us up, and we shall live in his
sight.** David orders Amasa to call together *all the
men of Judah on the third day,** because Christ orders
each and every prelate to call together and instruct
the faithful who worship and confess God, so that
they may prepare themselves for the third day, that
is the day of resurrection, in which they are going *to
render a reason* about their own deeds and to receive
what *each and every one* merits, *either good or bad.**

5. The king orders that Amasa himself be present
on the third day,** so that the prelate, of course, who
teaches others, may prepare himself for the third day,
for the day of resurrection, in which he is going to
return *a reason* not only *for himself*, but also for his
subordinates,** and so he may always be present for
himself (saying with the prophet, *My soul is always
in my hands*)** and so be prepared so that *when* the
Lord *comes and knocks* on his door,** he may be
found vigilant.

6. *Amasa went* and did not call the men of Judah
and did not come at *the time that the king had set*

*Jerome,
Int nom 68
(CCSL 72:145)
*2 Sam 20:5

*Rev 19:16

*see 2 Sam 20:4

*Jerome, Int nom
78 (CCL 72:157)

*Hos 6:3

*see 2 Sam 20:4

*see Rom 14:12;
see 2 Cor 5:10;
see Heb 13:17
*see 2 Sam 20:4

*see Rom 14:12;
see Heb 13:17

*Ps 118:109

*see Rev 3:20; see
Luke 12:36-37

for him.* In fact, a negligent and tepid prelate, who
acts halfheartedly, does not teach the faithful in his
charge as they must be taught and does not prepare
himself for the third day so that he may merit to hear
on that day, *Well done, good and faithful servant;
because you have been faithful in a small thing, I will
place you over many things. Enter into the joy of
your Lord.** Therefore on the third day, on the day
of the final examination, he will be deprived of the
promised honor and excluded from the glory of the
saints. The just judgment of God examines this, and
his decrees discern it, so that if the pastor has been
negligent in interior and exterior [matters], and in
his torpor has not carried out his God's precepts,
then he is demoted and his pastoral cares are taken
from him, so that a prudent and wise pastor may
advance, one who shall be concerned about his flock.

7. Well in fact, when Amasa delayed and did not
appear at the established time, the king *said to Abishai: Take the servants of your lord and pursue Sheba
son of Bochri, lest perhaps he find fortified cities and
escape us.** Abishai signifies a wise and vigorous person who is suitable and worthy to be in charge of
God's people. Amasa, when he is deprived of the
promised honor by his torpor—that is, when the
negligent and tepid pastor is removed from the pastoral dignity—then David orders Abishai to raise the
servants of his lord, because Christ provides a prudent and valiant pastor for his flock so that there
may be a leader and prince for his soldiers for pursuing Sheba son of Bochri.

8. *Sheba son of Bochri, that man Belial,* who
raised his hand against David (sounding a *trumpet:
We have no part in David, nor inheritance in the son
of Jesse*),* signifies the devil, who at once from the
beginning of his creation raised himself against
David, that is, his Creator. Through pride, as if he

*see 2 Sam 20:5

*see Matt 25:21,
23

*2 Sam 20:6

*2 Sam 20:1, 21;
see 1 Sam 17:23

sounded a trumpet, when he was in the presence of angels, he said with self-importance and presumption, *I will ascend above the height of the clouds. I will put my seat to the north. I will be like the most High.**

9. Sheba refused to be under David; rather, he persuaded the children of Israel to depart from the king and to imitate himself.* Similarly the devil refused to be under God but rather, as God, saying, *I will be like the most High.** And he persuaded the children of Israel (angels, that is, who happily enjoyed the vision of God before the Fall) to depart from the king, from their Creator and Ruler, and to follow him. He said to his own, *We have no part in David, nor inheritance in the son of Jesse.** We have no portion, no fellowship, no part with Christ. We have no inheritance in God's Son. We give up hope. Our sins having been examined, we are given into eternal death. We have no inheritance in heavenly places.*

10. This Sheba, that is, our *adversary, the ancient serpent,** *sounded a trumpet*† in Paradise, so that he could persuade the children of Israel, our first parents, to withdraw from their king, who had subjected to them Paradise and every tree therein except the tree of knowledge of good and evil.* Sheba sounded the trumpet of fraud in Paradise, saying to the woman, *Why has God commanded you not to eat from the tree of knowledge of good and evil?** To whom the woman said, *lest perhaps we die.*† And the seducer: *You shall not die. For God knows that on whatever day you shall eat from this tree, your eyes shall be opened, and you shall be as gods, knowing good and evil.**

11. Just as Sheba refused to be <subject> to David but persuaded the children of Israel to withdraw from the king and follow him, so also the devil refused to be subject to God, but rather [to be] like God, and

---

Margin notes (left column):

*Isa 14:13, 14 (as cited by Augustine *passim*)

*see 2 Sam 20:2

*Isa 14:14

*2 Sam 20:1

*see Eph 2:6

*see 1 Pet 5:8; see Rev 12:9 †2 Sam 20:1

*see Gen 2:16-17; 3:2-3

*see Gen 3:1; Gen 2:17 †Gen 3:3

*Gen 3:4-5

persuaded humans to desire in vain what he himself had desired presumptuously, so that they would be like gods.* Therefore just as the devil fell from heaven through pride and vainglory,* so humans were expelled from Paradise through the devil's persuasion by means of disobedience and illicit desires.*

 12. King David sent Abishai and a valiant army with him *to pursue Sheba son of Bochri.** David in this place signifies God. Abishai is the figure of a valiant and prudent man, who is in charge of others by God's provision and instruction, prudently guarding himself and wisely guiding the people subject to him. With his lord's servants he pursues Sheba, that is, the devil, rejecting the adversary and his ostentation, bravely fighting battles for his God,* subduing the flesh, suppressing vices, avoiding sins.

 13. With Abishai *all the valiant men went out of Jerusalem to pursue Sheba the son of Bochri.** Jerusalem the holy city (the city about which it is said, *Glorious things are said about you, O city of God)** happily already reigns partly in heaven, where there is a vision of peace and perfect glory of happiness, and partly on earth while she is traveling,* where there is misery: continual battle against Sheba, that is, the devil, who always takes up new weapons against the faithful and does not cease to attack Abishai and the servants of David. David sent many to pursue him: some before the law, some under the law, many during the time of grace.

 14. But Sheba son of Bochri could not be captured except by the advice of a wise woman who from the city said to Joab, *Is it not I who answer truth in Israel?** This wise woman signifies Christ, who is the Power of God and the Wisdom of God,* by whose advice and help Sheba is captured and his head cut off.* The head of the devil is the adversary's

*Gen 3:5

*see Isa 14:12

*see Gen 3:24

*2 Sam 20:7

*see 1 Sam 18:17;
25:28

*2 Sam 20:7

*Ps 86:3

*see 2 Cor 5:6

*2 Sam 20:19

*see 1 Cor 1:18,
24

*see 2 Sam 20:22

corrupt intention, which he always sharpens and raises against us. Let us cut off his head with the help and advice of God's Wisdom as often as we dash every suggestion of the devil *against the rock,** that is, Christ, and make it ineffective.

*see Ps 136:9; see 1 Cor 10:4

15. David sent Abishai *to pursue Sheba.** Sheba signifies the devil. Sheba is interpreted as *having gone out, he comes.** For the devil goes out from heavenly glory and honor by his pride and vain desire; he comes into misery and the captivity of eternal damnation. David, that is, God the Father, sent Abishai, that is, his Son, *to pursue Sheba*, that is, the devil, so that he would lead humankind (which Sheba diverted from God by fraud and perverse suggestion) back to David, that is, to God their creator.

*see 2 Sam 20:7

*Jerome, Int nom 40 (CCSL 72:108–9)

16. Our Abishai has come, Christ, leader of David's soldiers, and he found Sheba, that is, the devil, a strong and armed being guarding *his courtyard* and all that he possessed as if they were *in peace*. Abishai the *stronger* arrives, that is, Christ, *the Lord of hosts** and leader of God's whole army. He joined battle with the strong and armed Sheba,† that is, the devil, "whom, by conquering with stronger power, he casts out from his courtyard, that is, the world that had been *placed in wickedness,** in which Sheba, until the arrival of the Savior, was wickedly obtaining a peaceful empire, and as if all that he possessed were in peace, because in the hearts of the unfaithful, without any opposition, *the prince of the world,** the devil, was at peace."†

*Ps 23:10; see Josh 5:14 †see Luke 11:21-22

*see 1 John 5:19

*see John 14:30 †Bede, Luc 4.11 (CCSL 120:234)

17. Having conquered and ejected Sheba from his courtyard, our Abishai *tore away the weapons in which he was trusting and divided his spoils.** "The weapons of Sheba, that is, the devil, are treachery, spiritual wickedness,"* perverse suggestions, all that the wise and prudent Abishai tore away, because every trick of the devil, treachery, and perverse sug-

*see Luke 11:22

*Bede, Luc 4.11 (CCSL 120:234); see Eph 6:12

gestion, Christ made ineffective and reduced to nothing. "Sheba's spoils are people deceived by the devil, those whom the victor Christ divided, leading *captivity captive*,* giving *gifts to people,* ordaining *some apostles, some prophets, certain others evangelists, others pastors.*" *

18. Abishai, that is, Christ, leader of God's soldiers,† who by the command of the Father pursues Sheba son of Bochri, does not wish to have among his mercenaries and army anyone tepid and fearful, but all brave and warlike, according to what is written: *All the valiant men went out of Jerusalem with Abishai.* * Valiant men from Jerusalem, the city of God, are patriarchs, apostles, martyrs, and confessors, consecrated virgins and hermits and monks, all of whom go out with Abishai, that is, with Christ, imitating the obedience, humility, patience, mildness, steadfastness, and benevolence of Christ. These are the weapons of the valiant men going out of Jerusalem with Abishai.

19. The tepid and fearful do not go out with him, the lenient do not go out with him, the soft and epicene, but rather all the valiant. The stumbling and straying and undisciplined are sent back, those who run off impulsively as if frantic. The soft are carnal and self-indulgent, who are dedicated to luxuries and softness, embrace desires of the flesh, serving the belly before God and squandering transitory goods. The epicene are given to luxury, who, drunk on the dregs of lust, waste away in a pit of shame and ruin. These do not go out with Abishai, leader of David's soldiers, but withdrawing from the king they follow Sheba, that is, the devil, so that they are locked up with him in a city of damnation and a prison of death.

20. *All the valiant men* go out *of Jerusalem with Abishai. Joab's men went out with him to pursue Sheba.* * This is *the change of the right hand of the*

*Eph 4:8;
Ps 67:19

*Bede,
Luc 4.11, 22
(CCSL 120:234);
see Eph 4:11
†see Josh 5:14

*2 Sam 20:7

*2 Sam 20:7

*Ps 76:11

most High;* certainly this is divine work when Joab's men go out with Abishai. Joab is sometimes taken in a good sense, sometimes in a bad sense. In this one, where he fights his Lord's wars with manly vigor and saves victory for the king,* he signifies the chosen, and especially the apostles who bravely fought against the adversary of the human race, in all his works and virtues, seeking not his own glory but his Lord's.* But in the one where he treacherously killed two men better than himself, Abner and Amasa,* he signifies the devil, who oppresses the just, sets traps for the innocent, and seduces the just whom he can.

*see 1 Sam 18:17;
see Isa 42:13

*see 1 Thess 2:6
*2 Sam 3:27;
20:10

21. The men of this Joab are pagans, heretics, Jews, and all reprobates, from whom God's clemency calls many from error to truth, *from darkness to light*,* from disbelief to faith. And the men of David are made from the men of Joab, going in and going out according to the king's precept, manfully pursuing Sheba, that is, the devil, whom they were serving by faithlessness.

*see Acts 26:18

22. *Let us therefore*, my brothers, *cast off the works of darkness and put on the armor of light*,* so that rejecting Joab, that is, the adversary of the just, on the Day of Judgment, with the elect as our king rewards us, we may gain the pleasantness of eternal happiness. This may the *brave fighter*,* who everywhere conquers, deign to bestow on us, Jesus Christ our Lord, who with the Father and Holy Spirit lives and reigns, God through all ages forever. Amen.

*Rom 13:12

*see Isa 42:13;
see 1 Sam 18:17

Sermon 144

To Abbots

1. When Joab and Abishai and the
valiant men, who went out of
Jerusalem to pursue Sheba son of
Bochri, were <near the great stone that is in Gabaon,>
Amasa met them.* "Isaac, after *the Lord blessed him*   *2 Sam 20:7-8
*and he was greatly praised,** undertook a great work.   *see Gen 26:12-13
For he began to dig *wells that his ancestor's servants
had dug in the time of his father Abraham, but the
Philistines had plugged them and filled them with
earth."**   *Origen,
2. "Philistines hate water; they love earth. Isaac   Hom Gen 13.1
loves water: he always seeks wells, he always cleanses   (SCh 7*bis*:310);
old ones, he opens new ones, Isaac who for us was   see Gen 26:15, 18
offered as a sacrifice."* "Our Savior first of all wishes   *Origen,
them to dig wells that the servants of his father had   Hom Gen 13.2
dug. He wishes to restore the wells of the Law and   (SCh 7*bis*:312);
the Prophets that the Philistines had refilled with   see Eph 5:2
earth."*   *Origen,
3. "Who are these who refill the wells with earth?   Hom Gen 13.2
Certainly those who put an earthly <and> carnal   (SCh 7*bis*:314)
understanding into the law, and block up the spiritual
and mystical sense, so that they neither drink nor
permit others to drink. Hear our Isaac, the Lord Jesus
Christ, saying in the gospels, *Woe to you scribes and
Pharisees, because you have taken the key of knowledge, and you yourselves have not entered, nor have
you permitted others who wish to enter.** These are   *Luke 11:52;
those who refill with earth the wells that Abraham's   Matt 23:13
servants had dug, who teach the law in a carnal way,

and pollute the waters of the Holy Spirit, who have wells for this: not to bring forth water, but to put down earth."*

*Origen,
Hom Gen 13.2
(SCh 7*bis*:314)

4. Isaac approaches, I mean our Savior, to dig wells "that the servants of his Father had dug. A servant of his Father was Moses, who had dug the well of the law. Servants of his Father were David and Solomon and the prophets and all who had written the books of the Old Testament, that the faithlessness of the Jews had refilled with earthly and dirty understanding. When Isaac wished to cleanse the ancient wells, showing that whatsoever the Law and the Prophets had said was said about *him*,* the Jews *argued* with him.* And because he does not wish to be with those who refuse to have water in wells, but rather earth, he says to them, *Behold, your house shall be left to you desolate*."*

*see Luke 24:27;
see John 5:46
*see Gen 26:21

*Origen,
Hom Gen 13.2
(SCh 7*bis*:316);
Matt 23:38

5. "Therefore Isaac digs new wells, or, more correctly, Isaac's servants dig. The servants of our Isaac are Matthew, Mark, Luke, and John. His servants are Peter, Andrew, James, and all the rest of those who dig wells of the New Testament. But those who *sense earthly things** also wrangle about these; they do not allow new things to be stored or old things to be cleansed. They contradict the Gospel wells; they oppose the apostolic wells. And because in everything they contradict, in everything they challenge, it is said to them, *Because you have made yourselves unworthy of God's grace, from now on we shall go to the Gentiles*."*

*see Phil 3:19

*Origen,
Hom Gen 13.2
(SCh 7*bis*:318);
see Acts 13:45-46
*Gen 26:22

6. "Therefore Isaac dug the third well and *called its name Ampleness, saying, Now has the Lord expanded us and made us increase upon the earth.** Truly Isaac was expanded and his name increased upon all the earth when he fulfilled in us knowledge of the Trinity. For at first, only *in Judea* was *God*

known, and *in Israel was his name* called.* But now
*their sound has gone forth into all the earth, and
their words to the ends of the world.* For Isaac's
servants went out and dug wells throughout the
whole world, and they revealed *living water** to all,
baptizing all the nations in the name of the Father
and the Son and the Holy Spirit."*

7. "Each and every one of us who serves God's
word digs a well and seeks living water from which
to refresh listeners."† "We in fact, if we are Isaac's
servants, love wells and springs of living water; we
withdraw <from> the quarrelsome and false accusers,
and we leave them on the earth that they love. We,
however, never cease from digging wells of living
water. And indeed by striking down old things at one
time and new things at another time, we become like
that scribe in the Gospel about whom the Lord said,
*One who brings forth from his treasure new things
and old.*"*

8. "Every land has waters, but one who is a Philistine and senses *earthly things*† does not know how
to find water in every land, does not know how to
discover a rational sense and image of God in every
soul, does not know how one can find faith, piety,
reverence. What does it profit you <to have> learning
and not know how to use it, to have language and
not know how to talk? But Isaac's servants dig wells
of living water in every land; they speak God's word
to every soul and are fruitful."* Let us also dig with
Isaac's servants, so that we may likewise in the
present chapter meeting find living water, that is, the
spiritual sense.

9. *When Joab and Abishai and the valiant men
who went out of Jerusalem were near the great stone
that is in Gabaon, Amasa met them.** The great stone
in Gabaon signifies Christ who is the cornerstone,

*see Ps 75:2

*Ps 18:5

*see Gen 26:19

*Origen,
Hom Gen 13.3
(SCh 7*bis*:318);
see Matt 28:19;
see Mark 16:15
†Origen,
Hom Gen 13.3
(SCh 7*bis*:318)

*Origen,
Hom Gen 13.3
(SCh 7*bis*:320);
see Matt 13:52
†see Phil 3:19

*Origen, Hom
Gen 13.3 (SCh
7*bis*:320, 322)

*2 Sam 20:7-8

*Ps 117:22
†see Matt 7:25;
see Ant Ded eccl,
"Domus"
(Hesbert 3:2998)
‡1 Cor 10:4

*Dan 2:34, 35

*Jerome, Int nom
27 (CCSL 72:94);
see also Jerome,
Int nom 28
(CCSL 72:94)

*Matt 28:20

*see 2 Sam 20:7

*Matt 18:20
*2 Sam 20:8

about which the prophet says, *The stone that the builders rejected, this one has become the head of the corner.** He is the firm and solid rock,† about which blessed Paul says, *And they drank of the spiritual rock that followed them, and the rock was Christ.*‡ This is that *stone cut out of a mountain without hands* that *struck the statue on its feet of clay*, which Nebuchadnezzar had seen, and it broke *and shattered* the statue. *But the stone grew into a great mountain and filled the whole earth.** Behold how great this stone is.

10. This stone is in Gabaon. Gabaon, which is interpreted as *high hill* or *hill of sorrow*,* represents the church. It is rightly called a high hill because, although the church always strives toward lofty realities, it sojourns in lowness. The church is called a hill of sorrow, because penitents in it ceaselessly shed tears for their sins, and the perfect sweetly groan because they are delayed from entering the kingdom. The great rock is in Gabaon, Christ certainly in the church, just as the Son of the Virgin himself had promised to the primitive church: *Behold I am with you all days, even to the consummation of the world.**

11. Near this great stone are all the valiant men who, at David's command, went out of Jerusalem with Abishai *to pursue Sheba son of Bochri*,* because all the faithful follow the shepherd assigned to them by God, to pursue the devil, to fight against vice and sin. All these are near Christ, who promises them, *Where there are two or three gathered together in my name, there am I among them.**

12. And *Amasa met them.** Amasa does not go out of Jerusalem with the valiant men, but he meets them in Gabaon. Obviously one who through listlessness and idleness of mind conducts himself negligently does not prepare himself to fight against Sheba,

that is, the devil, but meets those who are prepared to fight in Gabaon. Because in all circumstances every lustful and negligent person who through idleness refuses to fight, coveting earthly and transitory things and embracing *desires of the flesh,** is hostile to religious men and those who bravely conduct themselves. Joab greets this one, because the devil loves and encourages such types.

*see Gal 5:16

13. Joab's greeting is the false and deceitful persuasion of the adversary, by which he entices the hearts of reprobates. In fact, so that he might persuade the reprobates [to commit] sins and crimes, in his seduction he promises longer life spans and, as if speaking to a friend, flatters in his deception: "Why do you refuse to carry out what the flesh desires? Behold how great is the sweetness, how pleasant and full of affection is the delight in pleasure of the flesh. Why do you tremble? Why do you have such dread? God has despised no one who repents and confesses! Use carnal pleasures while youth flourishes; you will repent in old age. Repentance is never too late." The devil, in his deceit putting forth this and ideas of this nature, is *Joab* saying *to Amasa, Greetings, my brother.*

14. *And Joab took Amasa by the chin with his right hand as if intending to kiss him.** Joab takes Amasa's chin with his right hand, because the devil rewards an impious and reprobate person with temporal and transitory goods as if he intends to kiss him. For the devil's friendship is not true, but rather feigned. Therefore in fact he helps in the present, so that he may punish in the future. He takes Amasa's chin with his right hand, because the devil works with the impious and reprobate for evil.* So the impious and ungrateful have plenty of temporal and transitory goods, and they overflow with riches and

*2 Sam 20:9

*see Rom 8:28

pleasures. But the Lord's servants in the present are afflicted with tortures and punishments. So the Lord says about his own, *You shall lament and weep, but the world shall rejoice.**

* John 16:20

15. The reprobates are designated by the name of *the world*, about whom the psalmist says, "*They are not in the toil of human beings, and they shall not be scourged with the just.** They recover from infirmity and wounds quickly; just people are shaken by the lashings of trouble. *Therefore pride has held them; they have been covered with their iniquity and their wickedness.** Through the arrogance that comes from good fortune, they are pressed by multiple injustices. *Their iniquity has come forth as if from fat.** As they have forgotten justice in the fatness of riches, iniquity has proceeded from them. Moses says about this fatness, *Jacob has grown fat and kicked back.** *They have passed into the affection of the heart,** as they do their own will and not God's."* Joab takes their chin, because the devil works with the reprobate for evil,† helping at present, punishing in the future.

* Ps 72:5

* Ps 72:6

* Ps 72:7

* Deut 32:15
* Ps 72:7
* PsJerome, Brev in Pss, Ps 72 (PL 26:1030C)
† see Rom 8:28

16. *Joab had on a tight coat of equal length with his habit.** The devil is armed and ready to fight against the chosen. He always *goes about seeking whom he may devour.** His coat is jealousy. The devil puts on this coat *of equal length with his habit*, because jealousy girds and surrounds the devil himself and all his members. This coat is tight because just as charity expands* and gladdens the hearts of the chosen, so jealousy restrains and hems in the hearts of reprobates. Over this coat is girded *a sword hanging down to his hip*. Over the devil's coat, that is jealousy, rightly hangs a sword *to his hip in a scabbard.** For *by the envy of the devil, death entered into the world.**

* 2 Sam 20:8

* 1 Pet 5:8

* see 2 Cor 6:11, 13

* 2 Sam 20:8
* Wis 2:24

17. His sword is his spiteful and perverse suggestion, by which he suggests always bad and never

good things to the good and the wicked and to whomever he can. This sword hangs down to the hip. Hips are near the shameful and virile members, in which the devil's suggestion is especially active, because through lust he boldly attacks not only reprobates, but even religious men. Joab's sword is held in a scabbard because the devil's suggestion penetrates the hearts of reprobates, who are always ready and quick to be persuaded by the adversary. The mind of reprobates is the devil's scabbard, in which hangs his sword, corrupt and perverse suggestion, obviously. From this scabbard, that is, the mind of reprobates, come forth quarrels, fornication, adultery, anger, wrangling, murder. These corrupt the body and kill the soul.

18. *Amasa did not take notice of the sword that Joab held.* In other words, the tepid and negligent one, who easily takes up the devil's suggestion, does not pay attention or consider the ruin of eternal death that the adversary prepares for him. And Joab *struck* Amasa *in the side and poured out his guts onto the ground, and he died.* Woe to the person whom Joab strikes on the side! One who is wounded on the side despairs of his life. A wound of the side is a criminal sin. The soul that is corrupted by Joab's sword, that is, the devil's suggestion, with a wound of the side, that is, with a criminal sin, dies immediately, and all her intestines are poured onto the ground.

19. Our intestines are a clean mind, a holy will, honorable thought, desire of eternal realities, pure intention, love of virtues. All these are poured out onto the ground if a soul is wounded by a criminal sin. In fact, the unfaithful and reprobate one, who is oppressed by criminal sins, does not raise his head to heaven, does not ponder what belongs to God so that he might consider heavenly realities, but, weighed down by a pile of sins, is always stooped to

*2 Sam 20:10

*2 Sam 20:10

the earth—nay rather, wholly changed into earth, made wholly earth—embracing nothing except carnal things, pondering nothing except earthly and transitory things. This one is *splattered with blood* *2 Sam 20:12   *and* lies *in the middle of the road.**

20. Our regular road is a protection, through which we are set upright and directed in choir, in the cloister, in chapter, and <in> every place. On this road the dead one lies splashed with blood, he who is wrapped in criminal sins, stained with filthy vice as with blood. This one, because he was already wounded in the side, hates *discipline* and throws *see Ps 49:17;   God's *words behind* his *back,** detesting the rigor of
see Isa 38:17   the Order, abhorring the monastery as though a jail, fleeing choir, avoiding the canonical hours.

*see 2 Sam   21. *On account of him, those who pass by* stop.*
20:12   Who are the people passing by? The faithful who eagerly run the roads of the Lord so that they may *see Phil 3:14   happily attain *to the reward** of Christ's promises are truly called Hebrews. With mouth and heart, they say with the apostle, *We have not here a lasting city,* *Heb 13:14   *but we seek one that is celestial.** Nevertheless they sometimes stop on account of Amasa, splashed with *2 Sam 20:12   blood, lying in the middle of the road,* because an out-of-step and disorderly brother is an obstacle and impediment to religious brothers.

22. *A certain man saw that the people stood still to look upon Amasa splashed with blood, so he removed him into a field, and covered him with a garment, so that those who passed might not stop on *2 Sam 20:12   his account.** The wise and discerning shepherd does this when he sees someone who is mentally unstable, straying, and undisciplined. "Lest one diseased sheep *RB 28.8   contaminate the whole flock,"* he moves him from the road into a field, that is from the cloister's protection to external business, covering him with a gar-

ment, entrusting to him, of course, some obedience in external responsibilities through which he might avoid leisure, which is an enemy to the soul.

23. Therefore brothers, let us not be restless, negligent, and tepid, lest what happened to tepid Amasa might happen to us, he who through negligence and listlessness has not followed the king's order and therefore lies pitiably dead. Let us eagerly go out of Jerusalem with the valiant men, bravely fighting with Abishai against Sheba, that is, the devil, resisting the devil and his servants in all things, so that with the valiant men who faithfully go in and out at the king's order, after David rewards the victory, we may take up the crown of eternal life, which may our King David, strong of hand,* deign to grant to us, who with his virtue has taken captive Sheba, that is the devil, and vanquished him with wonderful strength. To him be victory, honor, and power through everlasting ages. Amen.

*Jerome,
Int nom 68
(CCSL 72:145)

Sermon 145

On the Beheading of
Saint John the Baptist

1.

*Ant Nat JB
(Hesbert 3:3788);
see Mark 6:27

The unbelieving king sent his detestable
servant, and he ordered him to cut off
the head of John in prison.* The pride
of the unbelievers must be detested and execrated,
the cruelty of the impious, the presumption of the
reprobates who oppress, afflict, and kill God's servants. Herod, *the unbelieving king,* cruel persecutor,
devil's servant, friend of vice, enemy of virtues, *ordered to cut off the head of John in prison.* Although
he is said to be *saddened, because of his oath and
because of those who were with him at table,** he
was nevertheless not unwilling, but he voluntarily
killed John, whom he would gladly have destroyed
more quickly if he had not feared the people, who
venerated John as a prophet.*

*see Mark 6:26

*see Matt 14:5

2. So blessed Bede says about the impious Herod,
"Intellectually a hypocrite, and a skilled murderer,
he who had happiness in his mind was pretending
sadness on his face."* And Josephus, in his eighteenth
book, as he commends John the Baptist, includes
among other things, "But Herod killed this very good
man, who instructed the Jews to give care to virtue,
to cultivate justice, to preserve piety for God, and to
join together into one through baptism. And then
baptism shall be acceptable to God if it is not only
taken up for washing away sins, but also preserved
for chastity of the body, and justice and purification
of the soul. And when Herod had seen many people

*Bede,
In Marc 2.6
(CCSL 120:509)

98

flock to him, fearing that by John's persuasion the
people might depart from his reign, on this suspicion
alone, John, fettered in the castle Machaerus, is cut
down."*

3. So we have judged carefully that Herod did
not grieve, but rather he rejoiced when he perceived
a suitable cause, as it were, to justify killing John.
Just as his father Herod the Elder, under whose reign
Christ was born, killed the innocents so that he
would do away with Christ along with the innocents
lest he succeed him in his reign,* so this younger
Herod, a detestable son, an imitator of his accursed
father, destroyed the Lord's precursor, lest by John's
persuasion his kingdom be transferred to another.
Therefore both elder and younger Herods signify the
devil, who diligently keeps watch concerning this as
much as he can, lest in his reign, that is, among
human beings whom he possesses, Christ should rule.

4. *Herod* is interpreted as *skin* or *shape-shifter*,*
which is very fitting for the devil, on account of his
versatile cunning and multiple deceptions by which
he is effective against us. He certainly is *a ravenous
wolf*;* *a roaring lion*, who always seeks someone
whom he may devour;† the Leviathan,‡ sitting *in
ambush so that he may kill the innocent in secret*;#
a serpent more cunning than all animals;§ *the ham-
mer of the whole earth.** This spiritual Herod daily
sends *a detestable servant to cut off the head of John
in prison.** *John* is interpreted as *God's grace* or *in
whom is grace.*† In fact, every one can be called John
who has something in himself by which he might be
saved, because this is a gift and grace of God. Herod
is jealous of this person and sends against him *a
detestable servant to cut off* his *head.*

5. The spirit of fornication is a detestable servant,
the spirit of blasphemy, the spirit of contention and

*Rufinus, Eccl
hist 1.11 (GCS
91:77, 79), citing
Iosephus Flavius,
*Antiquitates
Iudaicae* 18.5.2

*see Matt 2:16-18

*Jerome,
Int nom 64
(CCSL 72:140)

*see Gen 49:27;
see Matt 7:15
†see 1 Pet 5:8
‡see Isa 27:1
#Ps 9:29
§Gen 3:1
*Jer 50:23

*Ant Nat JB
(Hesbert 3:3788);
see Mark 6:27
†Jerome, Int nom
69 (CCL 72:146)

anger, the spirit of quarreling and covetousness. And why shall we proceed further? There are as many instigators of evils as there are detestable servants of Herod, who all desire to cut off John's head, that is, Christ, who is life* and head of all the faithful, to separate [Christ] from his members.* But after Christ's blood was poured out* our enemies were made weak, so they no longer contend against us openly, but they attack us in prison, that is, in secret. They became bandits. Hidden by black darkness, they fearfully sit in ambush. And stealthily, in the manner of thieves, they grab our treasures, which are precious <vessels> of virtue.

*see John 14:6

*see Eph 4:15-16

*see Mark 14:24

6. Our value is great and ought to be extolled with highest praise. After God and angels nothing is more precious than a person for whom Christ's blood was poured out, to whom, if one persists in doing good, eternal royal powers are promised and shall be given. Nevertheless, let no one deceive himself, let no one suppose that he is going to run to the homeland of Paradise through a soft meadow.* We are surrounded by great columns of hostile forces, all things are filled with enemies, and our fragile flesh is also destined to be ashes. Therefore one goes astray and goes far astray who thinks that he can be just in this world without persecution. In fact *all*, according to words of blessed Paul, *who intend to live piously in Christ, suffer persecution.**

mollia prata:
Vergil, *Georgica*
2.384

*2 Tim 3:12

7. In this our misery and calamity, in this our exile, we are surrounded by double battle lines of enemies. On one side Herod with his servants assails us with arrows; from another side our own flesh disturbs us at close quarters. Myriad accomplices of demons, innumerable armies of vices besiege our camp. There would be no way of escaping for us nor any strength to resist if Christ our Lord did not do

battle with us and on our behalf. He is our refuge, our strength,* our victory, he our crown after battle. *see Ps 30:4 He fought beforehand and conquered, so that we might fight and conquer. So sacred Scripture invites us to fight: *Fight*, it says, *with the ancient serpent, because no one shall be crowned except one who struggles lawfully.** *see Rev 12:7-9; see 2 Tim 2:5

8. Herod, that is, our ancient adversary, before Christ's incarnation nearly subjugated the whole world to himself. But since the Lamb who took away our sins was raised on the cross,* the strength of the *see John 1:29 enemy has been diminished and the adversary can do nothing against us any longer, unless we render consent to him. To those who consent he is strong as a lion; to those who resist he is weak as an ant. So in sacred Scripture the same adversary is called an antlion,* that is, a lion of ants.† *myrmicoleon †see Job 4:11 (LXX) ‡ant #leo

9. For *Myrmix*‡ in Greek is called *formica* in Latin; a *coleon* is a lion,# so "*myrmicoleon* is a lion of ants. Or if we say it more expressly, he is equally an ant and a lion."§ "For he is as strong to those who consent as he is feeble to those who resist."* "But the antlion is a small animal that conceals itself under dust and kills ants as they carry their grain. So everywhere the apostate angel, *cast out* from heaven *to earth*, besieges" and *seduces*" "the minds of the faithful (who prepare the provisions of good works for themselves) on the road of their practice."* But he did not scare or seduce John the Baptist. §Gregory I, Mor 5.XX.40 (CCSL 143:246) *Gregory I, Mor 5.XXII.43 (CCSL 143:248) *see Rev 12:7-9 *Gregory I, Mor 5.XXII.43 (CCSL 143:248)

10. So as not to leave the truth unsaid, [John] despised Herod the most cruel, the brigand among nobles, the plunderer among allies, the thief in his own household, the murderer of common people, the killer of children, who drenched holy ground with blood. John was certainly preaching to him whatever was of justice, what was of the law, what

was a foundation not of hatred but of love, saying,
It is not lawful for you to have your brother Philip's
*Mark 6:18;
see 6:17 *wife.** So John offended Herod because one who
accuses guilty people incurs hatred. Herod beheaded
John on account of a holy and wholesome exhortation, him who was the teacher of life, pattern of holiness, monument of modesty, example of virginity.
see Matt 11:10-11 Who was greater than this person, equal to angels,
summit of the law, voice of apostles, silence of the
see Matt 11:13 prophets, handed over to an adulterer and beheaded
*see Ant "Puellae
saltanti," Nat JB
(Hesbert 3:4409) at the request of a dancing girl?* This is according
to the letter.

   11. Herod, who beheaded John, represents the
people of the Jews who persecuted Christ, the head
of the prophets, unto death. It is in vain that Christ,
destined to redeem the world, is exalted on the cross
see John 1:7, 15 while his precursor, imparting testimony to the
truth, is cut off at the head. John was beheaded,
because in the opinion of human beings (by whom
he was thought to be Christ) he diminished and was
determined to have been a human being and not
*see John 1:20;
3:28, 30; see
Luke 3:15-16 Christ.* But truly Christ is exalted on the cross, because he was considered a simple human being, he
whom the whole church now confesses as God and
human. "Their sufferings are consummated in a different order and a separate time by divine dispensa-
*Bede, Hom lib II, 2
(CCSL 122:354) tion."*

   12. "For just as [John] bore witness to Christ,
who was going to be born, going to preach, and
going to baptize, by being born first, by preaching
and by baptizing and also by suffering, he first indi-
*Bede, Hom lib II, 2
(CCSL 122:354) cated that <Christ> was going to suffer."* John was
finally beheaded because, in the minds of human
beings, he decreased, because he who was thought
to be the Christ is discerned to have been a prophet
and precursor of Christ. "Christ raised on the cross,

having his head raised to heaven, extended his hands over the earth, so to designate that he is Lord of heaven and that all the earth is subject to himself. The lowest parts of his cross penetrated to the hidden [regions] of the earth, so that the kingdom of the nether regions was transfixed by his suffering and recognized as destroyed."*

13. Therefore let us be humble with John, fasting and continually praying. Let us not resist being diminished before human beings, so that we can be exalted in Christ with John in heaven before God's angels. Amen.

*Bede,
Hom lib II, 23
(CCSL 122:355)

Sermon 146

On the Feast of Saint Benedict [1]

*Matt 19:27

1. **S**imon Peter said to Jesus, Behold, we have left all things and have followed you.* Because this gospel is read especially on the solemnity of blessed Benedict, which is celebrated today, let us show how reasonable this is and how it pertains to him and to his order specifically. Let superiors and subordinates listen and recognize that this gospel pertains to them also.

2. Because this gospel especially pertains to monks, it explains the double name of the one who asks. He who is described as asking this is called Simon Peter. Simon is interpreted as "obedient." *Petrus* in Greek speech is called *firmus** in Latin, but in Hebrew *agnoscens.** What does this Simon Peter signify (that is, obedient, firm, and acknowledging), if not the order of monks, whose mark of profession is obedience, who should not only obey but also acknowledge the virtue of obedience through discretion, so that through innocence they can stand firm?

*firm
*acknowledging;
Jerome, Int nom
62 (CCSL 72:141,
18)

3. Moreover, because Simon Peter was the first shepherd of the church, by Simon Peter one must understand the superiors. First, they offer their obedience to God, and then they must require it from

---

[1] Odo of Canterbury copied this sermon and included it among his own. The version included in CCCM 2C is based on the critical edition of Odo's sermons: Charles de Clercq, ed., *The Latin Sermons of Odo of Canterbury* (Brussel: Koninklijke Academie voor Wetenschappen, 1983), 227–40.

subordinates. It is fitting for them to be firm and understanding in obedience, so that they can instruct and strengthen their subordinates by word and example, to the point that the firmness of disciples' obedience can be acknowledged from the service and <discretion of> the erudition of the prelates. They do this rightly if they leave behind the world and things that are of the world for Christ, and if, following Christ himself with perfect charity, they strive to rouse their disciples to the same contempt of the world and love of heaven, so that they might form them as much by examples of holy life as by words of sound doctrine.

4. Such a person was our blessed father Benedict, whose feast we celebrate today on earth, being itself solemnized in heaven with the angels. In his works he stood out in obeying God and also strengthened the obedience of his disciples. If any who do not know [about this] want to know, let them read his life written by blessed Gregory, and let them find him saying to Jesus more by works than by speech, *Behold, we have left all things and have followed you.** *Matt 19:27

Let them find there how—obeying Jesus' words, *If anyone does not renounce all that he possesses, then he cannot be my disciple**—he left all the things of *Luke 14:33 the world by perfectly renouncing the world.

5. In fact, just as it was written in his life, when he was still in the world "he might have freely enjoyed it, yet even in his youth he despised the world as so much dust."* So, "having left behind his father's *Gregory I, home and property, he sought the habit of holy con- Dial II, Prol. 1 version."† He remained firm in obedience, because (SCh 260:126) once he began in it, so in the wilderness as in the †Gregory I, monastery, through holiness he persevered. So, wholly Dial II, Prol. 1 absorbed by the flame of divine love,* drawn by the (SCh 260:126) odor of Christ's ointments, he ran after him all the *see Song 8:6

*see Song 1:3
way into heaven.* Established there in that light through which all things were made, he merited to see below himself the world that he had perfectly left. So he was truly able to say to Jesus, *Behold, we have left all things and have followed you. What* *Matt 19:27 *therefore shall we have?** We left through humility, we followed you through charity. What therefore will you give to us in eternal happiness?

6. So that we may strive to follow Christ through humility, in his Rule he proposed for us twelve steps *RB 7 of humility.* The first of these is fear of the Lord, which keeps one from sin. The second step, rejection of one's own will. Third, choosing the will of another, that is, obedience. Fourth, in that obedience, to embrace severe and harsh matters with patience. Fifth, confession of sins. Sixth, contempt of the world, so that "a monk is content with the lowest and most *RB 7.49 menial treatment."* The seventh is contempt of oneself, so that one always judges himself as inferior to others. The eighth step is observance of the common rule. Ninth, keeping quiet, that is, *silence,* which is *Isa 32:17 *the service of justice.** The tenth step, strictness of mind, through which he is not readily given to laughter. Eleventh, seriousness in words and manners. Twelfth, constant memory of sins, so that at every hour, knowing that he is guilty, he considers himself as already standing before the terrible Judgment of God. This is the concept of humility written by blessed Benedict.

7. Twelve steps of pride are the opposite of these steps of humility. The first of these is forgetfulness of sins, which is accompanied by curiosity, which makes a person go astray through the eyes and other senses. The second step of pride, levity in words and manners, is observed through words inappropriately sad or happy. Third is a silly joy of mind, which is revealed in a readiness to laugh. Fourth is loquaciousness,

whose comrade is boasting, always expanded by excessive talking. Fifth is singularity, which always wants to show off. Sixth is love of self, to which is joined arrogance, by which one judges oneself to be better than others. Seventh is love of the world, for whom nothing is enough. Eighth is justification of sins. Ninth, impatience. Tenth, disobedience, which rebellion follows. Eleventh is love of one's own will, in which is the freedom to commit sin. Twelfth is shamelessness, by which sin becomes habitual. *When the sinner has come into* this *depth* by descending through the aforementioned steps of pride, *contempt.** *see Prov 18:3

8. Those bravely resist these steps of pride who truly can say to Jesus, *Behold, we have left all things and have followed you.** These were able to hear *Matt 19:27
with confidence, *Everyone who has left home, or father, or mother, or sons and daughters, or fields for my name's sake shall receive a hundredfold, and shall possess eternal life.** *Matt 19:29

9. Our home is the world, in which we dwell as in a home as long as we are detained in its vanities in mind and in body. The father of this household, whom we surely must leave, is the one who is called *prince of the world,** the devil in fact, through whose *see John 14:30
guilt we were all his children, as the apostle says: *Because we were all children of wrath by nature.** *Eph 2:3
Our mother is concupiscence, in which we were all begotten. Our brothers and sisters are perverse feelings, which can be called brothers according to the spirit, or which are taken by the name of sisters according to the flesh. In fact both affections, spirit and flesh, of course, beget concupiscence for us. Our wife is understood as pleasure,** from whose embrace we **uoluptas*
beget works that are according to pleasure,** like sons **uoluptatem*
and daughters. Generally by fields we must understand all riches, earthly possessions, and honors.

10. The Lord himself briefly expressed all these things, saying to Abraham, *Go forth*, he says, *out of your country, and from your kindred, and from your father's house.** By *country*, all earthly places that are considered among foreign [lands] are designated. By kindred (father and mother, brother and sister) all vices both carnal and spiritual are represented, those that by a certain natural kinship always cling to us. By the father's house is understood the world, in which by an abundance of evils the devil seems to preside like the head of a household. In the first place Abraham is ordered to go out from his country, in the second from kindred, in the third from his house.

11. In order to arrive at the country of the living, which the Lord is going to show to us,* in the beginning, as though going out from our land, we must leave behind all foreign things that we have on earth. Second, because "the cowl does not make the monk"* (rather, virtue does), we must strive to drive away from the entrance to the cloister all prior vices that by a certain right of kinship strain to follow us. For if they should enter with us into this cloister not as monks but as lay people, or rather, worse than lay people, we should live slanderously among our old kindred. Third, so that we may be perfect, going out from our father's house we must mentally transcend the world and all things that are of the world,* unwillingly to be detained in this world as if in a certain prison, daily desiring with Paul *to be dissolved* and *to be with Christ,** to live in the flesh contrary to the flesh, and although fettered by the body in the world, yet with a free mind to dwell in the heavens, so we can say with Paul, *But our way of life is in heaven.**

12. Now let us return to the words of the gospel. *Everyone*, says the Lord, *who has left home, or father, or mother, or sons, or daughters for my name's*

*Gen 12:1

*see Ps 26:13;
see Gen 12:1

*Proverbia 7:460,
#35860

*see 1 John 2:15

*see Phil 1:23

*see Phil 3:20

*sake shall receive a hundredfold, and shall possess
life everlasting.** Not all who come to the cloister for
the sake of the name of Jesus are allowed to hasten
to that place. In fact, many in the cloister do not seek
salvation of their souls, which this name of Jesus
signifies, but rather ecclesiastical honors. And those
in this generation who seem to leave behind all things
through religion are found to desire more distinguished status in the cloister through ambition, so
that status that they did not have in secular life, they
might find in the cloister through a certain pretense.

*Matt 29:29

13. Christ shows that the cloister is not to be
sought with such intention, but only for sake of his
name; that is, for love of eternal salvation, worldly
things are to be abandoned. But if superiors and subordinates will act according to the Rule of Blessed
Benedict, by following his humility and embracing
his charity, then they shall receive the blessing of
eternal beatitude from Jesus Christ himself, which,
by the merits and prayers of our Father Benedict,
may our Lord Jesus Christ deign to give to us, who
with the Father and Holy Spirit lives and reigns, God
through all ages forever. Amen.

Sermon 147

On the Feast of Saint Benedict [1]

*Ant and Resp,
Com conf
(Hesbert 3:1711;
4:6247);
see Sir 44:25
†see Heb 9:11
‡see Ps 28:10

1. **T**he Lord gave to him the blessing of all nations, and has confirmed his covenant upon his head.* This blessing, after Christ, seems to pertain to blessed Benedict. *Christ* our *high priest,*† who sits as *king forever,* who grants *virtue* to us and blesses *his people in peace,*‡ thus singularly blessed Blessed Benedict as he came to the blessing of ordination, while he consecrated him abbot over the whole of monasticism, so that besides the [blessing] that pertains to an abbot, he has also gathered together for him all the gifts of other blessings that he distributes singly to others individually.*

*see 1 Cor 12:11

2. According to the apostle, *to one is given the word of wisdom, to another knowledge according to the same Spirit, to another faith in the same Spirit, to another the gift of healing, to another the working of mighty deeds, to another prophecy, to another the discerning of spirits, to another various kinds of tongues, to another interpretation of speeches. One and the same Spirit works all these, dividing to each one according to his will.* These are the blessings in the book of the high priest, written by *the finger of*

*1 Cor 12:8-11

---

[1] Odo of Canterbury copied this sermon and included it among his own. The edition in CCCM 2C is based on the edition of Odo's sermons. See Charles de Clercq, ed., *The Latin Sermons of Odo of Canterbury* (Brussel: Koninklijke Academie voor Wetenschappen, 1983), 200–210.

God,* that is, by the work of the Holy Spirit. There   *see Deut 9:10
are other innumerable blessings written in the same
book, all of which he recited over the head of Benedict by reading the whole blessed book from title to
end. So blessed Gregory exclaims in exultation,
"Benedict was a man of the Lord, filled with the spirit
of all the just."*   *Gregory I,
   3. There is one blessing in which it was promised   Dial II.8.8–9
to Abraham that all nations would be blessed. *In*   (SCh 260:166)
your seed, says the Lord speaking to Abraham, *all*
nations shall be blessed,* which Paul explains thus: *Gen 22:18;
He did not say "in seeds," as in many, but as in one.   see Acts 3:25
*In your seed, which is Christ.** Human nature, de-   *Gal 3:16
livered to death by the curse of our first parent, is
promised to be blessed in Christ so that it could return to life. For that reason he is called Jesus, <that
is,> *Savior.** The baptized gain this blessing from   *Jerome,
Christ and through it arrive at salvation, if they pre-   Int nom 77
serve it whole after baptism by living rightly.   (CCSL 72:156)
   4. But because *narrow is the way that leads to life,*
and few people advance along it,* Christ saw that   *Matt 7:14
the greater part of the baptized, by withdrawing from
this way, did not in the least hold to the blessing that
he gave. So he established a vicar for himself, the
abbot Blessed Benedict, whom he consecrated thus
from childhood, so that he was "blessed by grace and
by name."* He it is whom *God the Father* to this   *Gregory I,
purpose *has blessed with every spiritual blessing <in>* Dial II, Prol. 1
heavenly places in Christ, so that he might be holy   (SCh 260:126);
and immaculate *in his sight in charity*.†   *gratia Benedictus*
   5. Christ *gave* to him *the blessing of all the na-*   *et nomine*
tions,* so that the blessing of baptism and of mo-   †Eph 1:3-4
nastic life might be one. Still, the blessing of baptism, *see Ant and
if well preserved, suffices to salvation without mo-   Resp, Com conf
nastic life. But the blessing of monastic life, except   (Hesbert 3:1711;
for those baptized in Christ, conveys nothing.   4:6247); see
                                                          Sir 44:25

Nevertheless, the great blessing of monasticism is also highly commended by a certain holy witness who said, "The same Spirit whom I saw over baptism, I have seen over the cowl." * The profession that a Christian who is about to receive baptism makes, and the one made by a monk about to receive the cowl, are one.

* *Vitae Patrum* 6, Verba Seniorum 1, 9 (PL 73:994B)

6. A Christian promises to renounce Satan and his pretensions and all his works. A monk promises conversion of his manners and stability in order to obey God. A monk promises nothing other than what he had promised as a Christian, but he repeats the same profession, which, because he could not preserve it in the world, he trusts that he might be better able to under the Rule of Blessed Benedict. By this reason *the blessing of all nations* that God the Father *gave** to Christ, Christ himself passed on to Blessed Benedict, so that by the same blessing by which those who come to Christ's baptism are blessed, all those who wish to serve under the Rule of Blessed Benedict are blessed. *

*see Ant and Resp, Com conf (Hesbert 3:1711; 4:6247); see Sir 44:25

*see RB 1.2

7. When God *confirmed his covenant upon* Benedict's *head,** he commanded <that> he put a new covering on his book, so that according to his Rule, just like a new reading from a new book, he more easily encourages lovers of new things (on account of the curiosity of people, who always gladly embrace new things). By doing this he most appropriately replaced three words that are the summit of the Gospel with three words in which consist the summit of the monastic Rule. In fact, just as in faith, hope, and charity* consists the <whole> strength of the Gospel, so the whole discipline of a regular monastery turns on humility, patience, and obedience. These three are reasonably placed so that the former three are in no way removed by the latter three.

*see Ant and Resp, Com Conf (Hesbert 3:1711; 4:6247); see Sir 44:25

*see 1 Cor 13:13

8. For humility harmonizes with faith, patience with hope, obedience with charity. For just as *faith is the substance of things to be hoped for,** so humility is the foundation of all virtues. *All that is not from faith is sin.** And everything that is not founded in humility is vice. Blessed Paul bears witness to the patience of faith, saying, *If we hope for what we do not see, then we await it through patience.** No wise person doubts that obedience is a sister to charity. Obedience is always eager for the task. And charity is necessary for faith in virtue, as Paul says: *Faith works through love.** And blessed Gregory says, "Charity is never idle. For if it works, then it is great."*

9. And so *the Lord gave the blessing of all nations** to blessed Benedict. Wherever the faith of Christ is received, there also the distinguished name of monks is known. In fact, every age, every situation, every sex, every tribe of human being has recourse to blessed Benedict's Rule, so that through it one might receive the blessing of eternal salvation. Therefore, following the principles of Blessed Benedict, they take refuge in the cloister, so that against temptations, which they cannot avoid in this world, they may more safely defend themselves in the cloister. This seems to me to have been prefigured in the first battle that David fought against the Philistines, after he was anointed to rule over Israel. David was not willing to await adversaries coming against him on the plain, but, in order to be safer, he fled to a stronghold, where, after consulting the Lord, he achieved victory over the enemy.*

10. For so the story goes, *The Philistines heard that David had been anointed king over Israel, and they all came up to seek him. When David heard of it, he went down to a stronghold. But the Philistines*

*Heb 11:1

*Rom 14:23

*Rom 8:25

*Gal 5:6

*Gregory I, Hom in Ev 30.2 (CCSL 141:257)
*see Ant and Resp, Com Conf (Hesbert 3:1711; 4:6247); see Sir 44:25

*see 2 Sam 5:17-20

came and spread out in the valley of Raphaim. David
consulted the Lord, saying, Shall I go up to the Philistines? And will you deliver them into my hands?
And the Lord answered, Go up, because, delivering
them, I will give the Philistines into your hand. Therefore David came to Baal Pharisim and conquered
them there, saying, The Lord has divided my enemies
2 Sam 5:17-20 before me just as waters are divided. Let us consider
how these verses that are said according to history
about the division of secular matters are appropriate
to the conversion of monks when understood spiritually.

    11. *David* is interpreted as *strong of hand,* or
*Jerome,
Int nom 68
(CCSL 72:145)
†Rom 1:3 desirable *to see.** And who is the ancient David if
not Christ, promised and born *from the seed of
David according to the flesh,*† who is truly strong of
hand, who conquered as *a stronger man* coming
*Luke 11:21-22
Ps 23:8 upon a strong, armed man, *the Lord strong and
mighty, the Lord mighty in battle!** Truly desirable
of face, when he himself is *beautiful with a beauty
above the children of human beings, on whom the
*Ps 44:3;
1 Pet 1:12 angels desire to look!** Infirm and ill-formed members should not be under so strong and so attractive
a head. For each and every one of the faithful who
*see 1 Cor 12:27;
see Eph 5:30 recognizes himself to be a member of Christ* should
be strong in fighting against vice, and should appear
desirable to the Lord's eyes, adorning himself with
virtues.

    12. Through Israel, which is interpreted as *man
*Jerome, Int nom
13 (CCSL 72:75)
†see Deut
26:18-19
‡see 1 Pet 2:10 seeing God,** because Israel is recognized as having
been God's people,† a multitude of spiritual virtues
is understood, a certain people of God as it were.‡
One who trains himself in virtues <becomes> a man
seeing God and is numbered with the people of God.
*see 2 Sam 5:17 *David is* anointed *king over Israel** when any faithful
person is consecrated in baptism by the anointing of

the Holy Spirit* to rule over the Lord's people. So
the apostle Peter says, *You are a chosen generation,
a royal priesthood, a holy nation, a purchased people,
so that you may declare the virtues of him who has
called you out of darkness into his marvelous light.*
13. Then the faithful one shows himself anointed
*king over Israel** when, wisely considering within
himself how great a glory and grace he received in
baptism and how he might preserve it after baptism,
he proposes and arranges to correct his life through
various duties so to rule himself as though [manag-
ing] a certain large family of virtues in the home of
his heart. By this wish to improve himself (though it
is not accomplished in a human being without the
anointing of the Spirit),* when he begins to deal
rightly with these matters within himself he is said
as it were to be anointed *king over Israel.**

14. *The* indignant *Philistines, hearing about this,
all came up to seek him.** *Philistine* is interpreted as
*those who fall by drinking.** These are spiteful spirits,
whom their master the devil inebriated with the
drink of pride. And because they were inebriated,
they were not able to find the steps of ascension, but
they fell when the devil first fell from the heights, he
who had ascended through pride, saying, *I will ascend above the height of the clouds, and I will sit in
the mountain of the covenant** opposite the Lord.
Whoever followed him to great heights, inebriated
with the drink of pride, has been cast down to hell*
with the confusion of destruction.

15. And so *the Philistines, hearing* that David was
anointed king *over Israel, all came up to seek him.**
When the spiteful spirits hear that some faithful person has the intention of living well in the world with
the helping grace of the Holy Spirit, and also, as
though a king, intends to gather a certain family of

*1 John 2:30, 27

*1 Pet 2:9

*see 2 Sam 5:17

*1 John 2:20, 27

*see 2 Sam 5:17

*2 Sam 5:17

*Jerome, Int nom 6
(CCSL 72:66)

*Isa 14:14, 13

*see Job 21:13

*2 Sam 5:17

virtues to the kingdom of his interior home, they, indignant about his good intention, rise up against him and come together in one conspiracy so to cast him down with every type of temptation.

16. So it follows, *And they came and spread out in the valley of Raphaim.** Who is this Raphaim, in whose valley the Philistines are spread out against David, assembled for battle? *Raphaim* is interpreted as *giant.** This is that renowned giant, powerful and enormous of stature,† who while he relied on *the might of his greatness‡* said, *I will ascend and will be like the most High.#* His valley is human flesh, which before the advent of Christ he possessed securely, like *an armed strong man.**

17. There are two parts in a human being, spirit <and> flesh, one of which, as the superior, is compared to a mountain, the other, as though inferior, is described as a valley. And although the Raphaim, who before the advent of Christ had possessed the whole human being, lost the whole human being through the victory of the cross after his advent, yet <because> he has an easier regress to flesh than to the mind, as often as he strives to invade <his ancient> possession through temptations, he still rightly retains his ancient name and can be called the valley of Raphaim.

18. In this valley, the Philistines spread out, coming together against David,* because spiteful spirits intend to join battle against the one who ascends to higher places by his mind. With an army of vices tempting him through the flesh's frailty, they securely mark out a camp in the valley, as it were. They are said to be spread out in this valley,* by which their abundant multitude is designated. For each and every leader of the army occupies each and every member for himself, moving the battles where they set up their battle lines.

*2 Sam 5:18

*Jerome, Int nom 9 (CCSL 72:70)
†see Bar 3:26
‡see Job 23:6
#Isa 14:14

*see Luke 11:21

*see 2 Sam 5:18

*see 2 Sam 5:18

19. The spirit of pride sets its tent in the heart, and around it each of its worst servants: a spirit of vainglory, spirit of envy, spirit of anger, spirit of resentment and hatred, spirit *of malice and wickedness.** And so this special place having been relinquished, each and every one of the rest chooses an apt place for itself in the rest of the members. The spirit of curiosity in the eyes, the spirit of appetite in the palate, the spirit of abuse, of slander, of lies, of loquaciousness, of empty and stupid talk in the tongue. The spirit of rapaciousness in the hands, a spirit of restlessness running about about in the feet, a spirit of fornication in the loins.

*see 1 Cor 5:8

20. Similarly the other spirits also occupy the rest of the human being's members; they fill the whole valley of weak flesh with their armies* so that they strike greatest fear against David the king of Israel, that is, against any faithful person proposing to ascend to the height of virtues. So David himself laments the infestation of all the enemies, saying, *I walked sorrowful all the day long.** And particularly he accuses the spirit of fornication, because it especially reigns in the world: *My loins*, he says, *are filled with illusions.** And as if unable to express the innumerable armies of the rest of the vices that were spread through the whole valley of his flesh, he generally laments about them all, *There is no health in my flesh.**

*see Matt 26:41

*Ps 37:7

*Ps 37:8

*Ps 37:8

21. What therefore remains for this one to do when surrounded by so great an army of vices, if not by the example of David, who fled from the field *to a stronghold,** also to flee from the world to the cloister? Just as David decided to take himself to the stronghold for sake of a more secure salvation rather than expose himself nakedly to the enemies in the field, so whoever understands sensibly, seeing that he cannot be secure in the world on account of waves

*see 2 Sam 5:17

of temptation rising up against him, because it is difficult to remain in fire and not be burned, he flies to a monastery as if to a stronghold, so that there he might restore through conversion the blessing that he had received in baptism (but later diminished by living wickedly) and thereafter might steadfastly guard by living regularly.

22. When he recovers himself, at once he consults the Lord, saying, *Shall I go up to meet the Philistines? And will you deliver them into my hands?** He then makes this consultation with the Lord, when he searches within himself meticulously and at length about making confession <and profession>. So certainly he will hear the Lord answering him, *Go up, because I will hand over and give the Philistines into your hand.** He said, as it were, "As long as you have not confessed sins that you have committed in the world, as long as you do not profess yourself to observe the Rule placed before you, then you still delay in the valley, besieged by vices. Similarly you will not be able to overcome the Philistines who are in the valley. If you wish to overcome those who set up battle lines against you in the valley below,* you, then, *go up higher!** By despising the flesh, go out of the valley! By following reason, climb the mountain! Make confession, make profession, because thus you shall see your revenge on your enemies."*

23. *Therefore David came to Baal Pharisim and beat them <there>, and he said, The Lord has divided my enemies before me just as waters are divided.** Having received such a great security from the response of divinity, *nothing <wavering>,** he fully confesses and firmly professes. Thus having received pardon for sins, made firm in the Rule, you shall merit to see division of all your adversaries, <that is, vices,> with the Lord's help.

*2 Sam 5:19

*2 Sam 5:19

*see 2 Sam 5:18
*see Luke 14:10

*see Jer 11:20

*2 Sam 5:20

*see Jas 1:6

24. Baal Pharisim, which is interpreted as *having division*, is a place where David struck his enemies. So he chooses the name, as Scripture testifies, because in that place the Lord divided David's enemies before him.* Moreover, it signifies monastic profession. A novice has the best division in himself because when he comes to it after confessing well, the Lord separates from him and divides before him all the vices that were previously <his> enemies.

*see 2 Sam 5:20

25. Vices are divided from the novice in profession as easily *as waters are divided.** For just as division of water is easy through liquidness of the element, so *forgiveness of sins** is easy for one who confesses well. And as a vessel of water is without difficulty divided by drops and sprinkled into a mist, so very easily every conspiracy of spiteful spirits <having been dissolved>, every attack of vices is reduced to nothing before a firm monk in profession with confession.

*2 Sam 5:20

*see Acts 13:38

26. *And there the Philistines left their idols.** These are the phantoms of worldly thoughts that frequently force themselves in after confession and profession. For although by confession and profession all vices have been separated, victors still emerge. Frequently however they raise mental images in thoughts that, like statues left behind by the conquered Philistines, weigh upon them in imagination through prior memory of sins. But there is nothing to fear from these, because as it is written, *David and his men took them away.**

*2 Sam 5:21

*2 Sam 5:21

27. The true David, Christ himself *strong of hand,** *who works among* the saints *both to will and to accomplish according to his good will,*† to whom he says, promising perfect liberation and freedom from all evils in both thoughts and actions, *If the Son shall make you free, you shall be truly free.** Excited

*Jerome,
Int nom 68
(CCSL 72:145)
†Phil 2:13

*John 8:36

and secure in this promise, the saints confidently shout out to God, *Free us from every evil, O Lord!** And especially against unclean thoughts, as it seems appropriate to remove them, forsaken in their past as though *Philistines' statues,** they pray, saying, *From unclean thoughts free us, Lord.**

28. The men of this David are all who act vigorously in the battle of vices,* whom the figurative David invites to himself, saying, *Act vigorously, and take courage, all you who hope in the Lord.** Paul plainly describes them, saying, *Those who are Christ's have crucified their flesh along with vice and concupiscence.** These are monks who boast in nothing except *in the cross of our Lord Jesus Christ, by whom the world was crucified* to them *and* they *to the world.**

29. *David and his men* remove the Philistines' statues,* because through Christ they are liberated not only from works and choices but also from bad thoughts; all who act vigorously in his service have confidence in him,* who may by the merits and prayers of Blessed Benedict defend us from enemies and lead us to eternal life, our Lord and King Jesus Christ, who with the Father and Holy Spirit lives and reigns God, through all ages forever. Amen.

*Lit 77, p. 826

*see 2 Sam 5:21
*see Orat div 162

*see 2 Sam 5:21

*Ps 30:25;
see 1 Cor 16:13

*Gal 5:24

*Gal 6:14

*2 Sam 5:21

*see 1 Cor 16:13

Sermon 148

On the Feast of Holy Relics

1. **T**_he saints shall rejoice in glory; they shall be joyful in their beds._* When the Lord was born in Bethlehem, _with the angel,_ who appeared to the shepherds, _there appeared a multitude of the heavenly army praising God and saying, Glory to God in the highest, and on earth peace to people of good will._* Behold, my brothers, a new song.* A song of glory, a song of angels, a song of saints who rejoice _in glory_ and are joyful _in their beds, praise of God in their throat._* All good angels, patriarchs and prophets, apostles and all saints continually sing this song. All jointly and harmoniously embrace peace, love peace, preach peace, cultivate and sing peace. The Holy Spirit invites us to sing this song to the Lord in the psalm: _Sing to the Lord a new song because he has done wonders._* He has done wonders by soothing anger, purging discord, _reconciling_ God and humankind, _making peace_* among angels and human beings, so that they may unite the earthly with the heavenly.

2. Children _of discord, children of anger_, children _of quarrels_ and dissension,* who sow _discord among brothers_,† who are puffed up with pride, impatient, temperamental, and disruptive, who do not obey the abbot, do not show respect to the prior, do not keep faith for the brothers, who are ungrateful to God, hateful to human beings, [and] disturbers of fraternal peace, do not know and cannot sing the songs of these wonders. They do not sing the Lord's song, but the

*Ps 149:5;
Graduale in festo Sanctarum Reliquiarum

*Luke 2:13-14

*see Ps 149:1;
see Ps 97:1

*Ps 149:5-6;
see Ps 149:1

*Ps 97:1

*see 2 Cor 5:19;
see Eph 2:15-17

*see Gal 5:20;
see Eph 2:3;
see Jer 15:10
†Prov 6:19

devil's song. They do not sing a song of glory, but a
song of quarrel, the song of Cain, who killed his
brother,* as they do to him spiritually every day
through jealousy and anger and slander, ambushing
and plotting evils against their brothers.* The *praise
of God* is not *in their throat,** but anger, quarrel,
blasphemy, treachery, and lies are in their throats
because *they knew not the way of peace, and the fear
of God was not before their eyes.** These *will* not
rejoice in glory but shall be saddened in punishment.
They will not *be joyful in their beds,** but they shall
be tormented in their tombs, that is, in hellish places,
in which Satan and his accomplices shall be burned,
where *there will be weeping and gnashing of teeth.**

3. But the saints whose relics are also preserved
in all our churches, whom we devoutly venerate
today, continually sing the *song of the Lord,** the
song of peace. In fact, they were harmonious in the
Lord's house, human beings of tranquil <mind> and
good will.* Let us follow these our patron saints,
who preceded us to glory. Let us strive to have tranquility of mind and peace. For thus we shall fruitfully
celebrate the feasts of the saints, if we imitate their
morals, their life and behavior. One who loves discipline, obedience, gentleness, patience, self-control,
sobriety, humility, and chastity,* one who loves God
above all things and his *neighbor as himself,** such
is the imitator of those whose relics are preserved in
our churches. This is one from the fellowship of those
who already rejoice *in glory* and are joyful *in their
beds.** For although he sojourns in the flesh on
earth,* nevertheless he conducts himself in heaven
through good will.*

4. "Just as our body exists in some place of earth,
in the same way our soul, according to its condition,
is in the selfsame place of earth. Just as we are cor-

*see Gen 4:8

*see Prov 6:14
*Ps 149:6

*Ps 13:3

*Ps 149:5

*see Matt 8:12

*see Ps 136:4

*see Acts 4:32;
see 1 Pet 3:8

*see Gal 5:22-23
*see Mark 12:32-33

*Ps 149:5
*see 2 Cor 5:6
*see Phil 3:20

poreally either in England, or Gaul, or Egypt, or
whatever other place of earth, so one soul is said to
be in Babylon, another \<in\> Egypt, another in Jerusalem, or wheresoever you will."* "A soul seems to
be in Babylon when she is confused, when she is disturbed, when with peace lost she sustains battles of
passion, when the uproar of wickedness roars around
her. To this soul the prophetic saying is directed: *Flee
from Babylon, and let everyone save his own life.**
One who is in Babylon can scarcely be saved."*

5. "In Babylon the instruments of the hymns of
God are idle. So it says through the prophet, *By the
rivers of Babylon, there we sat and wept while we
remembered Zion; on its willows \<in its midst\> we
hung up our instruments.** Our instruments have
been hung up on the willows of Babylon's rivers as
long as we are in Babylon. If however we should come
into Jerusalem, into the place of a vision of peace,
instruments that before were hanging idle are taken
up in our hands, and we continually play on the lyre,
and there is no time when we do not praise God with
instruments that we have in our hands."* "One who
is a sinner and oppressed by grave crimes remains
here in Babylon. Just as there are sinners in Babylon,
so in contrast there are just people in Judaea or Jerusalem."*

6. "Therefore this saying of God warns those who
are in Babylon, *Flee from the middle of Babylon.*†
Not step by step, not gradually, but with speed and
running, for that it is to flee. Whoever have confused
souls from suffering various vices, this saying is directed to them: *Flee from the middle of Babylon.*"*
"One who is also immersed in countless criminal
sins is an inhabitant of the middle of Babylon. But
one who leaves evil little by little, turning his nature
to better values, already begins to desire virtues;

*Origen,
Hom Ier 2.1
(SCh 238:336)

*Jer 51:6
*Origen,
Hom Ier 2.1
(SCh 238:336)

*Ps 136:1-2

*Origen,
Hom Ier 2.1
(SCh 238:338)

*Origen,
Hom Ier 2.1
(SCh 238:40-41)
†Jer 51:6

*Origen,
Hom Ier 2.2
(SCh 238:340)

although he may have fled the middle, nevertheless he has not yet departed from the whole of Babylon,"* but he still dwells as though within Babylon's borders.

*Origen,
Hom Ier 2.2
(SCh 238:342)

7. "It is another thing to remain in the center of Babylon, as out of every part there might be equal space, <and> so one might dwell in [its] navel as though in the middle of an animal's heart. In fact, just as in the Gospel according to Luke the middle of the earth is called *the heart of the earth*,"* so sinners who are walled in on all sides by crimes, vices, and sins are said to dwell in the midst of Babylon. "It is not said to them, 'Go out from the middle of Babylon,' as can be done gradually, but rather, *Flee from the middle of Babylon*,"* that is, with all haste and speed, *from the middle of Babylon*, that is, from the depth of vices, speedily turn away from the dwelling of perdition! *And let every one save his own life.**

*see Matt 12:40;
Origen,
Hom Ier 2.2
(SCh 238:340–42)

*Jer 51:6; Origen,
Hom Ier 2.2
(SCh 238:340)

*Jer 51:6

8. It does not suffice for us to flee from the middle of Babylon (that is, speedily to turn away from vice) if we do not give work to virtues after our flight from Babylon. So the psalmist says, *Turn from evil and do good.** And, in the law, the Lord says, *You shall not appear empty before me.** A person who lacks virtues appears empty. So after it says, *Flee from the middle of Babylon*, is added at once, *And let everyone save his own life.** Our soul† has been saved by the shedding of Christ's blood, which was shed *for forgiveness of sins*.‡ Also a human soul# is saved in baptism, in which sins are forgiven. But because after baptism *in many things we all offend*,§ we need to save our souls again.*

*Ps 36:27

*Exod 23:15;
see Sir 35:6

*animam suam;
Jer 51:6
†anima
‡see Matt 26:28;
see Heb 9:22
#anima humana
§Jas 3:2
*animas nostras

9. In baptism, as we said, we receive justification and salvation of soul, "from which afterward, coming to grief through sin, we go down into Babylon, that is <into> the confusion of vices. For this reason it is necessary for any of us to re-save* our soul, so

*resaluare

that we may begin to have through grace what we lost through moral failure. So blessed Peter says, *We shall bring back the end of faith, the salvation of souls. About this salvation the prophets have thoroughly investigated and searched, they who prophesied concerning our grace.** Indeed it is in us to flee from Babylon, and it has been put in our power to revive what is ruined in ourselves"* and to save our soul through repentance, through confession, through worthy satisfaction. Whosoever save their soul in this way shall be made *holy; they shall rejoice in glory and be made joyful in their beds.**

    10. Great is the glory of the saints! "There is no one who does not love glory. But glory of the stupid, that which is called popular, has the enticement of deceit, as any person who is moved to the praises of vain people* might wish to live so that he might be made known by whatever people in whatever way. So men and women as if driven insane—insane on the inside, puffed up on the outside—lose their own goods by giving them to actors, performers,"* comedians, and flatterers, because of love for vainglory and the favor of stupid people. They not only do not listen to the poor, but they even scorn them, paying no attention to that terrible rebuke of the Lord by which he struck the condemned: *I was naked and you did not clothe me.** *Because you did not do it for one of the least of these, you did not do it for me.**

    11. However, the saints who through their works do good not on account of human beings but because of God, how they shall rejoice in true and eternal glory it is not possible for us to explain. *They shall rejoice in* eternal *glory, and they shall be joyful in their beds.** The psalmist does not say that the saints shall be joyful in theaters or arenas, or in racetracks or frivolities, or in vain affairs of this world, but rather *In their beds.* "What is *In their beds*? In their

*1 Pet 1:9-10

*Origen, Hom Ier 2.3 (SCh 238:344)

*Ps 149:5

*see Matt 6:1

*Augustine, En in Ps 149:10 (CSEL 95/5:280–81)

*Matt 25:43
*Matt 25:45

*Ps 149:5

hearts. Listen to the apostle Paul rejoicing in his bed, that is, in his heart: *Our glory is this: the testimony of our conscience.** Nevertheless, any people should fear that they might become pleasing to themselves in their own view, and, like proud people, boast about their own conscience. For we must rejoice *with trembling,** because *it is the gift of God†* from which we rejoice, not our merit. There are many who please themselves, and who consider themselves to be just, against whom the divine page continues, saying, *Who will boast that he has a chaste heart? Or who will boast that he is pure from sin?**

12. Therefore because *in many things we all offend,†* we should always be fearful, so that we do not culpably despair through a fault, or vainly show pride through justice. "We have a certain way of priding ourselves in our conscience, so all of us may know that our faith is sincere, know that our hope is certain, know that our charity is without pretense."* Christ demonstrates this true and perfect [knowledge] for us, he whose charity stands out as so great that he died for his servants, and he interceded on behalf of his enemies on the cross.*

13. This Saint of saints, King and Lord of all, we venerate today; although in our nature he is wholly in heaven, sitting at the Father's right hand, interceding on our behalf,* nevertheless his Body is represented in our church daily. The *Queen of heaven, Lady of angels* and humankind,* commends to us true humility, she who, since she was so great that she could be mother and virgin, esteemed not herself but God, saying, *My soul magnifies the Lord, for he has looked upon the humility of his handmaid. Henceforth all generations shall call me blessed.** Today's solemnity is dedicated to her, our Lady, Mother of Mercy, because although her body was

*2 Cor 1:12

*see Ps 2:11
†see Eph 2:8

*Prov 20:9;
Augustine, En in
Ps 149:11
(CSEL 95/5:282)
†Jas 3:2

*Augustine,
En in Ps 149:11
(CSEL 95/5:282)

*see Luke 23:34

*see Rom 8:34;
see Heb 7:25

*see Ant "Ave,
Regina" (Hesbert
3:1542)

*Luke 1:46, 48

preserved whole—where and how the Lord knows—
nevertheless we possess something precious from her
hair or clothing among our relics.

14. *That disciple whom Jesus loved,** *a virgin
chosen by the Lord and more beloved among the
others,** *to whom the virgin Christ on the cross entrusted his virgin mother,** claims this solemnity for
himself by right, because his ring, which he sealed for
Blessed King Edward, we hope you have frequently
kissed among our precious relics. The prince of
apostles and shepherd of the church, our principal
patron, blessed apostle Peter, in whose faith and confession the whole church throughout the world is
consolidated and strengthened,* is not in the least bit
deprived by the solemnity of this day, in whose honor
the present church is dedicated and its precious relics
are abundantly enriched. Edward, the outstanding
confessor of the Lord, founder of this church, a virgin
before marriage, virgin in marriage, and after marriage persevering as a virgin, makes the present day
solemn for us, he whose virgin body remains happily
contemplated in wholeness before us.

15. For this reason, the apostles, martyrs, confessors, and sacred virgins, and the relics of whoever
are concealed among us, are devoutly venerated by
us today. Therefore let us strive to imitate the saints
whose relics we venerate today, rejoicing in our
beds,* that is, in our hearts, through a good conscience, so that we may join them in the life to come
through true glory, which the Saint of saints may
deign to grant to us, the Lord Jesus Christ, who with
the Father and Holy Spirit lives and reigns God,
through all ages forever. Amen.

*John 21:7

*Ant "Ioannes
apostolus"
(Hesbert 3:3494)
*Ant "Iste est
Ioannes"
(Hesbert 3:3423)

*see Matt 16:16-19

*see Ps 149:5

Sermon 149

On the Feast of
Blessed Mary Magdalene

1. *Your faith has made you safe; go in peace.** The giver and bestower of peace, *mediator of God and humankind, the man Christ Jesus,** who made peace between God and humankind* reassigned in peace the sinful woman* whom he liberated from sin. He releases us in peace* when he absolves us from sin. This is true peace: to be a human being cleansed of sin, and *servants of justice.** Whoever is oppressed by guilt is deprived of this peace. So it is written, *There is no peace for the wicked, says the Lord.** How are they said to be in peace who are always disturbed by confusion and contention of vices, who are continually intoxicated by the golden goblet of Babylon?

2. *The golden goblet of Babylon intoxicates all the earth.** We can understand the golden goblet of Babylon to be carnal concupiscence. This goblet is called golden, perhaps, because just as gold is cherished more earnestly than the other metals, so carnal concupiscence is taken up with more feeling than the other carnal realities. We can easily assess how this goblet has intoxicated all the earth if we consider its types of drink. We are intoxicated through this goblet sometimes by anger, sometimes by sadness, sometimes by vainglory, luxury, avarice, and various feelings of the passions. This goblet of Babylon* intoxicates all the earth because all the earth is full of sins.

*Luke 7:50

*1 Tim 2:5
*see Col 1:20
*see Luke 7:37
*see Luke 2:29

*Rom 6:19

*Isa 57:21

*Jer 51:7

*see Jer 51:7

3. Sinners, who delight in earthly matters without moderation, are designated by the name *earth*. Just people, however, when they are on the earth, because they have fellowship in heaven* refuse to be as intoxicated as they could be by this goblet. But all the earth is intoxicated by this goblet, because every sinner, who is rightly designated by the name of earth, is delighted more by vices than by virtues. So it is said to any person who is committing sin, *You are earth, and into earth you shall go.** On the other hand, it can suitably be said to a just person, "You are heaven, and into heaven you shall go," because such a person bears *the image of the heavenly.** Therefore, so I may briefly conclude, *the golden goblet of Babylon intoxicates all the earth,** because as long as we are earth, that is, as we covet earthly cares without moderation, we are intoxicated by the wine of carnal concupiscence.

4. "Just as when someone accepts a flow of wine beyond the need of thirst and moderation, we see the body of the drunk person agitated, feet staggering, temples and head weighed down, mouth loosened, tongue impeded, and with lips sticking, words cut short. So we see those who drink in this same way from the golden goblet of Babylon—how they are moved, unsteady of step, agitated in thought, debilitated in mind, holding nothing firmly—but inconstant, always driven by confusion."* These do not abide in a dwelling of peace, but in the disturbances of commotion. "So after Cain has sinned, Scripture says about him, *Cain went out from the face of God, and dwelled in the land of Nod opposite Eden.** Nod is interpreted as *commotion*. He who abandons God and quits the sense of thinking about God, such a one dwells in the land of Nod, that is, he lingers in disturbance of a wicked heart and commotion of mind."*

*see Phil 3:20

*Gen 3:19 as cited by Origen

*see 1 Cor 15:49

*Jer 51:7

*Origen, Hom Ier 2.10 (SCh 238:356–58)

*Gen 4:16 as cited by Origen

*Origen, Hom Ier 2.10 (SCh 238:358)

5. Mary Magdalene dwelled in this land of Nod when she was in the disturbance of a bad heart and commotion of mind, when she was moved by shame from what is wicked to wicked, from sin into sin, from iniquity to iniquity, when she was intoxicated by the golden goblet of Babylon,* serving carnal desires *by living luxuriously.** But after she learned that the Lord Jesus had come to Simon's house, without delay she spurned the power of the world and every adornment of worldliness, throwing herself down at the Savior's feet, wetting the Lord's feet with her tears, and wiping them with her hair.* Then *Babylon suddenly fell and was destroyed** in her heart.

6. "Let each and every one of us examine himself so that we might know whether Babylon has yet fallen within us. Christ has not yet arrived in one's mind if the city of confusion has not fallen in one's heart. So of course when he arrives, Babylon—that is, every confusion of vice—is usually ruined."* Let us imitate Mary, an example of pardon, hurrying to Jesus, "fleeing to the protection of prayers, begging that Jesus might come into our hearts and crush Babylon and make all its malice a ruin, and, in its place, might rebuild Jerusalem in the chief part of our heart, God's holy city,"* the city of peace, so that every one of us may merit to hear from the Lord, *Your faith has made you safe; go in peace.*†

7. Let us not dread rushing to Jesus on account of our sins, because he is *compassionate and merciful, long-suffering and rich in mercy.** "He is blasphemed by the impious, and yet *he makes his sun to rise upon the good and wicked.*"* The sinner Mary Magdalene was bad and infamous, yet the Lord made his sun to rise upon her. The Lord illuminated her with the sun of justice* unto repentance, and he melted and dissolved all blight of sins in her. Behold how great is the Lord's mercy.

*see Jer 51:7
*see Luke 15:13

*Luke 7:44
*Jer 51:8

*Origen, Hom Ier 2.11 (SCh 238:360)

*Origen, Hom Ier 2.11 (SCh 238:360) †Luke 7:50

*Ps 102:8

*Matt 5:45; Augustine, En in Ps 102:16 (CCSL 40:1466) *see Mal 4:2

8. "Everywhere he calls us to repentance and im-
provement. He calls us to repentance by imparting
a time for living and repenting. Sometimes he calls
us by favors, sometimes through lashings of correction, sometimes through the mercy of encourage-
ment, because *he is long-suffering and rich in mercy.**   *see Ps 102:8
Still, we very much need to tremble lest by using the
extent of God's mercy badly we store up for ourselves
what the apostle says: *wrath in the day of wrath <and
revelation> of the just judgment of God.** So the   *Rom 2:5
same apostle says, *Or do you despise the riches of
his goodness and long-suffering? Do you not know
that God's patience leads you to repentance?"**   *Rom 2:4;
                                                             Augustine,
9. Every iniquity displeases him. Sins are not   En in Ps 102:16
pleasing to him; still, through his mercy he awaits our   (CCSL
good works. By sparing us with his long-suffering,   40:1466–67)
he calls us to repentance. Let us not delay in turning
to him, lest the raven's voice speak in us: "Tomorrow,
tomorrow. Today I shall remain in pleasure and the
concupiscence of my flesh, and tomorrow I shall
abstain from desires." But when the next day comes,
because carnal pleasure pleases me more than bodily
affliction, perhaps tomorrow again I think, "Today
is not the last day; I shall remain as such the whole
day; tomorrow I shall be different." For those who
postpone a good conversion in this way, from tomorrow unto tomorrow, suddenly an unexpected death
intrudes upon them, and immediately they are
snatched into punishment, those who put off following Christ to glory. The raven was sent from the ark
one time and did not come back.* So the reprobate   *see Gen 8:6-7
are sent out of this life once, and they do not return
to the ark, that is, to the church, in which is given to
all the ability to repent, confess, and make satisfaction for sins.

10. "The Lord does not ask for procrastination
in the raven's voice, but for confession in the dove's

*Augustine,
En in Ps 102:16
(CCSL 40:1467)
sigh.''* For whoever humbly confess their sin are prepared to obey God, wherever they are sent; that is, with whatsoever exterior cares they are entrusted, they always return to the ark, that is, to the holy church, through holy devotion. But those who are hard-hearted, once they are sent out from the ark entangled in exterior cares, do not turn back to the ark, that is, to the strict life of the saints, but always put off a good conversion, "*according to hardness of their heart and their impenitent heart*, storing up for themselves *wrath in the day of wrath, and revelation of the just judgment of God, who will render to every person according to his works.*"*

*Rom 2:5-6;
Augustine,
En in Ps 102:16
(CCSL 40:1467)

11. Turning these things over in her heart, blessed Mary Magdalene did not put off a good conversion, but took care to finish well after a bad beginning. At once *when she knew* that Jesus had come to the house of Simon,* according to the law's precepts, she strove to change our firstborn of an ass for a sheep. *The firstborn of an ass*, it says, *you shall change for a sheep.** If we live indulgently, brutishly, and like a beast, then our firstborn are of an ass. If, however, afterwards <we live> chastely, wisely, religiously, patiently, fruitfully, not only for ourselves, but also for others, like a sheep that lives not only for itself but for others, then we redeem *the firstborn of an ass for a sheep*. How stupidly, how indulgently, how like a beast this woman lived, harming herself and many others!

*see Luke 7:37

*Exod 13:13

12. Mary Magdalene, "from whom blessed Mark the evangelist said that seven demons were cast out,"* had been oppressed by a great burden of sins. Even blessed Gregory, in his explanation of this gospel, says about this blessed sinner, "Mary, who was filled with all the vices, had seven demons."* Nevertheless, reflecting upon the stain of sins in her heart,

*see Mark 16:9;
Gregory I,
Hom in Ev 33.1
(CCSL 141:288)
*Gregory I,
Hom in Ev 33.1
(CCSL 141:288)

she wisely hurried to the spring of mercy to be washed. Having happily washed in this spring, she withdrew, hearing from the Lord, who is the spring of mercy, *Your faith has made you safe; go in peace.** When she had been oppressed by many sins, she refused to come to Jesus empty handed. She *brought* with her precious gifts: faith, hope, and charity—oil, a kiss, and effusion of tears.* As blessed Gregory says, "In fact she found as many sacrifices regarding herself as she had pleasures in herself." *

13. When previously she was intent on illicit acts, she had poured over her body ointment for the fragrance. Wisely she was now offering this to God. By pouring tears over the Lord's feet, she purified her eyes with which she had watched earthly affairs. Hair, which she had frequently brushed and woven into a bun* for a style accenting the beauty of her face, she rejoiced to dishevel with her tears. Her mouth, with which she used to carry on foolishly in company and in chorus with dirty humor and perversity, through repentance and holy confession in the house of Simon, she wisely kept quiet. Behold, as great as was her fault, just so great was her repentance; Mary Magdalene's satisfaction was as salutary as her pleasure was pernicious. Therefore let us love not the fault, but the repentance. Let us imitate not the self-indulgence but the devotion of this blessed sinner. Let us seek the Lord where Mary found him.

14. She did not find him in the city center or market, but in the house of Simon. Simon is interpreted as *obeying*; Jesus, *Savior* or *saving*.* Let whoever therefore desires true salvation strive to master obedience, because Christ, who is true salvation, says about himself, *I have not come to do my own will, but that of him who sent me, the Father.** And concerning Christ himself the apostle says, *Christ was*

*Luke 7:50

*see Luke 7:37-38

*Gregory I, Hom in Ev 33.2 (CCSL 141:289)

**pexuerat ad modum pilae*

*Jerome, Int nom 71, 13 (CCSL 72:148, 76)

*John 6:38-39

*Phil 2:8

made obedient to the Father unto death. * Coming to Jesus, let us diligently pay attention to what we should offer. Let Mary teach us. The wise woman had known that *without faith it is impossible to please God,* * and therefore in the beginning she offered the gift of faith to God, believing Jesus to be God's Son, believing him therefore to have come into the world *to take away the sins of the world,* * believing him to wish and to be able to free sinners from sins through faith. Through this faith she has earned salvation.

*Heb 11:6

*see John 1:29;
see 1 John 3:5

15. How great was this faith of Mary, the Lord declares in recompense: *Your faith has made you safe; go in peace.* * In this faith she offers hope to God, because through the faith that she had she was hoping to obtain forgiveness of sins from God. She also offered love, through which faith works.* * For she loved Jesus above all things, him from whom she received forgiveness of sins. The Lord himself, speaking to Simon, demonstrates how great was the love <of this blessed sinner>: *Therefore I say to you, many sins are forgiven her because she has loved much.* * After this she offered repentance. In fact, the cleansing of her tears makes manifest how much she repented about the sins in her heart.

*Luke 7:50

*see Gal 5:6

*Luke 7:47

16. Offering these her gifts to God, she prostrated herself at the feet of her Redeemer, because after she accepted a pardon, she faithfully walked in the Lord's ways. Journeys are completed with feet. Therefore we prostrate ourselves at Christ's feet whenever we walk in his ways sincerely. One who is a disciple of Christ *ought also to walk even as Christ walked.* * Finally, one who faithfully imitates the Redeemer's journeys is prostrated at his feet. Let us prostrate ourselves through devotion with Mary at the Savior's feet, offering precious gifts to him:* faith, hope, true love, repentance, and confession, so that with blessed

*1 John 2:6

*see Luke 7:38

Mary we may gain forgiveness of sins and eternal peace from Christ, which, by the merits and prayers of Mary Magdalene, may the Lord Jesus deign to bestow on us, he who with the Father and the Holy Spirit lives and reigns God, through all ages forever. Amen.

Sermon 150

On the Feast of Blessed Mary Magdalene

*Rom 12:15

*see Luke 15:7-10

*see Luke 1:14

*dilectricis

*Rom 2:4

*Ezek 33:11 as in
Resp Dere in quad
(Hesbert 4:6406)
†see Ezek 18:21-22;
Ezek 33:14-16

1. **T**he apostle urges us, *Weep with those who weep and rejoice with those who rejoice.** Since today there is joy in heaven,* and public happiness of men and women on earth, we should rejoice and exult in Christ.* Today the occasion of exulting is single for the residents of heaven, but for the earthborn it is double. The heavens no longer rejoice at the conversion of the sinner, but at the festive assumption of Christ's lover* into heaven. Let us also rejoice with a twin feeling of joy, two [things] that prove the evidence of the inborn gentleness in the Lord Jesus: that he patiently awaits a wrongdoer and that he mercifully accepts a penitent. A twin charm of sweetness surges in the heart: the longsuffering of the Lord Jesus in anticipation, and readiness in giving.

2. Concerning longsuffering, it reads, *Do you despise the riches of his goodness, and patience, and <longsuffering>? And again, Do you really not know that his kindness leads you to repentance?** According to this, for a long time he suspends the sentence of retribution upon one who pays no heed, so that he might display the grace of forgiveness in the penitent for a while. For *he does not wish the death of a sinner, but that he convert and live.** Concerning the easiness of forgiveness, it reads, *At any hour the sinner might cry with regret; if he has done true penance, then he shall acquire true pardon.*† So the

136

prophet says, *Let the wicked forsake his way and the unjust man his thoughts, and let him turn to the Lord and he will have mercy on him, and to our God because he is bountiful in granting pardon.** David, expressing both beautifully, says in a few words, *The Lord is longsuffering and bounteous in mercy.**

*Isa 55:7

*Ps 102:8

3. Blessed Mary Magdalene is put forth as an example of his longsuffering and readiness to grant remission of punishment, she who was a notorious sinner and rightly so called. As we learn in Luke's gospel, she heard that Jesus was reclining at table in the home of Simon, and without shame before the diners—with her hair down and her tears poured out, intending to gain pardon for her crimes—she prostrated herself before his feet.* The Savior's indescribable and wonderful mercy! "He does not flee from the leper, he does not avoid the unclean, so he can wash away the stains of humankind."* "The woman entered into Simon's house. She could not otherwise have been healed if Christ had not come to earth. This woman represents a species of soul or the type of the church."*

*see Luke 7:36-38

*Ambrose, Exp Ev Luc 6.13 (CSEL 32/4:236)

*Ambrose, Exp Ev Luc 6.13 (CSEL 32/4:237)

4. "Matthew introduces this woman pouring ointment over Jesus' head. And therefore perhaps he did not wish to say 'a sinful woman.'* For according to Luke, a sinful woman poured ointment over Christ's feet.* And lest the evangelists seem to have given contrary accounts"* (when the former says the woman poured ointment over the head and the latter says over the feet), "the question can be solved by the difference in time and merit. For a soul or the church does not change character, but rather makes progress. A faithful soul approaching God, not unknown to sin but lovingly serving the Word of God, having the confidence of immaculate chastity, ascends to the head of Christ and spreads the scent of

*see Matt 26:6-7

*see Luke 7:37-38

*Ambrose, Exp Ev Luc 6.14 (CSEL 32/4:237)

*see 1 Cor 11:3
*see 2 Cor 2:15;
Ambrose, Exp Ev
Luc 6.14 (CSEL
32/4:237)
†see Song 1:3

her merits.* For the life of the just honors God, fragrant with good odor."*

5. In fact, the just who obey God's precepts as much as they can run *in his odor*.† Christ has his own chariots, by which he transports his chosen ones. The devil has his own chariots, by which he subverts the reprobate.

6. "The chariots of God are the chariot of self-control, the chariot of innocence, and the chariot of wisdom. The chariot of self-control has two wheels: prayer and discipline. The horse that draws this chariot is devotion. A soldier of Christ sits on this horse, <contempt for self,> in a saddle of purity, having the discipline of the reins and a riding crop, the fear of God. The chariot of innocence has two wheels: the humility of one who does not wish to be in charge, and the meekness of one who wishes to be subject to others. A strong and gentle horse draws this chariot, love of peace, naturally. The rider of this horse is contempt for the world, sitting on the saddle of benevolence. His reins are zeal for truth; <the riding crop,> love of God and neighbor. The chariot of wisdom has two wheels, prudence and simplicity. The horse drawing this chariot is fortitude; the driver is the love of God, who sits in the saddle of vigilance; the rein is modesty; <the riding crop is zeal for

*William of
Saint-Thierry,
Brev com 23
(CCCM
87:181–82)
†see Job 1:7; 2:2

justice>."*

7. "Similarly, the devil has three chariots, in which he makes his rounds throughout the whole world.† The first chariot is luxury, the second is pride, the third is malice. The chariot of luxury has two wheels: gluttony and wantonness. *An untamed

*Sir 30:8

horse** draws this chariot, a violent urge of the flesh, you see. Love of self sits on the saddle of pleasure like a soldier on this horse. The horse's rein is want. The riding crop, by which the horse is goaded, is lust.

The chariot of pride has two wheels: presumption about oneself and audacity. The horse that draws this chariot is the appetite of vainglory. Love of the world sits on it, in a saddle of adulation. The rein is avarice; the riding crop is malice. The chariot of malice has two wheels: pretense and deception. The horse drawing this chariot is malevolence. The soldier that sits on it is a taste for the wicked, sitting in a saddle of fraud. The rein of this horse is negligence; the riding crop is anger."*

8. At one time that woman who was called a sinner in the city was conveyed by these demonic chariots. But after she entered into Simon's house so that she could prostrate herself at the feet of Jesus, immediately she turned away the chariot of luxury so that she could ascend into the chariot of chastity. She avoided the chariot of pride to follow Christ in the chariot of humility. She renounced the chariot of malice to be eagerly conveyed by the chariot of innocence, chastely and devoutly running *in the odor of* Christ's *ointments.** Let us run with that sinful woman *in the odor of the ointments* of God, because *we do not have here a lasting city, but we seek one that is to come.**

9. Let us not presume about what is said about us: *A human being was made to the image and likeness of God.** Through sin, we have disfigured and confused the Creator's image in ourselves, so the life of a human and of a beast was made *similar,** but the ultimate ends of each are not similar. For people are limited in the present, so that in the future they may end badly in punishment or well in glory. And a beast is limited in the present, so that in the future it may not appear at all. We are all fed by a similar corporeal bread in the refectory and by spiritual [bread] on the altar, but we shall be separated as we

*William of Saint-Thierry, Brev com 23 (CCCM 87:181)

*see Song 1:3

*Heb 13:14

*Gen 1:26; Gen 9:6

*see Ps 48:13

go out from the present chapter, just as we must be
divided in our death.* And what is more serious, we
know not who *is worthy of love or hatred.**

10. If only we would ponder these things! *If only
they would be wise and would understand*, says
Moses, *and would provide for their last end.** They
would understand what rewards await those who do
good, and they would provide for their last end,
namely, what punishments are prepared for those
who do bad. There are animals that trust in their
hoof.* Hooves are extremities of the body that signify our last end. Those cleaving the hoof are those
who ponder how they will go out from this life, and
when they must be put on the right or on the left.*
Finally, to cleave hooves is to provide for the last
things. Because Mary prudently did this, she changed
a bad beginning into a good end. Therefore let us
imitate Mary, the example of pardon.

11. One who has not yet renounced his own sins,
let him come, worship, and prostrate before Jesus
who made him,* since he can at least come to his
feet. He cannot come to Jesus' head. For a sinner
must approach the feet, but a just person to the head.
Mary brings ointment with her.* You, after sin, offer
also repentance! "Wherever you might hear the name
of Christ, run to him. You might have learned that
Jesus has entered into the interior of someone's
house: hurry also to enter! When you have discovered wisdom or justice reclining in someone's inner
chambers, rush to the feet, that is, seek the extreme
part of wisdom. Do not disdain the feet. *A woman
touched the hem of his garment** and was healed.
Confess your offenses with tears, so that the heavenly
justice may say about you, *With her tears she has
rinsed my feet, and wiped them with her hair.*"*

12. "Good tears <can> not only wash our sin, but
also rinse the footprints of the heavenly Word, so

*see Eccl 3:19-22
*Eccl 9:1

*Deut 32:29

*see Deut 14:6-8

*see Matt 25:33

*see Ps 94:6

*see Luke 7:37

*see Matt 9:20-22

*Luke 7:44;
Ambrose, Exp Ev
Luc 6:17–18
(CSEL 32/4:238)

that his steps are fruitful in us—good tears, in which are not only redemption of sins, but also refreshment of the just. For instance, the voice of the just is this: *My tears have been bread for me day and night.*" * "Also, let down your hair! One reads about a certain person who as long as he had hair could not be defeated.* What is more, it is not proper for a woman to pray with her hair shorn.* Therefore let a person have hair with which to cover the feet of Christ; with these braids one might wipe the feet of Wisdom's beauty and elegance. This woman is not one of mediocre merit about whom Wisdom says, *From the time I entered your house, she has not stopped kissing my feet.*" * "Blessed the one who can anoint Jesus' feet with oil, but more blessed the one who anoints with ointment. Having collected the grace of many flowers into one, such a one sprinkles the <varied> sweetness of scents."*

13. Therefore Mary is blessed and happy, she who deserved to anoint not only Jesus' feet, but also his head and whole body. *Mary Magdalene,* the evangelist says, *and Mary the mother of James, and Salome, bought aromatic spices so as to come and anoint Jesus.* There are three ointments with which blessed Mary anointed Jesus. With the first ointment she anointed his feet, with the second his head, with the third his whole body. The first is ointment of contrition, the second of devotion, the third of love. The first ointment expresses grief, the second mitigates grief, the third repels distress.*

14. "A soul entangled in many crimes prepares the ointment of contrition for herself when she begins to consider her ways.* She collects, gathers, grinds many and various types of her sins in the mortar of conscience, and within the boiling pot of the sinner cooks all at the same time with a certain fire of repentance and grief, so she can say with the prophet,

*Ps 41:4;
Ambrose, Exp Ev
Luc 6:18
(CSEL 32/4:239)
*see Judg 16:17
*see 1 Cor 11:5

*Luke 7:45;
Ambrose, Ex Ev
Luc 6.19-20
(CSEL 32/4:239)

*Ambrose,
Exp Ev Luc 6.21
(CSEL 32/4:240)

*Mark 16:1

*morbum

*see Ps 118:59

*Ps 38:4

*Ps 50:19
*see Ps 73:21

*Ps 50:19;
Bernard, SC 10.5
(SBOp 1:51)
*John 12:3;
Bernard, SC 10.6
(SBOp 1:51)

*see Luke 15:7,
10; Bernard, SC
10.6 (SBOp 1:51)

*Prov 31:10

*Jas 1:17

*see Ps 44:8;
see Ps 22:5

*Ps 49:23;
Bernard, SC 10.7
(SBOp 1:52)

*My heart grew hot within me, and in my meditation a fire shall blaze up.** That is the sacrifice by which a sinful soul ought to cleanse the beginnings of her conversion. In fact, the first *sacrifice* is *an afflicted spirit.** Therefore, like *the poor and needy,** as long as she does not have [the virtues] from which she might collect the better and more precious [ingredients], let her not neglect to prepare that ointment, although from common types, because *God will not despise a humble and contrite heart."** "What do we read about the ointment? *The house*, it says, *was filled with the odor of the ointment."** "She ought not to be entirely spurned, nor should an ointment of this type be reckoned as cheap, whose odor not only calls human beings to reform but also invites angels to exultation."**

15. "There is another ointment much more precious than this ointment, as it is composed from better types [of ingredients]. Our earth does not bring forth the aromatic spices of this ointment, but we seek them for ourselves *far off and from the most distant lands.** May that ointment be made from the divine benefits bestowed on humankind. Truly *every best gift and every perfect gift is from above, coming down from the Father of lights.** Happy those who take care eagerly to collect these aromatic spices for themselves and restore them <before> the eyes of their mind with the worthy acts of grace. Surely if these aromatic spices have been in the vessel of one's heart, bruised and crushed with the pestle of frequent meditation, and at last boiled with the fire of holy desire and anointed *with the oil of gladness,** then this ointment will be far more precious and excellent than the previous ointment. A sufficient proof is the testimony of the one who says, *The sacrifice of praise shall honor me."**

16. "It is said about the previous ointment [of contrition] that *God will not despise* it.* But concerning the latter [ointment of meditation], it is said that *it shall honor* God,* and it is therefore recommended all the more. So the latter is put on the head, the former on the feet. If on Christ the head is to be assigned to divinity (as Paul testifies, who says, *The head of Christ is God*)* then without a doubt, one who gives thanks anoints the head, because one touches God, not humankind."* "In fact, though, our entire hope depends on the human God, but not because he is a person; rather, because he is God. Accordingly, the former is rendered to God on the feet, the latter <on the head>. The humiliation of a contrite heart is appropriate for the humbling of the flesh, <and glorification befits majesty>."*

17. "There is another ointment that far surpasses both of these, which is called the ointment of piety, because it comes from the difficulties of the poor, from the anxieties of the oppressed, from the troubles of the sad, from all the hardships of any <miserable people>. These types seem despicable, but this is an ointment *above all aromatic spices** because it is made from them. Obviously it has a healing effect. For *blessed are the merciful, because they shall obtain mercy."** May the merciful and most loving Lord Jesus Christ deign to bestow that on us, he who lives and reigns with the Father and Holy Spirit, God, through all ages forever.

*see Ps 50:19

*see Ps 49:23

*1 Cor 11:3

*Bernard, SC 10.8 (SBOp 1:52)

*Bernard, SC 10.8 (SBOp 1:52)

*Song 4:10

*Matt 5:7; Bernard, SC 12.1 (SBOp 1:60)

Sermon 151

On the Feast of
Saint Peter in Chains

*Jerome, Int nom
65 (CCSL 72:141)

*Acts 12:5

*Acts 12:6

*Acts 12:4

*see Acts 12:7

*Introitus Missae,
"Puer natus est"
Missae in
Nativitate Domini
(see Isa 9:6)

*see Heb 1:14

*see Acts 12:7

*Eph 5:14

*see Acts 12:8
*see Matt 22:11
*Acts 12:7

1. **P**eter is interpreted as *recognizing.** That is, a rational soul understanding God through faith. *Peter* is held in jail* as long as a human being sojourns away from the Lord in his body, *bound with two chains,** certainly, that is, entangled in the twin chains of vices of the flesh and spirit. Such a one is handed over *to a squad of four soldiers** while suffering a hindrance from four elements, from four mixtures, from four arrangements, from four seasons. An angel visits this person and illuminates the jail* when the grace of Christ, who is *the angel of great counsel,** inwardly enlightens the divinely inspired mind of the person and assigns to him an angelic spirit for ministry,* that is, to teach him what should be done in all matters.

2. This faithful one, Peter, is struck *on his side* while he is reproved about his sleepiness,* and thus he is awakened, as the apostle says: *Rise, you who sleep, and arise from the dead, and Christ shall enlighten you.** At the angel's command, Peter prepares himself to go out of the jail, because the soul now brought to life and roused from the dead, now illuminated by inward aspiration, hurries to go out from the body at the Lord's urging. What does he do? He puts on the shoes of humility, he girds himself with the belt of chastity,* he clothes himself with *a wedding garment,** the garment of charity. At once *the chains fall from his hands.** Because as soon as he

began to be dressed in the works of charity, all the fetters of depravity were loosened.

3. *Going out* of the jail, he follows the angel,* because withdrawing from the servitude of sin that he was suffering in his body, he follows Christ, who leads the way in all matters. Peter *did not know* this was *true*, but *he supposed that he saw a vision.** In fact, *as long as* a human being sojourns *in the body*, he walks *by faith not by sight*;* he sees *through a mirror* and as if *obscurely*, not yet in that truth of vision that is *face to face.**

4. *Passing through the first and second guard post, they came to the iron gate that <leads to the city, which> opened to them by itself.** The iron gate is a very hard death, which leads just persons crossing through it into that heavenly city of the celestial Jerusalem.* The first and second guard posts that must be crossed before one comes to the gate are sins of the will and of necessity, or two fears, one concerning remorse for sins, the other concerning vision of malicious spirits, which one will have passed through with attending grace: *he shall not be confounded when he speaks to his enemies in the gate*,* because *precious in the sight of the Lord is the death of his saints.** Although this gate might be iron, nevertheless it opens by itself for the saints;* that is, willingly and without fear, with readiness and cheerfulness, one is taken up by those who want *to be dissolved and to be with Christ.** So David says, *In the river they shall pass on foot*, that is, they shall easily pass through death, because *in that place*, that is, in the land of promise, having crossed the river of death, *we shall rejoice in him*,* that is, in Christ our leader.

5. When they had proceeded on to *one street, the angel departed from him.** The first street that he meets after going out of the gate is Paradise, which,

*see Acts 12:9

*Acts 12:9

*see 2 Cor 5:6-7

*see 1 Cor 13:12

*Acts 12:10

*see Heb 12:22; see Gal 4:26

*Ps 126:5

*Ps 115:15
*see Acts 12:10

*see Phil 1:23

*Ps 65:6

*Acts 12:10

after temporal death, any saint enters. In that place the angel departs from him, because now he does not require an angel's service, he whom the chorus of saints in its assembly shall take up. There Peter is received *in the house of Mary,* where he meets *a girl*

*see Acts 12:12-13 *named Rhoda,** which means *rose.*

6. *We know that, <since> our house of this habitation on earth will have been demolished, we will have a building from God, a house not made with*

*2 Cor 5:1 *hands, eternal in heaven,** where the virgin mother of Christ reigns, where as we arrive at that place with great delight, she will meet us—she the church, which is virgin through integrity of faith and rose-colored on account of Christ's blood. Then all of us, understanding *what great things* the Lord *has done* for our

*see Ps 65:16 *soul,** in great joyfulness of heart shall cry out in praise of Christ with Peter, *Now I know truly, that the Lord has sent his angel, and has rescued me from the hand of Herod, and from every expectation of*

*Acts 12:11 *the people of the Jews,** that is, of the devil and his angels.

Sermon 152

On the Chair of Saint Peter [1]

1. **P**eter, <an apostle> of Jesus Christ, to the
chosen foreigners dispersed through
Pontus, Galatia, Cappadocia, <Asia,>
and Bithynia, according to the foreknowledge of God
the Father, unto the sanctification of the Spirit, unto
obedience and sprinkling of the blood of Jesus Christ:
May grace and peace be multiplied for you.* I am in
awe concerning blessed Peter, and I almost say about
him what the Jews said about the Lord: How does
this man know letters, when he has not learned?*
Behold, a fisherman without letters, not an orator,*
reared in a boat and not in a school, composed words
so finely in the introduction of his letter.

    *1 Pet 1:1-2

    *John 7:15
    *see Acts 4:13

2. According to history, he directs his reassuring
epistle to those who had arrived at Judaism from the
five places mentioned above. And afterward, through
the preaching of the apostles, they took up the faith
and, for sake of the same faith, having been dispersed
from Jerusalem at a time of persecution, they had gone
back to their respective places. Mystically, however,
he speaks to the church's five virgins, who although

---

[1] Odo of Canterbury copied this sermon and included it among
his own. The CCCM 2C edition is based on the edition of Odo's
sermons (Charles de Clercq, ed., *The Latin Sermons of Odo of
Canterbury* [Brussels: Koninklijke Academie voor Wetenschappen, 1983], 185–87). In this sermon, Raciti has supplied passages
missing in the Reading-Cluny manuscript of Aelred's sermon
from Odo's version of the sermon as found in the Clercq edition,
enclosing them in angle brackets (< >).

*see Matt 25:2

*Jerome, Int nom
73 (CCSL 72:151)
†Jerome, Int nom
72 (CCSL 72:150)
‡Jerome, Int nom
72 (CCSL 72:150)
#Jerome, Int nom
72 (CCSL 72:150)
§Jerome, Int nom
67 (CCSL 72:144)
*Wis 1:3

*2 Tim 2:19

*Ps 6:9; Matt 7:23

*Eph 5:10-11;
see Rom 12:17

*1 Cor 15:33

*2 Cor 9:2

*Ps 74:5-6

*Col 3:1

they were previously *foolish*, were afterward made *prudent*,* yet still called by the same names. The name of the first is Pontus, interpreted as *diverting*;* of the second, Galatia, which is called *transferred*;† of the third, Cappadocia, which is *redeeming for the Lord*;‡ of the fourth, Asia, which signifies *lifting up*;# of the fifth, Bithynia, that is, *useless*.§

3. The foolish one of the first name turns away from God through thought, as it is written: *Perverse thoughts separate from God.** But the prudent one turns away from the devil, as it is written: *Let everyone depart from iniquity who invokes the name of the Lord.** The foolish one of the second name is transferred to evil through works, to whom it is said, *Depart from me all you that work iniquity.** But the prudent one is transferred to good, to whom it is said, *Providing what is pleasing to God, have no share in the unfruitful works of darkness!**

4. The foolish one of the third name buys back others from the Lord by a perverse example and pernicious doctrine, that is, she takes away from the Lord, <as it is written, *Evil conversations corrupt good habits.** But the prudent one buys back others for the Lord with good example and sound doctrine, that is, she acquires others for the Lord, as it is written, *Your emulation has called forth many.>** The foolish one of the fourth name lifts herself up against God by her own stupidity. Against her the psalmist says, *I said to those who offend, Do not lift up your horn on high! Do not speak iniquity against God!** But the prudent one among her works always brings herself to contemplation of heavenly things on purpose, according to what was said to her by the apostle: *Seek the things that are above, where Christ is sitting at the right hand of God.**

5. The foolish one of the fifth name through desperation is now useless to all good purposes, as the

apostle says: *Those who despair have given them-*
selves up to lasciviousness, <unto> the working of
uncleanness.* But the prudent one, the more she progresses in heavenly matters, the more she is proved
useless in earthly matters, because *the world is cruci-*
fied to her *and* she *to the world.** Bithynia <truly,
according to what is fitting for the prudent virgin,>
is thus far interpreted as *little girl* or *daughter <of the*
Lord, or *daughter spouse.** In these three names are
denoted chastity, humility, and charity. If she is a
virgin, then indeed the apostle says, *I have betrothed*
you to one husband, to present a chaste virgin to
Christ.* But the daughter of the Lord is also a spouse,
as the prophet says: *Listen, O daughter, and see, and*
the king shall eagerly desire your beauty.>*

    6. <Therefore the apostle writes to all the *elect*
who are foreigners in *Pontus, Galatia, Cappadocia,*
Asia, and Bithynia, and likewise to those dispersed[2]
in *Pontus, Galatia, Cappadocia, Asia, and Bithynia.**
For those* were not born in the faith, but like foreigners they have come to the faith of Jesus Christ
from another place (that is, from the places listed
above, interpreted in the bad sense). For they were,
as Paul testifies, *at one time alienated, and enemies*
in their perception and evil works,* *alienated from*
the life of God,* *having no hope of the promise, and*
without God in this world.* Behold how far they
have come. But *now those who, at one time, were*
afar off, are made near by the blood of Christ,* *by*
him having *access in the* Holy *Spirit to the Father,**
made *citizens with the saints, and members of God's*
household.>*

Marginal notes:
*Eph 4:19
*see Gal 6:14
*Jerome, Int nom 72 (CCSL 72:150)
*2 Cor 11:2
*Ps 44:11-12; see Resp in Com virg (Hesbert 4:6142)
*see 1 Pet 1:1
*the foreigners
*Col 1:21
*Eph 4:18
*Eph 2:12
*Eph 2:13
*Eph 2:18
*Eph 2:19

---

[2] Aelred here contrasts foreigners who came to Christ from a sinful life with the elect, who are dispersed. Both groups are "sojourners in the body"; the difference between them is where they come from rather than where they now are.

7. <Nevertheless, although they may be citizens, still they are far removed from the heavenly Jerusalem;* in the places mentioned above (interpreted in the good sense), they are dispersed by the quality of their various merits, although joined by the unity of charity: *as long as* they are *in the body, they wander on pilgrimage from the Lord.** Peter himself testifying about this in the following verses speaks to all the faithful when he says, *I beseech you as foreigners and pilgrims.** And David in the person of some faithful person, sensing the same thing, says, *May you not be silent toward me, God, because I am a foreigner in your presence, and a pilgrim, as were all my fathers.>*

*see Gal 4:26;
see Heb 12:22

*see 2 Cor 5:6

*1 Pet 2:11

*Ps 38:13

8. <But there are all those whom he calls foreigners *from* the same places, and dispersed *in* the same places, chosen not for their own merits, but *according to the foreknowledge of God the Father,** because *whom he foreknew, he also predestined to be made like the image of his Son.>*

*see Pet 1:2

*Rom 8:29

9. <There are also those chosen *unto sanctification of the Spirit,** that is, that they may be sanctified by the Holy Spirit, chosen in Christ *before the foundation of the world, so that* they *should be holy and immaculate in his sight in charity.>*

*1 Pet 1:2

*Eph 1:4

10. <*In obedience to Christ*: that is, thus sanctified by the Holy Spirit that they may obey Christ. *Unto the sprinkling of his blood:** that is, through sprinkling of his blood, the usefulness of which is especially apparent in the end, so that freed from all temptations, they may go out from this world, just as the people of Israel through the blood of the lamb were freed from the Pharaoh's oppression and went out from Egypt.>*

*1 Pet 1:2

*see 1 Pet 1:18-19

11. <Therefore the apostle wishes for grace (which is also in forgiveness of sins and [in] gathering of

virtues through the Holy Spirit), and peace (which is in devotion of charity instilled through the same Spirit), to be multiplied for so long* on behalf of these chosen ones who go *from virtue to virtue* and who always progress along the way, until they arrive and see *the God of gods in Zion,** as he says in the second epistle, *May they be fulfilled** in the homeland. There, consequently, he immediately describes certain steps, ascending through which those who may wish to flee the *corruption* of this world may arrive at that place where they become *sharers in divine nature,** just as Peter himself bears witness. *You,* he says, *employing all care, serve virtue in your faith, knowledge in virtue, abstinence in knowledge, patience in abstinence, piety in patience, love of brotherhood in piety, charity in love of brotherhood.** And after some verses: *So an entrance shall be richly provided for you into the eternal kingdom of our Lord and Savior Jesus Christ.>**

*see 1 Pet 1:2

*see Ps 83:8
*see 2 Pet 1:2

*see 2 Pet 1:4

*2 Pet 1:5-7

*2 Pet 1:11

Sermon 153

On the
Assumption of Saint Mary

1. *A**rise, make haste, my beloved, my dove,*
*my beautiful one, and come.** Let us
all rejoice in the Lord,** because today
the Lord's mother, mother of our Redeemer and Savior, is invited and proceeds to heavenly nuptials.†
Today the *queen of the South* ascends into Jerusalem
*to hear the wisdom of Solomon,** the wisdom of the
glorious king who abounds *in riches* and glory *over
all the kings of the earth.** Today that most wise
queen, the Blessed Virgin Mary, obviously, who is the
ultimate queen of heaven and earth, offers to King
Solomon, to the king of peace,** to her Creator, as
many aromatic spices as were never before *brought*†
into that celestial Jerusalem‡ by any of Eve's daughters since the beginning of the world *unto this day,**
a day of exaltation and glorification of the Blessed
Virgin. Obviously *many* virgins and women *have
gathered together riches for themselves*; she however
has *surpassed them all.**

2. *Many* virgins *have gathered together riches for
themselves*, because many faithful souls with great
affection, much zeal, and immense toil, have sought
treasures of virtues as much as they could, so they
are adorned with their flowers and riches. But none
of them could be adorned and enriched with virtue
and grace as was the Blessed Virgin Mary. In her
womb as in his tent,** as also in <his> private bed
chamber,** or rather, as on his heavenly throne, dur-

*Song 2:10
*Entrance Ant of
Mass on the
Assumption
†see Matt 22:2-3

*see Matt 12:42;
see 1 Kgs 10:1-2

*see 1 Kgs 10:23;
3:13; see Prov 3:16

*Jerome, Int nom
63 (CCSL 72:138)
†see 1 Kgs 10:10
‡see Gal 4:26
*see Matt 11:23

*see Prov 31:29

*see Ps 18:6
*see Jdt 8:5

152

ing nine months the *Lord of hosts** and distributor
of grace rested *bodily*, Christ, Son of God and son
of the virgin. Finally, it is rightly said about this
Blessed Virgin that she surpassed all the virgins who
gather riches for themselves, because by a special
grace and singular privilege she stands out above all
virgins.*

3. In fact this bearer of life, mother of salvation,
temple of piety and mercy, conceived in her womb
Christ the king of heaven, in whom *the fullness of
divinity dwells bodily*,* by the secret will of God and
arrangement of the Holy Spirit, and at the suitable
time, at the time of giving birth,* *an eternal light for
the world she brought forth, Jesus Christ our Lord.*†
Therefore one must believe without hesitation that
even in this human body she was filled with every
grace and virtue,* through whose fecundity the world
was justified, humankind renewed, the exile led back
to the homeland. Her offspring redeemed the world,
justified the wicked,* raised up humankind that had
died in sin. For in fact, a person wrapped up in the
darkness of sins lies exposed to ambush and oppression of demons. But when the sun <of justice> arose
from the Blessed Virgin,* humankind was illuminated and, avoiding the snares of the enemies, now
powerfully tramples the strength of enemy power.

4. Therefore we must rejoice together, beloved
brothers, because our mediatrix, liberator of our
souls, supported by the services of angels and surrounded by a great army of virtues, today is happily
snatched away from this *valley of tears*,* and, *ascending above all the heavens*,* she is moved up all
the way to God's throne with immeasurable glory.
Every type of person, therefore, listless in oneself
from the sickness of vice and cut with the wounds of
outrageous deeds, because of continuing to be healed,

*Dominus
virtutum*;
see Ps 23:10

*see Prov 31:29

*Col 2:9

*see Luke 1:57;
see Gen 25:24
†Pref S Maria
(CP 366; CCSL
161A:101)
*see Luke 1:28

*see Rom 4:5

*see Mal 4:2

*see Ps 83:7
*see Eph 4:8, 10

renewed, and saved through this glorious Virgin, ought to praise the merits of this Virgin, to love [her] blessedness, to extol [her] highness, to proclaim [her] kindness and glory. For it is not to be doubted that she in heaven comes to help all who venerate her on earth.

*see Song 3:11

5. Congratulate, *you daughters of Zion*,* congratulate your queen; after Herod's persecution and the flight to Egypt, after many ambushes and atrocities of Jewish unrighteousness, after the toil and suffering that increase in this region of unlikeness, she is finally granted to say, *Turn, O my soul, into your rest, because the Lord has blessed you.** The Lord blessed Mary, he who rescued her soul from the corporeal prison and the hardship of this present life and established her in eternal happiness. The Lord blessed her, because today he conferred on her the calm of perfect tranquility, which she always sought with a devout heart. He who bodily rested in the tabernacle of her body today grants to her the rest of his heaven, inviting and guiding her to perpetual peace, to perfect tranquility, to eternal blessedness.

*Ps 114:7

6. For just as the bridegroom [invites] the bride or the father [invites] the daughter, so the Lord invites Mary to himself, saying, *Arise, make haste, my beloved, my dove, my beautiful one, and come.** You have been the tent of the king who was destined to fight in the world; you will be the seat of him who triumphs in heaven. You have been the inn for the traveler; you will be a palace for him who reigns. You have been the bedroom of the incarnate bridegroom;* you will be the throne of the crowned king. *Arise, make haste.** What is this? How does he who cleanses the unclean and justifies the wicked urge the queen of angels to arise, the mistress of the world, his mother? This word is customarily said to those

*Song 2:10

*see Ps 18:6
*see Song 2:10

who fall, sit, and lie down, who sleep in sins. To such
as those the apostle says, *Rise, you who sleep, arise
from the dead, and Christ shall enlighten you.** But
to presume this about Mary is a detestable sin. For
as far as the east is from the west, the Lord *has made
iniquities* and filth of sins far from her.*

7. Mary, the mother of light, the nurse of salvation, is naturally first and foremost among those who
continually meditate *on the law of the Lord** and
perfectly *keep the commandments of God.** For although she advanced through the hazards of the
present life, considering her life and manner I find
her advancement everywhere; nowhere do I read
about her slipping or falling. Yet she is invited by the
Lord to arise, not so that she might now be cleansed
from sins, but, having previously justified and sanctified her, he exhorts her to rise to be crowned. *Arise,
make haste.** Arise from your house of clay, from the
flesh that kindles war against the spirit,* from the
valley of human misery, in which spring many evils,
and enter into the rest of your Lord God!* Ascend
over all the heavens* to the throne of God! For he
who willed to have lodging on earth in your body
desires to put in you his throne in heaven. To you,
high queen, to you especially the Lord says, *Come,
my beloved, and I shall put my throne in you.**

8. *Arise, make haste.*† Listlessness does not hinder one who hurries to the Lord. Nothing can hinder
one who makes haste to God except sin and evil. But
what about you? There is no iniquity in you. There
is no offense in you. *Arise, make haste.* The soul who
loves more ardently runs more swiftly and arrives at
the kingdom sooner. Therefore make haste, Mary,
make haste, Blessed Virgin, make haste as a member
of the household, as one most dear, as you are singularly loved and specifically graced. *Arise, make*

*Eph 5:14

*Ps 102:12

*see Ps 1:2
*Rev 14:12

*Song 2:10
*see Gal 5:17

*see Heb 4:10-11
*see Eph 4:10

*Ant in Com
virg (Hesbert
3:5322–33)
†Song 2:10

*Song 2:10

*see Isa 34:4

*see Luke 1:28, 38

*Ps 74:5-6
*see Exod 15:4-5,
10

*see Ps 68:16;
see Isa 29:6

*1 Pet 5:6

*Song 2:10
*see Luke 1:28, 42
*Ant "Gen" in
Nat Dom (Hesbert
3:2938); Sedulius,
Paschale Carmen 2
(CSEL 10:48)
†Song 4:7

*Song 2:10

*Song 2:14

*haste, my beloved.** What, I ask, is more pleasant, what more kind, what more sweet than this invitation by the Lord? The Lord of all creation, King and commander of all kings, to whom *every army of heaven** yields with fear and reverence, called the humble virgin *my beloved*, the virgin who was once greeted by an angel and who humbly declared herself handmaid of God;* as if impatient of delay, the Lord hastens her arrival to himself with a holy invitation.

9. Learn, beloved brothers, learn to love humility from this mother of the Savior. In fact, this virtue enriches the poor, heals the crushed, lifts up the oppressed. *Do not lift up your horn,** do not mount horses and *Pharaoh's chariots,** the pride of Egypt's king, lest you be drowned in the depths of the sea, so you might not be swallowed up by the whirlwind and storm* of dreadful and eternal damnation. Go down into your very selves, so that you may ascend into God. *Be humbled under the mighty hand of God, so that he may exalt you* along with the Blessed Virgin Mary *in the time of visitation.** It will greatly benefit you to celebrate the solemnity of this Blessed Virgin if you imitate her works, life, and manners according to your small measure.

10. *Arise, make haste, my beloved,** beloved before all, *blessed* over all,* because *you are seen to be the first and last of your kind.** For *you are all beautiful*, all holy, all pleasing to me, *my beloved,*† through whose holiness sins are cleansed, through whose integrity incorruptibility is given, through whose virginity the human soul is reconciled to God. *Arise, make haste, my dove.** This is that beautiful and holy dove of God, whose prudence the bridegroom commends in the Song of Songs: *My dove in the clefts of the rock, in the hollow places of the wall.** In the manner of a wise man, who builds *upon rock* on

account of winds and stormy floods,* this dove, indeed the Blessed Virgin Mary, put her nest *in the
clefts of* that *rock*,* of which it is said, *And the rock
was Christ.*† Daily this wise virgin entrusts her life
and behavior to her Son, having all her hope in him
of whom it is written, *One who trusts in him shall
not be confounded.**

11. *Arise, make haste, my beloved, my beautiful
one, and come.** Beautifully here and everywhere he
says *my*. For although every creature ought to belong
to its creator, about none other does the Lord more
appropriately say "she is mine" than this Blessed
Virgin. No creature, except the humanity of Christ,
is more excellent than the Virgin Mary, none more
fortunate, none more pleasant, none more blessed,
none more holy. She is God's beloved friend, from
whom that holy and immaculate flesh <was> taken
up that was offered on the cross for the sins of all
peoples. Therefore the Lord of all, who *alone* is supremely *good*,* from whom <is> whatever is good,
addresses this Blessed Virgin as a father addresses a
daughter with great affection and wonderful sweetness of love, everywhere calling her his own: *Arise,
my beautiful one.** Truly *my beautiful one*, because
*you are beautiful and there is no spot on you. Wholly
beautiful*,* because perfectly and fully merciful, just
and powerful, strong and wise, singularly blessed
and admired above all women.*

12. *You are wholly beautiful*, through whose
fruitfulness the captive <has been> redeemed,
through whose child-bearing the world has been released from eternal death, through whose offspring
the condemned are saved and called back from exile
to the homeland. *You are wholly beautiful*,* because,
in soul and in body, humility does not forsake your
mind and purity of virginity keeps your body incor-

*see Matt 7:24-25

*see Song 2:14;
see Num 24:21
†1 Cor 10:10

*Sir 32:28

*Song 2:10

*see Luke 18:19

*Song 2:10

*Song 4:7

*see Luke 1:28, 42

*Song 4:7

rupt. For who among women is as humble as the
Blessed Virgin Mary, who, when she knew that she
was going to bear the King of heaven and earth,
humbled herself so much that, as if she were inferior
to the rest of women, speaking to the angel, was not
ashamed to call herself a handmaid? *Behold*, she says,
*the handmaid of the Lord; be it done to me according
to your word.** Who is as chaste as she who, in fervor
of love of the Holy Spirit, conceived and gave birth to
God's Son: virgin before the birth, virgin giving birth,
virgin after birth? She was full of virtue and grace,
who conceived with chaste womb and gave birth to
the King of virtues* himself, the generous giver of
grace. Therefore *you are wholly beautiful, my beloved,** endowed with every precious adornment.

13. *Arise, make haste, my beloved, my dove, my
beautiful one, and come,** because on account of
your extreme beauty, *the King* greatly desires *your
beauty.** *Come, my beloved, come* to your Creator,*
so that with your son, with whom you have sojourned on earth, you may reign eternally in heaven.
Therefore to you, our Lady, to you we commend our
souls and bodies. May your loving compassion be
upon us, so that we on earth who venerate your
exaltation according to our small measure may always experience your loving judgments in heaven,
with your excellent and beloved son our Lord Jesus
Christ, who with the Father, etc.

*Luke 1:38

Regem virtutum

*Song 4:7

*Song 2:10

*see Ps 44:12
*see Song 2:10;
see Ant in Com
virg (Hesbert
3:5322–23)

Sermon 154

On the
Assumption of Saint Mary

1. **T**oday the virgin Mary ascends into
heaven. Rejoice because she reigns forever with Christ.* While I reflect upon
the benefits of this Blessed Virgin, while I consider
the rewards and glory of this supreme queen, I am
not able to express in words how great the zeal, how
great the exultation, and how joyful the devotion
with which the hearts of the faithful ought to be
exhilarated on the day of her exaltation. For this is
that eminent and illustrious virgin who alone, out of
every human situation, reconciled her race to the
Lord. The world was saved through her fruitfulness
and giving birth, the exile was led back to the homeland, humankind was called back from error to truth,
from darkness to light, from death to life. Rightly,
therefore, we are invited to joy on the day of her
exaltation, because her election is our liberation, her
assumption is our reconciliation, her exaltation is
our glorification.

2. In fact, because of the manner in which the
mother of God was endowed, the fault of our first
mother was purged. For the serpent's malice surrounded and *seduced* the foolishness of the woman.
And so once Eve was made *foolish*,* she cut off the
taste of God's present sweetness for us. Obviously,
through the foolishness and illicit pleasure of the first
woman, that affectionate and most sweet pleasure
of seeing God has been turned into a great fear for

*Ant and
Resp Hod in
Ass (Hesbert
3:3105; 4:6851)

*see Gen 3:13;
see 2 Cor 11:3

*see Gen 3:8

humankind, so that the first man, after his transgression, fled from *the face of God** and hid himself among the trees of Paradise. So that proud enemy triumphed through the woman. After that, for a while, he rejoiced at having conquered, but since then, he grieves that he is conquered forever. For the wisdom of this Blessed Virgin laughed at and purged the cleverness of the serpent. For we who had been disfigured into foolishness through Eve have been reformed to wisdom through Mary. And now *wisdom*

*Wis 7:30

continually *conquers malice,** making foolish the sense of the flesh, purifying the understanding, healing the affection of the heart, so that nothing sweeter might be for human heart than to think about God

*see Ps 33:9

and to taste how *sweet is the Lord.**

3. The assumption of the glorious virgin is our reconciliation, because the Blessed Virgin, mother of mercy, way of reconciliation, temple of pardon, and source of life, *having been taken up to the celestial*

*Ant M Virg in
Ass (Hesbert
3:3707)

bedchamber,* reconciles us to her son by praying for us without ceasing, lest we be conquered by enemies, lest we succumb to vice and sin, lest we be cast down into the pit of death. Her exaltation is our glorification, because through her, our human nature is ex-

*Ant Exal in Ass
(Hesbert 3:2762);
Resp Beata
(Hesbert 4:6165)
†see Ps 44:10;
see Mark 16:19
‡see Ant and
Resp Hod in
Ass (Hesbert
3:3105; 4:6851)

alted *over the chorus of angels,** and, having been ineffably established in that heavenly happiness *on the right hand,*† she is honored. Therefore, rejoice! For *today she ascends into heaven,*‡ today while the <heavenly hosts> look on, the queen of heaven offers equally joy and vision about herself, so that she might hear the blessed spirits shouting with joy for her glory, *Who is this coming up from the desert,*

*Song 8:5

flowing with delights, leaning upon her beloved?*

4. The desert from which she ascends, a place *of*

*Deut 32:10

horror and vast wilderness,* a place of sorrow and

*see Ps 89:10

toil,* is the present world, in which many evils rise

up, in which there are fears and desires, where there are corruptibility and mortality, decline and success, doubtful happiness, fragile hope, perishable resources, empty and seductive prosperity. Therefore this place is well called a desert in which all these things become widespread, because all the saints have this place, that is, the present world, if not in body, then at least in mind. For thus they are in the world as if outside the world.* And although they dwell in the world, still they do not love but rather condemn the world,* and those vain things that are in it, they condemn in mind and cast aside. Today the Blessed Virgin ascends from this desert not empty* but full of virtues, honored by the service of angels, attentively received by God, exalted above all the hosts of heaven.†

5. *She ascends, flowing with delights.*‡ These delights are not carnal, but spiritual. There are two lives, one temporal, the other eternal. Each has its own delights. Delights of the temporal life include pleasure of the flesh, vainglory, luxury, desire, love of temporal goods, self-indulgence, etc. It is safer to keep silent than to speak about these. The world overflows with these delights. By these delights *the body is corrupted* and the soul is weighed down.* These delights have a sweet beginning, because the flesh takes pleasure in them, but their ends are *full of bitterness** and sink a person *into the depths of hell.*† That rich man in the Gospel had these delights in abundance, he who in this world *was clothed in purple and fine linen, and feasted sumptuously every day,** but afterward he was cruelly tormented in hell,* where he asked for just a little bit and a short time, and he did not get it, but rather it was said to him, *Son, remember that you have received good things in your lifetime, and likewise Lazarus bad things; now he is comforted, but you are tormented.**

*see John 17:15-18

*see 1 John 2:15

*see Song 8:5;
see Ant and Resp
Hod in Ass
(Hesbert 3:3105;
4:6851)
†Ant Exal in Ass
(Hesbert 3:2762);
Resp Beata
(Hesbert 4:6165)
‡Song 8:5

*see Wis 9:15

*see Prov 14:13;
see Lam 1:20
†see Prov 16:25
(LXX as cited
in RB)
*Luke 16:19
*see Luke 16:22-24

*Luke 16:25

6. Unhappy the soul who embraces these delights, by which she is oppressed and compelled to descend from evil to evil, from iniquity to iniquity, from this desert—that is, from the present world into hell—so that she presents to demons equally spectacle and joy over her, and she hears unclean spirits barking and jeering at her: *who is this coming up from the* [*]*desert, flowing with delights,** led astray by flatterers and her false friends? This is *the expectation of the* *wicked,** this the reward of the wicked, this the end of those who embrace worldly delights: to go down into hell, to be tormented and tortured in a lake *of* *fire and brimstone,** so in that place one who here loves illicit delights [there] endures eternal torture.

7. But what do we say about these delights today? This singular virgin, about whom we are glad especially on this day, avoids and abhors these delights. For she herself has her own delights in which she takes pleasure, not worldly and carnal, but spiritual and eternal. In these she abounds and overflows. Today, spectacularly adorned with these delights, she comes up from the desert of our sojourn,* so that she may reign eternally with her son in heaven, with whom she sojourned on earth. The delights in which the mother of the Lord overflows, the incomparable Virgin Mary, are delights of the soul, delights of eternal life, delights that do not hinder but adorn a soul, lest one appear filthy and naked in the sight of God, in the eyes of the Creator and his angels: faith, hope, love, humility, chastity, obedience, truth, peace, mercy, and the rest of the holy virtues by which a human soul is reconciled to her Creator. They are true delights, honorable delights in which she takes pleasure, in which a rational soul is restored and illuminated, in which a person is absolved from sins and called back to her homeland.

*Song 8:5

*see Prov 10:28

*see Rev 20:9

*see Ant and Resp Hod in Ass (Hesbert 3:3105; 4:6851); see Song 8:5; see Ps 118:54

8. *Foolish virgins,* whose *lamps go out,* lack these delights. Therefore they fail when they sleep, and they do not meet the bridegroom who is coming, and they are shut out from the wedding.* And to those who shout to the bridegroom, *Lord, Lord, open to us,* the bridegroom calls back to them, *Amen I say to you, I know you not.** That wretched one who was invited to the royal wedding had been deprived of these ornaments of the soul; he reclined in the royal home without *a wedding garment,** and therefore, rebuked by the king, *hands and feet tied,* was sent *into outer darkness.**

9. Therefore pay attention, beloved brothers, and diligently consider in what delights you abound, with what adornments you advance. If you feed on temporal delights, it will not be expedient for you, because they are corruptible, and, like smoke, they vanish and kill the soul. They are vulgar and unclean clothes of vanity, having corruption and filthiness. We ought not to come to that beautiful and well-adorned host of angels dressed in these clothes. *Rise up, shake off the dust,** cast off your old clothes, that is, carnal delights and ostentation of the world, and acquire for yourselves incorruptible clothes and new adornments: adornments of chastity and humility, adornments of peace and love, adornments of obedience and innocence and the rest of the ornaments of virtues.

10. These are her clothes, these are Mary's adornments, with which so adorned, *today she comes up from the desert flowing with delights, leaning upon her beloved.** With these delights, with these holy virtues, the singular virgin Mary overflowed and surpassed all women. For *many have gathered riches for themselves;* she however *has surpassed them all.** This is that virgin incomparably blessed to whom,

*see Matt 25:5-10

*Matt 25:11-12

*see Matt 22:11-12

*Matt 22:13

*see Isa 26:19; see Matt 10:14; see Isa 52:2

*Song 8:5; see Ant and Resp Hod in Ass (Hesbert 3:3105; 4:6851)
*Prov 31:29

by the celestial messenger, by the Archangel Gabriel, was given the singular grace of the greeting *Hail, Mary, full of grace, the Lord is with you, blessed are you among women and blessed the fruit of thy womb.**   *Luke 1:28, 42   This woman, mother and virgin, is filled with every grace, every wisdom, every virtue. It is she alone to whom no one can be compared, because she alone is embraced all at the same time by virtues that others particularly receive, she who without intercourse and the activity of a man conceived and gave birth to the King of virtues himself and Lord of glory, who is the Power of God and the Wisdom of God.*   *see 1 Cor 2:8; see 1 Cor 1:24

11. She is that eminent and exceptional friend of the bridegroom, singularly chosen and specially loved, whom he commends in the Song of Songs: *As a lily among thorns, so is my beloved among the daughters.**   *Song 2:2   All the daughters of Eve are like thorns in comparison to Mary, knotty and thorny trees, trees clinging to the earth and bearing earthly fruit. She alone among all the daughters of her mother is *as a lily among thorns.**   *Song 2:2   The flower of this lily is Christ, *the sun of justice* enlightening all things*   *see Mal 4:2; see John 1:9   and saving all together. Although that lily grows among thorns, nevertheless the thorns neither pierce nor choke her,*   *see Matt 13:7   because she has a powerful protector, her beloved, upon whom she leans.*   *see Song 8:5   This lily does not blossom in order to wither, but so that she may remain always green, may always blossom, may always bear fruit. She remains verdant through humility, blossoms through virginity, bears fruit through obedience.

12. All the hosts of heaven rejoice with our Lord today, and with exultation and jubilation proclaim, *Who is this coming up from the desert, flowing with delights, leaning upon her beloved?**   *Song 8:5   Who is the beloved upon whom this Blessed Virgin leans? Certainly Christ her son, lover and rewarder of virginity. He is

*beloved to God and humankind, a beautiful figure before the children of humankind,** on whom the angels desire to look,** about whose illustrious beauty the bride boasts, *My beloved is white and ruddy, chosen out of thousands.**

13. White, on account of gentleness and clemency, on account of mercy and loving kindness. White because *pleasant and meek,** as he testifies about himself: *Learn from me because I am meek and humble of heart.** White, because *his mercies are over all his works,** through which he saves his people.** Ruddy on account of fervor of charity. *For on account of his exceptional charity with which he loved us,** from the Father's bosom he descended into the virgin's womb; he came from heaven into the world, forsaking neither but dwelling in both at the same time, filling both, ruling both. He came to us so we would be enriched through him. And he was made *a sharer in our humanity so that* he would make *us sharers in his divinity.** Ruddy on account of *the pouring out of his blood*, which he shed for us, so that we would be cleansed of sins.†

14. Our queen leans upon this beloved. She refers all her glory, all her strength, all her virtue and wisdom to her son, saying with her mouth and heart, *The Lord is my strength and my praise.* My son, *my strength, was made salvation for me* and for all the world.** Certainly the glorious *salvatrix* of the world, prudent and vigilant, devoted to God, is discreet regarding herself, useful for us. Devoted to God: always adhering to him, having in her heart with the prophet, *It is good for me to adhere to God, to put my hope in <the Lord> God.** Behold how she leans upon her beloved: she does not withdraw from contemplation of him, does not withdraw from his love, filled with the Holy Spirit;** a virgin she conceives,

*Sir 45:1; Ps 44:3

*1 Pet 1:12

*Song 5:10

*see Ps 85:5

*Matt 11:29
*Ps 144:9
*see Matt 1:21

*Eph 2:4

*see Orat Nat Dom (CO 2:1692C; CCSL 160A:362); see Pref Asc (CP 528; CCSL 161A:147); see 2 Pet 1:4 †see Heb 11:28; 9:22; see Luke 22:20

*Ps 117:14; Exod 15:2; Isa 12:2

*Ps 72:28

*see Luke 1:28

and a virgin she gives birth. She leans upon her beloved, that is, upon her son, so that she consents to him for correction, so that she is enlightened <by him> for acquiring knowledge, so that she is transformed for him to wisdom, and formed unto glory.

15. Beloved brothers, let us also lean upon the Virgin Mary's beloved, because he is our beloved, he who so loved us that he put on our weak flesh for us, so to lay down his life for us, so to suffer for us, so to die and rise again for us.* Happy indeed the soul who leans upon this beloved! For every soul leans in vain who does not lean on him. For he says about himself, *Without me you can do nothing.** And the prophet says about him, *Unless the Lord builds the house, they labor in vain who build it.** We the infirm, who are girded about with corruptible flesh, are not raised up, nor do we succeed if *the Lord's right hand* is not extended to us,* so that he may raise and lead us, may also educate and guide us.

16. He leads us away from illicit desire, from wrong action, from perverse habit. He guides us so we do not fall, we do not falter, we do not wander off track. So that a bad person might turn into a good person, an impious person become pious, a cruel one become kind, it is not a work of human weakness, but *a change of the Most High's right hand** that strengthens those who falter, <fortifies> the feeble, justifies the impious, saves sinners. Let us lean upon the beloved, because for one who leans upon him nothing can be impossible, nothing difficult, but all things will be possible,* all things easy for one who leans upon him who can do all things. The apostolic word is, *I can do all things in him who strengthens me.* And: *All things are possible for one who believes.**

17. Blessed be the glorious lady the Virgin Mary, *who comes up from the desert flowing with delights,*

*see 1 John 3:16; see John 10:15; John 15:13

*John 15:5

*Ps 126:1

*see Job 14:15; see Ps 117:16; see Ps 138:10

*Ps 76:11

*see Matt 17:19

*Phil 4:13; Mark 9:22

leaning upon her beloved,* teaching that we also   *Song 8:5
may lean upon him, so that we may merit to come
up after her. This virgin ought to be imitated, because
she is the mother of mercy, a cause of pardon, a door
of life. Let us imitate her chastity, her humility, her
obedience. These virtues are necessary for all, but
especially for monks.

18. Outwardly, we all have indications of humility, but how I wish we kept these inwardly! Black
clothing, shaved heads, because we shave our beards
and necks: all these are signs of humility. But there
is no profit in having these signs in the body if there
is not true humility in the heart. For they should not
be rewarded but punished if under the skins of a
sheep, foxes and lions hide, that is, reprobate human
beings: foxes on account of fraud and deceit, lions
on account of pride and aggressiveness. Humility is
necessary for all, but especially for monks, who renounce the world and its ostentation.

19. Just as pride *is the root of all evil,** so humil-   *1 Tim 6:10
ity is the adornment of all virtues. Humility is never
alone, but rather, other virtues always accompany it.
For one who is truly humble is patient, judging himself worthily to suffer anything that happens, despising no one, judging no one, condemning no one. He
does not envy superiors; he lowers himself to inferiors, judging himself inferior to others than whom he
is higher. But the more humble and dejected a person
seems to himself, the more exalted and precious he
is before God, for whom the offerings of the humble
are always acceptable.

20. The rest of the virtues depend on this virtue
as on their steps.* Without this virtue the rest of the   **velut passibus suis*
virtues are either of little use or they soon fail. Hu-
mility endures all things, because patience accompanies humility, fortitude [accompanies] patience,
perseverance [accompanies] fortitude, which is the

completed work receiving a reward. Behold how the soul profits through humility and grows *from virtue to virtue** and presses toward the prize of eternal recompense.*

*see Ps 83:8
*see Phil 3:14

21. Therefore let us have humility in mind, chastity in body, going in and going out at the command of the supreme king, doing his precepts, always prepared and ready for obedience, so that through obedience we may be restored to him from whom we had been disfigured by disobedience. Let us ask Our Lady, the Virgin Mary, who is mother and worker of virtues, so that she might obtain humility, chastity, and effectiveness of obedience for us to the point that we are adorned with these virtues, leaning upon her beloved,* that is, upon Christ, who is the strength and reward of the saints. May we merit to reach that inestimable glory <where> Our Lady <is>, our queen, our *salvatrix*. May our Lord Jesus Christ deign to furnish this for us, Son of God and son of the Virgin, to whom be *honor and authority** with the Father and Holy Spirit through all ages forever. Amen.

*see Song 8:5
*see 1 Tim 6:16

Sermon 155

On the
Annunciation of Saint Mary

1. **H** *ail Mary, full of grace, the Lord is with you; blessed are you among women, and blessed is the fruit of your womb.** The sacred solemnity of this day ought to be taken up and venerated with the whole of devotion, all enthusiasm and reverence. For this annunciation is the beginning of our salvation. This is the first of all the Blessed Virgin's feast days in dignity and importance, rightly more excellent and more fruitful than a sacrament.

*Resp in Adv
(Hesbert 4:6156);
Luke 1:28, 42

2. Let us celebrate the conception of her who was going to conceive God's Son, because it has happened today. It is appropriate to celebrate the nativity of her from whom God's Son was going to be born, because it was announced by the angel today. It is religious to venerate the conception of her who was going to conceive God's Son, because it has happened today. Let us venerate her purification and the presentation of her son in the temple, because as it happens, they received their cause and origin from the sacrament of this holy annunciation. In the same way, if we attend other feast days of the Lord himself or of his saints, this holy solemnity is the beginning and origin of each one, if we consider it in the right way. For whatever was done today is divine and sacramental. Today the Blessed Virgin consented in order that she should be *full of grace.** *From that fullness,** honor and reverence have flowed to all the

*Luke 1:28

*see John 1:16

169

remaining feast days that the holy church celebrates. Today she conceived God and humankind, and would give birth with the integrity of her virginity unharmed.

*Col 1:26

3. This is *the mystery hidden from the ages,** promised by the prophets, hoped for by the patriarchs, rendered in the end, destined to be beneficial without end. Humans are ignorant of this mystery, wise people wonder, philosophers are astounded, angels venerate, stars speak,* *demons tremble,*† kings adore, Herod fears, children testify and proclaim by their death.‡ This mystery transcends nature, goes beyond codes of law, empties every custom, *surpasses all understanding,** however much it shatters precision, beats back every point of cleverness, permits no similar example; it demands from us only faith and reverence for God, rather than the investigation of human reason or assertion of arguments.

*see Luke 2:13-14;
see Matt 2:2, 9
†Jas 2:19; see
Matt 2:3, 11
‡see Matt 2:16
*see Phil 4:7;
see 2 Cor 10:5

4. A wonderful reality! A virgin becomes fruitful without seed, pregnant without a vector,* giving birth without intercourse, a mother without a father, conceiving a man without a man, bearing a son without detriment to her virginity. Wonderful reality, great reality, a new and unheard-of reality! This is that great thing about which Jeremiah says, *Behold, the Lord shall make a new thing upon the earth: a woman shall enclose a man.** This is that great thing about which Moses, when he saw the flaming bush not burning up, said, *I will go and see this great sight.** That great thing about which David says, *The stone which the builders rejected, this has become the cornerstone.** That wonderful and unheard-of enigma about which the prophet says, *Shall not Zion say, This person and that person was born in her?** A woman enclosed a new man, that is, she confined the whole of him within herself, that is, she conceived

*uectore

*Jer 31:22

*Exod 3:3

*Ps 117:22

*Ps 86:5

by herself, not by any husband's external activity or by means of seed.

5. *See the miracle*!* See the spectacular spectacle, the unprecedented prodigy and ineffable portent! A virgin gave birth, and God was born. Each one is remarkable, but each one is true. Each one seemingly supernatural, but relying on truth and joined by virtue. *Great and wonderful are your works, O Lord!** These are the works about which the prophet says, *Lord, I have heard <your> listening and was afraid. I have considered your works, and I became frightened.** See the dignity in the annunciation, newness in conceiving, integrity in giving birth. The virgin conceived God, Mary the Christ, the daughter the father, the latter the prior, the creature the Creator, the work the artist, the building the architect, the womb of the mother the Word of the Father, so that he might be one and the same son of humankind out of time and Son of God in eternity.

6. *O happy Mary and most worthy of every praise,* who first, nay rather who alone has erased the *handwriting** of perpetual slavery† that Adam had secured for the devil. And bearing the new human being, you have founded a new legal system, you have brought forth a new law. You have rendered a new liberty, having him in the womb who alone was found *free among the dead,** in whom alone is the true hope of liberty. So he himself says in the Gospel, *If the Son shall make you free, then you shall be truly free.** O sublime and pre-eminent feast of the bearer of God! *Today the church has been joined to the heavenly bridegroom,** while God's Son, in the bedchamber of the virgin womb, put our humanity into one part of his divinity, taking up from our [nature] so he might have a basis for compassion, retaining from his own so he might bestow the healing of consolation on us.

*Resp in Ann (Hesbert 4:7869)

*Rev 15:3

*Resp in Nat Dom (Hesbert 4:7274); see Hab 3:2

*chirographum; see Col 2:14 †see Resp in Ann (Hesbert 4:6725)

*Ps 87:6

*John 8:36

*Ant in Epi (Hesbert 3:3095)

7. Let us turn our attention to the mysteries by which the solemnity of this day has been sanctified, whose authority has consecrated the beginning of such great deeds. For just as in the first condition the work of the whole Trinity was expressed (where it says, *Let us make humankind to our image and likeness*),* similarly by one and indivisible work of the whole Trinity, the fall of our mortality was repaired and our condition restored. For *the Father has sent his Son into the flesh.** The Son descended into a woman, the Holy Spirit came upon the virgin, *and the power of the Most High* overshadowed her.†

8. Let us turn our attention to the dignity of the annunciation and the humility of obedience: one by an angel, the other in the Virgin. The former came down in divine power, the latter obeys in virgin sincerity. The angel announces lofty realities, the virgin responds in humble ways. *An angel was sent* to her,* a great messenger, the messenger *of the great king.** A messenger of a worthy matter, a worthy entrusting of the job from him who is sent and from him by whom he is sent; from him to whom he is sent, and from him for what he is sent. Who is sent? *The angel Gabriel*, which is interpreted as *God's strength*. From whom is he sent? *From God*. To whom is he sent? *To a* holy *virgin*,* modest, *chaste*.† After David in seed, but nearer to God in religion. Sent for what? For the salvation of the whole world, which the virgin who would give birth foretells.

9. Rightly therefore this feast is raised up for a singular celebration, which enriched the world with a singular benefit of divine compassion. For whatever of grace, whatever of sweetness and of love for her son we reserve in our hearts, this lady experienced wholly today in her praises, so that we love and praise her as much as we can and however we can.

*Gen 1:26

*see 1 John 4:14; see Gal 4:4; see 2 John 7 †see Luke 1:35

*Luke 1:26-27
*see Matt 5:35

*see Luke 1:26-27 †2 Cor 11:2

But what weakness lacks in possibility, may our devotion supply to a loving purpose. And just as we
need her constant influence, so may we venerate her
by constant deference, the lady of the universe, the
queen of heaven, who took away our servitude, restored our freedom, and furnished salvation and life
while she brought forth the Savior for us, our Lord
Jesus Christ, *who is God over all the blessed forever.
Amen.**

*Rom 9:5

Sermon 156

On the
Assumption of Saint Mary

1. **O**ur Lord does not want to let us have fastidiousness. Therefore he visits us sometimes through himself, sometimes through sacred Scripture, sometimes by our sermons in which we present something about that, sometimes by the example of good things that he has done for us through himself, and sometimes through those things that he has done through his own friends. These are our plates by which he feeds our souls, so that we neither suffer hunger, nor in eating do we endure any fastidiousness.

2. Just as among all the saints she is more distinguished, more blessed, and more sweet, and she now tastes his sweetness more intimately and pleasantly,* *see Ps 33:9; see 1 Pet 2:3 she who <is> now not only his creature, handmaid, friend, and daughter, but also his mother, so it is just that we take up her feast day with greater sweetness and pleasantness, and in her festivity we feed ourselves more abundantly with spiritual banquets. We ought to praise her always, to honor and recollect her sweetness with all devotion. And we ought to rejoice with her today even more, because her joy today was perfectly fulfilled.

3. She had great joy when the angel greeted her, when that remarkable union of God's Son and her flesh happened in her womb, so that he who was God's Son was also her son. She had great joy when she held such a son in her arms, when she kissed him,

when she ministered to him, when she heard his
words, when she saw his miracles. And because she
was greatly saddened in his passion, she had wonderful joy in his resurrection and even greater in his
ascension. But this joy that she received today surpassed all those joys.

4. There are two natures in our Lord Jesus Christ:
divine and human. These two natures are so perfect
in him that the divine nature was not diminished on
account of the human nature, nor was the human
annihilated on account of the divine. So he is both
equal to the Father and less than the Father—equal
on account of divinity, less on account of humanity.
It is a great good to recognize Lord Jesus according
to his humanity, to love him according to humanity,
to think about him and his nativity, <his> passion,
and his wounds as if in one's heart, to see his death
and resurrection. But those perceive a much greater
good who can say with the apostle, *And if we have
known Christ according to the flesh, now we know
him so no longer.** It is a great joy to see how he   *2 Cor 5:16
sucks the breasts, but it is <much> greater to see how
he feeds all things. It is a great delight to see him in
the arms of one girl, but much greater to see how he
contains all of heaven and earth.*   *see Wis 1:7

5. Up until this day the Blessed Virgin Mary knew
her son according to the flesh, because although after
her dearest son and Lord ascended into heaven she
had all her desire and love where he was, nevertheless
as long as she remained in this corruptible flesh,*   *see Phil 1:24;
those things that she had seen about him in the flesh   see Wis 9:15
could not slip from her memory. His deeds, his
words, always came to her mind. And above all, the
image of his beautiful face remained in her heart.
Today she crossed over from this world and ascended
to the heavenly kingdom.* Today she perfectly con-   *see Ant
                                                            Exal in Ass
                                                            (Hesbert 3:2762)

templates the glory, power, divinity of her son. Both
her joy and desire have been fulfilled, so that she can
truly say, *I found him whom my soul loves. I hold*
*him and will not let go.** Today the shadow of night
has withdrawn and the *light of light* has arisen for
her. In the night she did not cease from seeking, and
therefore since night has passed, she has found.

    6. *In my bed*, she says, *through the nights I sought*
him whom my soul <loves>; I sought him, and I
*found him not.** What is this bed? If it were corporeal, then it would not be <work> to search for a long
time. Perhaps this bed is that about which it is said
in another place, *Our bed is of flowers.** And what
was that bed if not her heart, where there were flowers of all the virtues? And indeed a bed, on account
of that wonderful rest and tranquility that she had in
her heart. For in that place there was no disturbance
of vain thoughts. In that place, there were no desires
of this world. There were no carnal passions and
wicked desires <in that place>. Where these things
are, there is no bed, because no one is able to have
tranquility who has these disturbances in his heart.

    7. Many people make a bed for themselves not
in the heart but in the flesh, because they do not have
any rest in their heart on account of a bad conscience,
but they lie down *in desires of the flesh,** and they
rest in the flesh as though in a bed. To such types the
apostle says, *Rise you who sleep, arise from the dead,*
*and Christ shall enlighten you.** But the blessed Mary
did not have rest in her heart, but in her mind, and
a good and holy conscience. There she was resting
from every care of the world, from the commotion
of vices, from every noise of vain thoughts, and still
she did not rest, because she was desiring and sighing, and with a groan and tears she sought the one
whom she loved. *In my bed through the nights I*

*Song 3:4

*Song 3:1

*Song 1:15

*see Eph 2:3

*Eph 5:14

*sought him whom my soul loves.** Let us see when   *Song 3:1
she began to seek.

8. Before the advent of the Lord she desired and
sought him. She sought so that she might come into
the land as he had promised, and that he might free
her with the rest from a miserable captivity. Nevertheless, she sought not in the city center, not on
market day, but in her bed, that is, in the secret bedchamber of her heart. This is that bed in which
Abishag the Sunamite warmed King David.

9. One reads in the Book of Kings that King
David had grown cold on account of extreme old
age. He was covered up with *clothes*, as Scripture
says, and *he was not warm. His servants said to him,
Let us seek for our lord an attractive girl to serve him
and sleep in his bosom and warm our lord the king.
So they found a virgin who was called Abishag, a
Sunamite, and she served the king and warmed him.
But the king did not know her.** King David signifies   *see 1 Kgs 1:1-4
our Lord Jesus Christ, who was born from his*   *David's
seed.* Spiritually he has a certain infancy and child-   *see John 7:42
hood, a certain youth and old age.   see Rom 1:3;
                                                           see 2 Tim 2:8
10. His infancy, as it were, was when he first
began to be born in the hearts of the holy fathers
who were before his coming. He was born in their
hearts in two ways, through knowledge and through
love. He was born in Abraham's heart when it was
said to him that such a one would be born of him in
whom all nations would be blessed, as we see fulfilled
only in our Lord Jesus Christ, who was from Abra-
ham's seed, in which all nations are blessed.*   *see Gen 22:18;
larly, in Isaac's heart he then began as if born when   Gen 26:4
his coming began to be known to him.* So also to   *Isaac
Jacob and the rest of the patriarchs. But thus far it
was his infancy, so to speak. Infancy is that age in
which a child can not yet speak. Now it was as if the

birth of Christ was known, but he was still not speaking, because the holy fathers Abraham, Isaac, and Jacob were not openly proclaiming his arrival to all. But although they did not speak about him openly, nevertheless they were keeping him warm, because *see 1 Kgs 1:1-4 they embraced him with ardent love.*

11. Afterward it was his childhood, as it were, when the law was given, when now his knowledge began to speak to all through various customs and sacrifices that were in the law. In these without a doubt Christ was speaking to all and making himself known to human beings as if <through> childish words, that is, through carnal observances and ceremonies.

12. Afterward he began to reveal his youth when he began to reveal more openly his strength, by which he had to conquer the devil, to plunder hell, to redeem the world, to arise from the dead, to condemn the wicked on the Day of Judgment, to crown saints. Of all of these our Lord himself has spoken through his prophets. These spiritual strengths, which the Lord Jesus Christ manifested, were signified by corporeal strengths and battles that David had made in his youth. One who can spiritually search out and discuss David's battles and victories would not find vain fables and simple narratives to be in sacred Scripture, but rather would see that all *sacramentis things are filled with great mysteries.* In these things, *see 1 Kgs 1:1 the more our David was warmed in his youth,* as it were, so many more were those who recognized, loved, and desired him.

13. Afterward Saint David began to grow cold, as it were. For *iniquity abounded, and the love of* *see Matt 24:12 many grew cold,* <so> that as the Lord's coming now approached, on account of the multitude of evils the *Ps 13:3 prophet says, They have all gone astray, etc.* Then

our *David was covered with clothes*, but *he was not warm.** Perhaps his clothes ought to have been high *see 1 Kgs 1:1
priests, priests, and all the Jews generally, whom our
Lord had spiritually joined to himself as though
clothes. He was in a way covered with these clothes
before his coming. For the Jews often visited the
temple; the high priests and priests made sacrifices
and celebrated festivals, Sabbaths, and new moons.* *see Isa 1:13
But all these were not keeping our Lord warm, because in their hearts there was not the warmth of
true love. Of course, many of them were doing these
things not through love but through hypocrisy, as
the Lord himself clearly proved.* Therefore it was *see Matt 15:7-9
necessary to provide a girl who was a virgin in whose
embrace that true David would rest, in whose bosom
he would sleep, who would warm him who was already growing cold and aged in his bed.* *see 1 Kgs 1:2

14. Our David provided this virgin for himself,
her who was more pure than all virgins, more holy
than all women, more valiant than all men, more fair
than the Sun, more fervent than fire. He knew her,
prepared her to be so excellent for himself, and
nevertheless willed to seek her through his servants.
Solomon, who asked, *who shall find a valiant
woman*,* sought her. Isaiah sought and found her, *Prov 31:10
and said, *Behold a virgin shall conceive*, etc.* Jere- *Isa 7:14
miah sought her and was astonished, saying, *The Lord
shall create a new thing upon the earth: a woman
shall envelop a man.** Finally, the angel Gabriel *Jer 31:22
sought her, found, knew, greeted, and invited her to
the embrace of the true David.* *see Luke 1:26-38

15. She alone was found to be the one in whose
bosom the true David might more intimately rest,
she who warmed him more pleasantly with her embrace, with whom he might sleep more quietly in
bed:* Our Lady Saint Mary, of course, in whose most *see 1 Kgs 1:2

sacred breast the flame of love had not grown tepid. As she loved more than all, so she desired more than all; therefore she searched more carefully. But the one whom her flesh then loved, her soul now and henceforth loves. So she says, *On my bed I sought him whom my soul loves.*

16. She does not say, "Whom my soul *used to* love," but *whom* it *loves.** For then her flesh used to love in a certain way. I mean, although the strength of divine love wholly possessed her most holy soul, so that she could rightly be called the Sunamite (Sunamite is interpreted as *scarlet;** scarlet is also the color of fire), preferring the flame of love, making red the fire of divine love—that is, although *her soul* therefore *wholly* loved *God,** nevertheless, because thus far she was solicitous about her own and the whole world's salvation, which he himself still had to work out through his flesh, she, desiring his humanity, still pondered him according to the flesh and sought him according to the flesh, and her soul loved him according to the flesh.

17. Indeed, she sought him whom her soul loved, but in a way according to the flesh, not wholly according to the spirit. In her first search, without doubt it was night, because the night of faithlessness had then occupied the whole world. *I have searched,* she says, *and I have not found.** What shall we say? Does she never find? Can it be that she, our Sunamite, has not embraced the true David? Not only in the bed of her heart, but also in the bed of her flesh, she sought and found him. Well then, what is this? Think, because these words do not fit according to that time when she understood God's Son according to the flesh, but according to the present time, when she ascended into heaven. For that reason, telling about the past, as it were, she says, *In my bed I sought him whom my soul loves.**

*Song 3:1

*Jerome, Ep 52.3
(CSEL 54:419)

*see Deut 6:5;
see Mark 12:30

*Song 3:1

*Song 3:1

18. Notice how astutely she puts the search in past time, *In my bed*, she says, *I sought*, but she puts love itself in the present time. And if she were to say, Then *I* only *sought him whom my soul loves*, and added, *I sought and have not found*,* how does she who   *Song 3:1 conceived him in her womb not find him, she who conceived and bore him with her chaste vital organs, who fed him with her breasts, kept him warm with her embraces? So beautifully Scripture says about Abishag the Sunamite, *The king did not know her.**   *1 Kgs 1:4

19. In no way do we read Abishag except as a virgin. For Adonias, brother of Solomon, who wished to defile* her in a brash stratagem, received a sen-   *incestare tence of death.* In the end, Abishag was a virgin   *see 1 Kgs 2:24-25 before the king's embrace, a virgin in the king's embrace, a virgin after the king's embrace. Behold how clearly the virginity of the most Blessed Virgin Mary is prefigured in this virgin, as even before the king's conception (in which God's Son was made a sharer in humanity), the seal of virginity was neither lost in conception nor unsealed in giving birth, and was still kept intact after the birth.

20. Let us hear what the most wise <Solomon> understood about the excellence of Abishag the Sunamite up to this point. When Bathsheba asked for Abishag the Sunamite to be given to Adonias, Solomon answered, *Why do you ask Abishag for Adonias? Ask for my kingdom for him also!** O, virgin of   *1 Kgs 2:22 wonderful excellence: she who merits his embrace also merits his kingdom! Why? Because if the king's embrace is not suited to this our Sunamite, then for whom was her most chaste womb preserved? How therefore did our Abishag not find the one whom she sought in the bed <of her heart> and received in the bed of her flesh?

21. Consider and speculate how much she understood about her very sweet son, to how much glory

she attained, and how perfectly love of divinity filled
her, so that before this time, she says that she has not
found him whom we all know she gave birth to from
her own womb. We have said these things about her
first search. She sought him again after his passion,
after his death. This search was full of pain, full of
anxiety. Then what Saint Simeon had foreseen about
her was fulfilled: *And a sword shall pierce your own*

*Luke 2:35   *soul.** A sword of pain, a sword of sadness, a sword
of compassion.

22. Then how great was the river of tears that
burst forth from her pure eyes when she saw her son
hanging on the cross, drinking gall, mocked by the
wicked and faithless! With how much pain she heard,

*John 19:26   *Woman, behold your son,** so that she might take a
disciple in place of her son, a servant in place of her

*see Ps 104:18;   Lord! So then *a sword* of pain *pierced her soul,**
see Luke 2:35   *reaching* mostly *to the division of her soul* and body.†
†Heb 4:12   Then her soul sought with affection the one whom
she loved, whom she sought with desire,* so she did

*see Song 3:1   not flee what the apostle lamented: *The flesh lusts*
*Gal 5:17   *against the spirit, and the spirit against the flesh.** In
fact I do not doubt that out of carnal affection she
then wished to free her son from that death, to silence
the derision of the Jews, or even, if she could, to
undergo death itself. Then also it was night, because

see John 13:30   her extreme adversity darkened her joy. She sought
then, but she did not find, because her carnal will
was not satisfied, that by which she wished that her
son would not suffer, that her eternal salvation would
not be fulfilled through her son's death.

23. Third, she began to seek him after his ascension. She sought, as I believe, in two ways. For those
things that she had seen in him physically were still
living in her memory; she pondered his delightful
way of life, pleasant speech, pleasing appearance,

and sweetest feeling of compassion. And because she still lived in her body, she often sought his physical presence. But sometimes she brought herself to more sublime realities, and drawing that heavenly mode of being to mind, she was accustomed to disdain earthly things in her rational soul, to sigh with all her feeling for heavenly things, and, lingering <on earth> *only in her body,** to abide there in her heart where she pondered that her son reigned over all things. Then indeed that absence of her son was night for her, and that cloister of her body that detained her as if by a chain, so that she could not wholly retain her son's embraces.

*see Resp Iste in Com conf (Hesbert 4:7009)

24. Therefore during these nights, <first> before his coming, then in his passion, and afterward when his ascension was completed, she sought him *whom her soul loves. I searched,* she says, *and I have not found.** And she added, *I will rise and go about the city, through the streets and the broad ways. I will seek him whom my soul loves.** Here I understand *the city* to be *the heavenly Jerusalem,** whose *broad ways are laid with pure gold, through* whose *streets* is sung, *Alleluia.** But what is it that she says: *I will rise and go about the city?*† Obviously on this day, *whether in the body or out of the body, I do not know, God knows,*‡ she ascended heaven and went about all that heavenly city with the vivacity of her mind. Today she entered that heavenly court, she saw the white robes of the virgins,* the red crowns of the martyrs, and the thrones of the apostles,† and among all these she found that her son reigned. She found him today so perfectly, so happily, that she admitted that previously she had not rightly found him. In fact, ascending beyond all heights, she arrived at such great knowledge of divinity that then for the first time she might boast that she had found him.

*Song 3:1

*Song 3:2
*see Heb 12:22

*see Resp "Plateae" (Hesbert 4:7390); see Tob 13:22; see Rev 21:21
†Song 3:2
‡2 Cor 12:3

*see Rev 6:11; Rev 7:9
†see Luke 22:30

25. So she says, *The watchmen who guard the city found me.** Watchmen are angels who guard the city of God, the holy church, of course, and protect it from the devil's invasions and treachery. It is certain that the whole army of angels has come to meet the most blessed Mary today. They found her in the world and brought her from the world. But although she had seen the luminance of angels and their glory, still this did not suffice for her, but she desired more greatly to see only him whom she loved above all. Therefore she says, *Have you not seen him whom my soul loves?**

26. And she added, *When I had passed by them a little, I found him whom my soul loves.** O blessed soul, who has passed by not only patriarchs, apostles, martyrs, confessors, and virgins, but even angels, thrones, and dominions, cherubim and seraphim, and *all the hosts of heaven,** and thus arrived at her most sweet son. She holds him and does not let him go.** She holds with the embraces of perfect charity, and never could she let him go, because she could never love less.

27. Beloved brothers, let us raise up our hearts to her, our lady, our advocate. Let us have great hope in her, because just as she is (after the humanity of her son) more excellent than every creature, so she is more merciful and kind than every creature. Therefore let us confidently beg her, who can help us by her merit and is willing through her mercy. On our behalf, may she impose on her son,* so that just as he deigned to be born of her, through her may he deign to have mercy on us, who with the Father and Holy Spirit, etc.

*Song 3:3

*Song 3:3

*Song 3:4

*see 2 Kgs 21:3
*see Song 3:4

*see Rom 8:34

Sermon 157

On the
Assumption of Saint Mary

1. <*I saw my fair one like a dove ascending above streams of water.>*</i> I know, dearest ones, how sweet this feast is to us and how well regarded, how much joy it confers, how much it raises our hope to heavenly realities. And no wonder. In fact, today our Lord Jesus Christ rescued his sweetest mother from the miseries of this life and raised her up to heavenly things and established her on a royal throne. It provides us with great cause for exultation. Our queen, our lady, our mother, our *bone and our flesh** is raised on high *above the chorus of angels,*† intending to pray for us. She is conveyed to the right hand of her son, intending to protect us. *If therefore she is for us, then who is against us?*‡

2. But perhaps you are astonished that we said she was taken up from the miseries of this life. What, for instance? Did she not exist in the miseries of this life? As far as I can estimate, no one sensed the miseries of this life more than she, no one wept longer, no one so suffered the burdensome dwelling of this human body. In fact, no one so loved that spouse who is *beautiful in appearance above the children of human beings,** no one so desired him. Therefore no one so longed for his presence, no one so wept at his absence. Who can comprehend how much this lady loved her son, how much she desired him? Therefore as long as she was in this life, on account of exceedingly great

*Resp in Ass
(Hesbert 4:7878)

*see Gen 29:14;
37:27
†see Ant and
Resp "Exaltata"
in Ass (Hesbert
3:2762–63;
4:6684)
‡see Rom 8:31

*Ps 44:3

185

desire for him, she was always in misery with tears
and moans, always in prayers and sighs, so that she
could speedily come to him for whom she longed.

3. Therefore a certain saint, who was able to see
her assumption with spiritual eyes, very properly
expressed a little of her way of life and assumption
when he said, *I saw my fair one like a dove ascending*
above streams of water. She was as beautiful as a
dove over streams of water. She was beautiful on
account of merit, a dove on account of moaning, over
streams of water on account of drinking from spiritual sweetness. *I saw my fair one.* She was fair who
did not have *spot or wrinkle or any such thing.*† She
was fair, because the Spirit had cleansed her *from all*
defilement of the flesh and spirit. Let us first consider in what matters there is beauty of the body, and
then let us see the beauty of the soul.

4. A person is beautiful according to the body,
which has whole members without any fault, and
then well colored, and finally well adorned. A fault
of the body is when out of a defect some member is
lacking to it that it should naturally have, or it has
some member that it ought not to have, as when
some people have six fingers on one hand, or when
a body has all the members that it should have and
no more, but still the members themselves are somehow corrupted and fit on the body otherwise than
they naturally should. If it has all the members that
it should have and no more, and they do not fit differently on the body than they should fit, and if there
is nevertheless some swelling, then it is not thought
to be beautiful. If people have these in good order
and are weak, even if nothing in the body is superfluous or corrupt or swollen, on account of weakness
they will not be able to do things as they should. If
they were to have all the things said above, and there

*Resp in Ass
(Hesbert 4:7878)

*Resp in Ass
(Hesbert 4:7878)
†Eph 5:27

*2 Cor 7:1

was whiteness where there ought to be, and redness where it was appropriate, if they go about naked and unadorned, then all that beauty will be either hidden and unable to be known, or it will displease. Therefore it is necessary to employ certain exterior adornments to be thought beautiful.

5. Now after this exterior beauty, let us consider what is within. A defect of the soul is ignorance of good. If <any>, in fact, do not know something that they need to know, then in what they do not know their soul is defective and lacks some member, as it were, that it is necessary for them to have. But for those who know whatever is necessary to know in this life, no member of their soul is lacking to them. But just as it is a defect of soul not to know what one should know, so it is an excess of soul to know what one should not. It is not for us to know incantations or magic arts or books of mathematicians or deceits and deceptions <of soothsayers> or self-indulgent songs of the pagans.* Those who have this wretched knowledge have certain superfluous members in the soul, as it were.

*see Lev 19:31; Lev 20:6; see Deut 18:10-11

6. There are those who have necessary knowledge, and they do not have a surplus. But they corrupt what proper knowledge they have, because through it they seek not spiritual goods, but temporal benefits. In addition, pride in the members of our soul is a swelling of which we must beware. For one who has all the members that one ought to have will in no way be beautiful if those members are puffed up. Thus there is no advantage in having knowledge or wisdom or a tenacious memory or an attentive intellect unless all these are without the swelling of pride. May we beware of weakness to the end. For what profit is there in knowing what ought to be done, and having members that are appropriate for

doing the task if one is hindered by some infirmity, so that one does not do what must be done? The whole of a soul's weakness, the whole of her health, is in love. If a soul loves what she should love and as much as she should, then the soul is healthy. A soul who does not love what she should love, or [loves it] less than she should, is weak.

7. But if any have whole and healthy members, let them see that they have color. Colors of the soul are interior virtues: chastity, tranquility, spiritual joy, and especially humility. Therefore whoever wash their soul in confession and wipe away dirt and stains of sin ought immediately to add the beautiful color of virtues. And because it is sometimes necessary for a virtue to be shown outwardly, it is necessary to have adornment. External behaviors are this adornment, in which there should be a certain beauty and a certain measure. Exterior adornment is maturity, gravitas, eyes without roaming, a tongue without loquaciousness, hands without pushiness. There is also exterior adornment in certain bodily obser-

*see 2 Cor 6:5

vances: *in fasting, in labors, in keeping vigil,** and other practices of this nature, with which our soul should be equipped. In this adornment measure must be preserved.

8. But now let us return to our most blessed lady and attentively consider her interior beauty, so that

*Resp in Ass
(Hesbert 4:7878)

we can individually say, *I saw my fair one.** Without doubt the fair one was her sweet soul, which had no vice from a defect, nor from excess, nor from corruption or disease. What wisdom or knowledge could be lacking in her soul in whom was abiding *corpore-*

*see Col 2:9
*Col 2:3

*ally** the one *in whom are hidden all the treasures of wisdom and knowledge?** Within her was Wisdom herself, who filled (may I say) all her internal organs with the light of spiritual intelligence, and poured

into that most hallowed heart the splendor of secret heavenly realities, and inebriated her with that wine of divine knowledge, so that even in this life she could feel that ineffable exultation that was promised to God's faithful. Therefore the prophet says, *They shall be inebriated with the abundance of your house,* etc.* Full of wisdom, she knew when she ought to speak, when to keep silent, what to say and what to leave unmentioned, to whom to speak, for whom to keep quiet.

*Ps 35:9

9. Let us come to the Gospel. The angel greeted her, the Holy Spirit filled her, the Son of God descended into her womb.* Did she, on account of the exceeding joy that she had within, run in the broad street so that she might promote herself, so that she might show her own joy in that place? She was utterly silent there. Therefore to whom did she tell her joy? Not to scribes and Pharisees, not to anyone who could thereupon doubt and accuse her of a lie or a boast. But she came to her relative Saint Elizabeth *and greeted* her, and at once *the infant leaped in her* *womb.** O how great the sweetness! Mothers greet each other, and infants in the womb leap for joy. If they could have embraced each other, what would they have done? Then Elizabeth says, *Blessed are you among women,* etc.* Then was the *time for speaking*† and showing her joy, the perfection of God's grace in her. Therefore *she says, My soul magnifies,* etc.* Again you read in the Gospel about her discreet silence: *But Mary <kept all these words, pondering them in her heart>,* etc.*

*see Luke 1:28-38

*Elizabeth's
*Luke 1:40, 41;
see 1:36

*Luke 1:42;
see 1:28
†see Eccl 3:7

*Luke 1:46

*Luke 2:19

10. Behold how she had all the members of her soul, that is, memory, intelligence, and knowledge, without defect and vice of failure. But because she cared to know nothing frivolous, nothing superfluous or corrupt, the members of her soul retained enough

room for their customary tasting of the consolation
of divine sweetness. In fact, in her wisdom and
knowledge, she was not held by desire of the world
or vanity of the age. But can it be that she was puffed
up through pride? Far be it! That humble voice ex-
cuses her from every swelling: *Behold the handmaid*
*of the Lord.** And that other one: *He has regarded*
*the humility of his handmaid.**

*Luke 1:38
*Luke 1:48

11. Now let us see how steadfast was her holy
soul in true love. She was proved to be true, because
it is written in the Song of Songs, *Love is strong as*
*death.** This is the sword of charity that penetrated
her interior and divided soul from flesh,* so that her
holy soul could <desire> nothing carnal. Charity occupied her wholly and wounded her with a sting of
inmost feeling, and was the death of every bodily
desire and every vanity of the world and glory of the
age. So she says, *I am wounded with love.** O sweet
wound, more pleasant than all health! O pleasant
death, and sweeter than all life! O delightful languor,
stronger than all virtue! *Daughters of Jerusalem*, she
says, *tell my beloved that I languish with love.**

*Song 8:6
*see Luke 2:35;
see Heb 4:12

*Song 2:5; 5:8
(LXX)

*Ant Anima in Ass
(Hesbert 3:1418);
see Song 5:8
*Resp in Ass
(Hesbert 4:7878)

12. Let us consider the beauty of this wonderful
soul with the one who says, *I saw my fair one*, etc.*
Consider the whiteness of her virginity and the redness of her charity. Her *cheeks are like the turtle-*
dove's. Her *neck like a necklace.** So her *cheeks are*
like a piece of a pomegranate. And her *lips are like*
*a scarlet ribbon.** If we knew all these things and
wished to explain how they come together in her
beauty, we would say, *I saw my fair one*, etc.* But
was that soul without exterior adornment? By no
means! No soul was ever so adorned, except the soul
of Christ. Her mien was chaste, her gait mature, her
speech serious. Her expression and likeness were
pleasant, so she merited to hear from her beloved,

*Song 1:9

*Song 4:3

*Resp in Ass
(Hesbert 4:7878)

You are entirely beautiful, my love, and there is no stain on you. *

13. Fair as a dove who has no gall.† This lady has no bitterness, no anger, no envy, but so sweet, so pleasant, so simple [is she] that she is even accustomed to care for sinners in hope that they may be converted to repentance. This is a sign of her wonderful benevolence. *This is the fair one among the daughters of Jerusalem,* without any bitterness, without envy and rancor. She turns *in her beds and in her gardens,* * where there is nothing hard, nothing harsh, nothing bitter, but only kisses and flowers and sweet odors and spiritual delights.

14. The dove does not sing but moans. It is a moan of pain and a moan of love. Raise your eyes to Jesus' cross, how she stands there next to his cross,* how she moans, how she sighs, how she weeps. The dove moans for pain, moans for anxiety. Although *she gave birth without pain,* * with pain she mourned the one to whom she gave birth. But when did she moan out of love? Certainly after the glory of the ascension. So she began to moan for love because she began to ascend. In fact, everywhere her son was, there was the sweetness of her life, pleasantness of her mind, refreshment of her spirit—there her heart remained. Therefore as long as she was on earth, she could not ascend, but after she ascended into heaven, she began to ascend. She ascended in heart, she ascended in love, she ascended in desire. But today she first came to that place where she ascended. Right up until this day, tears daily, moans daily, sighs daily. In all of these it says, *I saw my fair one like a dove ascending above streams of water.* *

15. Doves are accustomed to sit above streams of water in moaning and meditation, as it were. There is a certain refreshment for the one who loves

*Song 4:7;
Ant Tota in Ass
(Hesbert 3:5162)
†see Resp in Ass
(Hesbert 4:7878)

*Ant and Resp
in Com virg
(Hesbert 3:3416;
4:6994)

*see John 19:25

*see Ant and
Resp "Nesciens"
in Nat Dom
(Hesbert 3:3877;
4:7212)

*Resp in Ass
(Hesbert 4:7878)

to sit above streams of water, as if to meditate with moaning, and to desire because she loves. A private place, suitable for moans and tears, is next to streams of water. Therefore our dove sweetly passes time with a moan and desire, sitting there and diverting herself. There is the water of wisdom, which is found in holy Scriptures.* In that place is only refreshment and diversion of those who love and who moan. In that place are various streams of holy thoughts. With these the dove alleviated her pain. With these she refreshed her feeling. With these she spurred her desire to ascend.

*Sir 15:3

16. For who is able to doubt that often when she read the prophets in which Christ's humility, passion, resurrection, and ascension were foretold she was taken up into a certain departure of mind, so that she nearly became wholly outside her flesh, and her soul was taken up into heaven in the marvelous glory and sweetness of her son? But today this was fulfilled perfectly. Certainly Jesus, her son, with great festivity and joy, today comes to meet her. All pain ceased from this hour, all sadness was put to rest, all sorrow fell silent. Then tears went dry, and her beauty was made complete at <the hour> in which she ascended; the whole army of heaven, with her son, came to meet her.

*see Song 4:11

17. *The odor of* her *garments** had ascended before her; it so delighted all the holy society of angels that they desired the presence of her whose fragrance they had sensed. She had been anointed with all precious ointments, with every pleasantness of heavenly aromatic spices, every grace of spiritual pigment. Therefore *priceless fragrance was strong in her garments.** Her garments were her holy works, the adornment and clothing of her soul. It is written concerning these garments, *Blessed is one who protects his garments, lest he walk naked.**

*Resp in Ass
(Hesbert 4:7878)

*Rev 16:15

18. We work, and many work and do good works, but even if scented, nevertheless they are not fully scented. For a certain stench usually mixes in with our works, such as vainglory, love of pleasing other people, and things of this nature, which are like a certain stench in our garments. The most blessed Mary had no such works. They were filled with fragrance and pleasantness. The most precious myrrh of humility emitted its scent in them, the oil of an abundant piety, nard of a wholly intact virginity, aromatic balm of the sweetest charity. All without comparison, all without number, all without estimation. Therefore *priceless fragrance was strong in her garments.**

19. *And, like a spring day, flowers encircled her.†* A just comparison. In spring, all things that were as though dead in the winter begin to come to life. Consider more diligently what the world was like before this virgin. All things were dead, all cold, nothing green, nothing pleasant, generally nothing beautiful in it. In her, the world began to turn green, to blossom, and to produce fruit, so that rightly it is said *a spring day* that *flowers of roses, and lilies of the valley, encircled.** She is the rose of roses and the lily of lilies. A rose has the color of fire and signifies the fiery heat of charity. A lily expresses whiteness and the beauty of virginity. Although these virtues are mentioned at the same time, nevertheless one can exist without the other. In fact, charity can be without virginity, and virginity without charity. Where there is charity, there is also humility, patience, faith, hope, and all other virtues. Virginity alone can be absent. But just as she is the virgin of virgins, so too the rose of roses.

20. So rightly *flowers of roses, and lilies of the valley, encircled her.** All lovers of Christ are like flowers of roses, all holy virgins like lilies of the valley. All came to meet her today and encircled her and

*Resp in Ass
(Hesbert 4:7878)
†Resp in Ass
(Hesbert 4:7878)

*Resp in Ass
(Hesbert 4:7878);
see Sir 50:8;
see Song 2:1

*Resp in Ass
(Hesbert 4:7878);
see Sir 50:8;
see Song 2:1

drew her into that blessed rest to which today she ascended. Note that it does not say simply *lilies*, but *lilies of the valley*. For virginity is then a virtue if it is in the valley of humility, not on the mountain of pride. How great was the exultation in that heavenly court, what jubilation! Perhaps Jesus himself on this day increased the joy of his whole court (if it could still be increased) by conferring more sweetness on them and bestowing himself more copiously.

21. Therefore let us also, brothers, be among flowers of roses and lilies of the valley. Those who have the lily of virginity, let them have it in a valley, not on a mountain, in humility, not in vanity. But we who cannot have the lily of virginity, let us have what is necessary, the lily of chastity with roses of charity, and so let us encircle her who is the lily of lilies and rose of roses. Let us encircle her, and especially today. Let us encircle her so that she may be in our midst. That is, in our midst as though in common.

22. May she be our common joy, our common glory, our common hope, our common consolation, our common refuge, our common reconciliation. If we are saddened, let us flee to her so that <she may cheer us>. <If we are brought down, then let us flee to her so that she> may glorify <us>. If we despair, let us flee to her so that she may lift us up. If we are troubled, let us flee to her so that she may console us. If we suffer persecutions, let us flee to her so that she may protect us. If we sin, let us flee to her so that she may reconcile us to her son. May she be a guardian for us in this life, a protection for us in death. Now indeed may she guard us from sin, then present us to her son, who with the Father, etc.

Sermon 158

On the Nativity of Saint Mary

1. <*C*ross over to me, all you who desire me, and be filled by my generations. For my spirit is sweet above honey, and my inheritance above honey and the honeycomb.>* The   *Sir 24:26-27
apostle speaks about our Lord and says that <he is> the Power of God and the Wisdom of God.* He   *see 1 Cor 1:24
speaks to us in the Gospel: *Come to me, all you who labor and are burdened, and I will refresh you.* He   *Matt 11:28
who called us by himself calls also through his prophet: *Cross over to me*, etc.* It seems that he   *Sir 24:26
stands as though in some high place, so that he may see us as if far from himself, and he says, *Cross over farther and come to me.**   *Sir 24:26;
Matt 11:28

2. I do not know what there is between us and him that requires us to cross over. There seem to be three things between us and him that require us to cross over: one sea, one wall, one cloud. The sea is the danger of this world, the wall the habit of sinning, the cloud ignorance of good and evil. These three are between us and God's Wisdom, the Lord Jesus Christ.* We are required to cross over these so   *see 1 Cor 1:24
that we may come to him. One who wishes to cross the sea has to have a ship. One who might wish to penetrate a wall has to have an iron tool. A certain darkness is in the cloud, as it were, and therefore light is necessary.

3. All human beings are in the aforementioned sea for as long as they live. But some are drowned in it; others cross over. Those who have no ship, or who

jump ship, are killed. But not all who have a ship have an equally good ship. Ships without which no one is able to cross over ought to be made from one wood. This wood is the cross of Christ. In the faith of Christ's cross there are various ships, and not all are of one value, nor of one strength, nor of the same security. All lives and orders that are established in the holy church are like ships in the faith of the cross. Through each and every order, one who keeps himself well is able to cross over the sea, that is, the danger of the world. But, as was said, not all \<are\> of the same security.

4. Marital life is like a ship that is owned by those who have betrothed wives and have riches of the world. But it is not a strong ship; in it are many holes, so to speak, by which water is able to enter and sink it. Occupations of this world are like holes: care of the home, concupiscence that a person suffers even when he lives in chastity with his spouse. Nevertheless the one who keeps himself in this ship and does not jump out through adultery and fornication or other criminal sins and bails out all the water—that is, the sins that seep in through occupations of the world—drains it by alms and prayers, although with much danger, [and] is able to cross that sea concerning which we speak, and to come to him who says, *Cross over to me*, etc.*

*Sir 24:26

5. But one who has a spouse and slips into adultery and fornication is not able to come to the port of salvation, because he leaves the ship; he will be killed unless he regains his ship, or another better one, through repentance. But even if he does not fall by these damnable deeds, if nevertheless he is lazy about bailing out small drops through alms and good works, he will not be able to come to him who says, *Cross over to me*, etc.* In fact, that one will drive

*Sir 24:26

him away from himself who says, *Depart from me,
you cursed*, etc.* Why? Not because he engaged in   *Matt 25:41
adultery and fornication, but because *I was hungry
and you did not give me to eat*, etc.* Behold how   *Matt 25:42
great is the danger even for those who live chastely
in the world with their wives.

6. A certain other ship is stronger than that one,
that is, renunciation of the world, of course. One
who leaves the secular world behind and delivers
himself to any holy congregation enters the ship. But
just as there are ships of the same type, and one is
better than another, so there are many orders in
which a person can leave the world behind, and they
are not of the same perfection. But I will come to you
who have chosen a good and strong ship. In order
to keep yourself in it, beware of pirates, beware of
rocks, beware of Sirens, beware of storms. Temptations are storms, demons are pirates, scandals are
rocks, delights of this world are Sirens.

7. Certain animals in the sea that sing very beautifully are called Sirens, so that people who sail in the
sea, hearing that beautiful song, forget themselves
and without knowing hasten to death. Such are the
delights of the world. There seems to be in them a
certain wonderful beauty and pleasantness. When
people pay attention to this, they are enticed by this,
forget themselves, and leave their ship for the sake
of such enjoyment of delights, and so they endanger
their soul.* Therefore keep yourselves in the ship.   *see Prov 7:23

8. If temptations urge in this ship, they do not
force you out. If some scandals occur as rocks, do
not meet them, and do not jump ship! If pirates
come, that is, demons and vices fight against you, do
not jump ship towards them. Stay in the ship, and
you will be able to fight securely and win. If you hear
some blandishments of the world through some

thoughts or adulation of human beings, stop up your
ears,* stay in the ship, and you will come to him who
declares, *Cross over to me.**

*see Isa 33:15
*Sir 24:26

9. A wall is between us and him. This wall is bad
habit. It is a hard wall. We all know this; we have all
experienced it. We know how difficult it is to break
this wall. We need good and sharp tools. If anyone
was in the habit of wantonness, then he made a hard
wall between himself and God. But let him start to
break that wall. Let him take up abstinence from
food and drink, like sharpened steel, and let him
break that wall. Similarly one who was accustomed
to get angry and to quarrel made a wall between
himself and God. Let him take up silence, good and
sharp steel, <and> let him destroy that wall.

10. One who was accustomed to being restless
and idle out of habit, let him love the work and
practices of the Order, and let him destroy that wall.
One who was accustomed to being proud and envious built a strong wall between himself and God. Let
him begin to be humble and kind to his brothers, and
pleasant, and thus let him destroy that wall. One who
was accustomed to being greedy and desirous and to
steal another's property made a wall between himself
and God. Let him love only poverty, and whatever
he can carry off for himself, let him willingly bestow
it on others, and thus let him destroy this wall.

11. And we, brothers, if we arrive negligent and
lazy out of habit, if for the sake of some small cause
we get in the habit of staying away from Matins, and
we avoid the work of vigils, if for some small matters
we get angry, disparage, murmur, if we give ourselves
to levity and buffoonery and laughter, then this habit
is like a certain wall between us and God. But let us
cross over all these, so we can come to him who says,
*Cross over to me.**

*Sir 24:26

12. But up to this point a cloud hinders us, that is, ignorance. *For, as the apostle says, we know not what we should pray for as we ought.** We are often mistaken, and we know not what might be more expedient for us. Therefore it is necessary for us to have a lamp and oil. Let us aspire with the prophet: *Your word is a lamp for my feet.** When we are in some doubt, let us run back to the word of God, to the Gospel, to our Order, which was established according to the Gospel, and let us follow this lamp, so that we may come to him who says, *Cross over to me, <all you who desire me>.**

*Rom 8:26

*Ps 118:105

*Sir 24:26

13. See whom he calls to himself. Certainly those who desire him. They alone who desire Christ cross over to Christ. *And be filled by my generations.** Christ <is> the Power of God and the Wisdom of God.* The *generations* of Christ are the *generations* of Wisdom. The gospel today teaches us the *generations* of Wisdom. For thus it says, *The book of the generation of Jesus Christ. . . . From Abraham to David are fourteen generations.** Fill yourselves, brothers, with these *generations*, not carnally, but spiritually. Let us have in ourselves Abraham, Isaac, and Jacob, and the others from whom Wisdom, that is, Christ, was born.

*Sir 24:26

*see 1 Cor 1:24

*Matt 1:1, 17

14. Abraham signifies faith. This is the foremost generation of Christ. *Without faith*, in fact, *it is impossible to please God.** Faith is the foundation and foremost of all virtues, of all good things. Therefore, before all things it is necessary that we be firm in faith, as Abraham was. About him Scripture says, *Abraham believed God, and it was reputed to him unto justice.** Isaac is interpreted as *laughter†* and signifies the one about whom the Lord says in the Gospel, *Blessed are you who weep now, for you shall laugh.** This laugh does not signify buffoonery and

*Heb 11:6

*Gen 15:6;
Rom 4:3
†Jerome, Int nom
7 (CCSL 72:67)
*Luke 6:21;
see Luke 6:25

jokes, but a certain ineffable joy that we shall have with God. From this joy we ought to have some share in this life. Obviously we ought to rejoice in that hope that we should have in God and in those promises that he promised to us.

15. But someone cannot have this hope unless he sustains some labors for sake of Christ, because we can hope for as much reward from our Lord as we suffer for his sake. According to the apostle, *Every person shall receive his own reward according to his own labor.** Therefore after these generations we ought to have a third generation, that is, Jacob. Jacob signifies the work of patience, on account of that great labor that he sustained with Laban, just as he himself said to him: *Day and night was I parched with heat and with frost, and thus I have served you for twenty years.** It will take too long if we recount all those fathers about whom the Gospel speaks today. But in these three we can understand about the others, because all signify some mystery.

16. *Cross over to me, all you who desire me, and be filled by my generations.** Wisdom wants us to be filled by her generations, that is, her holy virtues. She does not wish it to suffice for us to have some small part of those virtues, but that we be filled with them. She wills that we be full of days. Fullness of days is death. And who can die perfectly to the world and to all vice, if not the one who was *full of days?** Vices are darkness, virtues are light, virtue is a day. Therefore one who is full of days is full of virtues. He can die, or rather *has died*, to all vice and *lives for God.** Be filled therefore, brothers, with Christ's generations,* so that you can experience what follows: *For my spirit is sweet above honey, and my inheritance above honey and the honeycomb.**

*1 Cor 3:8

*Gen 31:40-41

*Sir 24:26

*see Gen 25:8; 35:29; see 1 Chr 23:1

*see Rom 6:10

*see Sir 24:26

*Sir 24:27

17. None of the corporeal realities is sweeter than honey. So none of all the spiritual realities is sweeter than charity and love of God. The Holy Spirit especially is called love. Therefore whoever fills oneself with Christ's generations,* that is, with holy virtues, shall taste in this life the sweetness of the Holy Spirit, that is, the sweetness of God's love, and after this life the sweetness of inheritance *that* he himself *promised to those who love him*.* That is the inheritance about which the prophet says, *The Lord is the portion of my inheritance.** To this inheritance, through the intercession of his most sweet mother, may our Lord Jesus Christ himself deign to lead us, he who with the Father, etc.

*see Sir 24:26

*see Ps 30:20;
see Jas 1:12

*Ps 15:5

Sermon 159

On the Nativity of Saint Mary

1. **V**ery delightful and venerable is the nativity of this Blessed Virgin, from whom the salvation of the world has arisen,* from whom the Savior of all peoples was born, who first, or rather who alone deserved to be named *salvatrix*, who unexpectedly bore a son without a father, a man without a man. She is that *shoot from the root of Jesse* about whom Isaiah, being aware of future things in the Spirit, exulted as he proclaimed, *There shall come forth a shoot from the root of Jesse, and a flower shall rise up out of his root.** Christ is understood by the flower, he who is *the flower of the field and the lily of the valley.*† This *glorious queen of the world*‡ draws her ancestry equally from patriarchs and kings. So Matthew when declaring her generation identified the first of kings and greatest of patriarchs, saying, *The book of the generation of Jesus Christ, the son of David, the son of Abraham.** For the Blessed Virgin Mary was to give birth to him who is *the end of the law* and of the prophets,* in whom the prophecy of the prophets and <desire> or expectation of the patriarchs is brought about. The sense of the prophets, obviously, is Christ; the authority of patriarchs and all power of kings is from Christ.

2. Out of the great fathers, yet greater than all, this virgin came forth. So a certain wise person says, *As a thornbush brings forth a rose, so Judea <begat> Mary.** And in the Song of Songs, *Like a lily among*

*see Resp Hod nat in Nat SM (Hesbert 4:6854)

*see Resp Stirps in Nat SM (Hesbert 4:7709)
†Cant 2:1
‡Resp Beata M in Ass (Hesbert 4:6168)

*Matt 1:1

*see Rom 10:4; see Matt 5:17

*Resp Nut in Nat SM (Hesbert 4:6024)

thorns, so is my love among the daughters. * How much more beautiful is the lily or rose, pleasanter and sweeter, than a thornbush, so this sacred virgin in the beauty of her honor, the charm of her manners, the sweetness of her whole way of life surpasses that of all preceding fathers, proved so much better than they, in so far as she had been reserved by the Lord for greater fruits and better status. And so that no one be turned to doubt what Isaiah understood beneath this veil of words, in another place he explicitly declares it, saying, *Behold, a virgin shall conceive and shall bear a son, and his name shall be called Emmanuel* *

3. Rightly is this virgin designated by the name of *shoot*. For a shoot has three qualities: greenness, newness, flexibility. Vigor of greenness abounds so much more fully in a shoot, as it is neither dried up by old age nor divided up by many branches nor shrunk into the wrinkles of bark by a long heat. It has newness in age, because afterward it will grow up into an oak with branches. A tree is stronger than a shoot, it must be said. It is also flexible to the point that it allows its top to be bent back to the ground without injury to its tissue. Therefore these things are manifestly found in the Blessed Virgin: greenness in virginity, newness in holiness, flexibility in humility. Granted however that these same qualities might seem to fit certain others, blessed Mary claims them for herself by a singular prerogative, so that she is unique in virginity, exceptional in action, singular in humility.

4. There have been many virgins who have dedicated themselves to God, and by a ring of a pledge of faith, they present themselves to Christ. * But even if anyone had that much virginity in common with blessed Mary, still no one had the fecundity in virgin-

*Song 2:2

*see Isa 11:1;
see Resp Stirps
in Nat SM
(Hesbert 4:7709)

*Ant in Agnes
(Hesbert 3:1426)

ity as she did. For *she has a mother's joys* without losing the honor *of virginity, and there has never been one like her before, and none since.** A virgin before the birth, a virgin during the birth, a virgin after the birth, retaining nothing of a virgin that detracts from true motherhood, and adding nothing of motherhood that violates the enclosure of virginity.

5. But her humility, which is particular and singular, is apparent from <her> words when she says, *Because the Lord has looked upon the humility of his handmaid, for behold from this day forward all generations shall call me blessed.** She who merited the proclamation of blessedness in all generations was of great humility. Rightly so. In fact, when she heard great and wonderful things as the angel made his announcement, still she was neither elated in thought on account of its importance, nor injured in faith on account of her astonishment. Neither could move her soul to elation or shake her faith to despair. She was not elated in mind, she who undertook to return a word of humility, saying, *Behold the handmaid of the Lord,* etc.* She was not violated in faith to whom *Elizabeth, filled with the Holy Spirit,** gave testimony to her integrity, saying, *Blessed are you who have believed,* etc.*

*Luke 1:48

*Luke 1:38
*Luke 1:41

*Luke 1:45

6. So, concerning the holiness of her whom the Holy Spirit had sanctified, what shall I say? He chose and predestined her, making her so excellent and preserving her who alone was suitable, so that the salvation of the world was fashioned from her, as well as redemption of the human race, expulsion of the devil, and raising of the Christian people, destruction of death, <and> opening of Paradise. From her womb the Savior of the world has come *as a bridegroom from his bridechamber.** For who was so holy, so worthy as she who was *full of grace,* as the angel

*Ps 18:6

testifies?* She is *blessed* not only *among women,*†
but beyond all women: the former because of removal
of offense, the latter on account of her gathering of
favor. For she alone erased (with the knife of humility
and obedience) the ancient handwriting* of the
woman's reproach that Eve had written down with
the pen of disobedience, and in addition she sprouted
forth the author of eternal life for us.*

7. I dare not say that she lived utterly without
sin. That she was conceived without sin of concupiscence, or was born without original sin, is not to be
read, not to be discovered, especially when Scripture
says, *No one is cleansed of filth, not even an infant
whose life is but one day upon the earth.** Likewise
John: *If we say that we have no sin, then we are liars,
and the truth is not in us.** And there is not anyone
who is able to conceal himself from this voice, *And
in sins my mother conceived me,** except he alone
who was begotten without "human seed, but rather
by the Secret Spirit."* It is pious for certain ones to
feel differently. But thus piety must yield, so that
injustice is not inflicted upon truth. What I have discovered in Augustine, I believe and confess, because
after the Holy Spirit had sanctified her, and had
cleansed her so that God's Son was conceived in her,
just as she remained integral in body, so she remained
perpetually inviolate from every vice and sin, in mind
as in deed.

8. It is appropriate therefore to celebrate with supreme veneration the birth of her who was to conceive
and to give birth to God's Son, not so much because
of the good of conception as on account of the good
of the result, to the extent that we celebrate the birth
of John or his conception, as is the custom for most
people, not so much on account of the good of his
birth or conception as on account of the countless

*Luke 1:28
†Luke 1:42

*chirographum;
see Col 2:14

*see Isa 45:8

*Job 14:4-5
(LXX)

*1 John 1:8;
see 1:10

*Ps 50:7

*see Ambrose,
"Veni, redemptor
gentium," 484

and immeasurable goods that proceeded from them.

paranymphi If therefore the dignity of the bridesman is so great, then far greater and more excellent should be that of the bride herself, that is, of that mother of this bridesman's Lord, master of this disciple, judge of this herald, reality of this figure, truth of this shadow.

9. But you will say that John was conceived by *see Luke 1:11-13 the angel's announcing.* And how do you know if even greater or similar things happened in the conception of blessed Mary? One reads that *a heavenly benefit entered into Anna, from whom was born the* *Ant in Nat SM (Hesbert 3:1832) *Blessed Virgin.** And what is the heavenly benefit if not the grace of the Holy Spirit, which Anna received, so that she conceived her through whom the whole world received a heavenly benefit? It was great that *see Luke 2:28 Simeon received the Lord *into his arms.** Great that Blessed John immersed him with his own hands in *see Matt 3:13-16 the waters of the Jordan River.* Therefore it should be considered great that this sacred virgin carried him in her womb, warmed him on her lap, nursed him with her breasts, comforted him with hugs, pressed him with kisses, heard his crying, took him up as he sobbed, suffered in his trial, wept at his gibbet, and displayed all the services of maternal care with loving concentration and exacting diligence.

10. This holy lady and virgin, about whom we wretches and sinners presume to speak, can be understood not without cause through the shoot of Aaron, which in one night put forth leaves, blossomed, and *see Num 17:8 bore nuts.* For that shoot, after it was cut and uprooted and there was no moisture to ascend from the roots, began to swell into buds, sprouted into new *see Num 17:8 growth,* put forth fruit, and still received from divine virtue no less fecundity of bearing fruit. So also in blessed Mary there was no moisture of carnal mingling from which she might take on the substance

of reproduction, but only by the power and working
of the Holy Spirit did she interiorly conceive budding
strength by serving in faith, and she gave birth with
her virginity intact. And just as that shoot in a brief
interval of time received the effect of procreation, so
in the angelic annunciation this sacred virgin, through
the delight and love* of the Holy Spirit by which she   *dilectione
was inwardly inflamed, became pregnant and
brought forth the fruit by which all things are fed,
angels and humans are refreshed, the fallen are raised
up, the fettered are released, the saints are delighted,
demons are brought low, and hell is plundered.

11. Pay close attention to what I have said: by
means of the Holy Spirit's love. In fact, not without
cause is the Lord Jesus said to be *conceived of the
Holy Spirit*. As in the Gospel: *for that which is born
of you is of the Holy Spirit.** And likewise in the   *Matt 1:20;
Creed: "Who was conceived of the Holy Spirit." For   see Luke 1:35
although the works of the Holy Trinity are indivis-
ible, and the working of the Father and the Son and
the Holy Spirit is absolutely one and the same, nevertheless from most places in holy Scripture this work
of the incarnation is attributed to the Holy Spirit and
assigned more to his responsibility. So that it seems
easier, let us cross over to examples from nature; let
us see whether from their likeness any way can be
revealed for us to some understanding of this lofty
theory.

12. In the mingling of male and female, by the
carnal activity of both, the substance of generation
comes about, yet if there is love of both and the
consent of a mutual will, then pleasure also comes
between them. In fact, natural scientists say that if a
man joins himself with a woman, and yet, if possible,
imparts no compliance of love or feeling of pleasure,
then such an undertaking will be thoroughly fruitless,

and any effect of fecundity cannot come of it. "On the other hand, this tribute that nature expends, as if it were a certain debt to the design of the human body, is extorted not by necessity or constraint, but by pleasure* alone, and is provided as if by a certain voluntary charity."* And so love† and the pleasure of the thing that is done are the origin and a certain efficient cause‡ of that generation that follows, to the point that without love it cannot happen, nay rather, that out of love particularly and specifically it ought to happen, because when love is lacking, whatever is left comes together in vain and without fruit.

*dilectione

caritate; Hugh,
BMV 2:234
†*amor*
‡*efficiens causa*

13. This indeed allows the manner of generation in the Blessed Virgin to be more carefully considered. For when it was announced to her that she would conceive, where it says, *Behold you shall conceive and give birth to a son,** and when it says, *He shall be great and shall be called the Son of the most High,** and as it adds, *The Holy Spirit shall come upon you*, etc.*—when this, I say, was announced, soon she was delighted at the angel's words, she inclined her soul, granted her consent, kindled her desire, and bestowed her affection. She soon believed what she heard, loved what she believed, and with all her will desired to fulfill within herself what she loved, saying, *Behold the handmaid of the Lord. Be it done to me according to your word.**

*Luke 1:31

*Luke 1:32
*Luke 1:35

*Luke 1:38

14. Therefore she conceived more by faith than by her body, by charity* not desire, by love† more than work, rather out of the judgment of pleasure‡ than from the aid of masculine copulation. And because the Holy Spirit is love, with whose love this sacred virgin was inflamed, by whose grace and inner inspiration she was wholly ablaze, "rightly does it say that she conceived of the Holy Spirit. Not be-

caritate
†*amore*
‡*dilectionis*

cause she had the Holy Spirit as the genitor of her son, but because through the love and working of the Holy Spirit she received the material of fecundity in her flesh, and from her flesh she supplied the *substance* for the divine birth. For because in her heart love of the Holy Spirit singularly burned, the power* of the Holy Spirit made singular realities in her flesh. And his pleasure* in her heart did not permit a companion; his work in her flesh had no precedent."*

15. "Therefore Christ is said to have been conceived <of> the Holy Spirit, because the holy virgin conceived him through love and working of the Holy Spirit. He was born of the virgin, because from the flesh alone of the virgin, without mingling of a man's seed, he took on the substance of his flesh. And this is what was said to his mother through the angel: *The Holy Spirit shall come upon you, and the power of the most High shall overshadow you.** In fact, the Holy Spirit came over, so that through his power and working the conception would be fashioned. He overshadowed, so that the integrity of such great modesty might not not be burned with the passionate heat of carnal concupiscence in the conceiving."*

16. One may still contemplate the integrity of the Blessed Virgin with certain other similes. For just as a ray of sun passes through a glass window and pours its light to places beyond without harm to the substance of the glass, so the Savior's mother, <without losing> the integrity of her virginal womb, continually transmits a ray of unfailing light to us.* Look upon a crystal in the sun and cease being astonished at the birth of the virgin. In fact, a crystal heated by a ray of sun in a wonderful way takes up the generative strength of fire, feeds the fire within itself, and, after a few moments, when applied more closely, sets ablaze the same fire without consuming

*see Luke 1:35

*dilectio
*Hugh of Saint Victor, BMV (*L'oeuvre* 2:236)

*Luke 1:35

*Hugh, BVM (L'oeuvre 2:238)

*see Sir 24:6

itself. A crystal set alight by a ray of sun is the Blessed Virgin Mary, illuminated by the grace of the Holy Spirit, by whose pleasure* she was warmed, received fecundity, and conceived God's son in her chaste womb.

17. A fire in a crystal, a son in the virgin, whom after the completed time *she poured out for the world,** with the sign of her virginity unharmed. She bathed *every person who comes into this world*† and the entire creation with the true light. So it is written, *He has set his tabernacle in the sun, and like a bridegroom coming out of his bridechamber.** *There is no one *who conceals himself from the heat* of this fire.* This is the fire that God sent to earth, that he wills to be intensely set ablaze.* This is the fire that Moses saw in the flaming bush that did not burn, set afire but not consumed.* In fact, the same fire can be understood in both the bush and in the crystal: fire in the bush, offspring in the virgin. Light of fire, divinity of offspring. The bush was not burned up by the fire, nor the virginity violated by generation.

18. Still, look upon the morning star or some other star, and more firmly believe and more devoutly venerate the virginity of Christ's mother! "For just as a star emits rays from itself without being corrupted, so the Blessed Virgin bore her son without injury to her virginity. And the ray does not diminish the star's brightness, neither does the son take away the virgin's integrity."* So to her praise it was suitably said by someone, "As a star puts forth its ray, so in like manner did the virgin bring forth her son. And like the star by its ray, the Virgin is not corrupted by her son."*

19. On that account she is rightly called Mary, that is, *Star of the sea.* This world is *a great and spacious sea,** agitated by waves, stirred up by storms,

*dilectione

*see Pref S Maria (CP 366:5–6; CCSL 161A:101) †John 1:9

*Ps 18:6

*Ps 18:7

*see Luke 12:49

*see Exod 3:2

*Bernard, Miss 2.17 (SBOp 4:34)

*Seq "Laetabundus" str. 5–6, Nat Dom (PL 184:1327)
*Ps 103:25

and by incessant blowing of winds preventing all rest for itself. Even the mind of a person can be called a sea, which temptations agitate by continual commotion, tribulations compel, anger spurs, sadness disturbs, misery harasses. And if we wish to examine every single vicissitude of human fragility, just as the sea has no rest, so the mind has no rest, and no sure rest of the world will we be able to find in this life. Therefore in order to achieve a favorable judgment among such great dangers, fix your gaze on this star, set your eyes on the star of the sea, that is, on Mary. For she guides those who go astray, draws those who doubt, leads back those who wander, leads followers into the port of salvation, conducts seekers into the palace of the high King. Therefore in difficulties, in dire straits, in uncertain situations, call upon this star, follow her. Looking to her you shall not fear, following her you shall not stray, seeking her you shall rejoice forever.

20. She is the star about which the prophet says, *A star shall rise out of Jacob:** the star whose ray illuminates the whole world,* whose *light shines in darkness, and the darkness* does not comprehend it,* whose splendor *rising from on high* crosses over to the heavens,* penetrates hell, scans the earth, saves human beings, gladdens angels, fosters virtues, and dries up vice, and if any superfluity or enormity happens, it restores them to constancy. Therefore if winds should blow, if rivers should overflow their banks, if rocks should threaten, if temptations should strike,* if tribulations should arise, then look to the star, call upon Mary. If cupidity draws you, if avarice burns, if ambition rises up, if poverty overwhelms you, if a storm beats you down, if misery shakes you, if violence overthrows you, then fear not, despair not: look to the star, call upon Mary.

*Num 24:17
*see John 1:9
*John 1:5

*Luke 1:78

*see Matt 7:25

21. Whatever might happen, it will not be able
<to disturb> the house of your heart when it has such
a foundation,* and will not overturn the boat of your
conscience.† The destroying angel will not be able
to reach you if he sees the door of your heart marked
with this sign.* Therefore, so that a favorable judgment of her propitiation may always aid us, let us
never forsake the example of her way of life, and she
will reconcile us with Christ, *to whom* be *honor and
glory* through all ages forever.* Amen.

*see Matt 7:25;
see Luke 6:48
†see Matt 8:23-26

*see Exod 12:22-23

*see Rom 16:27

Sermon 160

On the Feast of
Saint Michael the Archangel

1. **T**he Archangel Michael triumphed over the dragon; let us also fight, so we can conquer.*[1] Our King, for whose stipends we serve as soldiers,† from whom we await not temporal gratuities but eternal rewards, is *a strong fighter,** as is the one about whom we read, *The Lord strong and powerful, the Lord powerful in battle.** He does not want to have unmanly soldiers; he does not seek lazy and uneducated fighters. He valiantly argues and teaches us what we should do in a conflict; he, girded with virtue and fortitude,* fighting *the Lord's wars* bravely and *valiantly,** doing the Father's will in all things,* has bravely vanquished the dragon that opposed him. Therefore Scripture says to us, *Gird your loins like a man and valiantly fight the wars of your God.** And the Lord himself says to all \<his\> servants, *Let anyone who serves me follow me.*† What is it "to follow me" if not "to walk in my ways"? If therefore I am holy, so also must *my servant* be. If I am chaste, then let *my servant** be a protector of chastity. If I have fought and conquered for you, then fight for me, so that you may conquer!

2. As long as we are on this pilgrimage,* we must always fight against the dragon, against offenses and

*Ant Vig Mich;
see Rev 12:7-8
†see 1 Cor 9:7

*see Isa 42:13
*Ps 23:8

*see 2 Sam 22:33
*see 1 Sam 18:17
*see John 6:38

*Job 38:3;
1 Sam 18:17
†see 1 John 2:6;
see Ps 24:4;
see Ps 127:1
*John 12:26

*see 2 Cor 5:6

---

[1] J. Lemarie, "Textes relatifs au culte de l'Archange et des Anges dans les Bréviaires Manuscrits du Mont-Saint-Michel," *Sacris Erudiri* 13 (1962): 113–52, here 121.

sins, against the weakness of the flesh, against the
see 2 Cor 11:3 · cunning of the serpent.* By what temerity will one
who is frozen and trembling with fear before a fight
hope or expect a crown? *One will not be crowned*
2 Tim 2:5 · *unless he strives lawfully.** The crown will be given
after the contest and victory. But perhaps the contest
in which you toil, in which you struggle and fight, is
loathsome to you. With great desire you await the
end of this contest. Still, this contest is not concluded
until *this mortal* puts on *immortality*, while *death is*
see 1 Cor 15:54 · *swallowed up in victory,** because *the last enemy,*
1 Cor 15:26 · *death, will be destroyed.** After the destruction of
death we shall fear no enemy whatsoever, because
there will be no hint of an enemy remaining with
whom we might struggle, no temptation, no assault,
see Josh 14:15 · but *the earth* will cease *from battles,** and we shall
rest secure in the kingdom of heaven with the angels,
dreading no enemy, because there will be neither *ad-*
1 Kgs 5:4 · *versary nor evil occurrence* in that place.* Therefore
let us fight that we may be crowned. In fact, *Michael*
triumphed over the dragon so we can conquer ourselves.

   3. And who is this *Archangel Michael*, if not the
one about whom we read, *And his name will be*
Isa 9:6 (LXX) · *called angel of great counsel,** the Son of God *whom*
John 10:36 · *the Father sent into the world** to vanquish the
see Eph 2:2; · powers of the air?* This is the angel of fortitude and
Eph 6:12 · consolation who rescues and saves *his people,** about
see Matt 1:21 · whom the psalmist says, *The angel of the Lord will*
encamp around those who fear him and will rescue
Ps 33:8 · *them.** This is the angel of life about whom John
says, *And I saw another angel ascending from the*
Rev 7:2 · *rising of the sun, bearing the sign of the living God.**
This angel is an archangel, <that is,> a prince of
angels, because *all things are subject* to him *through*
see 1 Cor 15:27; · *whom all things were made.**
8:6; see Col 1:16;
see John 1:3

4. *Michael triumphed over the dragon.* Michael is interpreted as "*Who is like God?*"* And to whom will this interpretation be assigned more aptly than to our Savior, about whom the psalmist sang, *Who in the clouds will be compared to the Lord? Who among the sons of God will be like to God?** Behold this Michael, "*Who is like God?*" *O Lord God of virtues, who will be like you? You are powerful, O Lord, and your truth encircles you.** Mary, sister of Moses and Aaron, astonished at the virtue and strength of this archangel, after the sinking of Pharaoh and his army in the Red Sea, *with her companions** singing a hymn with timbrels,† chanted to the Lord, *Who is like you among the strong, O Lord? Who is like you, magnificent in holiness, terrible and praiseworthy and doing wonders?** Behold, this Michael is everywhere. Who is like God in fortitude? Who is like God in virtue? Who is like God in counsel? Who is like God in power? Who is like <God> in salvation of his people?

5. *Michael triumphed over the dragon.* "*Who is like God?*" conquers everywhere, triumphs everywhere. Nothing *resists* him who does all his will *in heaven and on earth, in the sea and in all the depths.** *He triumphed over the dragon.* This *dragon* is *the ancient serpent who seduced the whole world.** This dragon was an angel whose excellence and prerogative of honor the prophet describes, saying, *The cedars in the paradise of God were not higher than he. The fir trees did not equal his summit. Every tree of Paradise is not similar to him, because God had made him more beautiful.** Through his excessive glory he slipped into pride, through which he was turned from an angel into the devil.

6. The dragon, cast out from the exalted seats of heaven, rushed headlong *into the abyss** of darkness

*Gregory I, Hom in Ev 34.9 (CCSL 141:307); Jerome, Int nom 56 (CCSL 72:129)

*Ps 88:7

*Ps 88:9

*see Judg 11:38
†see Exod 15:20

*Exod 15:11

*see Rom 9:19; see Ps 134:6

*Rev 12:9; see 20:9

*Ezek 31:8, 9

*see Rev 12:9; 20:3

*see Job 40:16
*Job 41:25

*see Wis 2:24;
see 2 Cor 11:3

and dwells in water and damp places.* *He is king over all the children of pride.* After his banishment he invaded our first parents through envy and *seduced them;** through this victory, by which he deceitfully triumphed over the first human beings, he was hoping that all flesh was subjected to him. This is because upon seeing Michael, that is, Christ, clothed in flesh, he attacked with presumptuous audacity to fight against him.

7. He fought against him when after he became hungry, he approached him and showed to him a pile of rocks, saying, *If you are the Son of God, then command these stones to be made bread.** But the Lord prudently resisted him and struck him down, saying, *Not by bread alone does a person live, but in every word that proceeds from the mouth of God.** *Again* he attacked him head on, when he transported *him onto a very high mountain and showed to him all the kingdoms of the world and* said, *All these I will give to you, if falling down you will worship me.** But Michael conquered. "*Who is like God?*" through his wisdom answered prudently: *You shall worship the Lord God, and him alone shall you serve.**

*Matt 4:3

*Matt 4:4;
see Deut 8:3

*Matt 4:8-9

*Matt 4:10;
see Deut 6:13

8. So this dragon, defeated everywhere, failed in his purpose, became empty and perplexed: discovering nothing in Michael about which he might rejoice, finding nothing in Christ that was of his own right,* drawing out from him nothing from which he would become more resolved. Still, when he saw himself defeated and mocked by Michael, he did not withdraw from the battle, but he armed his accomplices, the faithless Jews, with a view to his death. But here, that is, in death, our *Michael* ("*Who is like God?*") wonderfully *triumphed over the dragon.* Everywhere is the wonderful power of Michael, who vanquished

*see John 14:30

the prince of death through death. *He destroyed death* itself *through death.**

*see Heb 2:14;
see 2 Tim 1:10

9. The spiteful dragon thought he had conquered and thereupon suffered eternal defeat. In fact, through Christ's death, which he desired and induced, he squandered all his powers. He who before the Savior's death presumed to make a frontal assault against Michael himself no longer dares to join battle publicly against any of the least of Michael's angels, that is, those *least ones who believe in* Christ.* But like a serpent in a hedge, the hidden enemy secretly sets an ambush against us. Therefore let us have no despair, no dread of joining battle against this dragon, because *Michael triumphed over* him *so that we can conquer* and can reign together in heaven with the angels.*

*see Matt 10:42;
Matt 18:6;
Matt 25:40

*see 2 Tim 2:12

10. Today we call to mind the emblems of the angels, and therefore reason demands that we say something about angels. Sublime spirits of the heavens are sometimes called angels, sometimes archangels. Still, they cannot always be called angels or archangels, because they are only named angels or archangels when they are sent. "The Greek word *angel* is called *nuntius** in Latin; an archangel is a supreme *nuntius* or principal *nuntius*. And <it is> the name of their duty, not their nature."* Close to this is what blessed Augustine says: "An angel is a spirit by reason of what it is, but it is an angel by what it does."*

*messenger

*Gregory I, Hom
in Ev 34.8 (CCSL
306:182–84)

*Augustine, En in
Ps, Ps 103, S 1.15
(CCSL 40:1488)

11. "The angels were made before every creature. So it is written, *Wisdom was created before all things*." Not that supreme Wisdom who is the Word, because Christ, the Power of God and Wisdom of God,* is not created wisdom, but creating Wisdom, because through him all things have been created.* And he is coeternal with the Father, because the Father was never without his Wisdom. Angels are

*see 1 Cor 1:24

*see John 1:1-3;
see Wis 9:1-2

therefore created wisdom. "They are called wisdom because inborn Wisdom inheres in them." And this *wisdom was created before all things,** because "before all creation of the world, the angels were made. Concerning the apostate angel, Scripture is not at all silent; in fact it says, *He is the beginning of the ways of God.** The nature of angels is changeable, because if they had no changeability in their nature, the devil would not have come to ruin; but everlasting charity, to which they adhere, makes good angels unchangeable. So blessed Isidore says, "Grace, not nature, makes angels unchangeable." "For although they are changeable by nature, divine contemplation does not permit them to be changed."*

*Sir 1:4

*Job 40:19

*Isidore, Sent 1, 10.2–3 (CCSL 111:29–30)

12. Wicked angels must be detested and abhorred because they are inciters of vices and corrupters of virtues. They always foster vices and resist virtues. They continually set traps for us and plot death. Good angels are to be loved and imitated, because they are lovers and coworkers of virtues. They were assigned to us so that they might defend and guard us, might restrain wicked spirits lest they harm us as much as they want, might teach us what must be done, what must be avoided, might console us and help us on this our pilgrimage.

13. It is not within human ability to explain the happiness of good angels. In fact, so great is their blessedness that by no reasoning can it be estimated by a human being. These our happy fellow citizens await and desire our fellowship. And we ought to hasten with all diligence to their society, because there is the supreme and perfect beatitude. Therefore let us walk in the Spirit and extinguish carnal desires.* Let us walk in the Spirit because they are the spirits whose emblems we recall today. Let us walk in the Spirit so that our way of life may please the holy spirits.

*see Gal 5:16; see 1 Pet 2:11

14. Today let us venerate our pious protectors, the holy angels, *but especially Michael* the archangel,* because he is *the prince of the Lord's army,*† the standard bearer of the Lord's soldiers, the leader of the Hebrews out from Egypt. Let us call him so that he may come to our aid, so that he may do battle for us,‡ so that he may fight before us, so that he may attack on behalf of us, *so that we may conquer* and through him triumph *over the dragon. Defend us,* therefore, *blessed Michael, in battle, so that we may not be destroyed in the terrible judgment.** Lead us from this Egypt, from this land of affliction and misery in which we are pilgrims, where we are weakened and afflicted. And lead us into the land of promise, land of rest and happiness, so with you we may adore and contemplate God our creator, *to whom* be *honor and glory* through all ages forever. Amen.*

*see "Tibi, Christe, splendor Patris" in Mich (PL 112:1659, vv. 7–12)
†see Resp in Mich (Hesbert 4:6826)
‡see Ant in Mich (Hesbert 3:3754)

*see Ant and Resp in Mich (Hesbert 3:4716; 4:6117, 7578)

*see Rom 16:27

Sermon 161

On the Conception of Saint Mary

1.
A *star will rise out of Jacob, and a shoot will spring up from Israel and will strike the chiefs of Moab, and Idumea will be his possession.** Balaak, the king of the Moabites, seeing all that Israel had done to the Amorrhite, and that the Moabites were in great fear of him,* because *they were not able to sustain his assault,* brought *Balaam the seer, the son of Beor, to curse* Israel.* But because *the Lord* loved Israel, *he refused to hear Balaam, and he turned his cursing into blessing.** When Balaam saw that it pleased the Lord that he should bless Israel, as the Spirit rushed upon him he took up his parable.** Among the many good things that he had prophesied about God's people, he was clearly foretelling the future coming of the Blessed Virgin, whose conception from the seed of Jacob we celebrate today as well as the future birth of Christ from her. The star designates the virgin; the shoot designates her son: *A star will rise out of Jacob,* he says, *and a shoot will spring up from Israel.**

2. Today Balaam's prophecy has been fulfilled. Today *a star* has arisen *out of Jacob.** Today the ever-virgin Mary has been conceived *from the tribe of Judah.** This blessed virgin derived her origin equally from kings and patriarchs. Deservedly she is born from kings and patriarchs, she who was to give birth to Christ, Lord of kings and King of patriarchs.* He is the sense of prophets, authority of patriarchs, dig-

*Num 24:17-18

*Num 22:2-3, 5;
Deut 23:4;
see Num 23:7
*Deut 23:5

*Num 24:1-3;
see Num 23:18

*Num 24:17

*see Num 24:17

*see Ant Nat gl in
Nat SM (Hesbert
3:3850)

*see Dan 2:47

nity of kings. He is *King of kings and Lord of lords,** author and consecrator of the whole world, the pinnacle of kings and prophets.

*1 Tim 6:15;
Rev 19:16

3. Finally, out of the great parents, the Virgin Mary came forth greater than all. Although *many virgins have gathered together riches,* she *has surpassed them all.** The bridegroom commends the boundless dignity of this virgin in the Song of Songs: *As is the lily among thorns, so is my love among the daughters.** All the daughters of Eve in comparison to Mary are thornbushes, knotty and dark trees. But the Blessed Virgin is like a lily among thorns, she who surpasses all in beauty of honesty and attractiveness of manners; she was made so much the more worthy than all, as if she had been pre-selected for greater fruits and a greater place of honor.

*Prov 31:29

*Song 2:2

4. Indeed, it is appropriate to celebrate the conception of her who was to become the conceiver of Christ, the Lord of all the world. For she herself conceived through the Holy Spirit and gave birth to God's Son. Fertile without seed, pregnant without vector,* mother without father, conceiving a man without knowing the partnership of a man, giving birth to a son yet having no damage to her virginity. These events are unheard of and astounding through all the ages. From ages past *it has not been heard* * that any girl so conceived, so gave birth, that someone was a mother and remained a virgin. Nevertheless, Blessed Mary—queen of heaven, mistress of the world, mother of mercy, door of life, star of the sea— so conceived and so gave birth.

vectore

*see John 9:32

5. She is called star of the sea, because she escorts travelers, brings together the doubtful, leads back those who stray, guides followers to the gate of salvation. The sea is the present world, agitated by waves, stirred up by storms, and by the incessant blowing

of disturbances preventing all rest for itself. Even the human mind can be called a sea, which temptations shake with continual blows, tribulations compel, anger agitates, sadness disturbs, and misery harasses; it becomes bitter through malice, surges in waves of cupidity, puffs up through exaltation. And just as in the sea there is always toil and vacillation, so in the human mind, imagination of various thoughts never allows true rest to remain. Therefore, so that we might have some judgment among these dangers, let us fix our eyes on the star of the sea,* that is, on Mary. In dire straits, in tribulations, in temptations, let Mary always be in our hearts, in our affection, in our speech. We shall not fear when we have her. We shall not go astray when we gaze upon her. We shall be liberated from every danger when we follow her.

*see Jerome, Int nom 14 (CCSL 72:76)

6. Therefore Balaam says, *the person whose eye is stopped up* says, *the hearer of God's words* says, *he who falls and so his eyes are opened, A star will arise out of Jacob.** This is the star whose ray enlightens the whole world,† whose *light shines in darkness, and the darkness* does *not* comprehend *it*.‡ This light shone forth in darkness when Christ plainly showed his divinity to the Jews *with signs and wonders.** But *the darkness did not comprehend it*,† because the faithless Jews, seeing Christ's works, did not understand that he was the Christ, and therefore they crucified him. Then the prophecy was fulfilled: *O death, I will be your death!** As Christ died on the cross, on which *he wrought salvation for his people*,† *the sun was darkened, and there was darkness over all the earth.*‡

*Num 24:3-4, 15-17
†see John 1:9
‡John 1:5

*see Acts 2:22; see 2 Cor 12:12
†John 1:5

*Hos 13:14; see Ant in Sabb (Hesbert 3:4045)
†see Ps 73:12; see Luke 1:68
‡Luke 23:45, 44

7. Before an angel and a man sinned, the day was without night, a clear day, a bright day, a day without cloud and mist. For the angelic and human creation was made to gain knowledge of the Creator. But after

Adam fell, after the human was banished from Paradise, after the first parents were deprived of that blessed light in which they happily contemplated the glory of God's majesty, a dark night was made for them, and in it, for us all, a blackish-gray night, a night of sins enveloped in darkness. In this night patriarchs and prophets were like wandering stars to whom the Lord revealed secret mysteries* as much   *sacramenta* as he wished and as he wished.

8. But these stars, concealed by cloud and mist, gave a little light in a few, but no light in many. For they proclaimed the future's secrets in allegories. So the psalmist says about them, *Dark waters in the clouds of the air.** That is, the sense in the patriarchs   *Ps 17:12 and prophets is cloudy. But for us today *a star out of Jacob* has arisen. Splendor *arising from on high,**   *see Num 24:17; transcending the heavens, scanning the earth, pene-   see Luke 1:78 trating hell: the one who saves humans, gladdens angels, fosters virtues, destroys vices. This is the star about which Balaam says, *A star will rise out of Jacob.** Light of this star is *the Sun of justice,* the son   *Num 24:17 of Mary, *Christ our God,** who *enlightens every*   *see Mal 4:2; see *person who comes into this world.*† Certainly he says   Ant Felix and about himself, *I am the light of the world,*‡ the light   Nat tua in Nat of heaven and earth, the light of angels and humans.   SM (Hesbert
   3:2861, 3852)

9. *A star will rise out of Jacob, and a shoot# will*   †John 1:9 *spring up from Israel.*§ This is perhaps the *shoot*   ‡John 8:12 about which the psalmist says, *The shoot of your*   #*virga* *kingdom is a shoot of righteousness.** This is the   §Num 24:17 *staff** of Moses, through which *he brought forth*   *Ps 44:7 *water from the rock** for the children of Israel to   *virga* drink. This is the *shoot* about which Jeremiah says,   *Ps 77:16 *I see a shoot keeping watch.** Beautifully does it say that this shoot is keeping watch, because Christ, who   *Jer 1:11 is designated through the shoot, is Israel's guardian, about whom the prophet says, *Behold, he who*

*Ps 120:4

*Num 17:8

*Ps 2:9

*see Num 24:17

*see Gen 19:30-37

*Jerome, Int nom
73 (CCSL 72:151)

*see Isa 15:5

*Isa 15:1

*Jerome, Int nom
8 (CCSL 72:69)

*John 8:44; see
8:41
†see Num 24:17

*guards Israel will neither slumber nor sleep.** This is the staff of Aaron, not that which at one time blossomed and bore almonds,* but which blossoms daily in the church, daily puts forth leaves, daily bears fruit. It puts out leaves in faith, blossoms in hope, bears fruit in charity. It puts out leaves in teachings, blossoms in miracles, <bears fruit> in rewards. It puts out leaves through obedience, blossoms through patience, bears fruit through glory.

10. The psalmist speaks to the Son about this staff, in the person of the Father: *You will rule them with a staff of iron, and will break them in pieces like a potter's vessel.** Obviously he means the foreign tribes, the puffed up and proud chiefs of Moab.* Moab was the son of Lot, begotten of the elder daughter, in Segor, *in a cave* and at night.* This story is well enough known to us. And because the day is short and requires a brief sermon, I hold back some discourse and employ more succinct conclusions. Lot is interpreted as *deviating,** he who, according to the letter, deviated from God's judgment and from precepts of the law when through drunkenness he slept with his daughters. Segor can be called a wanton and fickle calf.* *Night* and *cave* are especially appropriate for the wicked, whom the gloom of impiety oppresses in the present, and in the future confusion of damnation will devour. Isaiah says about Moab, *Moab will be destroyed in the night.**

11. Moab is interpreted as *from the father.** Therefore chiefs of the Jews are designated by the leaders of Moab, the crucifiers of Christ, who said about them before his passion, *You are from your father the devil, and so you desire to fulfill the works of your father.** The shoot springing from Israel has struck them,† because the son of the virgin, from the seed of Israel, has laid low the pride of the Jews, first

by dying humbly, then by arising powerfully, and finally by ascending wonderfully as his disciples looked
on. In fact, the princes of the Jews, who seemed to
have conquered in the death of Christ, after the glory
of the resurrection, understanding themselves to be
defeated, failed in anguish and trouble. And Christ,
who seemed to be defeated, after his death ascended
to heaven victorious, adored by all.

12. The chiefs of Moab can be understood as
either heretics or demons, they who command the
reprobate *in the midst of a corrupt and perverse na-*
*tion.** Our shoot destroys them, because in the   *Phil 2:15
present Christ purges the doctrine of heretics and
weakens the power of demons, but in the future, a
sentence of damnation will strike and shatter the
latter and the former, when he will say to them, *De-*
part from me, you cursed, into the everlasting fire
*that was prepared for the devil and his angels.**   *Matt 25:41

13. It follows, *And Idumea will be* Christ's *pos-*
*session. Blessed be God!** Already Idumea has be-   *Num 24:18;
come Christ's possession, and not only Idumea, but   2 Cor 1:3
even the whole earth. So every church sings to him,
*The Lord <has reigned>; he is clothed with beauty.**   *Ps 92:1
Already we discern that that prophecy has been fulfilled in him, that Christ rules *from sea to sea and*
*from the river to the ends of the earth.** Already *we*   *Ps 71:8
*have heard and known** that *all power was given* to   *see Ps 77:3
him *in heaven and on earth.** This is the shoot   *Matt 28:18
springing up from Israel* through the Holy Spirit,   *see Num 24:17
arising in this temporal world from the Virgin, that
strikes the chiefs of Moab (meaning the faithless
Jews), heretics and demons, the puffed up and exalted, because God breaks all who are proud. And
Idumea has become *his possession.** To him the   *see Num 24:18
Father *has subjected all things,** and he conquers   *1 Cor 15:26;
everywhere with the Father and Holy Spirit, reigns   Ps 8:8
everywhere, commands everywhere.

14. Therefore let us take refuge in our star, let us call upon Mary, so that she may commend us to her son, and by his mother's prayers he may cleanse us of all sins, and he may fortify those who are cleansed on earth, so we may see and glorify him in heaven, *him to whom* is *honor and glory** with the Father and Holy Spirit through all ages forever. Amen.

*see Rom 16:27

Sermon 162

On the Nativity of Saint Mary

1. **S**olomon *made a great throne of ivory for himself and overlaid it with the finest yellow gold. It had six steps, and the top of the throne was round on the back, and two hands on either side holding the seat, and two lions stood, one at each hand, and twelve little lions stood upon the six steps on one side and on the other. No such work was made <in> all the kingdoms.** This eloquent preface, wonderful and pleasant, contains a mystery in itself, something that it might be childish to read aloud in the church, a ridiculous and huge laughingstock of excessive rashness. But because <*the glory*> *of a king is to conceal a word, and the glory of God is to reveal a mystery to his friends,** he *who reveals deep matters out of darkness and brings hidden matters into the light** brings you out into the light of knowledge, lays out the journey of understanding for us, and pours fourth from us and through you *a good word** and a sermon of wisdom.

2. *Solomon* therefore *made a great throne of ivory.** Solomon had three names: *Solomon*, which is peace-maker, *Ididia*, which is lovable,* and *Coeleth*,† which is preacher.‡ *Ididia* collates the customs of the citizens, *Coeleth* prescribes a legal system to the citizens, and *Solomon* peacefully steers the helm of the kingdom. But our *Solomon*, the consubstantial *Son of the Most high*,# is therefore called *Solomon* because *he is our peace, who has made both one,** who *through* his *blood reconciled* us to God the Father

*1 Kgs 10:18-20

*see Prov 25:2;
see Tob 12:7

*Job 12:22;
28:11

*see Ps 44:2

*1 Kgs 10:18
*see 2 Sam 12:25
†*Qoheleth*=
Ecclesiastes
‡Isidore, Ety 7.6;
see Jerome,
In Eccl 1.1
(CCSL 72:250)
#see Luke 1:32
*Eph 2:14

*see Col 1:20, 22;
see Eph 2:16
*see 2 Sam 12:25

*Matt 3:17; 17:5

*Isa 42:1

and pacified *both things that are in heaven and things on earth*.* *Ididia*, that is, *lovable to the Lord*,* is the one whom the Father clearly so named in the baptism and in the transfiguration: *This is my beloved Son, in whom I am well pleased. Listen to him*.* And prophetic eloquence promised, *He is dear to me*; he says, *I have placed my Spirit over him*.* He is called *Coeleth* because he wisely delivered <the cause> of human redemption that he had taken up as a priority, he diligently brought forth our case, he eloquently shut up the adversary,* he powerfully laid low the wicked one.

*eloquenter
conclusit
adversarium

3. Therefore he is a preacher by teaching useful things, lovable by conferring relief, a peacemaker by providing essentials. A preacher on the mountain, lovable by the sea, making peace on the cross. He imparted morals on the mountain. He bestowed benefits by the sea. He reconciled the world to the Father and to himself on the cross.* *Coeleth* in Judgment, saying, Go *into everlasting fire, you cursed*.† *Ididia*, that is, lovable, saying, *Come, you blessed of my Father*.* *Solomon*, when all things will be subjected to him, and he will hand over the kingdom to God the Father.* He is the preacher by giving terrible judgments to the impious. He is lovable by bestowing on each of his own a *mansion*.* A peacemaker by conferring ineffable glory through his vision.

*see Col 1:20; see
2 Cor 5:18-19;
see Rom 5:10
†Matt 25:41
*Matt 25:34

*see 1 Cor 15:24,
28

*see John 14:23

4. Therefore, so as to dissolve *enmity in his flesh*,* to reconcile the world to God,* so as *through* his *blood* to pacify *things that are in heaven and things on earth*,* our peacemaker made this throne for himself,* prepared a bedchamber, and built a palace in which he might diligently complete our cause and plead our case: a throne on which sitting by the power of Judgment, by the seriousness of counsel, by the test of virtue, he mercifully broke the bonds of sin, powerfully laid low the impious, conveyed the fallen

*see Eph 2:14
*see 2 Cor 5:19

*Col 1:20
*see 1 Kgs 10:18

to the lowest places. He built a bedchamber for himself <in> which he put on the habit of our flesh and
justly deceived the cunning enemy. In this bedchamber he showed his feeling towards us, so that he
might join the just to the convicted, the worm to
God, the highest to the lowest, light to mire, potter
to pottery, and Creator to humankind.

5. This throne is the unsullied womb of the Virgin
about which one reads in the psalm, *Your throne, O
God, is for ever and ever.* Not that the sacred Virgin's flesh was from eternity, but that God perpetu-
ated it as chosen before all the rest. About this throne
one also reads in another psalm, *And I will place
your seed*, it says, *and his throne as the days of
heaven forever.* As if he were to say openly, "From
the heavenly realm I shall send my Son by making
fertile the most pure womb of the Virgin. And what
will be born of the Virgin, with her I shall make as
a splendor to illuminate the firmament."

6. Likewise the prophet says about this throne,
*And his throne as the sun in my sight, and as the
moon, perfect forever.* As if in the voice of the
Father it is said in praise of the Virgin, "Without
wrinkle or stain, without dirt, without poison or dust
I have chosen the Virgin,* whose mind no illicit
thought will titillate, whose flesh no sort of action
will soil." For it is as if the Sun were the spirit of the
Virgin, and her flesh <as> the moon in the sight of
the Creator. Her mind burned with the fire of supreme love and shone with the light of wisdom in
knowledge of the Creator. And her flesh has suffered
no harm of corruption. Inwardly, innocent purity
glowed, and pure innocence; outwardly pure wholeness radiated, and whole purity.

7. Likewise, concerning this throne, it reads in
Revelation, *I saw, and behold, there was a chair set
in heaven, and one was sitting upon the chair.* A

*Ps 44:7

*Ps 88:30

*Ps 88:38

*see Eph 5:27

*Rev 4:2; see 4:1

*animus

chair was set in heaven, because the mind* of the glorious Virgin, reflecting on *all* earthly realities *as dung*,* was continually being astonished at the supreme things. *A chair was set in heaven*, because the Virgin's *way of life* was *in heaven*.* Concerning this throne, it adds, *And from the throne came forth lightning, voices, and thunder*.* These things just mentioned had come from the throne because the most brilliant* Virgin gave birth to God's Son, who mercifully rescued us from the bonds of the original fault, *from the empty conduct of the ancestral tradition*,* <and from> the rite of morally foul paganism,* challenging with the clarity of miracles, elucidating with the most gracious newness of preaching, and deterring with the most severe cruelty of eternal punishment.

*Phil 3:8

*see Eph 2:6;
see Phil 3:20

*Rev 4:5

*clarissima

*1 Pet 1:18

*gentilitatis

8. In fact, *the Lord* gave *goodness, and our earth* gave *her fruit*,* because the Merciful and Most High, through inherent goodness, created a fruitful virginity in Mary. And then our earth, which was previously barren* <and> only produced *thorns and thistles*,* has been turned into a healthy and pleasant fertility. So as you see, the pride of the apostate angel, the illicit presumption of Adam, and the insidious concupiscence of Eve were thrown down, poured out, and reduced to nothing, through the flower and fruit of Mary, while Mary's humility trampled Eve's pride, and her devout virginity subdued the concupiscence of the flesh.

*see Ps 84:13

*see 2 Kgs 2:19

*see Gen 3:18

9. *And from the throne came forth lightning, voices, and thunder*.* For what was the fruitful virginity in Mary if not an astonishing newness of a miracle unheard of from the ages?* What were the feelings of the angelic Virgin toward God if not voices of her most chaste and brilliant mind? What else was in her—desires of the heavenly kingdom, sighs for angelic glory, the fragrance <of prayers>,

*Rev 4:5

*see John 9:32

zeal for virtues, a most sincere hatred for the world and the flesh and sin—if not a certain terrible thunder, assaulting the world, the flesh, and the devil with fear? It was the miracle to which the Virgin gave birth: the cry of her mind, the love of a virgin; fervor for virtues was the downfall of vices.

10. *From the throne came forth lightning, voices, <and thunder>.** Because the most holy Virgin, who bore and suckled the Savior, who constantly stuck by his side, who always attended him as an inseparable companion, who was present all the time, saw more precisely, heard more secretly, recognized more quickly, she more readily retained and more lucidly proclaimed to the apostles and other disciples, reported more diligently, distributed better, delivered more faithfully. So it is that one reads about her in the book of Wisdom, *Many virgins have gathered together riches: you have surpassed them all.**   *Prov 31:29

11. For although <the Lord> spoke to the crowds in parables, although he made all things known to the apostles as to friends,* nevertheless one must believe that to the extent that he favored his mother before the rest, he thus taught her some things more readily, recounted certain other things to her more privately, often raised her up *to the mountain of myrrh** and the hills of Lebanon, and concealed her *in the wine cellar,** exactly as he knew and wished her to have revealed glorious <and> deifying knowledge of himself. Therefore *from the throne*, that is, from Mary, came forth *lightning, voices, and thunder,** because the mother more greedily drank up, more faithfully stored up, and more sincerely and more lucidly disclosed to others her son's parables, puzzles, sayings, works, and mystical deeds.

12. She was reverently preserved by nature, diligently venerated by the law, mercifully pre-selected by grace. Nature accordingly reserved for her the

*Rev 4:5

*see Matt 13:10-11, 34; see John 15:15

*see Song 4:6
*see Song 2:4

*Rev 4:5

flower of supreme virginity, the law reserved the honor of virginal fruitfulness for her alone, grace reserved before all things the beauty of divine maternity and the divine odor of spiritual matrimony: nature what is its own,* preserving virginity intact; the law by reverently distinguishing her from others; and grace by making virginity fruitful without seed. Nature by speaking in realities, not words, while in her it protected integrity, and the Lord of nature thundered from her, saying to the serpent, *I will put enmity between you and the woman, and between your seed and her seed.** The law proclaimed, while distinguishing her from others, *A woman who has received seed and bears <a man child> will be unclean for seven days.** Nature deferred to her when in the beginning the earth brought forth without a seed,* the law when *the bush* burned without fire,* grace when the Virgin gave birth.

*quod suum est
*Gen 3:15
*Lev 12:2
*see Gen 1:11-12
*see Exod 3:2

13. God dwells in her as the Creator does in the world, an emperor in the kingdom, a head of household in the home, a high priest in the temple, a bridegroom in the bedchamber. The Most High created her for himself as a most special world. In her mind, as in a sort of firmament, he placed a sun of reason and a moon of knowledge and stars of every sort of splendor: a sun that makes the light of divine cognition, a moon that with the stars restores a most splendid night of action.* And rightly so: *The Lord's is the earth and its fullness.** Therefore after creating the world, desiring a kingdom, he commanded the angel: *An angel was sent from God.** *The Spirit*, he said, *will come upon you, and the power of the most High will overshadow you.** So the head of the household entered the home, in which he took up the condition of our flesh, and he then offered it to God the Father on the altar of the cross as a sacrifice.

*see Gen 1:14-18
*Ps 23:1
*Luke 1:26
*Luke 1:35

He carries out his priesthood as a high priest in the temple. But because *Christ had to suffer and to rise again, and so to enter into his glory,** he had to carry the one hundredth sheep back to the flock† on his own shoulders,‡ *the people that walked in darkness* had to contemplate *a great light,** the world had to beam forth with the newness of his preaching and miracles. *Coming down from the Father of lights,** *beautiful in form above the sons of men,** having put on *a white robe, in a gilded garment,** *like a bridegroom* he came forth *from his bedchamber†* to the public.

14. In her as a sun in a constellation, rising in the evening, a craftsman lay hidden in his work: a work while she was being prepared for the king. [She was] evening while she was humbled by such great sublimity, a constellation while as the star of the sea she illuminated the ends of the earth. [He is] therefore the craftsman, adorning her, rising by being born, the sun by converting the world from error and offering her as an example for others. While such great and excellent matters are recalled of the bearer of God, still, for what it's worth,* a few things seem to exist for us. For she is ladder, bush, ark, constellation, shoot, fleece, bedchamber, rising gate, dawn. She is the ladder of Jacob, who when he put his head on the stone merited to see *angels ascending and descending.** Therefore, so that we might ascend to the society of angels, with arms and hands let us embrace the ladder of Jacob, that is, Mary, born from the seed of Jacob, keeping Mary in our heart, in our speech, and in our imitation. By her merits and prayers may our Lord Jesus Christ, who endured temporal death for us, grant us eternal life, he who with the Father, etc.

*Luke 24:26;
see 24:46
†see RB 27.9
‡see Luke 15:5
*Isa 9:2;
see Matt 4:16

*Jas 1:17
*Ps 44:3
*see Mark 16:5;
see Ps 44:10
†Ps 18:6

**rei pretio*

*see Gen 28:11-12

Sermon 163

On the Nativity of Saint Mary

*see S 162.14

1. **T**he ladder about which we spoke previously* has twelve steps between two sides. The right side goes from contempt of self up to the love of God. The left side goes from contempt of the world up to love of the kingdom. The twelve <steps> of this ascension are the steps of humility.* The first step is hatred for sin. Second is avoidance of fault. Third is dread of leisure. Fourth is to be subject to the Creator in all things. Fifth is to listen to one who is better. Sixth is to comply with one who is equal. Seventh is to yield to one who is lower. Eighth is to be subject to oneself. Ninth is to meditate continually on one's end. Tenth is always to respect one's own works. Eleventh is humbly to confess one's thoughts. Twelfth is to be moved through all things at hand and nod to the Lord's will. Through these steps, angels descend and human beings are raised up.* So the saints dispose *ascensions in their hearts** by making progress, and by ascending step by step, they will gain bright mansions *in the house of the Father.**

*see RB 7.5-9

*see Gen 28:12

*see Ps 83:6

*see John 14:2, 23

2. The bush that seemed to be on fire without burning up* signifies the virgin who would conceive by the Holy Spirit without loss of her virginity.* The bush that Moses dared not approach with his shoes on* points to the virgin who, amazingly, conceived without marital activity.* The tradition of the Hebrews asserts that the vision in this humble little bush was handed down so that the people would not be

*see Exod 3:2

*see Luke 1:30-31; see Matt 1:18

*see Exod 3:4-5

*see Luke 1:34-35

given to idolatry on some occasion. In the humble little virgin, a wonderful vision was presented to us, in which there was absolutely no occasion of any sort of fornication.

3. In fact, fornication is triple. One, you see, is human, a certain other is worldly, and a few pertain to a god. Human fornication happens by illicit touch, the worldly type by perverse affection, and the godly by wicked worship. The first one sins against neighbor, the second against oneself, the third against God. The first defiles the flesh, the second causes concupiscence of the world, the third idolatry. Mary employed individual remedies against each of these three. Against defilement of the flesh, <perfect> virginity; against concupiscence of the world, perfect humility; against idolatry, perfect charity. For Mary was most pure of flesh, most humble of heart, most devout of mind.

4. She is the heavenly constellation,* because the undiminished virgin brought forth her son for us, as a star* does a ray. As a ray from a constellation, as light from light, so a virgin comes forth from the Virgin, the light of the world.* Through Moses, it is said about this constellation, *A star shall arise out of Jacob, a person* shall rise up from Israel,** as if he were to say, "A virgin shall be born from the people of the Jews who shall give birth to Emmanuel."* Likewise it is said about this star through Job, *Can you bring forth the day star in its time, or will you make the evening star to rise upon the children of the earth?** The day star indicates the end of night and announces the approaching light. On the other hand, the evening star handles the reins at the edge of night as the light flees. Therefore *when the fullness of time came,** the All-Powerful, having pity on the fall of the human race, prepared the daybreak of the

*sidus

*stella

*see John 8:12

*homo
*Num 24:17

*see Resp in Ann (Hesbert 4:7338)

*Job 38:32

*Gal 4:4

unsullied Virgin who begat the Savior, put forth light for the earth, brought forth the Sun of justice for us, and drove out the disgraceful darkness of igno-

*see Mal 4:2

rance.* Therefore the day star is the birth of Mary; the evening star is the detestable originator of faithlessness. Of her a certain philosopher says, "From blood, the virgin's ray of most clear light shall go out, covering the filthiness of most souls, putting the

*source unknown

long-lasting darkness to flight."*

*see Jerome,
Int nom 14
(CCSL 72:76)

5. Mary is interpreted as *Star of the sea.** We read that there were two Marys in the Old Testament, but we discover a third in the grace and light of the eternal Gospel. The first was the sister of Moses. The

*see Eusebius,
Eccl hist 3.6
(GCS 91:209,
citing Josephus,
Bello 6.3)

second was the daughter of Eleazar.* The third was the mother, sister, and daughter of Jesus Christ. She was his mother through humanity, sister through humility, daughter through charity. Mother by begetting him, daughter by obeying his precepts, sister by contemplating his mysteries. Mother by bearing the flesh, sister by purifying her mind, daughter by mortifying her own will. Mother by teaching and examples of justice, daughter by affection for obedience to the paternal <will>, sister by desire for heavenly purity. Mary was mother, sister, and daughter, acting on precepts, keeping counsel, foretasting heavenly promises.

6. The first Mary, sister of Moses, relaxed the contracts of nature. The second devoured her own

*propria deuorauit
uiscera

flesh.* The third brought our nature up above the ether. The first opposed her own brother with her

*see Num 12:1

venomous speech.* The second raised her wicked

*see Eusebius,
Eccl hist 3.6
(GCS 91:209),
citing Josephus,
Bello 6.3

hands against her child.* The third made us blessed by giving birth to her most blessed son. The first had leprosy,† the second something freakish, the third, for all, was made most pure and gracious within

†see Num 12:10

herself. The first suffered punishment: she was put

outside the Hebrews' \<camp> for an interval of seven days.* The second suffered the most wretched faults, being alienated from the fellowship of the saints. The third dances in the glory of heaven, raised up in the presence of her son.*

*see Num 12:15

*see Eusebius, Eccl hist 3.6 (GCS 91:209), citing Josephus, Bello 6.3

7. The first represented the carnal synagogue, the second the killing letter, the third vivifying grace. Mary, the daughter of Eleazar, killed her child. But the mother of Jesus Christ called the human race back to life, because *the letter kills, the spirit gives life.** Therefore let the sister of Moses murmur, let the daughter of Eleazar murder, and let the mother and daughter of Jesus Christ give birth and liberate. May the synagogue grieve for its outcast self, and the letter suffer itself as void. Let Mary rejoice that she is pre-selected and raised up by grace.

*2 Cor 3:6

8. Adam, in name and sin, encompassed the four climates of the world. Mary, his daughter, both by grace and by various interpretations of her name, renewed all things according to that saying of the apostle: *As in Adam all die, so also in Christ all will be made alive.** The name \<Adam> encompasses the world in this way: four letters are found in his name. A, which is *anatole*, that is, the East. D, which is *dysis*, that is, the West. A, which is *arctos*, that is, the northern region. M, which is *mesembria*, is the southern region, of course. By sin, as one reads in the apostle, *Through one person sin entered into the world, and through sin, death, and so \<death> passed through all people.**

*1 Cor 15:22

*Rom 5:12

9. But in the name of the Virgin one reads a four-fold interpretation. For it is interpreted as *bitter sea*, or *myrrh of the sea*, or *star of the sea*, or *lady*. *Bitter sea* through contempt for the world, *myrrh of the sea* through contempt for oneself,* *star of the sea* through examples of justice, *lady* through love of

*see Jerome, Int nom 62 (CCSL 72:137)

wisdom. She attains the first through humility, the second through virginity, the third through charity, and the fourth through purity of contemplation. She attains the first through compunction, the second through mortification of the flesh, the third by enlightened divine thought, the fourth by being lifted up to invisible realities of God. Therefore may Our Lady herself, mother and virgin, lead us from the lowest to the highest, as she stands before her son, our Lord Jesus Christ, who lives and reigns through all ages forever. Amen.

Sermon 164

On the Nativity of Saint Mary

1. *All the glory of the king's daughter is within.** The glory of our Lady is described in this prophetic verse, and we gain no merit in silence. This daughter of the king is both daughter and mother: mother of humanity, daughter of divinity. For the King of heaven was born of \<his own\> daughter. He created for himself a mother in whom he would be conceived and from whom he would be born. For just as he founded a city for himself, about which David says, *The human was born in her, and the Most High himself has founded her* (that is, *in her he was born* as *a human, and* as *the Most High he founded her*),* so he created a mother for himself, from whom he was born as a human and whom he as God created."*

*Ps 44:14

*Ps 86:5

*Babion, Sanc (PL 171:901–2)

2. "Accordingly, David calls her the daughter of the king, whose glory he so described. The rest of the women, the remaining royal daughters, glory in their external beauty, but the glory of this daughter is from within. Concerning her the apostle says, *Our glory is this, the testimony of our conscience.** For she prefers to have the beauty of virtues in her conscience, rather than the fragile and transitory and empty form of the body, which is a temptation of the eyes. And that glory was *within golden fringes,** that is, in perseverance of good works. For the *fringes*, which are on the border of a garment, designate perseverance, and gold good works adorned with the light of charity. And although the glory of conscience

*2 Cor 1:12

*Ps 44:14

*Ps 44:15
was secretly hidden, nevertheless she was *clothed round with a variety** of many virtues. In fact, what she was wearing in her heart, she revealed in a display of deeds."*

*Babion, Sanc
(PL 171:902)

*Matt 6:1

*Matt 5:16

3. "The Lord who warned, *Beware that you not do your justice in the view of people, lest you be seen by them,** instructs us to let our *light shine <in the view of> people, so that, seeing our good works, they may glorify* God.* Therefore the service of works is not prohibited, but rather the doer's vain intention. But whose mind has been more pure, whose countenance more humble, whose speech more sweet, what virgin more chaste? She was an example of total goodness. She always used to call herself a handmaid: *Behold the handmaid of the Lord; be it done to me according to your word.** And again: *Because he has looked upon the humility of his handmaid.** She was *fair as the moon, chosen as the sun.** What specifically? *It seems no one has ever been, or shall ever be, like her."**

*Luke 1:38
*Luke 1:48
*Song 6:9

*Babion, Sanc
(PL 171:902);
Sedulius, Pasc 2
(CSEL 10:48);
Ant Gen in Nat
Dom (Hesbert
3:2938)
†see Luke 1:35
‡Ps 44:15

4. "In the first place she was brought up for the Lord, because he chose her whom the Holy Spirit overshadowed† before others so she would not sense the fire of any wicked will. *After her, virgins shall be brought to the king.*‡ The virgins in fact obtain the second place, because none can be made equal to her. The rest are able to follow; they are not able to catch up. Followers cannot be partners. And so *<the virgins> shall be brought*, but *after her.** But which virgins? Not just any, but those who will be *neighbors,** that is, imitators of her alone. For there are certain virgins who are chaste of body but corrupt of mind. These are not neighbors; these do not follow. These are not *brought to you,** O Lord. Nothing can have integrity of flesh without integrity of mind."*

*see Ps 44:15
*see Ps 44:15

*Ps 44:15
*Babion, Sanc
(PL 171:902)

*see 2 Cor 1:12

5. "There are other virgins who do not seek the glory of their conscience,* but the praise of human

beings. These, whose *glory* is not *from within,** desire the reward of their own virginity. Therefore they are not called followers of the daughter described above. These are *the foolish virgins* who have lamps and vessels but do not have oil in their vessels.* The lamps in their hands are works. Their vessels are the conscience of each one. Oil is the glory of works. *The prudent virgins* have with them *oil in vessels,** because they have glory in their consciences.* However, the foolish seek glory from human favor; therefore they do not have oil with themselves, seeking it from another place. But when the bridegroom comes the prudent virgins have shining lamps.* Yet *the lamps* of the others *are extinguished,** because then it shall be apparent that works that were desirous of vainglory give no light."*

6. "There are other virgins who, even if they might be chaste and free from the unclean enjoyment of luxury, are nevertheless overtaken by other vices. For the minds of certain ones are lifted up by pride, because they are either more prudent or more beautiful. These do not imitate Mary, who professed herself more a handmaid than a lady. And because they do not imitate her, *they will not be led after her.** For although she is the Queen of heaven, although she had given birth to the King, although she had carried her Creator, nevertheless she always considered that saying of Solomon, *However great you are, humble yourself in all things!** For her humble son (who *came not to be served, but to serve,** and who said, *Learn from me, because I am meek, and humble of heart,)** wished to have a humble mother, and wishes to have humble brothers. One who is not humble is not a son of the Father who is in heaven. So Mary says in her canticle, *He has put down the mighty and has exalted the humble.*"* Pride cast down an angel; humility led the human race back to heaven.

*see Ps 44:14

*see Matt 25:2-3

*see Matt 25:4
*see 2 Cor 1:12

*see Matt 25:10
*see Matt 25:8

*Babion, Sanc
(PL 171:902–3)

*see Ps 44:15

*Sir 3:20
*see Matt 20:28

*Matt 11:29

*Luke 1:52;
Babion, Sanc
(PL 171:903A)

7. "There are other virgins who wander freely outside while they stay in the cloisters; even if their body is detained in the cloister, still their mind wanders abroad. These are unlike her who *went into the hill country with haste*,* not delaying in the streets, not curious about the sights, not tempted by conversations. But in what things should she be detained? In the heavenly mysteries that she saw and heard. For Scripture says, *Mary kept all these words, pondering them in her heart*."*

*Luke 1:39

*Luke 2:19;
Babion, Sanc
(PL 171:903)

8. "There are other virgins who delight in empty conversations, slander, laughter; they are not eager for divine praises. They are not imitators of this one, who when she spoke with her kin did not do so about vain things, but about the secrets of heaven, praising and magnifying in these words: *My soul magnifies the Lord*."*

*Luke 1:46;
Babion, Sanc
(PL 171:903)

9. Therefore, brothers, let us imitate our blessed Lady, so that proclaiming and honoring her virtues, we can be sharers in her glory, which may our Lord Jesus Christ deign to provide for us by the merits of his mother, he who lives and reigns with the Father and Holy Spirit, etc.

Sermon 165

On the Annunciation of the Lord

1. **G**od created the first man pure and in freedom. The devil led the man astray, because he transgressed God's command, and took possession of him as a servant. But the man, now corrupted through sin, could not escape this servitude by his own power. Since, however, the man had <become> a servant by his own doing, if he were liberated through anyone other than a human, then it would be by violence, and the devil would justly protest that he had been wronged. On account of this, for the man to be redeemed, it was necessary to find a human in whom there was no sin, so that when the devil usurped power for himself over the one without sin, for whom (since there was no sin) he would have no reason for inflicting death (the punishment for sin)* by the usurpation of what was not his own, he would justly lose the human whom he had possessed through this presumption."*

*see Rom 6:23

*PsBruno, Exp Heb 2:14 (PL 153:500–501)

2. "But a person without sin could not be found among humans, because, born in concupiscence, all were subject to sin.* However, if (as certain people allege) angelic nature was incarnated, when each one—that is, angel and human—might have sinning in their nature, each might easily fall, since it may be agreed that each nature has fallen by itself. So it follows that human nature can in no way exist without sin unless divinity is united with it."* And so except through the mystery of the Lord's incarnation, the way for redemption of humans was not open.

*see Lev 22:9

*PsBruno, Exp Heb 2:14 (PL 153:501)

"Therefore God wished to be made human, so that he might make humans more subject to his love.* *I have loved you with an everlasting charity*, he says. *<Therefore,> pitying you, I have drawn you.*†

3. A great mercy, by which the supreme power* willed to be humbled and diminished. A great charity, by which divine majesty lowered itself.* *He lowered the heavens and descended.** He lowered the heavens when honor and strength* of celestial realities descended to a human being. A great dignity of the one descending, but what was the nature of the one descending? Hear the prophet: *He descends like rain upon the fleece,** he whom nothing could bear if he wished to be known in his unmitigated strength. He willed to descend gently, without any noise, into the womb of the virgin *like rain upon the fleece*, to show his strength more than if he had restrained it. *As light rain,** which descends with supreme gentleness in the manner of dew, pours upon the earth, doing no damage, so God descending into the virgin's womb brings fruitfulness and does not take away virginity. For as the virgin conceived, so the Word became flesh. He did not mingle himself with any <concupiscence> of the flesh, but as a husband was the Word, and hearing played the part of wife. She heard, she believed, and she conceived by faith.

4. "Why do you seek the rights of nature when you see the gift of incomparable grace? The angel says, *The Holy Spirit shall come upon you, and the power* of the most High shall overshadow you.** The Spirit did not, as certain misguided people suppose, take the place of seed in her, but rather so great was the force* of divine love granted to her, which so guarded her in mind and body, that no heat of carnal concupiscence prevailed over her. She alone merited to be chosen from whose immaculate flesh God's Son would put on an immaculate body for

*PsBruno,
Ex Heb 2:14
(PL 153:501B)
†Jer 31:3
*potentia

*see Phil 2:7-8
*Ps 17:10
*virtus

*Ps 71:6

*Ps 71:6

*virtus
*Luke 1:35

*vis

himself. So consequently it is said to the same virgin, *For the Holy that shall be born of you*, etc.* Certainly it ought to be holy, since it had to be offered for the sake of sanctifying sinners. It was fitting that this generation* should lack vice, since it brought about the purification of Eve's generation.* Eve brought together two evils for those who followed her: that in sin they would conceive, and in pain would give birth."* Mary experienced no fault in conception or anguish in giving birth. "For one who came to gladden a sad world should not have made sad the hospitality of the womb. By this splendor, God's Son is conceived; by this purity he is begotten."* *Who shall declare his generation?*†

5. *Just as it is not good for one who eats much honey, so one who is a searcher of majesty shall be overwhelmed by glory.** So therefore with a simple faith let us be content to leave her secret to the Virgin. She alone understands who promised to be alone. She herself knows indeed. What the church believes piously, this we believe, this we say and teach, that *a virgin conceived, a virgin gave birth, a virgin remained after the birth*.* "For if a Sun's ray passes through a crystal, neither by entering making a hole nor by exiting shatter, how much more at the entry or exit of the true and eternal Sun did the virginal womb continue closed and intact! So this was prefigured by Aaron's staff, which was neither alive <with sap> nor fertile with seed, which it does not have naturally, yet it sprouted flowers and fruit.* So that bush burning and unconsumed is shown to be read as a type of this Virgin.*

6. *The first <human> was made from clean earth, the second from the chaste Virgin*.† If you are astonished at the sequence of the births, then note the power of the one being born. He is the human who is thus born and the same God who arranges so to

*Luke 1:35

*generatio
*generatio

*see Gen 3:16;
Ivo of Chartres,
S 15, Ann
(PL 162:584–85)

*Ivo of Chartres,
S 15, Ann
(PL 162:585)
†Isa 53:8;
Acts 8:33

*Prov 25:27

*Resp Adorna and
Ant Senex in Pur
(Hesbert 4:6051;
3:4864)

*see Num 17:8

*see Ivo of
Chartres, S 15,
Ann (PL 162:585);
see Exod 3:2;
see Ant "Rubum"
in Pur (Hesbert
3:4669)
†see 1 Cor 15:47

be born. "The mystery is contained in this wonderful conception by which, with the handwriting of transgression erased,* the divine and human are united and become *two in one flesh*,* Christ and the church, of course. The bedchamber of this union was the virginal womb, from which with his wife (that is, with our flesh) the *bridegroom as if coming from his bedchamber* has placed his tabernacle (that is, the flesh he has taken up) *in the sun*."* "Invisible among his own, for our sake made visible among us."*

7. "And so through the condescension to our humanity he became among us like the milk of little ones,* he who in the sublimity of his divinity is the bread of angels.* For through his flesh we take in majesty. Just as loving mothers serve liquefied solid food through their breasts* to meet the needs of little ones, and it happens in them through breasts so that they do not lack in abundance,* when strengthened by the nourishment of milk, they become capable of chewing the solid food of bread.* So also our restorer and nourisher, far removed from himself in the region of unlikeness, willed to suckle us with the milk of his incarnation, by which he would make us grow up into the most sweet and ineffable taste of his divinity,"* to which may our Lord Jesus Christ lead us. Amen.

---

marginal notes:

*chirographo;
see Col 2:14
*see Eph 5:31-32;
see Gen 2:24

*see Ps 18:6
*see Ps 18:6; Ivo
of Chartres, S 15,
Ann (PL 162:585)
*Leo I,
Tractatus 22:2
(CCSL 138:91)
*see 1 Cor 3:1-2;
see Heb 5:13
*see Ps 77:25
*ubera

*uberibus

*see Heb 5:14;
see Ps 13:4

*Ivo of Chartres,
S 15, Ann
(PL 162:585–86)

Sermon 166

On the Nativity of Saint Mary

1. **A** *nd there shall come forth a staff* from* *the root of Jesse*, etc.* Today what had been promised through the prophet very long ago is fulfilled. Today that staff has sprouted from which sprang forth *the flower of the field and the lily of the valleys.* The holy root, the blessed fruit.** The staff is the Blessed Virgin Mary, the flower is her son."† "The staff presents uprightness; the flower presents beauty. The staff [signifies] uprightness of lifestyle, the flower the glory of reward. These are two: an upright life and a blessed life. O humankind, in these two all good has been upheld. Anything contrary to these is wholly vain and transitory. The mother is the upright life; the son is the blessed life. The son is born from the mother. So justice precedes; glory follows. Uprightness precedes; blessedness follows. Merit precedes; reward follows. Embrace the mother so that you may live <uprightly. Strive after the son, so you may live> blessedly. Hold to the uprightness of the staff; desire the beauty of the flower. Reach for this staff: perhaps it will give not only the flower, but also the fruit."*

    2. The staff proposes uprightness for you. She brings forth her growth from above. She extends herself in advance, as she desires goods to come. "She does not stray to the right, as that would give in to prosperity through self-indulgence. Nor to the left, as that would mean falling in adversity through impatience. Therefore by the example of this staff, let

*virga
*Isa 11:1

*Song 2:1
*see Rom 11:16;
see Luke 1:42
†Hugh of
St. Victor, Egred

*Hugh of
St. Victor, Egred

247

us raise our heart above, *where Christ sits at God's right hand.** Let us seek God diligently, because it is written, *How good is God to Israel, to those who are upright of heart!** Therefore because God is above, one who seeks God <ought> to have his heart above. One who loves the earth and takes pleasure in earthly goods has his heart below <and> does not attend to *how good God is to Israel,** because, with a contrary will, he has become bitter toward him. On which account, let the staff be upright of intention, so it may hasten above with desire. May it also be slim, so that it may pass <through> a narrow space, because our good is lofty and our passage narrow."*

3. "So the song of love says about the Virgin, signified by the staff,† *Who is she who goes up through the desert as a pillar* of smoke from aromatic spices of myrrh and frankincense?** Notice that he calls her not just a staff, but a pillar, so that he may show her to be not only upright, but more expressly elongated and thin. *As a pillar of smoke,* he says.* Smoke, when it is discerned, seems to be something. When it is touched, nothing is found. Thus every good soul in this world is apparent through its type of life, in which there is no intention of pleasure. You see a just and upright person who hastens above with purpose. In this life, drawn by necessity, not desire, stretched above this life by desire and love, he makes of himself a staff going up from the desert.* He seems to be on earth by his way of life; with delights left behind on earth, while he is compelled to labor for the necessity of this temporal life he is known to manage earthly goods, to possess things that will pass away."*

4. "Until such a type is discerned, he is thought to be a body in mind and desire, that is, he seems to adhere to corporeal realities. But let touch come near,

*see Col 3:1;
see Heb 10:12

*Ps 72:1

*Ps 72:1

*see Matt 7:14;
Hugh of
St. Victor, Egred
†*virgam*
**virgula*
*Song 3:6

*Song 3:6

*see Song 3:6

*Hugh of
St. Victor, Egred

<and> nothing of the kind is found. What is touch? Adversity. For we are touched by adversity. Adversity, an approaching touch as it were, tests if we are what we appear to be. Just people who have been touched are not found to be what they appeared, because as though possessing earthly goods in time of prosperity, they could have been considered lovers of the world. However, when the time of adversity suddenly arrives and they lose their possessions without sorrow, they then show that <they> have by no means succumbed to them through love."* "So Job was struck by a touch of the most grievous adversity; he who formerly mistakenly appeared fat to discerning eyes on earth showed himself to be a pillar by his contempt for earthly goods, saying, *If we have received good things from the hand of God, why should we not receive evil?"* *

5. "Let us hear where such a pillar comes from. *From aromatic spices of myrrh and frankincense.*† These two types signify two virtues. Myrrh signifies chastity of the flesh, frankincense devotion of mind. Chastity in flesh, humility in mind. Pay attention now to our pillar—virginal flesh in myrrh, a humble mind in frankincense—how she <goes up> through the desert of this world,* born from the land of human flesh through marriage,* elevated above the corruption of the flesh through way of life, joining all the ointments' powders to the myrrh of chastity and the <frankincense> of humility,* so that <she was> *full of grace,** replete with gifts of the Holy Spirit. On that account, myrrh and frankincense are sent ahead, because when chastity and humility go before, they are accumulated with all the following gifts of virtues."*

6. "She who is called a pillar in myrrh and frankincense is named a sheep, because she is the mother

*Hugh of St. Victor, Egred

*Job 2:10; Hugh of St. Victor, Egred
†Song 3:6

*see Song 3:6
*conditionem

*see Song 3:6
*see Luke 1:28, 35

*Hugh of St. Victor, Egred

of the lamb. A sheep is a gentle and pure animal. Gentleness signifies humility, purity signifies chastity. Humility and chastity are two. Humility destroys pride, chastity self-indulgence. Thus the sin of the world is taken away.* For by these two the world sins, and Pharaoh, king of Egypt, king of darkness,* is served *in straw and works of clay and bricks.*† Straw is pride; clay is self-indulgence. Pride perverts the mind, self-indulgence the flesh, and a person's whole nature *is fermented in the leaven of malice and wickedness* (malice through self-indulgence, wickedness through pride), until *the unleavened bread of sincerity and truth* is restored, impurity removed, pride purged."*

7. "These two evils separate us from true good. For impurity sets up a wall against God's purity, pride against truth. For all pride is a lie. Pride is to consider oneself greater than one is, or to arrogate for oneself what is from another. Moreover, one who says he is greater than he is, or that he has what he does not have, lies. Similarly one who says that he has from himself what he has from another lies. So it is proved that all pride is a lie. From the outside, pride shows the appearance of integrity, but it does not have the substance within. Therefore it lies, feigning what it is <not>. The primary truth is confession of crime, by which a sinner humbly confesses <what he is>."*

8. Therefore let us contemplate the staff that has come forth from the root of Jesse,* "so that we may advance properly. Let us consider the flower of the staff, so that we may live blessedly. O uprightness of the staff! O blessedness of the flower! The blessed staff that produced a flower so wonderful! Through Mary Christ is given, through Christ salvation is given."* The staff came forth from the root of Jesse.†

*see John 1:29

*Aegyptus tenebrae; Jerome, Int nom 73 (CCSL 72:151) †see Exod 1:14; 5:7

*see 1 Cor 5:8; Hugh of St. Victor, Egred

*Hugh of St. Victor, Egred

*see Isa 11:1

*Hugh of St. Victor, Egred †see Isa 11:1

Come forth you also, *daughters of Zion,** to contemplate the staff and the flower of the staff, to see our king, King Solomon, the peacemaker king. Come forth, that is, be brought out from those flocks of goats on the left* by the height of consideration and the virtue of good pursuits. Come forth, because you shall not see your king unless you come forth. This coming out happens in three ways. We come forth by abandoning the secular world and things that are of the world outside us, by abandoning deeds and feelings of sin that are within us, by abandoning and forgetting ourselves in contemplation and sweetness of those realities that are above us. Therefore *come forth*, holy souls, *and see* your *king.**

9. There are three visions of this sweet and delightful king: in the world, in Judgment, in the kingdom. He appeared gentle in the first vision, just in the second, glorious in the third. In the first he was seen <by> the good and bad but not by all. In the second <he is> to be seen <by> all, good and bad. In the third he is to be seen only by the good. It is said about the first, *Blessed are all who see what you see.** About the second, *All flesh shall see the salvation of God.** About the third, *You shall see him as he is.*† The impious are invited to the first vision, terrified about the second, prevented from the third. It is said to those who are invited, *O all you who pass by the way, listen carefully and see if there is sorrow such as my sorrow.** They are terrified to whom it is said, *They shall look on the one whom they pierced.** They are prevented as it is written: *Let the impious not see the glory of God.**

10. Everywhere he is called king. King in the world, king in Judgment, king in heaven. In the first vision he is director of morals: *Learn from me*, he says, *because I am gentle and humble of heart.** In

*see Song 3:11;
Jerome, Int nom
(CCSL 72:138)

*see Song 1:5;
see Matt 25:33

*see Song 3:11

*Luke 10:23

*Luke 3:6
†1 John 3:2

*Lam 1:12
*John 19:37;
Zach 12:10
*Isa 26:10 (LXX)

*Matt 11:29

the second vision he is discerner *of merits, saying to the reprobate, Depart from me, you cursed, into ever-lasting fire.** But to the chosen, *Come, you blessed of my Father, attain the kingdom.** In the third he is the distributor of rewards. Following this triple vision three names are assigned to him: Solomon, that is, *peacemaker;* Ecclesiastes, that is, *preacher;* and Idida, that is, *beloved of the Lord.* Solomon is in the first vision, when he pacified not only what things are on earth, but those in heaven.* Ecclesiastes in the second, when in Judgment he shall call *heaven and earth to discern his people.** Idida in the third, *when* after Judgment *he shall have delivered up the kingdom to God and Father.**

11. *Go forth*, therefore, brothers, *and see* the flower of the staff, the son of Mary, our King *in the diadem with which* his Father *has crowned him.** For the Father has crowned him with one diadem, his mother crowned him with another, his stepmother with yet another. The diadem *with which his mother,* the incorrupt Virgin, *has crowned him*, was of the flesh, composed from four attachments* of human nature, certainly from love and joy, fear and sadness. When he showed these to sinners as well ordered, he turned them from sin to justice by his example. For sin is nothing other than disordered affection,* and justice is none other than ordered affection. Disordered affection is when something is feared that should not be feared, or not feared that should be feared, or feared too much, or feared too little. The diadem with which his stepmother, that is, the Synagogue, crowned him is of thorns.* Even in the Judgment, that is, in the second vision, he shall appear crowned in these thorns when he reveals himself as terrifying to that irritating house.*

12. The third diadem, with which his Father crowned him, is the crown of glory. The psalmist says

Margin notes:
*Matt 25:41
*Matt 25:34

*see Col 1:20

*see Ps 49:4

*see 1 Cor 15:24

*Song 3:11

*affectionibus

*affectus

*see Mark 15:17;
see John 19:5

*see Ezek 2:5

about this, *You have crowned him with glory and honor, O Lord.** The angels always desire to look upon him in this diadem,† and the chosen are destined to see. So indeed, concerning all the just (under the *persona* of one just person) this saying is understood: *His eyes shall see the king in his beauty.** The perverse and reprobate are deprived of this delightful and blessed vision; in this life they do not seek God, but rather they strive for worldly and transitory goods more than divine ones. But those whose *fellowship is in heaven** shall see their king with the diadem of glory, and they shall glory with their king forever. For *there is* no condemnation *for those who are in Christ Jesus.** *For the law of the spirit of life in Christ* shall liberate them *from the law of sin and of death.**

*see Ps 8:6;
Heb 2:7
†see 1 Pet 1:12

*Isa 33:17

*Phil 3:20

*see Rom 8:1

*Rom 8:2

13. *The law of the spirit of life.** Not that which was given to Moses *on mount Sinai in the old books,** but that which was given through Christ *in newness* of grace.* For as you take delight in *God's law according to the interior person,*† what means would you have if *the law of the spirit of life in Christ* did not liberate you *from the law of sin and death*? O human mind, because you do not consent to desires of the flesh, because the law of sin does not set you apart from the citadel of justice, *the law of the spirit of life in Christ Jesus* liberates you.* May you not take pride in that. It does not say that the law of sin and death is that which was given on Mount Sinai, but the one about which blessed Paul says, *I see another law in my members, fighting against the law of my mind, and leading me captive in the law of sin.** The law given on Sinai is a *good* law, *a spiritual and holy law, a holy and just commandment.** *Was that which is good made death to me? God forbid. But sin, so it would appear as sin, through good wrought death for me, so that sin*

*Rom 8:2

*see Gal 4:24
*see Rom 7:6;
see John 1:17
†Rom 7:22

*Rom 8:2

*Rom 7:23

*see Rom 7:12,
14, 16

might become sinful beyond measure through the
*Rom 7:13   commandment.**

*Rom 7:8   14. Before the law, *sin was dead.** Why is it that
it was dead? It was hidden. It was not apparent, as
if the grave was not known. But when the command-
*Rom 7:9   ment arrived, *sin revived.** For *I would not know
concupiscence if the law did not say, You shall not
covet. But sin having taken occasion through the
*Rom 7:7-8   commandment wrought in me all concupiscence.**
So therefore, one who had been a sinner without
knowing it has been made a flagrant transgressor.
Therefore the law was given so that weakness would
be discovered, or rather, so that it would increase,
and thus a physician would be sought. For if the illness were slight, it would be disregarded, and a physician neither sought nor the illness cured. Therefore
*Rom 5:20   *where sin abounded, grace abounded all the more,**
which removed all that it found and provided aid for
our will so we do not sin, so that the will itself may
be praised not in itself, but in the Lord. For *in God
*Ps 43:9   we shall be praised the whole day.**

15. Therefore, brothers, so that we may praise
God himself and merit to be praised by him, let us
flee for refuge to the staff that comes forth today
see Isa 11:1   from the root of Jesse, that is, to the virgin mother
of the Redeemer. For she it is through whom salva-
tion appeared for the world, the mother of God and
of our Lord Jesus Christ. May he by the merits and
prayers of his most blessed mother lead us to eternal
life. Amen.

On the
Assumption of Saint Mary

1. *Y**ou are wholly beautiful, my beloved,
and there is no stain on you.** This
lover's commendation of praise about
his beloved can be applied to any holy soul, but he
especially looks to the Blessed Virgin Mary, whom
the Holy Spirit cleansed of every impurity of body
and stain of mind, so that she would be wholly beautiful,* beautiful in body, beautiful in mind. The son
of the Virgin and the bridegroom of virgins commends her on account of her incomparable beauty
of mind and body, saying, *You are wholly beautiful,
my beloved.**

*Song 4:7;
Ant in Ass
(Hesbert 3:5162)

*see Luke 1:28, 35

*Song 4:7;
Ant in Ass
(Hesbert 3:5162)

2. "Wholly sweet, wholly pleasant. Uniquely
beautiful and singularly lovely." "The bridegroom
himself declares the proclamation of the Virgin's
virginity; to be praised by him is so great that it is
scarcely possible for his praise to be mistaken for
that of anyone else. The lover of true beauty and the
author of truth commends the appearance of his beloved and confirms her charity. He admits that <he>
loves the one whom he made lovable, and boasts that
he glories in being loved by her to whom he gave
the sweetness <of love>. O wonderful reality! The
bridegroom himself and son of the Virgin, author of

---

[1] All portions of this sermon enclosed in quotation marks come
from Hugh of Saint Victor, *Pro Assumptione Virginis*, in *L'oeuvre
de Hugues de Saint-Victor* (Turnhout: Brepols, 2000), 2:134–58.

integrity and fruit of fecundity. He praises his loved one, commends the lovely one, invites his beloved. *You are wholly beautiful, my beloved.** O admirable lover* and singular lover!* What do you say? She is your mother,* she is your beloved." If she is your *genitrix*, how is she your beloved? If she is your beloved, how is she your *genitrix*? "Beloved because untouched; *genitrix* because fruitful. You, the son of integrity and beloved of fecundity, have a virgin mother and a beloved rejoicing in offspring."*

*Song 4:7;
Ant in Ass
(Hesbert 3:5162)
*amator
*dilector
*genitrix

*see Ps 112:9

3. "First your beloved, the virgin mother Mary, begat you. Afterward your beloved, the virgin mother church, was begotten from you. Coming into the flesh, you became son of your mother bride, by the body of the Virgin. Dying in the flesh, you became the father* of your bride, by the faith of the Virgin. By being born of your bride, you have received the substance of infirmity; by dying, you gave the sacraments of incorruption to your bride. Everywhere a wonderful lover,* everywhere a singular lover."* "One is your beloved, one your bride, one your dove."*

*genitor

*dilector
*amator

*see Song 6:8

4. "Therefore call your bride, invite your beloved. O handsome one, call <the beautiful one>, the lovely fair one, the only beloved! Praise her beauty, lest she fear to approach the Beautiful! Speak her comeliness, lest she dread to join herself to the most Beautiful. Say in what way you first came to her, loving and seeking love, so that she hastens to come to you, loving and returning love. Speak therefore, you who are loved, speak to your beloved about her loveliness, speak about your love, so that your loved one may love you who love, so that she may ardently desire to be loved even more and may more quickly hasten to be united. Say therefore, *You are wholly beautiful, my beloved.** Why do you hesitate? Why do you delay?"

*Song 4:7;
Ant in Ass
(Hesbert 3:5162)

5. "*Show your face.** Come out, so you may see the Handsome One, and you may be seen as lovely." "Remove fear, take away terror! I who call see you. I have you present, I who invite so that you might come. In fact, I do not call you so that I might begin to see you, but so that I may present myself to you to be seen manifestly." "By no means do I call you if I discern you as unready, if I should see that you are less worthy. I call the pure one, I invite the sincere one, I desire the wholly beautiful one. *You are wholly beautiful, my beloved.** O what excellent fellowship! The All Beautiful, and the wholly beautiful."

*Song 2:14

*Song 4:7;
Ant in Ass
(Hesbert 3:5162)

6. "I am Wholly Beautiful; you are wholly beautiful. I the Beautiful by nature, you by grace. I am all Beautiful, because everything that is beautiful is in me. You are wholly beautiful because nothing that is ugly is in you. You are wholly beautiful: beautiful in body, beautiful in mind. Beautiful in body by grace of virginity, beautiful in mind by virtue of humility." "Beauty left nothing in you that it does not possess. Elegance wholly obtains the whole, comeliness preserves, honor rules."

7. "*You are wholly beautiful, my beloved, and there is no stain on you.** O humble virginity and virginal humility!" "Thus you have elevated the humble one, thus you have made the Virgin fruitful, so the Virgin might give birth to God's Son, and the humble one might have God as a bridegroom. No other was suitable for such [a bridegroom], nor could another [bridegroom] be found for such [a bride].* O worthy [bride] of the Worthy, comely one of the Beautiful, pure one of the Incorruptible, exalted one of the Most High, mother of God, bride of the eternal King! How beautiful you are, how pleasant, whom the searcher of affections* approves,† whom the inspector of hearts praises, whom the author of beauty loves, to whom the teacher of truth gives tes-

*Song 4:7;
Ant in Ass
(Hesbert 3:5162)

*Nec alia talem
decebat, nec alius
tali inueniri
poterat

*renum
†see Ps 7:10

*Ps 44:11

timony. *Incline your ear** to his words. It is he who speaks, he who invites you: he wants you to hear. He says, *You are wholly beautiful, my beloved, and there

*Song 4:7

is no stain on you."* "Rejoice incomparably, Mary, be singularly glad. Hasten to come, hurry to meet and to receive the kingdom of the Bridegroom, to

*Ant in Ass
(Hesbert 3:5162)

possess the inheritance of the Son!"* "Notice by what sweetness he invites you, by what charity he awaits you!"

8. "*O my comely one*, O my love, *my dove, my

*see Song 2:10

beloved*.* I joyfully embrace you, I regard you pleasantly, because I see no stain in you, because I gaze upon you the wholly beautiful. But it delights me much more because I find you wholly full of sweetness. *Your lips are as a dripping honeycomb, honey and milk are under your tongue, the odor of your

*Song 4:11, 10;
Ant in Ass
(Hesbert 3:5162)

ointments is above all aromatic spices*.* Your lips, your tongue, your odor and ointments: all are sweet, all are pleasant, all are worthy of praise. Here he recommends three: lips, tongue, and ointments. A kiss on the lips, reassuring words on the tongue, odor and perfume in the ointments. The whole Trinity comes to the Virgin. It receives a kiss on the lips from the mouth of the Father, receives the Word of the Father on the tongue, receives the Spirit of the Father and Word in the ointments."

*Song 4:11;
Ant in Ass
(Hesbert 3:5162)

9. "*Your lips are as a dripping honeycomb*,* because they have fullness and sweetness." "Honeycomb has honey and wax: honey is divinity, wax is humanity. Honeycomb is *the Word made flesh* in the

*John 1:14
†Song 4:11;
Ant in Ass
(Hesbert 3:5162)

Virgin.* *Your lips are as a dripping honeycomb*.† In you divine and human nature, released from the ancient discord, were joined to perfect fullness and eternal union with a kiss of peace. In you divinity poured itself into humanity, whence the God-Man Christ emerges from you with true humanity and

perfect divinity." "How sweet and pleasant you are, who alone were worthy to receive the kiss of celestial sweetness in your conceiving, and you drip the sweetness of the whole world in your giving birth! *Your lips are as a dripping honeycomb, honey and milk under your tongue.* What is *honey and milk under your tongue?** The Word of the Father under your flesh." *Honey under your tongue*: the Word concealed under your flesh.

*Song 4:11; Ant in Ass (Hesbert 3:5162)

10. *"The odor of your ointments is above all aromatic spices.** Your sublimity conquers all; your dignity surpasses every perfection. You were singularly chosen, you were ineffably elevated, you could be like no one in grace; through you grace came upon all the children of humans. So *the angel said to her, Hail, full of grace, the Lord is with you. The Holy Spirit shall come upon you, and the power of the Most High shall overshadow you.** Your excellence is beyond every merit. You are more eminent than all, holier than all the world. No one has been so full of grace as you,* a virgin mother who *alone without precedent* gave birth;* you have both preserved the lily of chastity and obtained the fruit of fertility. The Holy Spirit uniquely rested in your humility, he who brought about a miracle in your virginity comparable to none. Therefore *the odor of your ointments is above all aromatic spices."**

*Song 4:10; Ant in Ass (Hesbert 3:5162)

*Luke 1:28, 35

*see Luke 1:28
*see Ant Beata in Nat SM (Hesbert 3:1563)

*Song 4:10; Ant in Ass (Hesbert 3:5162)

11. "You have received ointments for enjoyment. You have received ointments for beauty, you have received ointments for scent." "Some are anointed for healing, others receive ointments to be made strong, and all receive ointments at need. You, favorite daughter, and full of every grace, most precious in your charms, you have been anointed for elegance of beauty and as a sign of love. You have also been anointed so that he may excellently pour ointment

upon you first, which afterward in your <womb> he would singularly have to receive. Over you he received the fullness of ointment *before* all his *fellows.** You after him, pleasantness before all. Therefore *the odor of your ointments is above all aromatic spices."**

12. Come, therefore, *my comely one*, because *"winter is now past, <the rain> is over and gone. The flowers have appeared, and the voice of the turtle-dove is heard in our land.** O wonderful becomingness! Such things are becoming to such a one."† The beauty of the loved one, the sad exile, the sweet homeland were all mentioned." First the loved Virgin is praised, and then things that are hers are praised, and all this happens as an incitement of love. The winter and rain are mentioned so that she may hurry more ardently to the desire brought about and may hasten thereupon to go out where there is pain, where sadness remains, where grief is recalled, misery reigns. This is the whole exile. And then he praises his own homeland and tells what joys, what delights, how great the charms and pleasantness are there: *The flowers have appeared, the flowering vines have rendered their scent, and the voice of the turtledove is heard in our land."**

13. "All things are full of love. All resound with love: flowers, scent, song. There is nothing that does not enkindle the soul.** The mind takes fire from these things, desire is enflamed, the soul itself does not grasp its longings. Not without pleasure can be heard what is full of so much pleasure."** "The beloved is called so she may come, because one who does not come does not arrive. Therefore what was said is recounted, so that she may come."

14. "*Winter is now past, the rain is over and gone.** Miserable soul,† listen, diligently consider! *The world passes away, and its concupiscence.*‡ All

---

Margin notes:

*Ps 44:8;
see Heb 1:9

*Song 4:10;
Ant in Ass
(Hesbert 3:5162)

*Song 2:10-12;
Ant in Ass
(Hesbert 3:5162)
†*O mira decentia!
Talia talem decent.*

*Song 2:12-13;
Ant in Ass
(Hesbert 3:5162)

**animus*

*Hugh of
St. Victor, Ass

*Song 2:11;
Ant in Ass
(Hesbert 3:5162)
†*Misera anima*
‡1 John 2:17

things that you temporally love pass away." "So why
is that which passes away loved, I mean, that which
should not have been loved, even if it had not been
transitory? The world does harm while it stands,
deceives while it passes away: cruel in standing,
treacherous in passing away. Hear therefore why you
may rejoice: *Winter is now past, the rain is over and
gone.** Winter, because it restricts and obscures the
body with the fog of ignorance, is lazy about doing
good and cloudy for the purpose of observing."
"Happy that soul who gets to hear, *Winter is past!*
Winter always passes away, but not all are worthy
to hear this, except for those whom it passes and by
whom it is scorned until it is overcome. To these the
winter is serious, and summer in desire. These alone
merit to hear, *Winter is past,* so that in its passing
they may rejoice when they receive consolation, those
who in its previous condition were afflicted and
sighed."

> *Song 2:11;
> Ant in Ass
> (Hesbert 3:5162)

15. Therefore, brothers, so that the winter may
pass away for us, and every temporal affliction and
calamity flee from us, let us imitate the mother of
our Lord as best we can, not loving temporal and
transitory things, but hastening to eternal and celestial realities.* By the merits and prayers of his loving
mother, may the Son of the Virgin and bridegroom
of virgins deign to bestow these on us, our Lord Jesus
Christ, who with the Father and Holy Spirit lives and
reigns, God through all ages forever. Amen.

> *see 2 Cor 4:18

Sermon 168

On the
Assumption of Saint Mary [1]

*Song 2:11-13;
Ant Tota in Ass
(Hesbert 3:5162)

1. **W**inter *is now past, the rain is over
and gone, <flowers have ap-
peared,> the flowering vines have
given their scent, the voice of the turtledove <is>
heard in our land.** "O happy and desirable hour
above all, when along the way that heavenly bridegroom receives his beloved as she comes out from
the prison of the world after boundless longing, and
invites her to himself with gentle encouragement,
saying, 'Come out with delight, chosen one among
the daughters. Let putting aside the garment of corruptible flesh at death not seem harsh to you, you
who while living are acknowledged not to love corruption of the flesh. May you not tremble or become
frightened at all: you are avoiding exile, you are freed
from hardship. There will not be further *sorrow and
mourning* for you, because these *former things have
passed away.*"*

*see Isa 35:10;
see 2 Cor 5:17
*Song 2:11;
Ant Tota in Ass
(Hesbert 3:5162)
*Wis 9:15

*see Gen 15:17;
see Mal 4:2

2. "*Winter is now past, the rain is over and gone.**
No more will there be *what corrupts and weighs
down the soul,** because winter has passed, whose
heavy torpor and sad frost is now dispersed by the
southern breeze, and *dark mist* is scattered by the
rising sun of justice."* "If there had not been mortal-

---

[1] All portions of this sermon enclosed in quotation marks come
from Hugh of Saint Victor, *Pro Assumptione Virginis*, in *L'oeuvre
de Hugues de Saint-Victor* (Turnhout: Brepols, 2000), 2:134–58.

ity in you, then adversity would have prevailed against you. And therefore with death of the flesh, you remove the corruption of mortality. Thereafter you spurn the whole world and the adversarial evils of the world. On that account, *winter is past, the rain is over and gone, flowers have appeared, the voice of the turtledove is heard in our land.**

*Song 2:11-12;
Ant Tota in Ass
(Hesbert 3:5162)

3. "What are these flowers, what are the vines, what is the voice of the turtledove, what is his land?" "For if *his ointment** is in us, we know him and his land, and we can perhaps prudently give back an explanation about the flowers, about the odor of the vineyard, and about the voice of the turtledove. *Winter is now past, the rain is over and gone, flowers have appeared, the voice of the turtledove is heard in our land.** After sadness, joyful things follow. After what causes pain has passed, what gives pleasure follows. *Flowers have appeared in our land.*† A great responsibility threatens us: to speak about vines, about flowers, and about the voice of the turtledove. About winter, about rains and storms we know many things."

*see 1 John 2:27

*Song 2:11-12;
Ant Tota in Ass
(Hesbert 3:5162)
†Song 2:12;
Ant Tota in Ass
(Hesbert 3:5162)

4. "Rains are enemies to flowers, because extremely violent waves of rain can knock flowers off the vines. So because *the rain is over and gone, the flowering vines have given their scent.** Soon with the blossoming springtime and the vines spreading their scent, the turtledove gave his voice, and joy was fulfilled. So he says, *The voice of the turtledove is heard in our land.** He does not say 'my,' but *our*, so that he may share it with us." In exile, in which each and every one obtains one's own portion by lot, we do not say 'our,' but 'my,' because the greedy and reprobate do not share their property with others but protect their own uses.

*Song 2:11, 13;
"Tota pulchra"
(Hesbert 3:5162)

*Song 2:12;
Ant Tota in Ass
(Hesbert 3:5162)

5. Therefore "our exile is called an impassable land without water,* a foreign land, where the song

*see Ps 62:3

*see Ps 136:4
*see Ps 136:1

of the Lord is not sung,* but *upon the rivers of Baby-lon* we sit and weep, remembering Zion.* There are never flowers here, or flowering vines, but sterile willows, having leaves and no fruit. By no means is the voice of the turtledove heard here, but *we hang up our instruments,** and we cannot sing *the song of the Lord in a foreign land."** This exile in which *we wander** is a foreign land, to which we have been expelled by driving sins. *In our land,* that is in heavenly Paradise, *flowers have appeared, flowering vines have given their scent, and the voice of the turtledove is heard.**

*see Ps 136:2
*see Ps 136:4
*see 2 Cor 5:6

*Song 2:12-13;
Ant Tota in Ass
(Hesbert 3:5162)

6. "Three things are mentioned here: flowers, scent, and song. Flowers pertain to appearance, scent to fragrance, song to pleasantness. Appearance refers to vision, fragrance to sense of smell, melody to hearing. These senses of the body were chosen before all and named because each has its own singular pleasures and draws up eternal joys with a certain flavor. So it is written, *Taste and see that the Lord is sweet.** And *I shall be satisfied when your glory shall appear.** And *You shall make them drink from the torrent of your pleasure, O Lord.** One who tastes already enjoys and has arrived at desire. Thus certain beginnings of everlasting life are signified."

*Ps 33:9

*Ps 16:15
*Ps 35:9

7. As the bride, that is, any faithful soul, impatiently runs to the scent of the bridegroom, she is invited so that she may come.* "What is more, after she stepped out of the tabernacle of her home so that she might hasten to her bridegroom, his eyes were revealed. And behold, from afar, as the land, as the homeland, as the enjoyable region all this while invisible and more beautiful than all sights, full of elegance and delights, where all the realities that are truly beautiful shine forth incorrupt." "To this view, therefore, the bride, transfixed with the whole of her

*see Song 1:3;
2:13; see Ant Tota
in Ass (Hesbert
3:5162)

desire, collecting herself to herself, ardently desired to know more fully from where such wonderful beauty had suddenly shone forth. Whenever the whole of herself is inflamed in this purpose and does not catch herself because of joy, behold, the sweetest of scents has flowed in, and certain sweet songs are heard, also wholly wonderful beyond what is familiar."

8. "Therefore the flowers, scent, and song are mentioned. By all these the sweetness of invisible goods and delightfulness of eternal goods are designated." "Flowers, because they draw attention to appearance. Scent, because it pours out delightfulness. Song, because it expresses sweetness." "Whatever is seen there is beautiful, is charming, and pleasant. But it is as though still from afar. Therefore it is not perceived by tasting nor handled by touch. And yet from a distance the composition is heard, smelled, discerned, and wonderfully restored, and draws the soul into eternal desires. So she implores, *Draw me after you; we will run to the scent of your ointments.*"* "Eternal joys are designated by flowers, scent, and song. For they restore all things from afar, and they give delight from a distance to the arrangements."

*Song 1:3

9. "There are many things that ought to have been said beyond these, but we are lacking and limited in knowledge and speech, and we are not qualified for matters so vast and high beyond our power." "For just as the eye is fed by the appearance of things without defilement, and just as the ear is delighted by the charm of voices without corruption, so those eternal joys pour in charm and do not induce corruption. They always restore, never fail. They feed and continue undiminished. They present themselves for full enjoyment and remain incorrupt."

*Song 2:12;
Ant Tota in Ass
(Hesbert 3:5162)

10. "*The flowers have appeared in our land.**
What sort of flowers? Lily, rose, violet, and in that
place is no flower that does not have its own appearance or singular beauty. There is where every beauty
is the pinnacle of beauty. There is one good, and
every good is in it. If you say flowers, if you name
fruit," all is the Power of God and the Wisdom of

*see 1 Cor 1:24

God himself.* He is the tree and the wood of life, as

*arbor est et
lignum uitae;
see Gen 2:9
†lignum uitae
‡Prov 3:18

was said about Wisdom,* as it was said about wisdom, *He <is> the wood of life†* *to those who grasp
him, and one who shall possess him is blessed.‡ The
wood of life was planted alongside running waters,
which will give its fruit in due season, and its leaf*

*Ps 1:3;
see Gen 2:10
†arbor uitae

shall never fall off."*

11. The tree of life† "has leaves, has a flower, has
fruit. Leaves cannot be lacking to it, because it has
shade not for darkness but for cooling. The bride is
made joyful by the shadow of the bridegroom, saying, *I sat under the shadow of him whom I have*

*Song 2:3

desired, and his fruit is sweet to my palate.* So what
can we seek in that place that we might not find
there? Only what is nothing is not in that place. For
all things were made by him" who is the Wisdom of

*see 1 Cor 1:24
†John 1:3

*Rom 11:36

God,* "*and without him nothing was made.†* *Because from him, and by him, and in him, are all
things.*"* "Hear Wisdom enumerating his favors and
delights: *I have brought forth the charm of scent*, he
says, *and my flowers are the fruit of honor and in-*

*Sir 24:23

tegrity.* *<I was raised up> like a cedar in Lebanon,
and like a cypress tree on Mount Zion, like a palm
tree in Kadesh, like an olive tree in the fields, and like*

*Sir 24:17-18, 19

a sycamore near water in the courtyards."*

12. "But lest perhaps this abundance cause us to
be forgetful, and, leaving the flowers behind, to count
trees (for rigidity and hardness seem to belong to
trees), we turn to flowers. *Flowers have appeared in*

*our land.** It happens by contemplation of eternal Wisdom, whose aspect, full of every pleasantness and splendor, draws the soul into everlasting desires. *One who enters through me,* Wisdom says, *shall go in and go out, and shall find pastures.** The pastures are within. There is the land in which flowers appear, whose perpetual vigor never withers." "In fact, as great as you may imagine is the beauty in contemplating eternal Wisdom, where the appearance of all realities thrives without failure, remains without passing away, stands fast without corruption, is eternal without mutability!" *"Flowers have appeared in our land.** This is invisible to those who only see visible things. This is the land where the light shines that the eyes of the impious cannot see."

13. *"The flowering vines have given their scent.** The flowers appear first; only now, behold, they are perceived. Pleasantness is in the flowers, usefulness in the flowering vines. Pleasure in the former, refreshment in the latter. First the sight appeared for pleasantness, but now scent itself and sweetness itself pours itself out according to its charm." "Nevertheless, the bride still stands outside and has to be led *into the wine cellar.** The [unfermented grapes] are not as yet ready for the wine press,* nor does the grape juice ferment in the presses so that the wine might be poured into new skins. For these are large and are saved for the delights of the following feast." So *arise, make haste, my love,** because *the vines in flower have given their scent, and the voice of the turtledove is heard in our land.*†

14. "The voice of the turtledove is appropriate for love and delight.‡ For the turtledove has a singular delight for which he sings either in joy when present or in affection when absent. So the voice of the turtledove is about love, and the turtledove does

*Song 2:12;
Ant Tota in Ass
(Hesbert 3:5162)

*John 10:9

*Song 2:12;
Ant Tota in Ass
(Hesbert 3:5162)

*Song 2:13;
Ant Tota in Ass
(Hesbert 3:5162)

*Song 2:4
*Non adhuc
torcularia
nominantur

*Song 2:10;
Ant Tota in Ass
(Hesbert 3:5162)
†Song 2:13, 12;
Ant Tota in Ass
(Hesbert 3:5162)
‡amori . . .
dilectioni

not know anything except love." "The voice of the turtledove is a song of love." "Therefore what does the voice of the turtledove say? He makes one sound and always utters it and never disdains it. The turtledove never varies his voice, never alters his song. He always sings the same, he always holds dear the same song. *The voice of the turtledove is heard in our land.** O voice of the turtledove, how sweet you are! And who will be worthy to hear the turtledove's voice?"

*Song 2:12; "Tota pulchra" (Hesbert 3:5162)

15. "The turtledove sings in solitude, and the turtledove always holds dear his solitude, because he seeks a singular delight. The voice of the turtledove is not heard in streets, and he does not put forth his call externally. It resounds within; he sings internally, and people cannot hear the turtledove except those who are on the inside, who remain in solitude, who dwell in secret, who rest in silence. *In the horror of a nocturnal vision, when deep sleep usually overcomes human beings,** then the turtledove opens the hearts of men and women, and they hear his voice. There he reveals the hidden word to his friends, and they perceive the innate quality of his whisper and keep his secret. And he allures and leads his <bride> into solitude and <calls> with sweet encouragement, so that he may go out and speak *to her heart** and give her to understand charity."

*Job 4:13

*see Hos 2:14

16. "O splendid one among the daughters! You have heard the voice of the turtledove, and you have understood." Therefore love your bridegroom! Love is threefold: natural, carnal, spiritual. Natural love is that by which parents embrace their children and children their parents; by right of relationship, kindred embrace their kin. Carnal love is that by which carnal people carnally join themselves to the carnal. Spiritual love pours out spiritual sweetness with

sweetness for spiritual people. It makes the sweet and desirable voice of the turtledove for those who listen. The turtledove is a lover of one. And the whole progression of sacred Scripture invites us to the sweetness of one love, teaches one, preaches one, commends one God to all. It calls and leads all the faithful to one joy, to which may the lover and redeemer of souls, our Lord Jesus Christ, generous giver and rewarder of virtues, lead us, he who lives and reigns with the Father and Holy Spirit, God through all ages forever. Amen.

Sermon 169

On the
Assumption of Saint Mary

1. **T**he glorious solemnity of the present day is celebrated and made a feast day not in one city, not in one nation, not in one corner of the earth, but in the whole world. *From the rising of the sun to its setting*, let the *praiseworthy name of the Lord** resound this day in the lifting up of the Lord's mother, and *through* all *quarters and streets of the city* that the *Most High has founded** the blessed Son of Mary is blessed, he who exalted the blessed woman *among women*,† or rather, above all women, *over the chorus of angels*,‡ and *blessed with every spiritual blessing in the heavens*.#

*Ps 112:3

*see Song 3:2;
see Ps 86:5
†see Luke 1:42
‡see Ant Exal in
Ass (Hesbert
3:2762)
#Eph 1:3

2. Today *the splendid woman among the daughters of Jerusalem goes up from the desert* of this age, *overflowing with delights, leaning upon her kinsman.** Today the mother of the supreme emperor, *daughter of the prince*, whose *steps are beautiful in shoes*,† goes up like a dove *over streams of waters*,‡ and most honorably stationed in the seat of majesty next to the Son, even now takes care to see the very powers of heaven. These joys of today's feast are to be revered—annually for us, continually for angels. Today they gladden terrestrial beings by the sweet memory of the Virgin to be venerated, and they continually bless the heavenly beings by her glorious presence. O illustrious day, illuminated by the Virgin's ascension, how beautiful, how pleasant the spectacle

*Resp Spec in Ass
(Hesbert 5:6994);
Song 8:5
†Song 7:1
‡Resp Vidi in Ass
(Hesbert 4:7878)

you present to angels and humans! With a sweet melody you soothe the ears of the young people who run after the bridegroom.*

*see Song 1:2-3

3. Let a diligent contemplative now lift up the mind's eyes, and today, with delight, admire how *the most beautiful of women,** adorned with necklaces of virtues,** surrounded on all sides by ministering spirits,† *comes forth as the rising dawn‡* and, wonderfully passing beyond the paths of light, enters into the ways of eternity.# She even approaches the pinnacle of glory, because *the Lord Sabaoth who sits upon the cherubim§* with all the heavenly princes and elders of his court, wholly delightful and wholly festive, gloriously meets her who bore him, sweetly greeting and embracing her with that right hand that *contains* and rules *all things.** The noble Virgin, inflamed by these first fruits of joy, spreads the secret of her heart, saying to the inspector of hearts, *Show me, whom <my> soul loves, where you feed, where you recline in the midday.**

*see Song 5:9, 17
*see Isa 61:10; see Resp Orn in Ass (Hesbert 4:7340)
†see Heb 1:14
‡Song 6:9
#see Hab 3:6
§Ps 98:1; see Rom 9:29

*see Wis 1:7

*Song 1:6

4. Behold how elegantly this Virgin begins the conversation, how wisely she pleads and efficaciously she concludes. Let us not wonder if the mother and nurse of Wisdom speaks wisely with Wisdom.* But the order of her words is this: *O whom my soul has loved, show me,* etc.* Mary had understood, taught by the divine Spirit, how God and God's Son ought to be loved, when the law says, *You shall love the Lord your God with your whole <heart>, and with your whole soul, and with all your strength.** Because she had fulfilled the mandate of the law—because [she was] *the mother of beautiful love**—she said out of the sentiment of her heart, *O whom my soul has loved.**

*see 1 Cor 2:6

*Song 1:6

*Luke 10:27; Deut 6:5
*Sir 24:24

*Song 1:6

5. Why is it that she says *has loved,* and not *loves*? Is it possible that now she does not love the one

whom she has only loved before now? Brothers, that *has loved* does not remove *loves*. This past does not take away the present, but preferably places, completes, and increases. And what is more, if she were to say openly, "The love with which I love you is not immature, it is not a novice, not for an hour, but raised with me and the same age as me, it began with me, grew with me, has persevered with me. From this I have been able to know you. I have laid bare all my interior for your love, and thus my soul has loved you."

6. Notice, brothers, that in this paucity of words the most prudent Virgin not only supplicates but instructs, <asks,> and edifies. She supplicates her superior, instructs inferiors, asks her bridegroom and son, and edifies young women, of whom *there is no number*,* that is, souls who believe in Christ. The teacher of true love instructs and says, "If any decide to ask something from my son, then let them first set the roots of charity in their soul. And just as was said by a certain wise person, 'Have charity and do whatever you will,'* so now I say, 'Have charity and ask whatever you will.' " This is the word that draws the Word, this chain that binds the invincible, the arrow that wounds the invulnerable: the word, chain, and arrow of charity.

7. What is said first (*whom my soul has loved*, I mean to say)* can even represent an ingratiating preface,* which usually is said first by one experienced in speaking, before the request, to prepare and gain the sympathy of the mind of the listener. This is done when something is said that commends the character or cause of the petitioner, or that looks to the praise and glory of the one who is asked. Saying therefore, O *whom my soul has loved*,* beautifully and elegantly she persuades her most sweet Son,

*see Song 1:2;
see Titus 2:4;
see Job 9:10

*Augustine, In
Ep Ioh, tract 7.8
(SCh 75:328)

*Song 1:6
*captationis

*Song 1:6

\<mindful\> of that admirable, of that incomparable work of mercy and piety that *he has wrought in the midst of the earth** for the redemption of the world, not from necessity but from charity alone. He then took up this work to be fulfilled when *he bowed the heavens and came down,** and the Word was made flesh and dwelt* in her, so that by means of her he might dwell *among us.**

*see Ps 73:12

*Ps 17:10

*John 1:14

8. Although Mary's soul always loved God, nevertheless her act of love (the effect and the fruit) is ascribed especially to that hour in which, at the entry and greeting of the heavenly messenger,** by the arrival of the Holy Spirit and the overshadowing power of the Most High,** the soul of the Virgin was intoxicated by such a great flood of charity that in the flesh and from the flesh, not touched and not known by a man, the mother of the Savior wonderfully (or rather, ineffably) furnished the material of flesh for the Son of the Most High. Behold, having said this alone, Mary's glorious merits are recalled to memory and are demonstrated as if to the eye, marvelously commending her character and cause, that is, her prudence and humility, virginity with fecundity, and charity drawing and consummating the entire event.

*see Luke 1:28

*see Luke 1:35

9. Likewise this little word represents the glorious proclamations of the one who is implored: the redemption of the world, certainly, the renewal of the fallen, the banishment of the prince of the world, the plundering of hell, the liberation of captives, the opening *of the gates of Paradise,** the restoration of the angelic fall, and many other wonders that would be too long to describe in detail. It is pious and worthy to discuss these often (or rather, continually), to believe and to venerate them with a devout mind. *Ask* now, Virgin, with such an ingratiating preface;

*see Ant in Ass
(Hesbert 3:4215)

whatever you will shall be given to you, I do not say

*see Mark 6:22-23 *half the kingdom,* * but rather the loftiness of the throne, the whole honor of the kingdom and fullness of your Son's glory, so that you co-reign as queen with him who rules, and may you see him alone above yourself, he who intends to make you more exalted than all the creatures that he has restored. *Show me*, she says, *whom my soul has loved, where*

*Song 1:6 *you feed, where you lie down in the midday.* *

10. Behold, now she asks, but she still does not

*Song 1:6 stop trying. *Show me where you feed.* * I seek the place where you feed. For I know the place where you used to be fed, and by whose service you were fed in the days of your mortality and indigence. Behold, I am your mother. *Behold* your *handmaid* and

see Luke 1:38 nurse, * I who have carried you in my bosom, nursed you with my breasts, put you to bed most attentively, mollified [your] wailing and weeping with kisses and blandishments. I served you, as you yourself know, in your infancy, in boyhood, in adolescence, in youth up until the cross, with as much diligence as I could. While you hung on the cross I drank tears and sob-

*Ps 39:8; 1 Sam 3:5; Song 1:6 †Ps 25:8; see Exod 33:18 *see Ps 67:4 bing. *Behold I have come. For you called me. Show me where you feed.* *

11. *Show me the place where your glory dwells,*† where *the just feast* and exult *in your sight and are delighted with gladness,* * whom you feed and intoxicate and restore with the sweetness of your presence. Your bed during the night was my womb, in which you rested before you shone forth, illuminating the world. Your morning bed was that noble manger, in

see Luke 2:7; 9:58 which you laid your head with morning light of your visitation already beaming forth. Your evening bed was that precious tomb, in which, after the hard

see Matt 27:60 labor of the cross and fall of death, you descended and fell asleep. I know these three beds. The first was

the bed of my integrity, the second of my poverty, the third of my worry. I seek the fourth bed.

12. Show to me the mid-day bed, that is, the bosom and secret of paternal majesty,* the dining couch* of the supreme Trinity, where you recline at mid-day,* that is, at the pure and full and true day, where there is clear light and true peace and full happiness. This is the best part, which the chosen and pre-selected Mary *has chosen*, which today is conveyed to her by her Son, that *which shall* never *be taken away from her*.* *The blessed fruit of* her *womb** has borne this fruit for her, the joy indeed that *surpasses every sense*.* Today she is ineffably raised up by him, sitting at his right hand on a throne of glory, as *the queen in gilded clothing, surrounded by a variety* of virtues.*

13. So blessed Augustine proclaims, in a certain sermon about this glorious assumption of God's mother,* saying, "How much I behold, how much I understand, how much I believe that the soul of Mary fully enjoys Christ's brightness and the glorious visions of him, honored with a special prerogative from her Son: possessing in Christ the body that she gave birth to, now glorified at the Father's right hand. And if not her own [body], through which she gave birth, at least his, to which she gave birth. And why not her own, through which she gave birth? If authority will not prevent [it], I truly believe it also to be that through which she gave birth, because such great holiness is more worthy of heaven than of earth. God's throne, the Lord's bedchamber, and Christ's tabernacle* is worthy to be in that place *where Christ is*.* Heaven is as worthy as earth to preserve a treasure so precious. Incorruptibility does not follow such great integrity with any unraveling of decay."*

*see John 1:18

triclinium

*see Song 1:6

*see Luke 10:42

*see Luke 1:42

*see Phil 4:7

*see Ps 44:10; see Resp Orn in Ass (Hesbert 4:7340)

genitrix

*i.e., Mary's body

*see Col 3:1

*PsAugustine, Tract Ass 6 (PL 40:1146)

14. Blessed Jerome seems to feel otherwise. For he says, "Although the church does not deny that the resurrection of the body is complete in the mother of the Lord, nevertheless it chooses and judges it safer to reckon this among secret realities and piously not to know rather than to define for certain what it holds as uncertain."*

*see PsJerome, Ep 9:2 = Paschasius Radbertus, De Ass 2:12 (CCCM 56C:114–15)

15. Jerome neither denies nor affirms that the resurrection of the body is fulfilled in Mary, because authority that might lend support for this does not object. Augustine not only does not deny, but believes and affirms, because authority that might contest [it] does not object. Therefore let *anyone who is fearful** and scrupulous sit at the tomb of the Blessed Virgin; let him embrace and kiss an empty stone. However, let those who have more ardent zeal take up *wings like eagles** and ascend to gaze upon that eminent vessel of divinity, the virginal body, I say, glorified in heaven. Therefore by her merits and prayers may we attain the heavenly realm. Amen.

*see Judg 7:3

*see Isa 40:31

Sermon 170

On the Feast of Saint Edward [1]

1. **E**dward, *since he saw himself dedicated to the Lord, from his first years strove to avoid guilt.** It is a holy, pious, and necessarily sought-after zeal by which evil is avoided and good is begun and achieved. Amos the prophet recommends this zeal to us: *Seek good,* he says, *and not evil, that you may live, and the Lord of hosts will be with you.** Would that my soul would forget her *people and* her *father's house!** Would that she would eliminate and spurn earthly business and carnal desires!** Would that she would put the baggage and enticements of this world far from me, so that I could have leisure for God, leisure for myself, leisure for this pious and holy zeal, so that with blessed Edward I might busy myself *avoiding guilt,* avoiding sin, avoiding death!

2. But by doing what shall I avoid death?* Is this not the way of all flesh?* *Who is the person,* Lord God, *who shall live and not see death?*† Certainly I shall avoid death by avoiding sin, because the cause of death is sin. For *through sin, death entered into the world.** Therefore, although it may be impossible for someone to avoid death of the flesh, still one who strives with blessed Edward *to avoid guilt* shall avoid death, because dying he shall not die, but through

*Resp in Vig nat S Ed

*Amos 5:14
*see Ps 44:11

*see 2 Tim 2:4;
see 1 Pet 2:11;
see Gal 5:16

*see Luke 18:18
*see Gen 6:13;
see Josh 23:14
†Ps 88:49

*see Rom 5:12;
see Wis 2:24

---

[1] Saint Edward the Confessor, king of England 1042–1066; f.d. Oct. 13. Aelred wrote his *Vita S. Ædwardi* after Edward's canonization in 1161 (CCCM 3A:85–181; CF 56:123–243).

death he shall move to life, and when he has died, he
shall live! Dead to the world, alive to God.* *see Rom 6:10-11*

3. Therefore this wise man, desiring to avoid
death, first *strove to avoid* the cause of death, *to
avoid guilt*. For what is the cause of death if not what
was said to our first parent, who sinned in Paradise:
*Because you have eaten of the tree from which I had
commanded you not to eat, shall you die the death?** *Gen 3:17; see 2:17*
Certainly the cause of death is disobedience; the
cause of damnation is pride, because *the root of every
sin is pride*.* The cause of death is transgression and *Sir 10:15; see 1 Tim 6:10*
violation of God's precepts. The cause of death is any
mortal sin that corrupts and kills the soul.

4. In fact, blessed *Edward, since* (that is, after) *he
saw himself dedicated* (that is, sanctified) *to the Lord,
from his first years* (that is, from the cradle) *strove
to avoid guilt*.* Let no one wonder that *he strove to* *Resp in Vig nat S Ed*
avoid guilt from the cradle, when before his days in
the cradle, as the Lord appointed and sanctified his
boy, still enclosed within his mother's body, he had
been chosen as king equally by clergy and the people.
Therefore this holy boy *strove to avoid guilt*, fearing
and avoiding every illicit deed, chastising his body
and subjecting it to servitude,* keeping his heart with *see 1 Cor 9:27*
all watchfulness,* so that he would please him to *see Prov 4:23*
whom he had devoted himself.

5. *He strove* clearly *to avoid guilt*, loving good
and hating evil, imitating and accomplishing the full
precept of the Lord, who said through the prophet,
*Love good and hate evil, and establish judgment in
the gates, if by chance the Lord of hosts may have
mercy on the remnant of Joseph*.* Do you wish to *Amos 5:15*
know how anxiously, how eagerly, how perfectly he
strove *to avoid guilt? He scorned all things that give
service to the flesh*.* There are two things that espe- *Resp in Vig nat S Ed*
cially give service to the flesh: pleasures and riches.

This saint avoided pleasures, feared pleasures, spurned pleasures. But how did he who abounded in riches scorn riches?

6. In his days, the glorious *king exceeded* his predecessors, *all the kings of* his *land, in riches and wisdom.** There was no king before him in England who could be compared to him in wealth and glory. After the Danish battles, after the madness and tyranny of the Danes, who were attacking and assaulting our kingdom, like the great Solomon himself, Edward restored times of peace for us, times of calm, times of tranquility, enriching his people and kingdom with gold and silver, peace and justice, riches and glory, because *God was with him and set in order all his works.**

*see 1 Kgs 10:23

*Gen 39:23

7. Therefore how did he spurn riches, he who prided himself in his scepter and royal power, overflowing with honor and glory, power and family and every abundance of goods? Nevertheless he spurned riches, serving God and not wealth, loving God and not money.* His riches were like public goods, according to what we read in his *Life,* because his treasure was a public treasury of the poor. Finally, he had boundless properties, and still he spurned riches, as though having nothing and possessing all things,* using riches not so much as suggested by pleasure of the flesh, but more sparingly, as prudence in the situation required.

*see Matt 6:24; see Luke 16:13

*see 2 Cor 6:10

8. So, by all means, *he scorned all things that give service to the flesh.** The pomp of the world, suggestion of the enemy, pleasure of desires, enticement of temporal delights all serve the flesh. Edward, the Lord's strong athlete, scorned all these. Still it is astonishing and extraordinary how the glorious king could scorn these, he who was exalted in royal power, eminent in authority, great in glory, glorious in

*Resp in Vig nat S Ed

power. Pay close attention to how he scorned all these things. The exalted prince humbled himself *under the mighty hand of God*,* small to himself, but great in the Lord's eyes, lord and servant, lord of many peoples, restraining and curbing the madness and attack of the tyrants, but a servant of the one and only God, *for whom to serve is to reign.**

9. The Lord's saint *strove to avoid guilt*, ruling powerfully and serving faithfully, seeing *himself dedicated to the Lord** with a purpose, with a vow, with affection and effect. He had been dedicated to the Lord for a purpose, because understanding God's great gifts, in which he prided himself and was blessed before the rest of the kings of the earth,* and frequently vowing with himself lest he be found ungrateful for God's kind deeds, he proposed in his soul to withdraw from evil, avoiding and turning away from crooked and perverse ways that drive one to death, holding and walking the royal way* *that leads to life.*† In this good purpose he made a vow to the Lord with his will more than with his words to extinguish carnal desires and the fire of pleasure in himself, thus embracing purity of flesh and heart, so that he preserved not only <chastity> but even virginity in marriage, humility in his reign, uprightness and truth in judgment.

10. Therefore, what celebratory praise shall we give to this our king, our patron, our attentive protector? There is nothing that comes to mind at present more aptly than what the Lord at one time said about his servant Job: *Have you not seen my servant Job, that there is none like him on earth, a simple man, upright and avoiding evil?** Behold this other Job, who had no follower in his own days, *a simple and upright man, and avoiding evil*, humble under the scepter, chaste in marriage, upright in judg-

*see 1 Pet 5:6

*Orationes Oro pace (CO 2:1110; CCSL 160A:120)

*Resp in Vig nat St E

*see 1 Kgs 10:23

*see Num 21:22; see Matt 7:13 †see Prov 12:28; see 14:12

*Job 1:8

ment. Simple in uprightness, upright in simplicity, devout in love, strong in faith.

11. Job, the praiseworthy servant of God, had at some time said, *I made a covenant with my eyes, that I would not so much as think about a virgin.* And still he begat sons and daughters. But this *true Israelite, in whom was found no guile,* truly made a pact and kept it perfectly, so that he did not think about a virgin, because, although he had a wife, nevertheless from the day of his birth until the hour of his passing on to the Lord, he kept his virginity chaste and intact in the flesh. He did not care about the virgin, he who, sleeping in the embraces of a tender and most beautiful virgin, could perhaps have been attacked but not plundered, or tempted but not conquered. For although flesh was with flesh every day, still he did nothing carnally in deed.

12. For he had heard and frequently read, *Make a vow and give back to the Lord your God; all you who are round about him bring gifts.* And therefore he preserved *his vessel* pure, sanctifying his offering in a most sweet whole-offering to the Lord,* offering to him daily a pleasing sacrifice, a turtledove and a pigeon:* abstinence and innocence, humility and chastity—humility of heart, chastity of body. Virgin in heart, virgin in deed, virgin in flesh. Therefore, to whom will he be more suitably likened than to the holy innocents and sacred virgins, who *follow the Lamb wherever he goes*, playing the lyre and singing *a new song*, which no one could sing in a harmonious voice except a virgin?*

13. Thus *he saw himself dedicated* with a purpose and vow.* He even saw with affection, because all the good things that he did in his life, he did cheerfully, not unwillingly but with devotion, not by coercion but by free will, not with fear of the law, but

*Job 31:1

*John 1:47;
see 1 Pet 2:22

*Ps 75:12
*see 1 Thess 4:4
*see Num 28:27

*see Lev 5:7

*see Rev 14:2-4

*Resp in
Vig nat St E

with sincere love of the Creator. He was therefore
see Judg 16:17 that Nazarene dedicated to the Lord, as was said,
with a purpose, a vow, affection, and effect. Loving
above all, and very much beloved by them—Jesus,
Mary, John, and Peter. He always had them in his
heart, in his speech, and in his work, through whom
*see Gen 39:2   *he was a prosperous man* in all his ways and works.*

14. He thus had a familiar relationship with *the
John 21:20   disciple whom Jesus loved, so that he saw him
bodily at the dedication of the church of that same
apostle and evangelist, who asked something from
the blessed king under the name of blessed John. To
him the generous king, since at the moment he had
nothing more readily available to give, removed a
ring from his royal finger and handed it to the pilgrim
who had asked. The blessed evangelist sent it back
Edward's   to the glorious king as the end of his *transitus* approached, indicating to him through a messenger that
the dissolution of his body was imminent, promising
to him his fellowship in heaven, him whom he venerated on earth before the rest of the saints.

15. How *blessed are the clean of heart,** who
*see Matt 5:8   merit to see not only God's saints, but even God
himself. This saint did that while still living in the
flesh. For since he was chaste of body and pure of
heart, on account of his purity of flesh and heart he
merited to see his Savior Jesus himself. In this monastery, at the altar of the holy Trinity, not only with
the eye of his heart, by which he always regarded
Jesus, but also with the eye of the flesh, through
human appearance, *he saw* his Lord God *face to face,*
*see Gen 32:30   *and* his *soul has been saved.** Eye to eye he saw
God's Son in a vision of a boy, whose blessing he
merited.

*see Ps 134:9   16. *Signs and wonders** that he did in his life
make evident and proclaim his excellence and holi-

ness: giving light to the blind, curing paralytics, driving out many illnesses by many and various methods. He predicted the future just as if present, and he knew those events that were happening in remote regions, just as easily as those being done secretly in his bedroom in the present. By these and things of this nature he grew strong and flourished in his life. But these remarkable signs of miracles were not lacking to him in death. For while he was still closed up in the burial mound, while he was hidden *in the heart of the earth,** as if one from the dead, *he worked miracles in the sight of the children of humans,** so that it may be known that he lives *in the sight of angels.*†

*see Matt 12:40
*see Sir 48:15;
see Ps 30:20
†see Ps 137:1

17. Giving great testimony in his *Life* to confirm this are those seven blind people whom the saint fed, whom a certain one-eyed man preceded, offering to lead the way for them. In the gloom and misfortune of their blindness they provided a wonderful spectacle for the people, with one being conducted by another. When these were afflicted equally with blindness and starvation, they arrived together at the tomb of the blessed king, and, filled with faith, they most devoutly asked to be freed from their present misery by his merits. By the merits of the glorious confessor, they were all immediately given light, going back with joy, *praising and glorifying God** and his holy confessor Edward.

*see Luke 2:20

18. Concerning the rest of the miracles that this wonder-worker performed in his life, and concerning those that happened at his tomb, because they are many and great, we, being reluctant to afflict you with the tedium of a prolonged sermon, shall stay silent at present and invite all to rejoice with us in this sacred solemnity of this illustrious friend of God. Let no one on earth hesitate to praise and glorify this confessor of the Lord, whom God so splendidly glorified

in heaven. But how did he have such great excellence, such great glory, such great power of signs? Certainly because *from his first years he strove to avoid guilt, scorning all things that give service to the flesh.**

*Resp in
Vig nat S Ed

19. Therefore, brothers, let us imitate him, our patron. Let us strive *to avoid guilt*. But because we have not done this *from* our *first years*, oppressed and afflicted by Pharaoh's yoke in Egypt and Babylon, at least in these final days, converted to the Lord, let us strive *to avoid guilt*: lying, deceit, hatred, and whatever is contrary to divine precepts. Edward the glorious Confessor of the Lord invites us to this. Generous to the churches, lavish to the needy, compassionate to the wretched, devout to God, humble to the clergy, gracious to the people, from his days in the cradle *he strove to avoid guilt, scorning all things that give service to the flesh.**

*Resp in
Vig nat S Ed

20. Holy in infancy, sincere in boyhood, chaste in adolescence, perfect in old age, today he merited his wage, receiving *the reward of his labors.** Today he moved from death to life, ascending from earth into heaven, where he sings with the virgin saints *a new song in the sight of God,** exulting and rejoicing with the glorious kings in heaven, where he glories in eternal happiness. May the all-powerful Lord lead us to that glory and happiness by the merits and prayers of his beloved friends. To whom be honor, etc.

*see Matt 20:2;
see Wis 10:17

*see Rev 14:3;
see Ps 67:4

Sermon 171

On the Feast of Saint Edward [1]

1. **T**he just person shall burgeon like a lily and shall flourish forever before the Lord.* This world in which we sojourn,† although it may be a place of exile, however much it may be a valley of tears,‡ is nevertheless where we must sow so that we may flourish in the future life. *For what a person will sow, this also shall he reap;*# because *the just Lord* shall give *to each person according to his work.*§ Woe to the wicked, whose garden does not germinate, whose seed rots in the ground,* not dying, so that it might come to life, but utterly failing, so that it eternally perishes! For they sow in the flesh, carrying out carnal desires, so that they also reap corruption from the flesh.* Departing from this life, they bring nothing with them besides sins, their evil seeds, with which *they shall be punished forever,* according to what is written: *The seed of the wicked shall perish.**

2. But *men of mercy, whose righteousness shall not be forgotten,** by whose labor and doctrine the church of Christ is educated and strengthened, in this life afflict themselves *with fasting, vigils, and labors** and the rest of the established, strict discipline, sowing in blessings, so that they also reap from blessings not corruption, but rather immortality, life, and blessing.* A faithful people always seeks the Lord

*Ant and Resp Com conf (Hesbert 3:3549; 4:7060)
†see Ps 118:54; see 1 Pet 2:11
‡see Ps 83:7
#Gal 6:8
§see Ps 61:13; see Prov 24:29; see Rev 2:23

*see 1 Cor 15:36; see Gal 6:9

*see Gal 6:8; 5:16; see 1 Pet 2:11

*Ps 36:28

*Sir 44:10 (LXX)

*see 2 Cor 6:5

*see 2 Cor 9:6; see Gal 6:8; see 1 Cor 15:53

[1] Saint Edward the Confessor, king of England 1042–1066; f.d. Oct. 13, canonized 1161.

their Savior through works of piety and justice, so that they may merit to arrive at him who says, *Come to me, all you who labor and are burdened, and I will refresh you.** This is the chosen generation, about whom it is written, *The generation of the righteous shall be blessed.**

*Matt 11:28

*Ps 111:2

3. In this generation, ruled and loved by God, our pious patron gained destiny and fellowship. I mean the illustrious King Edward, whose glory we celebrate, whose proclamations we lean upon today, by whose good deeds we are supported, by whose examples we are urged on to eternity. He is that outstanding king whose whole life from childhood to old age shone bright with virtues. This is the light that, kindled by the Lord, put to flight the darkness of depravity,* dispersed the cloud of vices, and illuminated the world with many rays of virtue. For as one necessary to all, the Lord's outstanding Confessor Edward, at every age, in every situation, left examples of a pious and holy way of life. Obviously the Lord found Edward *a man according to* his own *heart** and *magnified him in the sight of kings, and gave to him* grace in the eyes of all the people,† so that all might see individually in him what they might imitate and love, might see what in him they might admire, and rejoice.

*see Matt 5:14-16;
see Luke 11:33-36

*see Acts 13:22;
1 Sam 13:14
†Ant and Resp
Com conf (Hesbert
3:3671; 4:7059);
see Sir 45:2-3

4. Indeed, to this end the Lord willed to make obvious the virtues of certain people, so that among many weak people, he would show that certain people have been perfected, by whose teaching and example the less experienced might be taught and led to eternal life. Again, *narrow* and arduous *is the way that leads to life.** And therefore if there were not perfect people who had walked this way before us, we, the weak and crippled, would in no way presume to take it up. *Therefore,* so that we *not* march

*Matt 7:14

as though despairing through that broad way *that leads to death,** the way that is walked upon without difficulty, or rather with a certain delight of the flesh (which is more dangerous), the life of holy fathers is laid out for us, so that we not follow the flesh *that leads to death*, but by example of the perfect we faithfully take up the narrow and arduous way *that leads to life.** *Matt 7:13

*see Matt 7:13-14

5. This glorious king is put before kings and princes of the earth, teaching *mercy and judgment,** ruling his people in gentleness and fairness, showing himself pious to the gentle, humble to the humble, and more severe to the proud and fierce, just as the rigor of justice demands. *To the rich* he preached more by deed than by speech *not to hope in the uncertainty of riches,** not to *store up* for oneself *treasures on earth.** Certainly his treasures and wealth, which the Lord had given in his hand—now by building churches, now by refreshing Christ's poor—by lavish generosity he stored up faithfully in heaven.* *see Ps 32:5

*see 1 Tim 6:17
*see Matt 6:19
*see Matt 6:20

6. Therefore this *just person shall burgeon like a lily, and shall flourish forever before the Lord.** Sacred Scripture orders us to put our hands to a feast with diligence when we have been invited to a meal of any wealthy person. Now behold, today we are invited to the meal of a certain wealthy person,* to the meal of the glorious King Edward, of our pious patron and devoted founder of this church. Let us put our hands to the feast with diligence, so that he may feed us deliciously, because he is rich in virtues. Let us put our hands to the feast with diligence, so that in this meal we might take something from which we may be fed interiorly, from which our spirit may be sustained and revived. In fact, for this purpose the words and deeds of the saints are recalled

*Ant and Resp Com conf (Hesbert 3:3549; 4:7060)
*see Prov 23:1 (LXX)

to us frequently, so that by their example we may be inspired to holy pursuits, pious works, and essential lessons.

7. The meal of this wealthy person about whom we speak is the life of the illustrious confessor and friend of God, King Edward, *who pleased God in his days and was found just.** The feasts by which he restores us in this meal are the holy virtues in which he wonderfully abounded in the present life. For *in the time of wrath he was made reconciliation.** Having halted the attack of enemies who were assailing his kingdom, after grave and various disturbances to the kingdom, he restored peace to his people, with frequent prayer and pious service reconciling his household to his Savior, the Lord of armies. The sincere life of the prince held fast so that no malice of the enemy prevailed <over> the people. For in the days of this peacemaking king, the people enjoyed peace as well as riches, because for the sake of the devout king the Lord protected his people, overthrowing their enemies and reducing the foes to nothing.

8. The *just* king *burgeoned like a lily.** The man is held in high esteem because he was enriched with *glory and honor above all the kings†* who preceded him, because he was filled with the spirit of prophecy, because he gave light to the blind, because he restored paralytics to their pristine health, because he, this apostolic man, performed many other extraordinary deeds of virtue. Therefore he was so great because *he burgeoned like a lily.** What is it for a just person to burgeon *like a lily* if not to tread upon carnal desires, to keep his flesh spotless without any dregs or dirt of corruption, and to live in the flesh as though outside the flesh? Chastity is designated by the lily, whose root lies hidden in the ground, whose

*Ant and Resp Com conf (Hesbert 3:2544; 4:6609); see Sir 44:16-17
*Sir 44:17

*see Ant and Resp Com conf (Hesbert 3:3549; 4:7060)
†see Ps 8:6; see 1 Kgs 10:23

*see Ant and Resp Com conf (Hesbert 3:3549; 4:7060)

flowers are white, like incorruptible virtue, clear virtue, angelic virtue. This virtue lies hidden in the flesh against the flesh.

9. And so what has been put forth is beautifully assigned to this blessed king: *The just person has burgeoned like a lily.** In fact, his whole life was chaste and holy. Although he had a wife, nevertheless from the day of his birth until the day of his passing on to the Lord, he faithfully persevered in holy virginity. O treasure more precious than any gold, preferred to all power! For what could be more sweet, what more desirable than that which unites a human being with angels and makes one an imitator of Christ? It has been truly written about virgins, *These are they who follow the Lamb wherever he goes, for they have remained virgins.**

10. *The just person shall burgeon like a lily.** In the Song of Songs, concerning a holy soul, a virgin soul, a soul who has been darkened by no blackness of corruption, one reads, *Like the lily among thorns, so is my love among the daughters.** It is great and precious to burgeon like a lily, but it is much more excellent to burgeon like a lily among thorns. The thorns are the riches and pleasures of this world. Therefore *the just* Edward *burgeoned like a lily among thorns,** because among riches and pleasures, in which he abounded and was affluent, he guarded virginity in his body and humility in his mind. Finally, your merits are great, blessed King Edward, you who reserved your treasure of incorruptibility in a fragile vessel, in the tabernacle of your flesh!

11. Let anyone who can carefully assess how great the devotion, how great the praise, how great the veneration with which that glorious body should be revered and venerated, in which, like God's angel among human beings, without stain and far from

*Ant and Resp Com conf (Hesbert 3:3549; 4:7060)

*Rev 14:4

*Ant and Resp Com conf (Hesbert 3:3549; 4:7060)

*Song 2:2

*see Luke 8:14

defect of sexual desire, this precious confessor conducted himself. His flesh, which should have been naturally corrupted, persevered incorruptible against the nature of the flesh, by means of secretly working because it lay hidden in him incorruptibly. Therefore, *behold the odor* of God's friend, *like the odor of a*
*Gen 27:27
*plentiful field which the Lord has blessed.** With the odor of pleasantness, with the odor of sweetness, with the odor of holy and sincere chastity, the life of this just man permeated Christ's church, he who in
*Ant and
Resp Com conf
(Hesbert 3:3549;
4:7060)
†see Eph 6:12
‡see Dan 13:56
this fragile life *burgeoned like a lily,** fighting against flesh and blood,† against riches and pleasures, lest perhaps his heart be overthrown‡ and consent to vice.

*see Luke 11:21
12. And because this wise man did not guard an empty courtyard,* but one filled with virtues, malicious spirits who jealously attack virtues continually lay in ambush against him. The soldier of Christ prudently fought against them so that he would keep inviolable his treasures (humility in his reign and chastity in marriage); he endured repeated martyrdom in his flesh. Certainly there is no greater battle, no more serious struggle, and no more precious victory than to feel the attacks of intrusive temptations and not consent. Therefore let us imitate this brave athlete of Christ, vigorously contending against vices of the flesh, carefully and cautiously fortifying ourselves against ambushes and wickedness of malicious spirits.

13. Let us follow this rich man to whose meal we are gathered today, he who today deliciously feeds us with incorruptible food, invisible food, spiritual food. The feast that this rich man puts before us in
*see Prov 23:1
(LXX)
his meal* refreshes souls, fends off eternal hunger, leads to perpetual satiation. These are the holy virtues: chastity, humility, charity, faith, repeated prayer,

continual devotion, patience, fortitude, and other virtues of this nature that the life of this true Israelite preached to us.* These are a holy feast, a delicious feast, a feast necessary to the soul. These are the clean and white garments* with which human souls are adorned, holy souls, so they do not return to their Creator naked or empty.* These are the strait ways through which *the Lord led the just man and showed him the kingdom of God.**

14. Let us imitate this imitator of Christ, who shows us the ways of life by his pious habits. Let us love and imitate the chastity, humility, patience, and charity of this friend of God. Let us praise and venerate him with all devotion, and because he desires holy and honest compliance (so that the speech of our mouth may be pleasing to him),* let us keep to his ways, because his paths are strait paths,* just paths, paths through which the Lord drew him and introduced him into his kingdom.* May we merit to arrive at his kingdom by the merits and prayers of this glorious confessor, as our Creator provides, to whom be authority and glory through all ages. Amen.*

*see John 1:47

*see Rev 3:4-5

*see 2 Cor 5:3;
see Sir 35:6

*Ant and Resp in
Com conf
(Hesbert 3:3541;
4:7059);
Wis 10:10

*see Ps 18:15;
see Sir 2:19
*see Isa 26:7

*see Wis 10:10

*see 1 Pet 4:11

Sermon 172

On the Feast of Saint Edward [1]

*Ant in Com mar (Hesbert 3:3544); Sir 39:6

*see Col 3:1-2

*see Ps 118:133
*see Ps 36:27
*see 1 Tim 4:7; see 1 Cor 7:32

*see Ps 118:133

1. *A*t daybreak the just person will give his heart to keeping watch for the Lord who made him, and he will pray in the sight of the most High.* Beautiful and honest, to be venerated and proclaimed, is the occupation and way of life of the just person who seeks *things that are above, not things that are upon the earth.** Misfortunes do not weaken, good fortune does not cause to exult, enticements of the world do not seduce, desires of the flesh do not diminish his praiseworthy strength. For the just person carefully directs his *steps according to the speech* of his God, *so that no iniquity might have dominion over him.**

2. One who avoids evil and does good* directs his steps, exercising himself* in matters that are of God, inciting his soul to obedience, to discipline, to holy meditation. Therefore, as was said above, the occupation of the just person is pious and honest. Such a one always desires not temporal things but eternal ones, not corporeal but spiritual, not earthly but heavenly; this person always thinks, always chooses, and continually aspires to these.

3. The just person directs his *steps according to the speech* of his God,* humbling himself *under the*

---

[1] Saint Edward the Confessor, king of England 1042–1066; f.d. Oct. 13. After Edward's canonization in 1161, Aelred wrote *Vita Sancti Ædwardi, Regis et Confessoris* (CCCM 3A:85–181; CF 56:123–243).

mighty hand of God,* obeying the precepts of his superiors,* not doing his own will but that of theirs, imitating his Lord, who says, *I have not come to do my own will, but his who sent me, the Father.** The just person directs his *steps according to the speech* of his God,† avoiding and fleeing *works of darkness,** so his ways do not become *dark and slippery,** as he always remains vigilant and fights against flesh and blood and the devil, the inciter and accuser of vices.*

4. Why, *lazy one, do you sleep? The just one* gives *his heart to keeping watch:** he is not lethargic, does not rest, does not act halfheartedly, but keeps watch. He keeps watch in prayer, in work, in fasting, in difficulty and affliction, seeking his Lord, who, as Job says, *is not found in the land of those who live pleasantly,** that is, of those who walk according to the flesh, *who are clothed in soft garments,** who follow the desires of the flesh and embrace their own will. God is not found in their land. So the bride says in the Song of Songs, *In my bed I sought him whom my soul loves. I sought him and found him not. I found him not,* she says, *in bed.** Although *his place* may have been *made in peace,** nevertheless it is discovered with labor. Not those who sleep, but those who keep watch find him. He dwells in high and steep places. On that account *narrow* and steep *is the way that leads to life.**

5. For us, therefore, who have the Lord as a helper (as it is written that God cooperates with all who do good),* the *yoke* of Christ becomes *sweet, and* his *burden light.** Let us not continually shrink back at the rigor of the established Order. Let us put forth the twofold life before the eyes of the human condition, and sin will not be enticing. Behold, brothers, aroused from sleep, we hesitate to arrive at eve-

*see 1 Pet 5:6
praelatorum

*John 6:38
(as in RB 5.13);
see John 6:39
†see Ps 18:133
*see Rom 13:12
*see Ps 34:6

*see Rev 12:10

*Prov 6:9;
Ant in Com mar
(Hesbert 3:3544);
Sir 39:6

*Job 28:13
*Matt 11:8

*Song 3:1
*see Ps 75:3

*Matt 7:14

*see Rom 8:28
*see Matt 11:30

ning. Again yielding our bodies to rest, we are
ignorant about the arrival of light. Everywhere mindful of nature and also of fickle life, let us understand
that we are guided by God's providence.

6. Considering these matters, we shall not fall
short, we shall not be ravaged by some fleeting lust,
but neither shall we go around collecting earthly
treasures; on the contrary, with daily fear of retreat
and with continual meditation expecting the end,
we will tread upon all perishable things. Love of
women will cease, the fire of sexual desire will be
extinguished, we shall forgive each other's debts,
always having before our eyes the advent of the
ultimate retribution. So indeed greater dread and
horrible fear of punishments dissipate the induce-
ments of the slippery flesh. So it is, that saying of
Solomon: *Son, constantly ponder your last end, and*
*you will never sin.**

*Sir 7:40

7. Therefore let us press on to the end of our
purpose with all toil. Let no one who is *looking back*
imitate Lot's wife,* because the words of Truth are,
No one putting his hand to the plow and looking
*back is fit for the kingdom of God.** To look back is
nothing other than to regret what you have begun
and to be caught up in desires of the world again. In
this the children of Israel are blameworthy, they who
while in the desert desired to return to Egypt, where
they had sat *over the flesh pots.** But we, brothers,
having come out of Egypt, tonsured and clothed in
our habits, renouncing Pharaoh and his works, let
us not go back with desire into Egypt, let us not covet
flesh pots, illicit and dirty desires of the flesh.

*see Gen 19:17, 26;
see Luke 17:32

*Luke 9:62

*see Exod 16:3

8. In fact, sacred Scripture tells what the children
of Israel endured when they desired only meat and
not God: *Their meat was still in their mouth*, it says,
and the wrath of God came upon them, and killed

*the fat ones among them.** These things happened to the children of Israel, who, after receiving the manna, abandoned God. These things happen even now in the church. If anyone is refreshed by the flesh and blood of Christ and immediately turns away to vice, he will know that God's Judgment threatens him, just as the apostle Paul says: *Whosoever receives the body and blood of Christ unworthily exacts judgment upon himself.** On that account, *the just person*, lest he be condemned with the world, resisting carnal desires,* *gives his heart at daybreak to keeping watch for the Lord who made him.**

9. Daybreak is when darkness is divided at the beginning of the dawn. *At daybreak the just person will give his heart to keeping watch*, because having cast out the darkness of sins, and at the beginning of the dawn of virtues, the devout and constant person keeps watch in prayer, saying securely with the prophet, *Give <ear>, O Lord, to my words.** "No one has this confidence except the just. One who is a sinner has not dared to say, *Give ear, O Lord, to my words*. One who is angry and curses dares not say, *Give ear, O Lord, to my words*; rather, he hopes that God will close his ears."* But the just person confidently prays, saying, *Understand my outcry, O Lord.**

10. "An outcry in the Scriptures is not of the voice but of the heart. So the Lord says *to Moses, Why do you cry out to me?** In no way does he cry out with the sound and noise of his voice. And the apostle says, *Crying in your hearts: Abba, Father.** One who cries out does not cry in his heart, but on his tongue. When therefore our groans* and conscience beseech God, we cry out in our hearts, and God hears this outcry. So also Jeremiah says, *Let the pupil of my eye not be still.** For sometimes the pupil of the eye also cries out to God. Just as we cry out in our hearts,

*Ps 77:30-31

*1 Cor 11:27, 29

*see 1 Pet 2:11

*Ant in Com mar (Hesbert 3:3544); Sir 39:6

*Ps 5:2

*Jerome, Tract Ps 5.2 (CCSL 78:12)
*Ps 5:2

*Exod 14:15

*see Gal 4:6

*see Ps 37:10

*see Lam 2:18

*Jerome,
Tract Ps 5.2
(CCSL 78:12–13)
†Ant in Com mar
(Hesbert 3:3544);
Sir 39:6
‡Ps 5:3

*Jerome, Tract Ps
5.3 (CCSL 78:13);
see Rom 6:12

*see Phil 3:19

*Jerome, Tract Ps
5.3 (CCSL 78:13)

*Ant in Com mar
(Hesbert 3:3544);
Sir 39:6
†Ps 5:4

*Jerome, Tract Ps
5.4 (CCSL 78:13)

*Ps 54:18

*see Ps 53:9
†see Ps 54:19
‡Eph 2:14

*Ant Com mar
(Hesbert 3:3544);
Sir 39:6
†see Ps 68:18;
see Ps 101:3
‡Ps 5:4

when we beseech God with a groan, so when we pour out tears to God, the pupil of our eye cries out to God."*

11. *At daybreak the just person will give his heart to keeping watch for the Lord who made him,*† crying out from the heart to his Creator, *My King and my God.*‡ "He alone truly says, *My King and my God*, for whom *sin may not reign in* his *mortal body.*"* The just person says with great confidence, *My King and my God.* "May you reign in me, seeing that sin may not reign in me because you are my God. [My] belly is not my God,* gold is not my God, sexual desire is not my God. You are virtue, and I want to have virtues; therefore you are my God, because you are my virtue."*

12. *At daybreak the just person will give his heart to* prayer.* And in the morning the Lord will listen to him, according to the psalmist, *In the morning you will listen to my voice.*† "What then? Does he who listens in the morning not listen in the evening? Does he not listen at midnight?"* Scripture says in another place, *Evening, morning, and at noon I shall tell and declare, and he will listen to my voice.** Evening, when Christ undertook the passion for us. Morning, when he was resurrected. Noon, when he ascended the heavens having fulfilled the glory of his virtue. Every just person devoutly venerates and faithfully declares these times. *I shall tell*, therefore, *and declare*, because he rescued me from tribulation of death, redeeming my soul from enemies* in peace,† that is, in Christ, who *is our peace, who made both one.*‡

13. *At daybreak the just person will give his heart to keeping watch,** and the Lord in the morning, that is, *swiftly*, will listen to him,† according to the promise of the psalmist, who says, *In the morning you will hear my voice.*‡ "As long as I remain in the error of faithlessness and darkness of sins, you do

not listen to me. But in the morning, that is, as the sun of justice appears in my heart,* immediately as the darkness of sins begins to flee, immediately in the beginning of good work, you listen to me."* *At daybreak*, finally, *the just person will give his heart to keeping watch for the Lord who made him, and he will pray in the sight of the most High.**

14. God himself is the most high, under whom all things are placed, and who created the universe, and gave what he willed and as he willed for all things to be. In his sight the just person prays with confidence, saying, *Do not turn away your face from me.** The sinner and the impious dare not say this, but say instead, *Turn away your face from my sins.†* Our first parent, the old Adam,‡ after sinning, wished to hide himself <*from God's face*> among the trees of Paradise,* saying to the Lord, *I heard your voice in the middle of Paradise, and I was afraid because I was naked.** And Cain, after the fratricide, was cast out *from the face of the Lord*, made *a vagabond and a fugitive on the earth.**

15. A sinner flees from *the face of God*, because *everyone who acts badly hates the light.** The place of darkness is far from the region of lights. Far from the region of the living is the region of unlikeness, the dwelling of sinners, because *salvation is far from sinners.** The impious one is cast out *from the face of God* by sins that drive out.* The just person, approaching God by good works, *prays in the sight of the most High, at daybreak* keeping watch for *the Lord** and attending to God in the morning, according to the psalm: *In the morning I shall stand before you, and will see, because you are not a God who wills iniquity.**

16. "Not in the evening, not in darkness, but *in the morning I shall stand* constantly *before you,* and I shall imitate Moses;* *I shall stand before you,* not

---

*see Mal 4:2

*Jerome, Tract Ps 5.4 (CCSL 78:13)

*Ant in Com mar (Hesbert 3:3544); Sir 39:6

*Ps 101:3; see Ps 26:9
†Ps 50:11
‡see 1 Cor 15:45

*see Gen 3:8

*Gen 3:10

*see Gen 4:12, 14, 16

*John 3:20

*Ps 118:155
*see Gen 4:14, 16

*Ant in Com mar (Hesbert 3:3544); Sir 39:6

†Ps 5:5

*see Exod 24:12, 18

before another. As the light of virtues begins in my
soul, I shall not sit, I shall not lie down, but *I shall
stand before you*, and you will set *my feet upon a
rock*,* and then I shall merit to see you, *because you
are not a God who wills iniquity.*"* Therefore I flee
iniquity and follow justice, running *in the way of
your commands*† and with the prophet sighing for
you: *As the deer longs for springs of water, so my
soul longs for you, O God.**

*Ps 39:3

*Ps 5:5; Jerome,
Tract Ps 5.5
(CCSL 78:14)
†see Ps 118:32

*Ps 41:2

17. When a deer finds a snake he draws it out
with his nose, and after this, beginning to burn, in
order to extinguish his thirst he hurries to a spring.
Therefore a human being who spends a long time in
a venomous deed, when he looks back at himself
polluted with the filth of fornication and the stench
of vices, preceded by God's grace and stung with
contrition, hurries to come to Christ, who *is the
fountain of life*,* so that once cleansed in him, he
receives the gift of forgiveness and is made just from
unjust, holy from a sinner. And so having extinguished the vices, the just person is inflamed with the
desire for contemplation of the Lord, saying, *As the
deer longs for springs of water, so my soul longs for
you, O God.** Having left the world, I want to cross
over to you. *When shall I come and appear before
the face of my God?** When will be the time that in
that glory by which the saints are conformed to your
glory, I may appear in splendor with them?**

*see Ps 35:10

*Ps 41:2

*Ps 41:3

*see Phil 3:21

18. In this way, *at daybreak the just person* gives
*his heart to keeping watch for the Lord who made
him.** In the desire of seeing God and so that he
might appear to his face in splendor, the glorious
king has faithfully persisted—Edward, beloved of
God, giving *his heart to keeping watch for the Lord
who made him, in the sight of the most High** press-
ing on with devout and constant prayers. God in-

*Ant in Com mar
(Hesbert 3:3544);
Sir 39:6

*Ant in Com mar
(Hesbert 3:3544);
Sir 39:6

spired a love of chastity in Edward from his infancy,
hatred for vice, passion for virtue, desire for heavenly
things, contempt for earthly ones.

19. He presented himself as a fellow to his household servants, humble to priests, gracious to common
people, compassionate to the unfortunate, generous
to the needy. His treasure, as we read in his *Life*,
was seen as public property of the whole region, a
common treasury of the poor, because if he was
asked, the king made available all that he had, sup-
posing it to be not only his but everyone's; if he was
received, then he remained silent, a modest receiver,
a cheerful giver. So it was as though possessing all
things and having nothing,* he judged his goods to
be communal property for all.* He was poor among
riches, sober among pleasures, humble under the
purple, and under the gold crown a despiser of the
secular world.

20. What was the manner of the origins of this
blessed king's holiness? Even though it might not be
within our ability to explain, nevertheless we should
not be completely silent about what we have truly
heard and faithfully read about him. This saint, while
enclosed within his mother's womb, was preferred
to the legitimate and grown sons by him who does
all things according to the counsel of his own will;
he who reigns in a kingdom of humans desired to
give that to whomever he might wish. For the eminent king Edeldred,* father of our blessed patron,
having two sons (Edmund, surnamed Iron Side,†
from the daughter of Earl Thoretus, and Elured‡
from Queen Emma), being threatened by an enemy
sword, anxiously considered which of them should
succeed him in royal power, and whom he would
more safely leave after himself as defender of the
kingdom in such difficult times.

*see 2 Cor 6:10

*see Acts 2:44;
4:32

*Æthelred II
(r. 978–1013,
1014–1016)
†Ferreum Latus,
Ironside
‡Alfred

21. Finally, at the king's instruction, there was a great gathering of bishops, of counts, and of nobles, and a large crowd of common people in his presence. And when the king asked advice of each and every one quite earnestly, on account of various opinions from various leaders, he weighed the matter in question. For some chose Edmund on account of his strength of body, and others preferred Elured to Edmund on account of the power and military service of the Normans.[2] But the Foreknower of all things that were to come, choosing neither of them to be king, overturned the votes of all in favor of Edward, who was not yet born. Still enclosed in the womb and chosen as king, the one not yet born was preferred to the one already born. And he who was not yet received by the land was designated lord of the land.

22. And so the chosen boy was born and bathed in the sacred font, made into an abode of the Holy

*see Wis 1:5

Spirit, and nourished in his discipline.* Chaste in body, frugal in words, simple in deed, pure in affection, with wonderful benevolence and gracious services he won over the love of all his contemporaries for himself. Meanwhile, as the barbarians were invading England and laying waste a large part of the island in slaughter and burning, the queen was transferred to Normandy with her children.

23. And so as the enemy sword raged in England, churches were set afire, monasteries were laid waste, and the bishops were put to flight from their sees; lamenting the common misery, they took refuge in deserted places. One of these, Britwold, the bishop of Winchester, entering the monastery at Glastonbury, took time for psalms and prayers. Between his prayers and tears he grew weary. When sleep over-

---

[2] Elured's mother Emma was Norman, and both he and Edward grew up in Normandy.

took him, he saw through a dream blessed Peter situated in a lofty place. There also seemed to be a man of splendid countenance before him, dressed in royal emblems. With his own hands the apostle consecrated and anointed this man as king; commending to him a celibate life, he revealed that he would be [celibate] for as many years as he reigned.

24. Astonished by this vision, blessed Britwold asked the holy apostle for the secret of this vision to be revealed to him. Blessed Peter said to him, "*The Lord* will choose *for himself a man according to his own heart, who will do all* his *will,*** who with my help will secure the kingdom of the English and will put an end to the Danish madness. For he will be accepted by God, gracious to human beings, terrible to enemies, lovable to citizens, useful to the church." All of this was fulfilled in blessed Edward.

*see 1 Sam 13:14; see Acts 13:22

25. Therefore let your charity carefully consider of what great honor he is worthy, he whom the Lord so honored* that before he was born, he was designated lord of the land. Not yet anointed by a human, he was spiritually consecrated as king by Blessed Peter. Such prophecies preceded our patron before he was born. In the end, after he was born and consecrated as king, Edward, the man of God, was made into an abode of the Holy Spirit. No one ever saw him either puffed up with pride or unhinged with anger or disgraced with gluttony. But an appearance of sanctity continually shone in him, he who appeared pleasant in his countenance, serious in his gait, simple in his affection.

*venerabatur

26. How shall I praise his modesty? His gracious chastity persevered in exile as a companion in adversity, an inseparable comrade for him in prosperity. So great was his purity of heart that he would contemplate God's Son in visible form. *Blessed are the pure of heart, for they will see God.** So this saint

*Matt 5:8

has done, not only with the eye of his heart, by which he continually contemplated God, but even with the eye of his body he visibly discerned the invisible.

27. For in this monastery, before the altar that is consecrated in honor of the deific Trinity, as the most Christian of kings, attending the mysteries of our sacrosanct redemption while the mystery was being conducted on the heavenly altar and the divine sacraments were touched by the hands of the priest, behold, *beautiful above the children of men,** Christ Jesus, standing on the altar, appeared to his bodily <eyes> and, extending his sacred right hand over the king, depicted the sign of the holy cross in blessing him.

*Ps 44:3

28. Wonderful, many, and great are the deeds that divine power did through him. If any desire to know them, let them read the book of his miracles, and they will regard with wonder the remarkable <human> above humankind. By his merits and prayers may the holy and supreme Trinity lead us to eternal life, to whom is honor and power through all ages forever. Amen.

Sermon 173

On the Feast of Saint Martin [1]

1.   *Fear not, little flock, because it has pleased your Father to give you a kingdom.** If   *Luke 12:32 only your charity would turn its attention, my beloved brothers, to how loving, how concerned, how full of affection is God's compassion toward us. What is promised to us today is great, great and to be embraced with much desire. In fact, all of you, according to Christ's solemn promise, according to the promise of Truth, are going to become kings, not of each one's kingdom, not of an earthly and transitory kingdom, but of the heavenly kingdom that has no end, of the eternal kingdom. But he who promised the kingdom has laid down a condition, if you have preserved humility, of course. I mean, to whom has he promised a kingdom? Certainly to the little flock, implying that no one can attain to the kingdom unless he strives to have humility in his heart. So it says in another place, *Blessed are the poor in spirit, because theirs is the kingdom of heaven.**   *Matt 5:3

2. Therefore because *the kingdom* promised to us *is not of this world,** and we still sojourn in the   *see John 18:36 world,* and we long for our homeland, for our inheritance, for our kingdom, as though from afar,*   *see 2 Cor 5:6   *see Heb 11:13 our loving Lord by consoling our humility *lest we falter along the way** shows us the ease of arriving   *see Matt 15:32 at the kingdom, saying that it is pleasing to his Father

---

[1] Saint Martin of Tours, 316–397, f.d. Nov. 11 or 12.

to give us the kingdom, if we are from his little flock.* Therefore let us see who this little flock is and why it is called little, who is the shepherd of this flock and where he feeds his flock, from where he leads it in the morning, and to where he leads it back in the evening.

*see Luke 12:32

3. This little flock* is the Christian people, the Nazarite people, *consecrated to God,* a chosen generation, a purchased people.* This flock is called little in comparison to the greater number of the condemned. In fact, the chosen are few and like a little flock in comparison to the condemned, because *many are called, but few are chosen.* Or it is called little by the effect of humility, because however much it is multiplied by a great number, however much it is raised up by perfection of virtue, nevertheless it always continues in humility, keeping the precept of Scripture: *The greater you are, humble yourself the more in all things, and you shall find grace before God.*

*see Luke 12:32
*see Judg 16:17
*see 1 Pet 2:9

*Matt 20:16

*Sir 3:20

4. The shepherd of this flock is the pious *Samaritan*, who, *making a journey near* Jericho, put a man who had been wounded and plundered by robbers on his mule and *brought him to an inn and* compassionately *took care of him.* This is the shepherd *of souls, the good shepherd,*† who gives *testimony* about himself, *and we know that his testimony is true.* *I am the good shepherd. The good shepherd lays down his life for his sheep.*† This shepherd does not feed his flock by the *rivers of Babylon,*‡ lest perhaps it be carried away and overwhelmed by its waves in a confusion of vices,* but he feeds his flock *by the waters of the Jordan,* in spiritual fields, in the progress and conveyance of virtues, in the sweetness and pleasantness of love, in the harmony of peace.

*see Luke 10:30, 33-34
†see 1 Pet 2:25

*John 21:24;
see John 10:8
†John 10:11
‡see Ps 136:1

*see Isa 40:11
*see Num 13:30

5. In the morning, that is, *in the beginning*, he leads out his flock* from the ignorance and error of faithlessness. Obviously in the morning, that is, among the first things, Wisdom, which *reaches from end to end boldly and orders all things pleasantly,* enlightens humans* to acquire knowledge,* then confirms them in faith, but in the evening, that is, in the end, he blesses them through eternal reward in glorification.

*see John 10:3; see John 1:1; see Gen 1:1

*Wis 8:1

*see John 1:9

6. Or in the morning, that is, in the beginning, he leads out his flock from enjoyment of the flesh and desire of earthly cupidity.* This is the establishment of the Lord's way: to renounce the flesh, to renounce cupidity, to renounce corrupt habits. This renunciation is rough and harsh, but necessary and worthy of much reward.

*see John 10:3

7. This is the emigration of Abraham *from the land of the Chaldeans*, so that he might come into the land that God was going to show him.* Here is the departure of the Hebrews from Egypt, so they might come into the land *of promise*. We cannot reach *the land flowing with milk and honey,* we do not deserve the kingdom promised to us, unless we spiritually leave Egypt with the Hebrews, unless we leave our *land and kin* with Abraham, that is, from a worldly and carnal way of life and illicit cupidity and corrupt habits. The Lord thus invites us to emigrate when he says, *Let anyone who wishes to come after me deny himself and take up his cross and follow me.* Behold how rough, how harsh, how difficult and troublesome this departure is for the flesh. For what is more difficult for a person than to deny oneself, to fight against pleasure, against habit, against one's own will?

*see Gen 12:1; see Acts 7:4

*see Exod 3:17; see Heb 11:9

*see Gen 12:1

*Matt 16:24

8. In the evening, finally, that is, after this battle by which the spirit labors against the flesh and the

*see Gal 5:17

flesh struggles against the spirit,* our shepherd leads his flock to tranquility by a journey to the homeland, from toil to rest, from exile to the kingdom. Therefore, *Fear not, little flock, for it has pleased your*

*Luke 12:32

*Father to give you a kingdom.**

9. Blessed Martin was a great member of this little flock, by whose commendations we are supported today, for whom the Lord faithfully fulfilled his promise today. Today he bestowed on him the kingdom promised to us. Today Christ mercifully raised up Martin to the joys of the kingdom of heaven. Today *happy Martin is received in the bosom of Abraham and honored with heavenly hymns. Martin,*

*Ant and Resp in Mart (Hesbert 3:7311; 4:7132); Sulpicius Severus, Vita S Mart, Ep 3.21 (SCh 133:344)

*this poor and modest one, enters heaven a rich man.**

10. Happy and necessary, voluntary poverty, which scorns the world, flees vainglory, restrains luxury of the flesh, nourishes self-control, fosters sobriety, and inflames love of God in the human heart, happily attains eternal reward without hindrance. Blessed Martin loved this, preferred it to riches and status; on account of this he scorned the palaces of kings, he discarded his soldier's belt. But after corporeal military service, he transferred himself to the spiritual battle and, girded with the sword

*see 1 Sam 18:17

of God, vigorously fought the wars of his God,* fighting against *flesh and blood and the leaders of*

*see Eph 6:12

*darkness.**

11. So not long after his conversion, on a journey he came to meet a spiteful spirit who envied his sanctity and the glory of his merits, and as an adversary threatened the holy man wherever he went. But the Lord's man Martin, fervent with charity and filled with faith, despised the horrible beast, taking refuge

*Ps 117:6-7

in God's garrison and saying, *The Lord is my helper;** I do not fear your threats. Great was the fortitude of this athlete of the Lord, who while near to death

looked at the devil, who was standing nearby, and did not fear. Recalling his past life, and discovering nothing in his conscience about which our *adversary the devil** should boast,* secure about his merits, he proclaimed, "What are you doing here, you blood-thirsty beast? Nothing in me, deadly one, will you discover. May the bosom of Abraham receive me."

*see 1 Pet 5:8
*see 2 Cor 1:12

12. This true *Israelite, in whom there is no guile,** ought to be honored. For if we diligently examine his life and behavior, he was fervent in charity, strong in faith,* frequent in prayer, perfect in humility, eager in obedience, truthful in speech, efficacious in deed, powerful in the accomplishment of miracles. I do not read, I do not find anyone after the apostles who could be compared to blessed Martin in virtues, in miracles, *in signs and wonders.**

*see John 1:47

*see 1 Pet 5:9

*see 2 Cor 12:12

13. So that we may glean a few things about many matters, fringes of his clothing and threads of that goat-hair garment liberated many <people> from various illnesses. Beautiful and pleasing to God was the praise of God in Martin's mouth, who cleansed a leper by a kiss. When the man of God happened to meet a leper at the gate of the city of Paris, taking pity equally on his deformity and on his sickness, he did not shrink back from his horrible appearance; rather, the man [of God] kissed the leper and immediately cleansed the leper through the kiss. Indeed, rightly enough through the touch of his mouth the leprosy was put to flight, because *the law of his God* was *in his heart*. His *mouth* contemplated *wisdom,** because there was "never anything on his mouth except peace, except Christ, except compassion."*

*see Ps 36:31, 30

*Sulpicius Severus, Vita S Mart 27.1–2 (SCh 133:314)

14. He gave light to the blind, restored hearing to the deaf, healed paralytics, raised the dead, commanded flames, trees, birds, and beasts. Martin the

*see John 4:48

priest of God worked these and many other bound-less *signs and wonders** while he still lived in the mortal flesh. Therefore, what great things do we be-lieve that he can do now that he is joined to his Creator, from whom he received so that he was ca-pable of these and similar things? Certainly, as I may truly confess, he is capable of all things in God the all-powerful, to whom now he eternally adheres, be-cause he has served him faithfully, in person, regard-ing temporal matters.

15. Therefore let us flee to him, because he is loving and generous to all who entreat him. He has not been accustomed, not known to deny his benefits to those who ask of him. Therefore protect us, chosen and beloved priest of God, Martin, so that with your merits lending support, may we deserve to attain to that blessed rest that today you have happily entered, to which, by the merits and prayers of blessed Martin, may our Lord Jesus Christ deign to lead us, who with the Father and the Holy Spirit lives and reigns through all ages forever. Amen.

Sermon 174

On the Feast of Saint Katherine [1]

1. **T**his is the wise virgin whom the Lord finds keeping watch.* Today we celebrate the birth of the blessed virgin Katherine and her glorious victory. Thus we celebrate so as to make progress, recalling that it has been written, *Sing wisely.** We extol the wise virgin; let us wisely praise her. Who praises wisely? Those who imitate whomever they praise, those who accomplish in deed what they preach in speech. Those praise wisely who praise in voice and heart. Thus celebrating the feasts of the saints benefits us if we strive to imitate their life, their habits, and their virtues that we preach. If our work differs from our speech, the Lord will say about us what was said about a perverse and reckless people: *This people honors me with their lips, but their heart is far from me.**

*Ant and Resp in Com virg (Hesbert 3:3007; 4:6809); see Matt 25:4, 6; see Luke 12:37 *Ps 46:8

*Matt 15:8; Isa 29:13

2. Therefore let your charity pay attention to what we put forth in praise of the glorious virgin: *This is the wise virgin*, etc.* We have spoken briefly, and we have said much, and it is wholly true what we have said. Three things are proposed here: that she is *a virgin*, that she is *wise*, that *the Lord* found *her keeping watch.*

*Ant and Resp in Com virg (Hesbert 3:3007; 4:6809); see Matt 25:4, 6; see Luke 12:37

3. That she is called *virgin* is the beginning of praise, or rather it is great praise by the addition of

---

[1] Saint Katherine of Alexandria, ca. 287–ca. 305, f.d. Nov. 25. Katherine was tortured on a wheel known as a breaking wheel or a Katherine wheel.

what follows, that she is *wise*. Virginity without wisdom is not virginity, but foolish and undisciplined virginity. It does not make a virgin but corrupts her even more, because it also makes an <undisciplined> and foolish virgin. Therefore when you say that she is *a virgin*, the mind of listeners is still ambivalent. They still weigh judgment, because there are *foolish* virgins, and there are *prudent* virgins.*

*see Matt 25:2

4. When you say <that> she is a virgin, you have a gem, as it were. Accordingly, virginity is rightly compared to a gem, which is a shining thing but in itself fragile, and it can easily be ruined, unless some more dense material, such as gold or silver or something of this nature, encircles it and strengthens it against external harm. Therefore, seek gold and encircle the <fragility> of your gem, and say that she is *wise*. O how well they come together, wherever they come together, such a gem and such gold! Behold an ornament more precious and more beautiful than every necklace, than every earring, than every braided necklace, more than any womanly ornament: virginity with wisdom.

5. From this gem and this gold that precious ring was fashioned, the seal of love and chastity* by which the *wise virgin* prided herself as betrothed when she said, *With <his> ring my Lord Jesus Christ has betrothed me.** This is that treasure hidden *in a field*, to which *is likened the kingdom of heaven, which a person found and then hid and, for joy thereof, went and sold all that he had and bought that field.** The field in which that treasure is found is zeal for heavenly discipline.

*see Song 8:6

*Ant in Com virg
(Hesbert 3:1426)

*Matt 13:44;
see Matt 13:24

6. This blessed virgin found this desirable treasure in this field, because through zeal for heavenly discipline she arrived at love and knowledge and desire for virginity and wisdom, even to the embrace

of the one who is a virgin, the son of the Virgin, bridegroom of virgins, the Lord Jesus Christ, who is the Wisdom of God the Father.* Having found this treasure in this field, *she sold all that she had and bought that field,** because for the sake of zeal for heavenly discipline she renounced all enjoyments and worldly desires and ample possessions, and the kingdom and delights, so that she could truly say, *I have disdained the kingdom of the world and every adornment of the age on account of love of the Lord Jesus Christ, whom I have seen, whom I have loved, in whom I have believed, whom I have held dear.**

*see 1 Cor 1:24

*see Matt 13:44-45

*Resp in Com virg (Hesbert 4:7524)

7. Pay attention also to the virgin's prudence. Consider what this wise businesswoman has done. See what *she sold and bought.** She sold earthly things, and she bought heavenly things. She replaced her earthly kingdom for the heavenly kingdom. She chose God's Son to be her bridegroom instead of a bridegroom who was the son of a human being. Instead of fallacious and momentary glory she acquired for herself the joys that will remain without end. Therefore let this prudent virgin say, *I wished, and understanding was given to me. I called upon God, and the spirit of wisdom came upon me. And I preferred her before kingdoms and thrones and esteemed riches to be nothing in comparison to her.**

*see Matt 13:45

*Wis 7:7-8

8. Behold how truly, how rightly, how worthily it has been said about this blessed virgin, *This is the wise virgin whom the Lord found keeping watch.** Behold the conclusion, behold the consummation of all praise: this praise is the praise of perseverance. What does it mean that she was found keeping vigil by the Lord, if not that in proper faith and good works and holy way of life *she persevered to the end?** Often in divine Scripture, the end of the present life is represented by the arrival of the Lord,

*Ant and Resp in Com virg (Hesbert 3:3007; 4:6809); see Matt 25:4, 6; see Luke 12:37

*Matt 24:13

so that the Lord may be said to come to those whom he calls from life in this world through death of the flesh, either to punishment or to rest, everyone *according to his works.**

*see Ps 61:13

9. O how cautiously, how providently this virgin had ordered her life, had aptly equipped her lamp, had reserved oil in her vessel, had led the whole sleepless night of the present life, so that when he came the Lord would find her *keeping watch.** Why do I say she had reserved? Nay rather, so great an abundance of oil filled her vessel, so that oil would not fail in the vessel of her body *even until the present day,** and not just any kind of oil, but sweet oil, holy oil, saving oil, just as on this day you sing, *A flood of salubrious oil flowed from her virgin members.**

*see Matt 25:4-6;
see Luke 12:37

*see Matt 27:8

*Resp in Vig Cath

10. Accordingly, beginning from the top, let us say, *This is the wise virgin whom the Lord finds keeping watch.** But I have said very little with respect to "the Lord finds her keeping watch." I will say more, and I will speak truly with respect to this prudent and vigilant virgin, who by urgently and ardently seeking preceded and found the Lord, who was as though absent, making a delay,* as it were. For she who had been *wounded by charity*, she who was languishing with love,* she who was crying out the whole day, *When shall I come and appear before the face of my God? Daughters of Jerusalem, declare to my beloved that I languish with love!**—she could not bear the bridegroom's *delay.*† But as though she were saying in her heart, *I will rise and will go about the city, through the streets and the broad ways, I will seek him whom my soul loves.**

*Ant and Resp in
Com virg
(Hesbert 3:3007;
4:6809);
see Matt 25:4, 6;
see Luke 12:37

*see Matt 25:5

*see Song 5:8

*Ps 41:3; Song
5:8; see *Ant*
Anima in Ass
(Hesbert 3:1418)
†see Matt 25:5
*Song 3:2

11. Consider the life of this virgin before her passion,* and you will see that she completed a certain wonderful career in a brief time, while with ardent zeal and vehement desire she sought her beloved, her spouse, her God. Pay attention to her life and her

passionem

holy behavior before her passion. See whence she advanced. Go forth and see the sequence of her passion. Behold by which route she crossed over. *Raise your eyes, and see* her established in heaven *at the right hand* of her bridegroom,* *as a bride adorned with her jewels.*† Behold where she has arrived.

*see John 4:35;
see Acts 7:55
†Isa 61:10

12. She crossed over from rest to rest through labor: from the rest of contemplation to the rest of full enjoyment by means of the labor of suffering.* Out of the constant meditation of contemplation, the fire of desire to see God ignited in her heart.* In fact, it is the strength and the nature of contemplation that the more anyone progresses, the more ardently one thirsts to enjoy the reality of that presence that one attains only by vision of the mind through desire; nevertheless one senses oneself to be removed from its enjoyment and laments: *I shall go over into the place of the wonderful tabernacle, even to the house of God.** Behold where she crossed over to: *even to the house of God*, to God's presence, to God's glory.

**passionis*

*see Ps 38:4

*Ps 41:5

13. By what route has this virgin crossed over, eager *to run the way*?* By a laborious way, a humiliating way, rugged and inaccessible, through the hands of sinners, through excessive and exquisite types of torment. So she was able to say, *All your heights and your waves have passed over me.** Even the superiors who tormented her seemed to prevail. For they seemed to utterly extinguish and oppress her with torments, but the torments passed over, they vanished, they lost their effect, and nothing had any effect on her. They passed over by failing where she crossed over by succeeding.

*see Ps 18:6

*see Ps 41:8

14. But by what leader, by what helper did she cross over unharmed, did she overcome unconquered? *God* was helping *her by his face*, by his presence. *God is in the midst thereof; it shall not be moved.** God in her, God with her, God for her. In her,

*Ant and Resp in
Com virg (Hesbert
3:1282; 4:6042);
see Ps 45:6

strengthening her; with her, leading her; for her, protecting her, just as in the psalms it is written, *You have protected me from the assembly of the malicious, from the multitude of those who work iniquity.**

*Ps 63:3

15. I find this crossing over clear enough in the Song of Songs, so that it seems to me that this girl is discussing her beloved with herself or with one of her companions, and about her absence and delay she laments, *In my bed by night I sought him whom my soul loves.** What does it mean that she sought in her bed if not that in the peace and quiet of contemplation, which is signified by her bed, she had time for God alone, to whom she aspired with the whole intention of her heart, desiring according to the apostle's wisdom *to be dissolved and be with Christ?** And she does not have leisure, because it says *by night*, because while other people have been lulled to sleep by the pleasure of vices, she was spending the night in good works and holy habits. So she deserved to be called prudent and vigilant.

*Song 3:1

*see Phil 1:23

16. *I sought him, and I found him not. On my bed* I sought and did not find, because he had already *turned away** by taking away his presence, as it were, so that he would be sought more ardently. In fact, her bridegroom had already prepared for her a way of seeking and finding him other than by rest and peace: the way of suffering,* a harsher but more glorious way. It is as if her bridegroom were to say to her, "In vain do you seek me *in your bed*. For there you will not find me. But *arise and make haste, my love, my dove, and come.** Follow the way on which I have gone before, if you wish to come to me." So as she was advised and invited by her friend, she joins in, saying, *I will rise and go about the city, through the streets and the broad ways, seeking him whom my soul loves.**

*see Song 5:6;
see Song 3:1-2

*passionis

*Song 2:10, 13

*Song 3:2

17. When do you think she did these things? When she arose from her private bed and went forth into the public, forgetting girlish timidity and modesty as well? Then indeed when she is afire with the fervor of Christian religion, inflamed with love of the bridegroom, having left the throne of her father, she prostrated herself amid a sinful nation* and fearlessly presented herself to a cruel tyrant who sacrificed to idols. Then with a free voice, she cried out, "These are demons." When rhetoricians and grammarians debated against her, the conquering virgin taught the faith of Christ and pointed out martyrs worthy of God. *I sought him, and I found him not.** Truly she had not yet found her bridegroom, because she had not yet completed her *course.** A hard and *great way* still remained.*

*see Isa 1:4

*Song 5:6; see Song 3:2

*see Acts 20:24

*see 1 Kgs 19:7; see Ps 16:4

18. Go forth, therefore blessed virgin, indicate to us whom you have found on the way, nay rather, who has found you, before you found your beloved. *The watchmen who guard the city found me; they struck me and wounded me.** Does this really need an explanation? Who has doubts about this, except perhaps one who has not heard about the suffering of this glorious virgin or not read or not understood? *The watchmen of the walls took away my cloak.** Right order, and true. According to the truth of the story, having found her *they* first *struck and wounded* her, and afterward *they took away* her *cloak*. By decapitating her, of course, they stole the cloak of her flesh, as it is written: "After many punishments, the kind martyr was led away to be decapitated."

*Song 3:3; Song 5:7

*Song 5:7

19. But we must not in silence pass by what is said: *Watchmen of the walls*. Who are these *watchmen of the walls*? These men were in charge of guarding the public jail and other places of punishment, to whom had been assigned guarding and torturing

holy confessors of Christ's name. These confessors
are steadfast and sturdy walls because they are holy
and brave in warding off all of the assaults of tor-
mentors and the blows of the persecutors. These
confessors are founded *upon the solid rock* who is
Christ,* who was called *a wall* by the prophet: *Zion,
the city of our strength; a Savior, a wall and a bul-
wark, shall be set therein.**

20. Was not this girl about whom we speak an
impregnable wall, whom neither that machine of
wheels nor exquisite types of tortures could over-
whelm or penetrate at all? And what more could
really be done against a wall of stone or bronze? She
remains immovable, taking no interest in either
gentle or harsh [treatment]. The queen and noble
Porphyrius, with the white-clad army of soldiers,
were strong walls.* Also those fifty orators,[2] who all,
vigorously standing fast *in faith* and for the faith of
Christ,* by their death conquered death and the author of death.* *Watchmen* of these *walls took their
cloak* from our virgin.*

21. It follows, *When I had passed by them a
little,** soon *I found* the bridegroom, because having
removed the garment of the flesh (which had been
more an impediment to her than an adornment),
soon she found her beloved, whom she had sought
through so many and such great dangers. *And the
king brought* her *into* his *bedchamber,** just as he
had promised through an angelic voice. For *a voice
from the heavens thundered,** "Come, my beloved,
into the bedchamber of your bridegroom."† So now
in possession of a fulfilled vow, having secured the

*see Ant and
Resp Domus in
Ded eccl (Hesbert
3:2998; 4:6801);
see Matt 7:25;
see 1 Cor 10:4
†Isa 26:1

*see Rev 3:5

*see 1 Cor 16:13
*see Heb 2:14
*Song 5:7

*Song 3:4

*Song 1:3;
see Song 3:4

*see Matt 3:17;
see Ps 28:3
†see Ps 18:6

---

[2] The emperor summoned fifty philosophers to debate Katherine, some of whom she won over to Christian faith and were
therefore executed.

reward of her labors, she erupts into an expression of confidence, saying, *I hold him and I will not let go.** She truly holds him, now joined and united to her bridegroom, and she does not let him go. In fact, under no condition can she be separated from the fellowship of Christ, she whom *a sword* could not *separate from the charity of Christ.**

*Song 3:4

*see Rom 8:35, 39

22. Let us imitate this glorious virgin, brothers, and if we cannot do so by that wonderful way by which the Lord her God led her, then at least let us seek our beloved *in* our *bed*, according to her example;* that is, let us through a pure conscience and the quiet of contemplation and holy living seek God, so that *when the Lord comes* to us, he may find us *keeping watch.**

*see Song 3:1

*see Luke 12:37

23. And because we do not know the hour of his arrival, let us always be mindful of it,* as if always saying in our hearts, "Behold, presently he will come; behold, presently he will come." And so let us always be cautious and prepared when *in the middle of the night*, that is, suddenly and without warning, *a shout will be made, Behold the bridegroom comes*! Let us run *to meet him* with lamps lit,* and let us enter *with him to the marriage** of eternal exultation, and let us live with him through all ages forever. Amen.

*see Matt 25:13;
see RB 4.47

*see Matt 25:6

*see Matt 25:10

Sermon 175

On the Feast of Saint Andrew

*Matt 4:19;
Ant in And
(Hesbert 3:5357)

*see Matt 19:21

*see Matt 16:24

*2 Cor 8:9;
see Zach 9:9

*see Matt 11:5

*see Acts 4:13

*see 1 Cor 1:26-27

*see Matt 4:18-19

1. *Come after me, and I will make you become fishers of men.** A sacrifice of perfect justice takes its beginning from the Gospel. From where the Gospel begins to be proclaimed, voluntary poverty is commended.* This is the first sacrifice that we must offer to God: to leave behind our own, and not only our own, but rather our very selves,* that is, our individual counsel, individual will, and individual consent, and to follow the Savior, who *when he was rich* among his own for our sake *became poor** among us.

2. Obviously, when God's Son came into the world, King of heaven and earth, Lord of all, he chose not the rich but the poor for preaching. So speaking to the disciples of John, among the rest of his miracles of power, although it was not the first, nevertheless he added it as though most important: *The poor have the gospel preached to them.** Among the greatest signs of his mighty deeds, it was a great miracle, because through the lowly, poor, and uneducated,* he converted the noble, rich, and wise to himself. Through the needy and simple, he subjugated kings and emperors to himself.*

3. But where were our shepherds and leaders, specifically Peter and Andrew, when the heavenly master called them? On the sea, of course, and not just any sea, but the sea of Galilee.* Nothing here is in vain, nothing useless, nothing superfluous. Peter and Andrew were on the sea, because devoted to love

of the world, they coveted temporal gain, and in Galilee because they were living in restlessness and mutability,* pursuing earthly and transitory things; rarely did they think about heavenly things—they were not preaching eternal values, on account of the boat and nets. From this sea, that is, from love of the world, the lover of angels and human beings recalled them, he who *emptied himself, taking the form of a servant** so that he might teach us not to pursue riches but to spurn vainglory, to flee the pomp of this age, and not to love the world.

4. Because we have spoken about the sea, let us see what the sea has within it. Certainly it has in it bitterness, depth, instability, and swells. Accordingly, the sea beautifully signifies the world, which is bitter from ill will, deep from duplicity, unstable through cupidity, swelling through glorification. Whoever therefore loves the world, *the charity of God is not in him,** since one who loves the world does not love his neighbor. And if *one does not love his brother whom he sees, how* will he love *God, whom he does not see?**

5. And so a lover of the world is bitter, through malice hating his neighbor, and therefore *he is in darkness,* because everyone *who hates his brother* remains *in darkness.** The heart of such a one has depths because of duplicity, one who *in his heart and heart,** that is, *with a double heart,*† speaks to his neighbor, saying one thing and thinking another. Such a person is one thing and pretends to be something else. He says that he is a brother and yet agrees to be a persecutor of his brother. He feigns friendship and nurses anger; by his expression he promises a favorable decision, <and> yet *in his heart plots treachery.** He preaches charity and follows avarice. He is unstable through cupidity. Such a person is like

*see Jerome, Int nom 64: *Galilaea uolutabilis aut transmigratio perpretata* (CCSL 72:140)

*Phil 2:7

*1 John 2:15

*1 John 4:20

*1 John 2:11

*see Ps 11:3
†see Sir 2:14

*see Prov 6:14

*see Matt 11:7

a reed shaken by the wind:* he turns in whatever direction so as to gain what he wrongly desires or to avoid what he foolishly dreads. He swells through pride, seducing equals, despising inferiors, envying superiors.

*1 John 2:15

6. Such a one is a lover of the world, not of God.* *The adversary* of humankind fishes for a human being of this type in this large and wide sea that is the world.* And so the reckless hunter, that is, the devil, has his seine, his net, and also a hook for fishing in this sea.

*see 1 Pet 5:8;
see Ps 103:25

7. So Habacuc the prophet, in the appearance of the king of Babylon, speaking about the devil, says, *He lifted them all together with his hook, he drew them in his seine, and he gathered them into his net.** "How does the fisherman cast his hook, net, and seine so that whomever <the hook> cannot, the net catches, and those who evade the net are confined by a wider seine; thus the devil, ravaging all of them, made the whole human race his prey before the advent of Christ."* "He had *human beings like fish* and ravaged all *like creeping things that have no ruler.*† That cunning enemy cast a hook, to which Adam was attached, and drew him outside Paradise with his net and overwhelmed him with his seine, that is, with complex deceits."*

*Hab 1:15

*Jerome, in
Hab 1.1 (CCSL
76A:594)
†see Hab 1:14
(LXX); see
Judg 6:4

*Jerome, in
Hab 1.1 (CCSL
76A:594)

8. *He will be glad and rejoice over this. For this reason he will offer victims to his seine, and he will sacrifice to his net.** "Not with a hook, which is understood to be perverse speech, but with his net, because he catches very fat victims in it. And *by one person,* a sinner, *many became sinners,** and in Adam we *all* have died;† thereafter all saints have been equally cast out from Paradise with him.‡ So it says about him through blessed Habacuc, *His food is choice.** According to another prophet, he seeks *his*

*Hab 1:15-16

*see Rom 5:12,
19; see Luke 5:8
†see 1 Cor 15:22
‡see Gen 3:24

*Hab 1:16

meat from God, * wishing to subvert prophets and
apostles. And because he deceived the first human
being, daily *he does not cease to kill* the <whole>
human race." * This is what the prophet adds, saying,
*For this cause he spreads his net and will never cease
to slay the nations.*†

*Ps 103:21

*Jerome, in
Hab 1.1 (CCSL
76A:594–95)
†Hab 1:17

9. The adversary's hook is understood to mean
corrupt suggestion. For just as meat is displayed on
a hook and the sting of the barb is hidden, so by a
diabolic suggestion pleasure is promised and future
punishment is left unmentioned. For the spiteful one
suggests loving the appearances of the present age:
the sweet tastes, pleasant sounds, fragrant odors,
pleasing touches, worldly honors, transitory happiness, all of which recede and pass away *like a
shadow.* * So all of these offer pleasure, like meat on
a hook. Obviously they have a sweet beginning, but
a most bitter end. In fact they deceive those who love
them and send them into abominable misery and
eternal damnation. Such is the devil's hook, display-
ing meat and hiding punishment, promising life and
inflicting death.

*see Wis 5:9;
see Job 14:2

10. Consent is represented by the devil's net,
which has many meshes on account of the body's
five senses. For just as the net has various meshes
woven into it, so consent of the five senses has
various feelings conspiring with it. For who knows
with which and how many [feelings] vision toys with
consent? Who will explain how many and what sort
of sounds and imaginative tales the sense of hearing
presents to it? So taste, smell, and touch: each uses
its own functions. So just as heads of households stay
in the house when they propose some project, they
speak with leaders and elders of their household to
use their advice; thus the soul, remaining within with
her own advisers as it were, uses these five senses for
any project.

11. Vision presents to the soul comely figures and very beautiful sights, so that she may take pleasure in them. It urged this concupiscence of the eyes to our first mother in Paradise and deceived her, as it is written: *The woman saw the tree that* was beautiful to see and pleasant to eat from; she took its fruit and *ate and gave to her man.** From this has appeared disease, pain, trouble, and our every misery. Similarly taste, in order to deceive, offers sweet flavors; hearing, pleasant sound; the sense of smell, fragrant odors; touch, soft and pleasing caress. Therefore just as a fish is enclosed by a net and entangled by interwoven mesh, so a soul is entangled in misery by consent of these five senses and held captive through pleasure.

*Gen 3:6;
see Gen 2:9

12. By the seine, which is bigger than the rest of the nets because it encompasses the width of a river, reaching to both shores, cupidity or appetite for human acclaim is represented. *The adversary spreads his net** over every nation, because in the whole human condition rarely is found one whose mind is not touched by cupidity, or who does not sometimes stray toward appetite for human acclaim. *The adversary* is delighted and rejoices *over this*, and therefore *he will sacrifice to his net,** "because he catches very fat victims in it."†

*Hab 1:17;
see 1 Pet 5:8

*see Hab 1:15-16;
see 1 Pet 5:8
†Jerome, in
Hab 1.1 (CCSL
76A:594)

13. So the devil raises his hook when, through perverse suggestion, he diverts anyone from God's precepts and brings them down to sin. He draws *in his seine and* gathers *into his net* when, out of pleasure of sin, he persuades anyone to wicked consent and an illicit deed. Therefore it is well said through the prophet, *He lifted up the whole on his hook; he drew them in his seine and gathered them into his net. The whole,** that is, the human race, *he lifted up on his hook*, because through perverse suggestion in Adam he hooked the whole human race for himself.

*Hab 1:15

*He drew them in his seine and gathered them into his net,** because out of wicked and perverse pleasure in the first parents, he led the whole of their posterity into the shame of death through malign consent. *Hab 1:15

14. But *the Lord is compassionate and merciful;** lest the human creature whom he had created to know <him> should utterly perish, *he sent his Son into the world,** so that *the stronger* would vanquish *the strong,** and he might liberate the human being from the power of the malicious one. In short, *a mediator of God and human beings** showed in himself and through himself how the adversary should be vanquished.** Nevertheless he chose as preachers Peter and Andrew and the rest of the disciples, through whom he led the race of humans from darkness to light, from error to truth, from *the worship of idols** to the worship and faith of the one and true God.

*Ps 102:8

*see John 3:17
*see Luke 11:21-22

*1 Tim 2:5

*see 1 Pet 5:8

*see 1 Cor 10:14;
see Wis 14:27

15. See whom the Lord chose for the work of preaching: not the rich, not philosophers, but the poor and simple, sending fishermen against kings and princes and the wise of the world. These are the fishermen about whom Scripture speaks: *Behold I send many fishermen, says the Lord.** The first and principal of these are Peter, prince of apostles, and his brother Andrew, whom the Lord saw *next to the sea of Galilee** and called, saying, *Come after me! I will make you fishers of men.**

*Jer 16:16

*see Matt 4:18
*Matt 4:19

16. Through them the Lord willed to liberate souls from the sea and to lead [them] from the waves of the world to the blessedness of the eternal kingdom. Fish die when they are hauled out of the water with seines or nets <or hook>. Blessed are those who, having been caught by the apostles' nets, seines, and hook, are led away from the sea of the present age. They die continually, not to God but to the world.

They die to sin, so that rising up they may live to Christ God.*

*see Rom 6:11

17. "We therefore, brothers, because we have already been drawn out from the waves of this age by the Lord's disciples, let us reform the vices of the body, let us reform perverse understanding, let us reform worldly affection. Let us not be fish who dwell* in the salty waves, but led out from the deep whirlpool of evils, let us always be converted to better things, according to that apostolic saying: *But as we all contemplate the glory of the Lord with open face, let us be transformed into that same image from glory to glory.*"*

*versantur; also "whirl around"

*Origen, Hom Ier 12.1 (PG 13:439A); 2 Cor 3:18 as cited by Origen
†Matt 4:19

18. Consider carefully what the Lord says to Peter and Andrew: *Come*, he says, *after me*.† The Lord does not wish his disciples to remain on the sea. He does not mean for them to delay any longer among the waves and storms. He orders them to disembark and follow him. "We, therefore, because we are liberated from the sea waves through that Redeemer and his disciples, let us not return again to the deep, but let *our conversation** be in the mountains. Thus we have <no> need of fishermen who might remove us <again> from the waves."*

*see Phil 3:20

*Origen, Hom Ier 12:1 (PG 13:439B)

19. He called two brothers, so to recommend the unity of fraternal love to us. For however much the Lord commends all virtues to us and exhorts us to each one, still there is one virtue that he more especially loves in us and sees as more gratifying in us. It is unity and fraternal love. No <other> virtue establishes us so in concord with God <and> terrible to the devil. Therefore he called two in one calling, and he chose [them] for one, that is, for one preaching of the kingdom of heaven.

20. But whom did he choose? "Peter and Andrew. *Peter* designates *recognizing*,* and *Andrew* is inter-

*Jerome, Int nom 65 (CCSL 72:141)

preted as *virile.** How well these names fit the personalities of preachers: Peter and Andrew, *recognizing* and *virile.* For only those become suitable for the work of preaching who are enlightened by the light of wisdom, and what they preserve by teaching and doing, they suggest for others to undertake and do with bravery and virility."* Finally, if anyone desires to come after Jesus, he ought to be Peter and Andrew.

21. Such a one ought to be Peter so that he may recognize himself, so that he may be careful and circumspect <in> all his ways, considering how much he can do, saying with the prophet, *My soul is always in my hands.** For imitators of Christ should continually meditate on their final end,* because they do not know when their *Lord is going to come.** One who so acts does not fall short. So it is written, *Visiting your beauty you shall not sin.** In fact, those who thus examine themselves, by lamenting the bad deeds that they have committed and by giving thanks for good things that the Lord has conferred upon them, observe themselves well. Such a one is to be called Peter, that is, *recognizing.**

22. To this purpose, one ought to be Andrew, that is, *virile,** so that he may bravely resist deeds of the flesh, vices, and sins, and vigorously fight the battles of his God.* Certainly that is what the Lord's brave athlete has done, our pious patron Andrew, whose proclamations we venerate today, who could not be swayed from the truth of the faith by threats or promises. Obviously *founded upon firm rock, he contended* vigorously *for the law of his God,** not fearing the wicked Aegeus; rather, he paid no heed.

23. See how this saint comes after Jesus. The Lord himself speaks to all: *Learn from me because I am meek and humble of heart.** Behold, one reads con-

*Jerome, Int nom 66 (CCSL 72:142)

*Rabanus Maurus, *In Matthaeum* 2.20 (CCSL 174:112–13)

*Ps 118:109
*see Sir 7:40
*see Matt 24:42

*Job 5:24

*Jerome, Int nom 65 (CCSL 72:141)

*Jerome, Int nom 66 (CCSL 72:142)

*see 1 Sam 18:17

*see Ant and Resp "Iste" in Com Mar (Hesbert 3:3434; 4:7010); see Matt 7:25

*Matt 11:29

*see Resp
"Vir iste" Ant in
And (Hesbert
4:7899)

*Ant in And
(Hesbert 3:1863)

*Passio Sancti
Andreae Apostoli
12 (Acta
Apostolorum
Apocrypha 2.1)

*see 1 John 2:6

*see Matt 4:20

cerning this saint that he was *the meekest* of saints.*
That he was meek and gentle, the faithful testified as
they cried out to Aegeus, *Relinquish to us the just
person, give back to us the holy person, lest you kill
a person who is dear to God.** "A holy man, chaste,
rich in character, a good teacher, modest, and rational,
should not suffer such things."*

24. He was meek in speech, humble in heart,
chaste in body, strong in faith, devout in preaching,
complete in charity. In all these he came after Jesus.
For what is it to come after the Savior if not to love
what he himself loved, to teach what he taught, *to
walk as he walked.** In fact, the one who conforms
himself to Christ by his habits and life as much as he
can comes after Christ. This blessed Andrew has
done. For just as Christ mercifully willed to be crucified on behalf of Andrew, so Andrew faithfully allowed himself to be affixed to a forked cross on
behalf of Christ.[1]

25. Brothers, let us imitate this leader and our
patron; let us strive with him to come after Jesus. Let
us withdraw with him from the sea, that is, from love
of this age, leaving nets, that is, all impediments of
the world, so that *having left our nets,** that is,
earthly and transitory matters, we may gain heavenly
and eternal realities. May our heavenly master, Jesus
Christ our Lord, deign to bestow this upon us by the
prayers and merits of blessed Andrew. Amen.

---

[1] Saint Andrew is depicted in art with or on an X-shaped cross.

Sermon 176

On the Feast of Saint Vincent [1]

1. *I* *shall give hidden manna to the victor.** A brief word, but an extensive and deep sacrament. A great and huge gift, because here the Lord promises to the servant, the Creator to the creature, God to the human. What is promised here by the Lord is not given to all—not given to those who sleep, not given to the negligent, not given to those who walk according to the flesh, not given to the self-indulgent and effeminate. But to whom is it given? To those who fight, who conquer,* who pray. One who continually cries out and prays, *Depart from me, evil ones, and I will search out the commandments of my God,** one who walks in the *Spirit* and *does not fulfill the desires of the flesh** shall have *hidden manna.** The *hidden manna* is not given to beginners, but to those who persevere, because *but the one who perseveres unto the end shall be saved.**

2. *I shall give hidden manna to the victor.** The battle precedes, victory is anticipated, the crown is put forth, eternal life is promised. If therefore you desire life, do not shudder at death. If you seek rest, do not flee toil. If you aspire to glory, do not detest ignominy. If you love a crown, do not dread battle. For by what rashness shall one who trembles before

* *Vincenti;*
Rev 2:17

* *vincenti*

*Ps 118:115
*see Gal 5:16
*Rev 2:17

*Matt 10:22
*Rev 2:17

---

[1] Saint Vincent of Saragossa, 3rd-century protomartyr of Spain; d. 304; f.d. Jan. 22. The name *Vincentius, Vincent* is derived from *vincere* "to conquer," and is cognate with the name *Victor*, meaning "winner" or "conqueror." This sermon and S 177 contain numerous echoes of the name *Vincentius* and cognate verbs and nouns, e.g., *vincere, victoria, victor.*

*2 Tim 2:5

battle hope for a crown? *One will not be crowned unless he strives lawfully.** In the beginning a battle, after the battle a victory, after the victory a crown will be given. For *I shall give hidden manna to the*

*Rev 2:17

*victor.**

3. What is *hidden manna*? The Word of the All-powerful Father. Therefore *hidden*, because secret. For *who knows the Father if not the Son*, or who

*see Matt 11:27

*knows the Son if not the Father?** So accordingly the prophet says about the divine begetting, *Who shall*

*Isa 53:8
†Rev 2:17

*declare his begetting?** *Hidden manna*† is the Father's Word, because it is sacred and deep and covered by a sacred veil. This *manna* is the Power of God and

*see 1 Cor 1:24
*Ant Maior adv
(Hesbert 3:4081);
Wis 8:1

the Wisdom of God,* *reaching from end to end bravely and ordering all things sweetly.**

4. When the children of Israel were in the desert, which could not be cultivated or sown, *they cried to*

*Ps 106:6

*the Lord** so they would not be consumed by starva-

*Ps 77:24; see
Wis 16:20; see Resp
Adduxi in Dom IV
Quad (Hesbert
4:6030)
†see Exod 16:15
‡see Matt 15:32-33;
see Mark 8:4;
see Ps 118:54
#see Ps 110:5;
see Ps 77:24;
see Resp Adduxi
in Dom IV Quad
(Hesbert 4:6030)
§Gal 4:4; John 3:17;
see 2 Cor 5:18-19;
see Fortunatus,
"Pange Lingua,"
str. 4.1 (PL 88:88B)
*see Resp Adduxi
in Dom IV Quad
(Hesbert 4:6030)
†Isa 9:6; see
Resp in Nat Dom
(Hesbert 4:7450)
‡see John 6:33, 35

tion, *and manna from heaven rained down for them.** When the Hebrews saw it, not knowing *what it was, they said, Manhu? What is this?*† Similarly *in the desert* of this present age, lest we grow weak *in the solitude of* our *pilgrimage*,‡ we cried out to the Lord, and he sent a Savior for us. *He gave* us heavenly *food, manna from heaven rained* for us.#

5. For *when the fullness of the time had come, God sent his Son into the world*,§ to reconcile the human race to himself.* Then *manna from heaven* was given to us, when according to the prophecy of Isaiah *a child was born to us, and a son was given to us.*† Our Lord himself, Jesus Christ, is the manna: heavenly food, refreshment of those who hunger,‡ relaxation of those who labor, renewal of those who are lost, victory of those who struggle, life of mortals, redemption of sinners, rejoicing of the chosen, glory and blessing of angels.

6. Therefore as long as we are *in* this *desert*, as long as we dwell in *houses of clay*,* as long as we are *in the solitude* of mortality, we always have need to cry out with the Hebrews, *Manhu? What is this?** For there is no one in this mortality of such great knowledge, of such great acuity and prudence, who can perfectly search out the power of the divine Word. So the psalmist says, *A human being shall come to a deep heart, and God shall be exalted.**

*see Job 4:19

*Exod 16:15

*Ps 63:7-8

7. For the more attentively, the more subtly and more perfectly we ponder on this Word, so much the more sublimely and vehemently we wonder at his incomprehensible majesty. In fact, he is *hidden manna*,* because the Word of God is unsearchable. His depth exceeds every understanding. So blessed Paul says in his Epistle to the Romans, *O the depth of the wisdom and knowledge of God! How incomprehensible are his judgments, and how unsearchable his ways!**

*Rev 2:17

*Rom 11:33

8. *I shall give hidden manna* only *to the victor.** What the Lord here promises to his servant is great and should be sought with no small desire. But this is not promised to just any servant. It is not promised to the vanquished, but to the victor. The victorious athlete is honored by his Lord. For him a procession is prepared, great honors and ample possessions are lavished upon him. But one who is vanquished in the field, disgracefully stripped of his weapons, cruelly trampled on, *with hands and feet tied** is dragged to jail or torture.

Vincenti;
Rev 2:17

*Matt 22:13

9. Our Lord and God has placed us all in the field so we might bravely do battle* for him against his adversary. The field is this world, in which we are never safe; we are never without misfortune, without misery, without battle. So it is written, *The life of a man upon earth is warfare.** We all serve in combat

*see 2 Macc 13:14

*Job 7:1

for one king. Each one of us has entered into combat for God against a strong athlete, a cruel combatant, a wicked and grievous fighter: against the devil. Let each person diligently attend to how he conducts himself in the field, how he holds his shield, how he raises his staff, which <stones> and what sort of blows he might hurl against the adversary.*

*see 1 Sam 17:40, 49

10. The shield by which we are protected and boldly armed against the devil is faith.* Without this shield no one emerges a victor, no one conquers,* no one overcomes. For *without faith it is impossible to please God.** Our staff, which we must raise against the adversary, is the cross of Christ. Against all diabolical suggestions and invasions, in every temptation one must have recourse to the passion of Christ, one must call to mind the Savior's cross. By the sign of the holy cross we must fortify the heart and brow, the eyes, the ears, and the rest of our members. For the Lord's cross is the sign, or rather the reality itself, in which God's Son triumphed over the devil.

*see Eph 6:16
*vincit

*Heb 11:6

11. The blows by which we must push down and beat the devil are our prayers, with frequent sighs from the heart and secret and holy meditations. Nothing so perturbs and bewilders the devil as does sincere and holy prayer. It is that smooth stone from the stream with which David while still a boy struck down Goliath,* a brave man and *warlike* from boyhood.† By the power of prayer and of faith the adversary of God's people is torn and destroyed.

*see 1 Sam 17:33, 40, 49
†see 1 Sam 16:18

12. Therefore *be brave* men,* because if you conquer, then I shall give you a great reward. Not one city, not one country, not only heaven and earth, which certainly shall pass away,* but I shall give you *hidden manna*:* my Word, which *remains forever.*† I shall give you eternal life. I shall give you my Son, through whom I have created all things, and in him

*see 1 Sam 18:17; see Ant in Com apos (Hesbert 3:2684)
*see Matt 24:35

*Rev 2:17
†see Ps 118:89

and with him I shall give all things to you.* For one who has him has all things.

13. Blessed Vincent happily sought this promise of happiness and glory, he whose martyrdom we celebrate today. He according to his own name was truly victorious.* Victorious in promises, victorious in threats, victorious in punishments. *He strove for the law of his God even unto death, and he did not fear the words of the wicked*, because *he was founded on solid rock.** He did not fear the threats and punishments of Dacianus.

14. So Dacianus, that blood-thirsty and cruel persecutor of the church, when he could not turn Vincent away from the faith of Christ, "with trembling breast, grim and menacing eyes, began to shout to the soldiers, 'What are you doing? I do not recognize your hands.'"* "'Tie Vincent to the rack, stretch his members, and tear apart his whole body. Let him endure this punishment before the torments.'"* Finally the holy "athlete of Christ is tortured, flogged, and burned with fire,"* but is not conquered. Faithfully he contended, vigorously he fought, bravely he conquered. He conquered the world, he conquered the devil, he conquered Dacianus, he conquered the executioner, he conquered the flesh, he conquered prison, he conquered fire.

15. So it is that he merited to see heavenly light in a dark prison, and "surrounded by a holy company of angels, he was warmed and soothed by angelic solicitude and encouragement. He heard from angels, 'Recognize, O Vincent most invincible, for whose name you have faithfully struggled. He who made you a victor in punishments keeps a crown prepared for you in heaven.'"* Today *a crown of justice, a crown of glory*† was given to blessed Vincent, a crown of eternal life. Today *hidden manna* was given to him.‡

*see Rom 8:32

**uincens*

*see Ant and Resp
Iste in Com Mar
(Hesbert 3:3434;
4:7010);
see Sir 4:33;
see Matt 7:25

*Acta S *Vincentii*
2.9 (Acta SS, 395)

*Acta S Vincentii
2.7 (Acta SS, 395)

*Acta S Vincentii
2.12 (Acta SS 396)

*Acta S Vincenti
3.14 (Acta SS 396)
†see 1 Thess 2:19;
see 2 Tim 4:8;
see Jas 1:12
‡Rev 2:17

Today, instead of earthly and perishable goods, on him were bestowed heavenly goods that remain without end.

16. Therefore let anyone who desires *hidden manna* imitate Vincent. And so it has been determined by the holy fathers to celebrate the feasts of the saints, so that we might call to mind their life and behavior and imitate their examples. For how does it benefit them if we sing or read about them? Can it be that we make them better or holier by this? But it profits us much more in faith and holy devotion to celebrate their solemnities if we diligently imitate their works. One who faithfully follows his chastity, patience, and charity profitably celebrates the feast of blessed Vincent.

17. If temptation rises against me, if by chance it suggests to me that I sleep when I ought to keep vigil, or that I eat when I ought to fast, or that I speak when I ought to keep silent, then thinking about blessed Vincent I shall say in my heart, Blessed Vincent mortified his flesh on account of Christ: he did not do his own will, he fasted when he wished to eat, he kept vigil when he wished to sleep, he became silent when he aspired to speak, he spurned youth and bodily beauty and all the world's pomp, he rejected earthly and transitory goods like dung.* In all these I ought to imitate him according to my small measure. If thus I have thought and so I have done, then I did well to read about blessed Vincent.

18. And if Dacianus, that is, the devil, should come suggesting to me some illicit deed, flattering me with promises of success or frightening me with threats of adversity, and I call to mind the suffering of blessed Vincent, then I shall say in my heart, "I despise your flattery or even your threats, Dacianus, *get behind me, Satan*;* prosperity or adversity will

*see Phil 3:8

*Mark 8:33

not be able to call me away from the way of my God. Rather, on account of Christ I shall mortify and subdue my flesh" (saying with blessed Paul, *The sufferings of this time are not worthy to be compared with the future glory that will be revealed in us**), so no one will be able to divert me *from the charity of Christ** by love or fear, flattery or threats.

*Rom 8:18

*see Rom 8:35, 39

19. "There are two movements of the heart by which the rational soul is driven to every purpose that it does. One is fear; the other is love. When these two are good, they accomplish every good. Through fear bad deeds are avoided; through love good deeds are practiced. Through bad fear one withdraws from good; through bad love one carries out bad deeds. Therefore these two are like two gates, through which death and life enter. Death certainly when they open for evil life, when they are unlatched for good."*

*Hugh of S. Victor, De sac 2:13 (PL 176:527BC)

20. The blessed Vincent had good love and fear, he who was not frightened by threats and not mollified by flattery. So despising the flattery of Dacianus and spurning threats and punishments, he confidently responded to the tyrant, "The servant of God is prepared for enduring all torments for the sake of his Savior."*

*Acta S Vincenti 2.7 (Acta SS 395)

21. Therefore brothers, by the example of this great soldier of Christ, let us *bravely* fight *the Lord's battles*,* so that vigorously resisting the devil and his servants, we can be victors, and with blessed Vincent we may merit to gain the crown of eternal life, which may the Lord Jesus Christ deign to bestow upon us by the merits and prayers of his martyr, he who with the Father and Holy Spirit lives and reigns, God through all ages forever. Amen.

*see 1 Sam 18:17; see 2 Macc 13:14

Sermon 177

On the Feast of Saint Vincent[1]

*militia; Job 7:1

*militiam

*see 1 Cor 2:14

*militandi

*see Luke 8:13;
see Sir 6:8; 37:4
†see Matt 12:30

1. *T*he life of a man upon earth is warfare.* On this illustrious solemnity of this particular soldier of Christ, the subject teaches and the reward persuades to take up spiritual warfare.* Five things are necessary to practice this warfare: rank, skill, fortitude, weapons, and the enemy. But please do not understand these things in a carnal way, but rather spiritually.* Rank is profession, skill is instruction, fortitude is steadfastness, weapons are virtues, the enemy is the foe of virtues.

2. Rank bestows the dignity of fighting,* skill care in usage, fortitude the security of conquest, weapons help in guarding oneself and harming adversaries, and the enemy the substance of a quarrel. One who struggles against vices without a Christian profession fights without rank. One who is not instructed in Scripture is without skill. One without fortitude is *one who* fights *for a time and in time of* <tribulation>* either flees or breaks off the fight. One who does not gather virtues† is without weapons. The enemy is never absent but is always at hand, always imposing himself, and if at any time he is conquered, again and again he tries his weapons.

3. If he is vanquished by one weapon, he tries another. If he is overcome by self-control, then he tries vainglory. If he is pushed back by abstinence,

[1] Saint Vincent of Saragossa, 3rd-century protomartyr of Spain, f.d. Jan. 22.

then he assails with pride. If he is restrained by the austerity of religious life, then he harasses with lust for praise. When the character of the person whom he attacks is greater, then all the more powerfully does he vex. He scorns worldly people, as if he were not concerned about them. He disregards those who are entangled in worldly *business*,* as though common prey. So the Lord says to blessed Job about the adversary, *He eats grass like an ox.** Understand grass as those who are given to feelings of carnal desires and worldly pleasures, whom the devil cuts off and devours as *an ox* does *grass.* Isaiah says about this grass, *All flesh is as grass, and every glory thereof as a flower of grass.** And, *Truly the people is grass.*†

4. But the devil, who *eats grass as an ox*,‡ does not touch coals, especially when kindled, about which the prophet says, *Coals were kindled by it.** Therefore they become coals, so that first the trees are set on fire and then extinguished, and afterward they are burned for various uses. Coals are the minds of the faithful, first extinguished by the water of concupiscence and then enlightened by the grace of the Holy Spirit. The devil avoids these coals, although reluctantly.

5. Nevertheless, many times he assails and treads upon the holy and perfected, such as blessed Job, but only with permission, not of his own power. So the devil said to the Lord about blessed Job, *Does not Job fear the Lord in vain?** And the Lord said to him, *Behold, all that he possesses is in your hand.** Blessed Job testifies that the devil assails and treads upon the saints, saying in another place, *He strews gold under him as mud, and brass as rotten wood.** Understand the gold to be wise people who have been strengthened by maturity and religion; understand the brass to be preachers singing the praises of God in <deed>

*see 2 Tim 2:4

*Job 40:10

*Isa 40:6; see 1 Pet 1:24
†Isa 40:7
‡see Job 40:10
*Ps 17:9

*Job 1:9
*Job 1:12

*Job 41:21, 18

and word of faith. But the adversary assails the former and the latter. So Saint Job says, *He will drink
up a river and will not wonder, and he has confidence*
*Job 40:18 *that the Jordan may flow into his mouth.**

6. But to avoid this, the enemy's disturbance,
those five that we previously spoke of are necessary.
Of them, four ought to be sought in need: rank, skill,
fortitude, and weapons. But the fifth, the enemy of
course, must be assaulted with the whole of one's
effort. How do we say these five are necessary? Isn't
the enemy necessary? By all means! How? For prov-
ing, testing, victory. Where there is no fight, there is
no victory, and where there is no victory, there is no
glory. Therefore five are necessary: rank of course,
which is profession, and skill, which is instruction,
and the others. Let us see about each one more fully.

7. Of professions, some are general, some special,
others singular. General profession is the observance
of the common aspects of Christianity, without
which Christian warfare is not practiced. Special
profession is the perfect conversion of those in a
religious order, with which Christian warfare is more
perfectly practiced. Singular [profession] is the singular intention of solitaries, withdrawn from others.
Without any of these three professions Christian
warfare is not practiced.

8. Of skill, some is natural, other doctrinal. The
natural is an innate disposition of the soul; when it
thrives in certain people, they are more perceptive
than the rest and more skillful. However, when lacking in others, they are ignorant and more simple. The
former are more inclined to Christian warfare and
more eager; the latter are slower. Doctrinal skill is
what we seek with the support of practice, by revelation of God, or by disclosure from teachers, or by
studying books. By these three methods we find the
skill to do battle against demons.

9. Fortitude, that is, steadfastness, which we have put in the third place, exists for warfare to begin, likewise while practiced and guided, and again while it is embraced unto the end. For a good beginning is of no benefit for a human being unless there is also a consummation. Steadfastness has many types: perseverance, obviously, and long-suffering, patience, truth of speech, and self-control of all one's members. Just as steadfastness is of most value to Christian warfare, so inconstancy is most harmful. So it is written, *A double-minded man is inconstant in all his ways.** And again, *Woe to the sinner who walks the earth in a double-dealing way!**   *Jas 1:8   *Sir 2:14

10. For these three—rank, instruction, steadfastness—to have fortification and protection, weapons are necessary. For an unarmed soldier of whatever status, diligence, and fortitude is easily overpowered, wounded, and killed by that armed strong man who has guarded *his courtyard.** When someone goes to war without weapons, will he not be judged as arrogant and reckless? These weapons of ours are not carnal, but spiritual, just as our warfare is spiritual.   *see Luke 11:21

11. The apostle says about these weapons, *The weapons of <our> warfare are not carnal,** but spiritual. And again, *Put on the armor of God, that you may be able to stand against the deceits of the devil.** And, *Take up the armor of God, that you may be able to resist in the evil day.** *Stand therefore, having your loins girt about with truth, and having on the hauberk of justice and your feet shod in the preparation of the gospel of peace, in all things taking up the shield of faith, with which you may be able to extinguish all the fiery darts of the most wicked one. And put on the helmet of salvation and the sword of the Spirit, which is the word of God.** Behold how the apostle arms his soldier. Behold by what names he indicates weapons.   *2 Cor 10:4   *Eph 6:11   *Eph 6:13   *Eph 6:14-17

12. By the shield of the Christian soldier, which fortifies the hauberk and protects in front, faith is accepted,* which is the foundation of all virtues and the first of all. In fact, *without faith it is impossible to please God.** In order to hold up the shield of faith, one needs a right hand, by which the works of faith are designated. For in fact, *faith is dead* and idle, unless there have been works.* By the hauberk, which fortifies the whole body, in front and behind, on the right and the left, charity is understood,* which fortifies on all sides and protects and defends from every projectile of the adversary. For one who has charity has all; one who does not have it has nothing. "Have charity," says Augustine, "and do whatever you will."* By the helmet, which is raised up and tends at all times toward heaven, hope is accepted.†

13. By iron greaves, chastity. One wards off [an attack] with a lance that pierces the enemy, and so that he cannot come near the hauberk and shield, holy prayer is taken up, which pierces the devil *in the forehead,** so that he cannot injure faith or charity, or weaken the other virtues. By the horse on which one sits is represented the flesh or sensuality. Over this, reason, that is, the superior part of the soul, should preside as though master. Lest this flesh become disobedient or wanton, it must be restrained with a bridle, which is the supervision of discipline. Reason's two reins are judgment and mercy. When one of these tries to gain control for itself beyond measure, the other strives to recall it lest it be excessive; that way reason is not too severe through judgment or too lax through mercy. The saddle, placed upon the back of this horse, is *the sweet yoke* of the Lord and his *light burden.** Spurs, by which this horse is goaded, are repentance and abstinence.

14. A Christian soldier ought to acquire these weapons for himself so that he may do battle against

*see Eph 6:16

*Heb 11:6

*see Jas 2:17

*see 1 Thess 5:8

*Augustine, In Ep Ioh, Tract 7.8 (SCh 75:328)
†see 1 Thess 5:8

*see 1 Sam 17:49

*see Matt 11:30

the enemy with them. For the enemy is strong because it is triple, that is, the flesh, the world, and the devil. The flesh strives to take the soul captive, the world to take away heaven, the devil [to take away] God. Concerning the battle of the flesh against us, it is written, *The flesh lusts against the spirit, and the spirit against the flesh.** Concerning the battle of the world, *All that is in the world is the concupiscence of the eyes*, etc.* Concerning the battle of the devil, *Your adversary the devil, like a roaring lion, goes about seeking whom he may devour.** These three leaders—the flesh, the world, and the devil—have many soldiers against us.

*Gal 5:17

*1 John 2:16

*1 Pet 5:8

15. Against us, the soldiers of the flesh are those that Paul mentions, saying, *Mortify your members upon the earth: fornication*, etc.* The soldiers of the world against us are excess, vanity, curiosity. Excess consists in four aspects: in things undertaken, in things set aside, in things postponed, in things stored up. Vanity also [has] four aspects: in exaltation, in vainglory, in favoring oneself, in disdain for others. Curiosity similarly consists in four things: in ambitions, in attitudes, in profits, in acquisitions. And because there are many types of these, there are many soldiers of this world against us. That the devil opposes us, no one doubts, since we continually sense uneasiness about him. His accomplices are those that Paul mentions, saying, *Our struggling is not against flesh and blood, but against principalities*, etc.* Not that we have no battle against vices of the flesh and soul, but in regard to the battle of the devil, there seems to be no battle of vice.

*Col 3:5

*Eph 6:12

16. With these three enemies, three wars need to be undertaken, and three victories must be had. Let the flesh be attacked through self control, the world through contempt, the devil through humility. A dignified, trained, brave, armed soldier, fighting a triple

war with this triple enemy, is busy denying himself by dominating the flesh, rejecting his own possessions by overcoming the world, conciliating himself to himself by triumphing over the devil. Let him deny what he is, let him deny what he has, let him deny the one who holds him.* One who so lives is a soldier of Christ, and one who wishes to be a soldier of Christ should thus live.

*see Matt 16:24

17. One who is immersed by the flesh and entangled by this age and overwhelmed by the devil does not practice Christian warfare and does not have life, but is the living dead,* as the one *who has a two-edged <sword> in his mouth** says *to the angel of Smyrna:** You have the name of being alive, and you are dead.* Our *life is warfare*, and not just any life. But a life of military service is not everywhere, but *upon the earth.** For life in heaven is not warfare; rather, it is the wages of war, the triumph of victory, eternity of glory.

*see 1 Tim 5:6
*Rev 2:12
*see Rev 2:8
*Rev 3:1

*see Job 7:1

18. Note what he says, *the life of a man*. But not of woman, not of livestock, not of a brute animal, not of a bestial creature, but of a man. A man is sometimes a characteristic* of carnality, sometimes of virility, sometimes of fickleness, sometimes of distinctions of sex. Of carnality, as in Genesis: *My spirit shall not remain in a man forever, because he is flesh.** A man is a sign of manliness, as in the present, *The life of a man upon earth is warfare.** And in Leviticus: *A man, if he offers a sacrifice of the cattle, shall offer a calf without blemish,** and in many other places. It is a sign of changeability, as in the Book of Kings: *He is not a man, that he should do penance and change his plan.** It is about distinctions of sex, as when Jesus is called *Son of Man*, that is, son of Mary.†

*nota

*Gen 6:3

*Job 7:1

*Lev 1:2-3

*1 Sam 15:29;
see Num 23:19
†Matt 9:6
‡Job 7:1

19. And so *the life of a man is warfare*,‡ that is, one who is virile and brave must in his whole tem-

poral life take up Christian warfare and live according to it. Moreover, there are three lives, as Augustine says: the life of cattle, the life of a human, the life of an angel. The life of cattle is a life that is deficient; the life of a human is progressing; the life of an angel is fulfilled. The life of cattle is satisfaction of the belly, the life of a human is acquisition of salvation; the life of an angel is knowledge of divinity. Therefore *the life of a man is warfare*; the life of cattle, idleness; the life of an angel, glory. *The life of a man is warfare*—not the life in heaven, which will be equal to that of angels,* but that on earth. *see Luke 20:36

20. In warfare, according to the variety of wars, they slay and are slain, they wound and are wounded. At various events they flee or they counter-attack, they destroy and are destroyed, according to what David says concerning Joab: *Various are the effects of war; the sword consumes now these and then others.** So it is in human life. Now one succumbs to *2 Sam 11:25 enemies, then one triumphs over enemies. Not only people who are condemned, or those who are only partially good, have this situation, but even the chosen and the perfect now fall now and then get back up.

21. For *a just person falls seven times in a day and seven times rises again.** Certainly wicked people *Prov 24:16; see Luke 17:4 fall but do not rise again at all, because they are *a dry tree*, cut off at the roots.* But *a tree*, as Solomon *see Isa 56:3; see Ezek 17:9 says, *in whatever place it shall fall, either to the south or to the north, there it will remain.** Because people *Eccl 11:3 cut off by death, in whatever acts they are found, whether in good acts with God or in bad deeds with the devil, in them they will remain. In fact, because there has not been a dispensation in the present through repentance, in the future they will remain with those acts in torment.

22. Finally it is a most perfect warfare to live here in Christ, that is, in the commandments of Christ. It is also a most perfect warfare to die for the sake of Christ. A proven soldier sometimes dies for sake of his leader. Our King has died for his soldiers, because that was the need. Let a soldier die for sake of his king when there may be need.

23. Dearest brothers, let us seize spiritual, victorious, and glorious military service, and let us act so strenuously in it that in battle we may achieve victory and deserve everlasting glory in the kingdom, which may our Lord Jesus Christ, our fighter and remunerator, deign to bestow on us, who with the Father and Holy Spirit lives and reigns God through all ages forever. Amen.

Sermon 178

On the Feast of Saint Gregory[1]

1. *Cry out, cease not, lift up your voice like a trumpet, and declare to my people their wicked deeds, and to the house of Jacob their sins.** *Why are you troubled and thoughts arise in your hearts?** Do I seem forgetful of today's solemnity? And you say *within yourselves,** "We ought not to rebuke our wicked deeds today, ought not to declare sins, but we ought to recount the merits of our blessed father Gregory, commend his <proclamations>! What you say is for Lent, not for a feast day. They are mournful rather than festive words, not suitable for this occasion." But so far none of our solemnities, my brothers, can present pure joy to us, because pure justice is not found in us. *All our justice is like the rag of a menstruating woman;** therefore all our *laughter* is mixed with *sorrow,** all feast days are full of bitterness.* When will come that full and pure festivity that was desired by the one who said, *That my glory may sing to you, and I may not regret?**

2. *Cry out, cease not,* etc.* God spoke this word to a prophet and now speaks it continually to a faithful soul, whose cry he hears and may always be willing to hear. I suppose this [applies] to our father, and

*Isa 58:1
*Luke 24:38
*see Matt 3:9

*Isa 64:6
*see Prov 14:13
*see Tob 2:6;
see Lam 1:20

*Ps 29:13
*Isa 58:1

[1] Saint Gregory the Great (Pope Gregory I), ca. 520–604, original feast day March 12, the day of his death. Since 1969, it is celebrated in the Western church on Sept. 3, the day of his episcopal consecration in 590.

if not singularly, nevertheless specifically words of this sort.

3. *Cry out, cease not.** While *a person looks to appearances, God however regards the heart,** so a person's ear [hears] the sound of a voice, but divine attention penetrates internal things and comprehends interior realities. As he says to the happy soul, *Let your voice sound in my ears, show me your face, for your voice is sweet, and your face comely.** Many make noise outwardly; within they are quiet. Moses is silent outwardly, and he hears, *Why do you cry out to me?** Let us beware, my beloved ones, let us beware, we who are occupied by duties, lest he say about us, *This people honors me with their lips, but their heart is far from me.** Our voice is not sweet to him if our interior does not sing with our exterior, if our minds are not in harmony with our voices.*

4. Some speak to him as though with a quiet voice, a humble prayer, a meager feeling, a modicum of devotion. In the end, there is need for God to incline his attention to anyone who thus speaks* in order politely to pay attention, mercifully to condescend. God's ear *hears all things,** and yet *he stops his ears lest he hear blood.** He condemns, he detests, and he does not say to a soul of this type, *Cry out, cease not.** He is not well pleased† by the cry of that one to whom he says, *Be silent, and go out from him.*‡ Neither does he accept the cry of him to whom he says, *Why do you cry out to me? Your wound is incurable.** Moses blames his modest or thin voice,† but however humble he is, God does not reject or ignore hearing the voice of piety, and if that voice is not strong enough to ascend, then he does not refuse to descend.

5. Any feeling of piety is a voice acceptable to him, but more acceptable is a voice crying out when the fervor of love, when the vehemence of desire, when

*Isa 58:1

*1 Sam 16:7; see Resp Quae de Sap (Hesbert 4:7457)

*Song 2:14

*Exod 14:15

*Matt 15:8; Isa 29:13

*RB 19.7

*see Ps 16:6; see Ps 114:1-2

*see Wis 1:10

*Isa 33:15

*Isa 58:1
†see Matt 12:18; Isa 42:1
‡Mark 1:25

*see Jer 30:15, 12
†see Exod 4:10

the power of love is more ardent. Who thus cried out, who loved so affectionately, who prayed so piously, who so delighted heaven's attention as this blessed Gregory? For what did he seek that he did not merit to obtain? Rightly then do we think that it was said to him, *Cry out, cease not.** In fact, God does not turn his ear away from his cry,* does not *set a cloud so that prayer does not pass through.*† Because he says, *Cry out,* he calls forth confidence. Because he says, *Cease not,* he encourages perseverance.

*Isa 58:1

*see Lam 3:56;
see Ps 21:25
†see Lam 3:44

6. No one can persist in the pursuit of contemplation without the training of action, just as action itself without contemplation is less valued, less wise, less useful, less pure. So you have *Be not over just, and be not excessively wise, lest you be stupefied.** Justice dwells in service; wisdom dwells in contemplation. In an allegory of service and contemplation one reads that Saint Jacob of old had two wives,* and the sacred gospels testify that two sisters complied with the Lord's will.* And to be sure, I admit that I do not recall reading in the New or in the Old Testament that in this life one is recommended without the other. Certainly it is alleged that *Ephraim is a heifer taught to love threshing.** And the one who says *"I love God" but does not keep his commandments* is proved to be *a liar.**

*Eccl 7:17

*see Gen 29:15-30

*see Luke 10:38-42

*Hos 10:11

*see 1 John 2:4;
4:20

7. Such is what we mentioned above: *Be not over just, and be not excessively wise, lest you be stupefied.** That is, may you not get too entangled in activity, for while you want to satisfy everyone, inside you become empty. And may you not give yourself wholly to the pursuit of contemplation, so that you forget yourself as a human being, as it were, and do not keep the duties of the common life, *seeking* only *what is useful* for yourself, not *what is for the many.** It is best to moderate both, according to what we read: *desiring wisdom,* may you serve *justice, and the Lord*

*Eccl 7:17

*see 1 Cor 10:33;
see RB 72.7

*Sir 1:33

*will give her to you.** This saying also recommends [wisdom and justice] to us in turns: *If I lie down to sleep, I say, When shall I arise? And again I shall look*

*Job 7:4
*Isa 58:1

*to the evening.** The following exhortation pertains to this, *Lift up your voice like a trumpet.**

8. For as a voice is louder in an instrument, so prayer is more effective with service, and contemplation more fruitful with action. Otherwise, *he who turns away his ear so not to hear the law, his prayer*

*Prov 28:9

*shall be detestable.** So Truth says concerning himself, *Why do you call me, "Lord, Lord," and you do*

*Luke 6:46
*Isa 58:1
*Isa 62:6

*not do what I say?** *Cry out* therefore, faithful soul, *cease not,** as the prophet admonishes, saying, *You who are mindful of the Lord, do not be silent.** As often as you fall out of contemplation as a result of the burden of human weakness, recover yourself by sacred action, so that, having recovered your strength, you may return to it stronger.

9. Consider some form of sacred action in the appearance of a trumpet. A trumpet is narrower in the mouthpiece, wider in the hand, widest beyond one's hand. In that part that is applied to the mouth, the trumpet is narrower, wider in that which is held by the hand, so that each part makes the sound louder. Beyond the hand a trumpet must have more ample width, so that each faithful person may say less, do more, and <desire and attempt the most>.

10. There are various types of trumpets. Some are wooden, others ceramic, others horn, others bronze. Among the people of Israel, the people were called

*see Num 10:1-2

together with silver trumpets.* Sacred Scripture also reminds us to sound *the trumpet on the new moon,*

*Ps 80:4

on the day of our *solemnity.** The new-moon trumpet was that by which the Jews were accustomed to designate the beginning of a month at the new moon. So the name itself also expresses the newness of the moon.

11. If by the trumpet, as was said above, service is designated, it will be a silver trumpet if it is in harmony with divine words. For divine words are suitably enough compared to silver.* We can understand in silver the generosity of almsgiving, in horn tolerance of tribulation, in the new moon sacredness of life. One who disperses and spends money sings to the Lord with the silver trumpet.* For as long as *one has mercy on the poor, he lends to the Lord*.†

> *see Ps 11:7

> *see Ps 111:9; 2 Cor 9:9
> †Prov 19:17

12. How well you cried out to the Lord, most blessed father, and did not cease, you who, as we read, "although you nearly wasted away with fatigue every day, nevertheless you wanted to give no rest to your body; you would either pray or read or write or dictate."* How well you have cried out, by whose prayers "the restless boy," whose extremities were already dead, was freed from the dragon. To you he cried that "he was given to be devoured," and then, "he was free from death and acquired salvation."* How well you have cried out. We read that you wept for so long over the error of the most pious prince Trajan, until you received a favorable response concerning him.*

> *Johannes Diaconus, Vita S Greg 1.8 (PL 75:66A)

> *see Johannes Diaconus, Vita S Greg 1.38 (PL75:78B–79A)

13. How quickly you sounded *the new moon trumpet*,† for whom "there were difficult studies for you already at an early age."* And when your father died "obtaining an unhindered opportunity for distributing goods, you constructed six monasteries in Sicily."* And "in your own house" within the city you constructed a seventh monastery and in that same place took up the monastic habit.† How boldly you sang out *with a long trumpet, and the sound of a trumpet made of horn*,‡ when you so afflicted your body by chastening and subjecting it to servitude# that "your life-giving spirit" was hindered.§ Finally, how fortunately you exalted your voice with a silver

> *see Johannes Diaconus, *Vita* S Greg 2.44 (PL 75:105B)
> †see Ps 80:4

> *Johannes Diaconus, Vita S Greg 3 (PL 75:64A)

> *Johannes Diaconus, Vita S Greg 1.5 (PL 75:65A)
> †see Johannes Diaconus, Vita S Greg 1.6 (PL 75:65AB)
> ‡Ps 97:6
> #see 1 Cor 9:27
> §see Johannes Diaconus, Vita S Greg 1.7 (PL 75:65BC).

*see Isa 58:1

trumpet:* when you offered your mother's silver dish to a needy person, you bestowed it on an angel, whom afterward, as the thirteenth among strangers that you received as guests, you alone merited to see, you alone to speak with, you alone to be consoled and instructed by him.*

*see Johannes Diaconus, Vita S Greg 1.10; 2.23 (PL 75:66C, 96AD)
*see John 21:17

14. Accordingly, you stood out as worthy, truly like the loving disciple to whom the Lord entrusted the care of the flock and feeding of the sheep.* In fact, aptly could he remove *a beam* and *a straw* from the eyes of his neighbors, he who had cleansed his

*see Matt 7:3-5

own eyes of both.* Therefore after pursuit of prayer, after practice of action, aptly is the duty of preaching taken up. *Declare to my people,* says the Lord, *their*

*Isa 58:1

*wicked deeds, and to the house of Jacob their sins.**

15. Beloved brothers, as I judge, by this *house of Jacob* the present Scripture distinguishes us from the people of God, us whose *life upon earth* in this in-

*see Job 7:1
*see Eph 6:12

terim especially professes warfare,* us for whom the conflict ought to be a continual clash and *struggle,** not *against flesh and blood, but against the spirits of wickedness.* So then, as unsuitable as it is to rebuke secular people about trivial negligence, and while swallowing a camel to admonish them about strain-

*see Matt 23:24

ing a gnat,* so it is unworthy if any among us might wish to have a sermon about correcting <or> avoid-ing more serious crimes among us, *if fornication or uncleanness, if indecency or buffoonery is considered*

*see Eph 5:3-4

unbecoming of the saints.* In fact this holy pontiff carefully furnishes individual examples in appropri-ate categories, and his *Liber Pastoralis* presents them.

16. Now, to bring this sermon to an end, in all these words it must be considered—that is, it must be kept in mind that we should take care by the di-vine admonition and equally by the example of so great a father to strike the ears of the judge with

constant crying out,* always by pious intention and
the fervor of internal desire. And so that our prayer
may be found more effective and more acceptable,
let us strengthen it by holy actions. Finally, contending *in the struggle* like the house of Jacob, let us
tremble and refrain *from all* sins as much as we can.*

17. Indeed place, habit, nourishment, celebration
of sacraments, teaching of morals, discipline of our
elders, examples of the saints—all amount to an ac-
cumulation of blame if we have been negligent. Place,
on account of the usual reverence of sanctity. Habit,
because it displays evidence of innocence and humility, and *the appearance of piety*.* Nourishment, because we must always remember with concern that
it is from the alms and offerings of the faithful for
sins.* Celebration of sacraments because in them,
just as each humble and God-fearing person obtains
grace,* so one who is irreverent and unworthy merits
wrath. Teaching of morals, which is heaped upon us
repeatedly, *conveniently and inconveniently*,* as the
apostle advises. Discipline of our elders, which is
practiced so sedulously around us. Examples of the
saints, of which an abundance is shown to us every
day. Would that these might all work together *for
the good* of us all,* supplied by that one who *alone
is good*, without whom *no one is good*,* *God who
is blessed over all things forever* and ever. *Amen.*†

*see Luke 18:6-7;
see Matt 7:7;
see Isa 58:1

*see Gen 32:24-29;
see 1 Cor 9:25

*see 2 Tim 3:5

*see Heb 10:8, 18

*see 1 Pet 5:5;
see Luke 18:14

*see 2 Tim 4:2

*see Rom 8:28

*see Matt 19:17;
see Luke 18:19
†Rom 9:5

Sermon 179

To Nuns

On the Thursday after the Week of the Resurrection

1.   **A***rise, O north wind, and come, O south wind. Blow through my garden, and let its aromatic spices flow.** That holy woman, O daughters, who believed the Lord to be a gardener† was not much mistaken. For *from the beginning* he planted *a garden of pleasure,** and in the end times he willed to be buried *in a garden,** like *the tree of life* planted *in the middle of Paradise.** He loves gardens and the splendor of gardens; he delights in lilies and roses.*

*Song 4:16;
Ant in Com virg
(Hesbert 3:5070)
†see John 20:15
*Gen 2:8
*see John 19:41-42
*see Gen 2:9

*see Song 6:1-2

2. Happy is the garden where lilies are resplendent and fragrant, so that viewers are edified by the example, and *good odor** prompts to virtue those who are far off. The brilliance of purity and sanctity is agreeable to Christ. *Good testimony from those who are outdoors** is pleasing to him. His *delights* are *to be with the children of humankind,** chiefly those whom *incorruption* made near.* This garden has a cloister;* it has protection and ample diligence. In fact, where virginity is more cherished, it is less neglected, more eagerly fostered, more diligently guarded. Precious grace and virtue are to be embraced: integrity of flesh, model of angels, and the form of resurrection.*

*see 2 Cor 2:15

*1 Tim 3:7
*see Prov 8:31
*see Wis 6:20
*see Song 4:12

*see Luke 20:36

3. You do not ignore how the bridegroom ignores the foolish virgins and says to those who knock, *I do*

*not know you.** Whom do we consider foolish if not
her who does not know God? Utterly not knowing,
she *will not be known.** No wonder if we fear ourselves, O daughters, if indeed Paul himself fears *that
just as the serpent seduced Eve by his cunning, so* our
*sense may be corrupted away from the integrity that
is in Christ,** to whom he betrothed us as chaste virgins, *to present* one *virgin to one husband.** Because
the apostle fears that the integrity of our sense in
Christ is corrupted, he admonishes us not only about
preserving integrity of virginity in our flesh, but much
more about the integrity of our sense in Christ.

4. Integrity of the flesh preserves inviolable the
bridegroom's garden,* Christ's abode, *the sanctuary
of the Holy Spirit, the temple of God.** *If anyone
should violate* this, *then God shall destroy him.*†
Integrity of sense thinks *about the Lord in goodness,
and* seeks *him in simplicity of heart.** *In goodness,*
it thinks about him who *alone is good;** *in simplicity
<of heart>*, it seeks him who is nothing except good.
In goodness, it thinks about him who is singularly
good; *in simplicity of heart* it seeks him who is simply
good. What is *simply? In whose presence there is no
change, and no shadow of alteration.**

5. Integrity of sense always recognizes mercy and
truth in Christ.* It is moved by mercy to love, by truth
to fear. She who said, *My beloved is white and ruddy**
had recognized him as such. Lovable and terrible. In
ruddiness is terror, in whiteness of vision gentle charm.
But why lovable if not out of mercy, out of goodness,
out of grace? Why terrible, if not out of his judgment,
out of his justice, out of his severity? So the apostle
says, *See the goodness and severity of God.**

6. These are the two millstones that the law forbids to be taken from a debtor as a pledge,* so that
however much anyone might fail, a superior might

*see Matt 25:12

*see 1 Cor 14:38

*2 Cor 11:3
*see 2 Cor 11:2

*see Song 4:16
*see Ant Beata in Ass
(Hesbert 3:1563)
†see 1 Cor 3:16-17

*see Wis 1:1
*see Matt 19:17;
see Luke 18:19

*Jas 1:17

*see Ps 24:10
*see Song 5:10

*Rom 11:22

*see Deut 24:6

never remove the love or fear of God from him. These two are the springs that we read the father Caleph added for his daughter when she sighed,* so that a faithful soul is equally inspired by love and fear. Here is that north wind and here the south wind that the bridegroom calls *into his garden*, saying, *Arise, O north wind, and come, O south wind.**

*see Josh 15:18-19; see Judg 1:14-15

*Song 4:16; see 6:1

7. *From the north*, as Scripture says, *every evil breaks forth.** The *wind* is cold, strong, and *violent*,† as though rising from the region of midnight, oppressive and fierce out of hell. This is the spirit of fear that compels one to say, *I shall go to the gates of hell*,* which already heaps up all hellish* torments upon a trembling soul, as it were: the worm that does not die, inextinguishable fire,* dread of exterior darkness, binding hands and feet, weeping and gnashing of teeth, the company of demons,* snow water and everlasting fire.*

*Jer 1:14
†see Job 1:19

*Isa 38:10

*gehennalia

*see Mark 9:43

*see Matt 22:13-14

*see Job 24:19; see Matt 25:41

8. The wind from the south suggests to the soul who desires where the bridegroom reclines and feeds,* happy and warm, those many dwellings that *are in the Father's house*,* and the *delights at* God's *right hand even to the end*:* joy and happiness, thanksgiving and the voice of praise,* a torrent of pleasure,* fullness of light, vision of divine majesty, fellowship of angels, communion of saints, and finally what *eye has not seen and ear has not heard.**

*see Song 1:6

*see John 14:2

*Ps 15:11

*see Isa 51:3

*see Ps 35:9

*1 Cor 2:9

9. Carefully turn your attention to the words themselves: *Arise*, it says, *O north wind, and come, O south wind.** The former arises as severe, the latter comes as modest, as pleasant, as gentle. In fact, from this twin breeze flow precious aromatic scents of the spiritual garden as often as a remorseful soul softens either from fear or love, and thereupon melts into tears of salvation. The Lord, desiring to find these in us, not only in the Song of Songs but also in the

*Song 4:16

Apocalypse, makes known what he desires: *Would that you were hot*, he says, *or that I would find you cold!** Who is hot if not one upon whom the south wind blows?* Who is cold if not one against whom the north wind comes up? He who does not need our good things* chooses these for us, and we do not want [them]?

10. If only he would always find us so hot or cold, and never tepid, lest God start *to vomit** or abandon us! If only *mercy and truth would not forsake* us! If only we would put *them around* our *neck and write them on the tablets of* our *heart!** For these are what he wishes for in us, these are what *God loves*, and in one whom he finds them, *the Lord will give grace and glory.** The one who advised against fear as well as love of the Lord wills to make us tepid. Envious and *false* and *father* of the lie,* *by* whose *envy death came into the world,** he persuaded us that God was false and envious, projecting his own offenses upon him, just as until today even on this side *they imitate him who are from his side,** so they disgrace others with their own squalor.

11. God, the lover of human beings, who *alone is* supremely *good,** in these things that he created for human uses made all things good and *very good;†* desiring nothing except good, he forbade only the tree *of knowledge of good and evil,** not jealous of anything good, but warning to beware of evil in the good, punishment in pleasure, death "standing at the entrance of enjoyment."* *God from the beginning* planted *a garden of pleasure*, providing a place of happiness for humankind, and *placed the human* in it.* How therefore would God be jealous of humans, whom he not only created from nonexistence but gave to them that they might be in charge of the rest of what he had created?* *You have crowned him*

*Rev 3:15

*see Song 4:16

*see Ps 15:2

*see Rev 3:16

*see Prov 3:3

*see Ps 83:12

*see John 8:44
*Wis 2:24

*Wis 2:25

*see Matt 19:17;
see Luke 18:19
†see Gen 1:31

*see Gen 2:16-17

*see RB 7.24

*see Gen 2:8

*see Gen 1:26

with glory and honor, it says, *and set him over the*
*Ps 8:6-7
*works of your hands.**

12. God commanded the humans *to cultivate the*
*see Gen 2:15;
Gen 2:8
*garden of pleasure and watch over it.** In any garden
of the Lord, in any cloister, in any Paradise where
there are God's *delights to be with the children of*
*see Prov 8:31
*humankind,** let us acknowledge idleness as the
*see RB 48.1
soul's enemy.* *You may eat*, he says, *from every tree
of Paradise* (which is to enjoy every pleasure); *you
may not eat from the tree of knowledge of good and*
*Gen 2:16-17
*evil.** Flee only that in which evil follows good. As
the wise one says, *There are ways that seem good to
people, the end of which plunge into the depths* of
*Prov 16:25;
RB 7.21
hell* (when what pleases him is not expedient); thus
is it mixed like a hook in bait, or poison in honey.

13. Therefore he does not prohibit good as if he
were jealous, but he prevents evil in his providence,
as it were. God wanting the good for you, he desires
to find you thoroughly free of evil. If good pleases
you, then let <not> what accompanies evil be pleasing. *Laughter will be mingled with sorrow*, says the
wise man, *and mourning will overtake the end of*
*Prov 14:13
*joy.** Good laughter is not mixed with sorrow, good
joy does not have a mournful end, good joy is not
destined to be found passing away. The Creator
wishes the knowledge of good and good for you, he
furnishes it, he commends it, so that you are finally
conveyed from the place of this temporal pleasure to
a superior place and more desirable position of eternal happiness.

14. The jealous one, *by* whose *jealousy death
*Wis 2:24
entered into the world,** wishes knowledge of evil
and evil for you, so that, in rancor of soul and affliction of body, you may store up *for yourself wrath
*see Rom 2:5
unto the day of wrath** and may be crushed *with
*see Jer 17:18
double destruction;** your torments beginning for

you here, which may hereafter into eternity admit no end. But because *vexation* usually gives *understanding* to many* and evil is fled at first sight, whereas a better hope for a future good does not always convince, it is hoped that you are leading your *days in good things* rather than *in a moment* descending *to hell.** As Ambrose testifies, "enticing vices deceive many, but sad and extremely severe cruelty diverts many more from itself."* So even the good Lord, also desiring only good things for you, presented the tree of knowledge of evil and good as a remedy. In the meantime, it is less pleasant but healthy, bitter but medicinal, punitive but useful: this tree of the cross, not pleasurable but fruitful, salutary rather than pleasing.

*see Isa 28:19

*see Job 21:13

*Ambrose, Exp Ps CXVIII 16.45 (CSEL 62:376)

15. Moreover, as the first way of human destruction in the tree *of knowledge of good and evil** snatches those whom transitory pleasure (*vapor that appears for a little while*)* drags to eternal punishment, now the second [way] holds them who also hurry through temporal bitterness toward neverending punishments, as if in some experience of evil and evil. So for us the first return out of that region to life by means of the tree of knowledge of evil and good, through redemptive affliction, stands open. Later and loftier is the way that was proposed only to our first parents, through knowledge of good and good; in this we discern some people, even now for the most part flowing with spiritual delights,* with great joy playing a role in their own salvation. So as our blessed father Benedict bears witness, only by narrow beginnings is the way of salvation begun, which however *with the passage* of time *is traversed with the inexpressible delight of love.**

*see Gen 2:17; Gen 3:6

*Jas 4:15

*see Song 8:5

*RB Prol. 48-49

16. Accordingly, so that we may briefly sum up, there is a tree of knowledge of good and good, sweet

and equally salutary charity; of evil and good, a discipline that at first is not of joy but of lamentation;

*see Gen 2:17
*of good and evil,** that is self-will, whose *end plunges*
*Prov 16:25; RB 7.21
*into the depths of hell;** and of evil and evil, impatience and murmuring and hatred, which are not useful or pleasant.

17. Therefore, when *that wicked one, more cunning*
*see 2 Thess 2:8; see Gen 3:1
*than other living creatures,** heard that God had forbidden to the man the taste of this tree under threat of death, he rejoiced in having found an opportunity, so that once the man was convinced by a lie to transgress, he would not in turn experience either the mercy or the truth of God, but inevitably God would be found either merciless if he punished relentlessly or deceitful if he should pardon. Just as he cannot be loved by anyone who has not experi-
*see Orat Def (CO 2.1140–44; CCSL 160A:133–35)
enced mercy or pardon,* so also he would not be feared if in his threat he had not spoken truly and did not act.

18. Therefore he attacked humankind, but in the weaker sex. He was cunning; he knew at which part he would apply his most powerful battering ram of temptation. Striking first in word, and not receiving a definite response from the woman, immediately he employed every impetus of his malice, and as though biting slowly at first, right on the spot he poured on all the venom of his unfair persuasion. *Why has God commanded you not to eat from every tree of Paradise?* "From the trees of Paradise," she says, "we may eat; *from the tree of knowledge of good and evil* God
*see Gen 3:1-2; Gen 2:17
told us we may not eat, *lest perhaps we die."** And God did not say to them, "Perhaps you will die," but,
On whatever day you will eat from the tree of knowl-
*Gen 2:17
*edge of good and evil, you will die the death.** Be-
*death and perhaps
tween *morte* and *forte** there is little difference in sound, but much difference in meaning.

19. God asserts, the woman doubts, the serpent denies: *By no means will you die*, he says. *For God knows*, etc.* He spoke against *the severity and goodness of God* with one speech,* so that he should be neither feared nor loved, as if he were a liar and equally spiteful. Or do the man and woman shudder? If only then they had shuddered. Or even now, if only we would shudder as often as that spiteful one says something to us against *the goodness and severity of God*.* He is trying to dissuade us from fear or love of him. *By no means will you die*, he says.* Therefore is he who said, *You will die* a liar? But perhaps without knowing he deceived, or wishing to take counsel, by a certain dutiful falsehood he wished to detract from that which was not expedient. And if this is agreed, then indeed God is to be reverenced less, or rather should not be loved deeply, he who wished to take counsel even to the detriment of truth.

20. "It is not so," he says. *For God knows that in whatever hour you will eat, you will be as gods*.* Therefore he is jealous and a seducer, who attempts to hinder so great a good and, by this, the appearance of giving counsel. The enemy assigned to the Creator two great crimes, falsehood and iniquity, for he wished to block both the north wind and the south wind from that garden,* so that [God] would not be feared, [as one] whose threat was false, or loved, whose *counsel* was so harmful, *such fraudulent counsel*.* That *wicked* liar the devil† knew that one millstone without another does no good, one foot without another does not suffice—if God is not believed, neither mercy without truth nor truth without mercy benefits a human to salvation.

21. As for the rest, *there is no counsel against the Lord*,* and fraud contradicts itself. God was immediately known as truthful in carrying out the sentence,

*Gen 3:4-5
*see Rom 11:22

*see Rom 11:22
*Gen 3:4;
Gen 2:17

*Gen 3:5

*see Song 4:16

*see Prov 12:5
†see John 8:44

*see Prov 21:30

*see Ps 110:10

so that *fear, the beginning of wisdom*,* persuaded
the humans, and that false liar (who had said, *By no
means will you die**) is found out as a liar. But what

*Gen 3:4; see
John 8:44
†see Ps 76:10

do we do about mercy? *God* has not forgotten *mercy*.†
Certainly the sentence of unchanging truth stands,
because *in Adam all die*, and *his mercy is confirmed

*Ps 116:2
†1 Cor 15:22
‡see 2 Cor 6:2

upon us*,* because *in Christ all shall be made alive*.†
This is that *acceptable time* and *day of salvation*,‡
by which, according to the prophet, *mercy and truth
have met each other*, and yet not as adversaries, as
they seemed till now, but more as embracing, as it

*Ps 84:11

adds: *Justice and peace have kissed*.*

22. This time was foreseen by the one who said,
*You will arise and have mercy on Zion, because it is

*Ps 101:14

its time for mercy, because the time is come*.* Abraham exulted that he might see the day* of the Lord.

*see John 8:56

He saw, and he rejoiced.* The psalmist says about
this day, *This <is> the day that the Lord has made;

*Ps 117:24
*see Ps 34:27

let us exult and be glad in it*.* Therefore *let* everyone
exult and be glad in it;* let *all the nations* praise and
extol, saying, *For his mercy is confirmed upon us*, he

*Ps 116:1-2
*Isa 12:6
*Ps 100:1

whose *truth remains forever*.* *Exult and praise, O
dwelling of Zion*,* singing psalms and saying, *Mercy
and judgment I shall sing to you, O Lord*,* and in
each situation I shall try to respond with appropriate
feelings.

23. How indeed you ought to be feared, O Lord,

*see Ps 93:1
*see Exod 34:14
*Ps 65:5
*see Matt 10:28
*see Zeph 1:12
*see Ps 95:13

God of vengeance:* *God*, your *name* is *the jealous
one*,* *terrible in counsels over the children of human
beings*,* who when you kill the body have the power
of destroying *the body and soul in Gehenna*,* who
are going to search *Jerusalem with lamps** and are
going to judge *the world in fairness*,* to the point
that not an idle word passes by without rendering

*see Matt 12:36
*see Ps 85:5;
see Joel 2:13

an account.* How you ought to be loved, *O Lord,
pleasant and* merciful,* ignoring sin *on account of*

repentance,* not wishing *the death of sinners, but that they be converted and live,* *you who have mercy upon all and hate none of the creatures that you have made.*† How you ought to be loved, you who so love souls that you chose to die rather than not pardon the sinner. Therefore let us fear and love Christ God as much as we can, he who is truly terrible and lovable, *white and ruddy, chosen out of thousands;* he is one with the Father and the Holy Spirit, *God over all things, blessed forever. Amen.*

*Wis 11:24
*Ezek 33:11;
Resp "Tribularer"
in Heb I Quad
(Hesbert 4:7778)
†Wis 11:24-25

*Song 5:10
*Rom 9:5

Sermon 180

On the Feast of All Saints

1. **A**lthough our Lord commends all the virtues to us and urges them upon all of us, nevertheless there is one that he especially loves and sees in us with more satisfaction. This is unity and fraternal love. No other virtue makes us so in accord with God and so terrible to the devil. He now <preaches> this virtue in words, now shows it to us in examples, and invites to its excellence in many ways.

2. For what does it mean that through the year we sometimes celebrate the feast of Blessed Mary, sometimes of Saint Michael, sometimes of John the evangelist, sometimes of Peter, sometimes of John the Baptist, sometimes of Paul, another time the feast of that apostle, of that martyr, of that confessor, of that virgin—<and> today it has been established that we celebrate not only one, but the feast of our Lord God himself, and of all his saints? I think this is the greatest reason: that the unity and concord of that holy city is commended to us. It is a great sign of unity to dedicate one day, one glory, one feast to all at the same time. This is the blessed city that unity unites, concord preserves, charity nourishes, love governs. Blessed is the society in which there is nothing dissonant, nothing divisive, where there is no place of jealousy, where nothing of discordance is evident, where there is one mind, one will, one desire: all things are tranquility. *Blessed is one who has a part in* this city.* *My portion is in the land of the living.**

*see Rev 20:6
*Ps 141:6

360

3. There is the land of the dead, the land of the dying, the land of the living. The land of the dead is where there are none except the dead and severely dead. This is the land where death is without death, which Saint Job, desiring to avoid, said, *Release me, O Lord*, etc.* This land is hell, where there are none except the dead, who are not able to praise God, just as the prophet says: *The dead shall not praise you, O Lord*, etc.* Our confession† is praise‡ of God. The dead are not capable of this. For *confession from the dead perishes as if it might not exist*.# O pitiful land! Woe to those who place their portion here!* Woe to those who build dwellings for themselves in this land! In this land a house is built for adultery, fornication, impurity, hatred, discord. For in that place *no order*, no peace, no concord, *but everlasting horror dwells*,* perpetual anguish in soul and body, continual discord between body and soul.

4. Contrary to this land is the previously mentioned land of the living, where *all are living*,* as the Lord says, *I am the God of Abraham, the God of Isaac, the God of Jacob. He is not <the God> of the dead, but of the living*.* How they live, who can say, who can even imagine? How excellent is the life of angels there, who, as though God's advisers, see in him what he is going to do and, when he so orders, announce it to others! How excellent is the life of the prophets there, who see in reality what with such great joy they awaited in hope! Rightly do they say, *As we have heard, so have we seen*, etc.*

5. How glorious is the life of the apostles there, who present to the Lord so many crowds saved through their teaching! How excellent the splendor of martyrs there, who hold out their wounds to the most victorious Lord! There are also confessors, monks, and hermits there, who through vigils, labors,

*Job 10:20-22

*Ps 113:25
†*confessio*
‡*laus*
#Sir 17:26
*see Ps 49:18

*see Job 10:22

*see Luke 20:38

*Matt 22:32;
see Exod 3:6

*Ps 47:9

and self-control conquered the devil and subdued their own flesh! What shall I say about the virgins, who *follow the Lamb wherever he goes*, who sing that *new song* that *no one can say, except* those who are not *stained* with any ugliness of the flesh?*

*see Rev 14:3-4

6. O how blessed is mother church, which divine honor so illuminates! She *is our mother*, the heavenly Jerusalem, *holy land*, land of the living,* where although there might be a diversity of merits, there is nevertheless one peace and one accord, common joy. And what could be a greater peace, greater accord, than that all—each and every one—love the good of another as much as their own, delight in the happiness of another as much as their own?

*see Gal 4:26;
see Heb 12:22;
see Exod 3:5;
see Ps 141:6

7. Between these two lands, one of the dead, the other of the living, is the middle land of the dying. It is the land in which we are. Here there are none but the dying. The dying are those who are not completely living and not completely dead. Those who are in the land of the dead are completely dead. Those who are in the land of the living are completely living. We are between the two. Therefore it is necessary that we so examine ourselves that we might avoid perfect death and come to perfect life. We ought to do this here.

8. Let all—each and every one—see what and how much they send ahead to that place where they will always remain. Let us see if we can say, *My portion, O Lord, in the land of the living.** Who is it whose *portion* is *in the land of the living*? Certainly those who through God's mercy are so prepared in this life that they are worthy to dwell in that sweet and pleasant city, about which we spoke above.

*Ps 141:6;
see Ps 118:57

9. Carefully pay attention to what Solomon did after he wished to prepare those vessels that he had designed to adorn the temple. *The king cast all the*

vessels, it says, *in a clay ground on the plains of the Jordan.** Let us carefully consider the place and method by which these vessels are prepared. Behold the place: *In a clay ground on the plains of the Jordan.* Behold the method: *He cast them*, it says. There is no need to explain to you who is the true Solomon and the true *peacemaker.** Certainly you know who is not only our peacemaker but even *our peace, who made both one.**

*1 Kgs 7:46;
see 1 Kgs 7:45

*Jerome, Int nom
63 (CCL 72:138)

*Eph 2:14

10. Moreover, I believe it is not unknown to your charity what the temple is for which he prepares appropriate vessels. It is that which is constructed on high from living stones.* An angel was created for the adornment of this temple, and a human being was created; they were created as the best and chosen vessels, so to speak, suitable for divine uses.† But because the human defiled this beauty and rendered himself unworthy of God's temple, it pleased Solomon to reform the deformed, to adorn the disgraceful, and thus to restore vessels for his temple. But where? *On the plains of the Jordan.**

*see Hymn "Urbs
Ierusalem beata,"
str. 1 (Chevalier
2:20933);
see 1 Pet 2:5;
see Heb 1:3
†see Acts 9:15

*1 Kgs 7:46

11. The Jordan signifies baptism because the sacraments of our baptism were established there. That water, the first of all waters, was consecrated by the baptism of Christ himself. The plains of the Jordan signify the extent of the church, in which the water of baptism is certainly retained as though it were the river Jordan. Therefore these vessels are prepared in the church. Whatever is prepared outside the church, whatever is cast, is not fit for the heavenly temple. *On* these *plains of the Jordan* those vessels have been prepared; concerning their excellence we rejoice today. And what more? *In a clay ground.**

*see 1 Kgs 7:46

12. A clay ground is more tenacious* than other grounds. It is hardened by fire and rendered solid. By a clay ground, we here understand the fragility

*tenacior

of the flesh. It certainly is foul and tenacious; the one
wanted to be liberated from its tenacity who said,
Unhappy man that I am, who shall deliver me from
*Rom 7:24 *the body of this death?** Brothers, we have experienced, and often experience, how tenacious this
ground is and how damp, which if not baked in the
fire of tribulation easily soils us. However, those vessels are prepared in this ground, in this flesh, in this
body. For as long as we are in this body we need to
be prepared and molded so that we may be fit for
the beauty of the heavenly temple.

13. Let us see now what he means by these vessels
being molten. When vessels are melted, first a certain
form is made to which the vessels must be molded.
And then once the metal is melted in fire, it is cast in
the form and receives its likeness. You know that we
have been created *according to the image and like-*
*see Gen 1:26-27;
Gen 5:1 *ness of God.** We have disfigured this form in ourselves and strayed from the very form in which we
were created. But this form, the very Wisdom of God,
has remained intrinsically whole, whole in heaven,
whole in the angels. And who would ascend into
heaven to adapt himself again to that form? Therefore the form came to us, indeed the very Power of
see 1 Cor 1:24 God and the Wisdom of God demonstrated in his
life, in his behavior, a certain form of living to which
we need to be molded if we wish to put on our pristine elegance again.

14. But how does our Solomon mold us to this
form? He employs fire; he melts metal. In fact, whoever wishes to be adapted to this form must be inflamed with the fire of charity in order to set aside
the former hardness, to be softened by loving kindness, so that by dying to self one may run back whole
to the form to which one must be formed. Therefore
our Solomon comes *to cast fire on the earth*, which
*see Luke 12:49 he wills *to burn,** and anything in us that is ancient

he kindles and sets on fire. Whatever is tepid or cold becomes hot.

15. Therefore brothers, to speak more plainly, our Solomon melts us by two methods, by the fire of charity and the fire of tribulation. By this double fire we are liquefied and conformed to him. Listen to Paul speaking about one fire: *If we suffer, then we shall also be glorified.** It is as if he were saying, "If we have been melted by the fire of tribulation, then we can be conformed to him." Concerning another fire, listen: *We ought to bear the infirmities of others, and not please ourselves.** This indeed is nothing except to die to self for the sake of charity. So also we can be conformed to our form, that is to Christ.

16. For he was melted, in a way, by a certain fire of charity, when *he emptied himself, taking the form of a servant.** Likewise melted by the fire of tribulation, he cried out on the cross, *My God, my God, why have you forsaken me?** If therefore we wish to be vessels *for an honorable purpose** in that heavenly temple, then let us not avoid being melted in the double fire, let us not avoid being conformed to our form, as long as we are *on the plains of the Jordan*, that is, in the church, as long as we are *in* this *ground of clay,** in this mortality of the flesh.

17. Thus these saints whose feast we celebrate today have been melted. Thus the true Solomon conformed them to himself. Thus their sufferings, thus their works of charity, thus whatever it is they have suffered for Christ and whatever they have done. Know, beloved brothers, that whatever we suffer for Christ in this life, whatever we do according to his charity, we shall wholly recover in that city, *in* that *land of the living.**

18. Accordingly, let us say, and let us say truly, *My portion is in the land of the living.** Not <in>

*Rom 8:17

*Rom 15:1;
see Matt 8:17

*Phil 2:7

*Matt 27:46;
Ps 21:2
*see Rom 9:21

*1 Kgs 7:46

*Ps 141:6

*Ps 141:6

gold, not in silver, not in expensive clothing, not in glorious houses, but *in the land of the living*, where they are truly living, truly rejoicing, where there are those whose feast we celebrate today, well conformed to Christ regarding the soul.* For they have regained *the image and likeness** that had been deformed in them, through the fires of charity and tribulation, by which they have been tempered and melted *on the plains of the Jordan*, that is, in the church of Christ, when they were *in a clay ground*,* that is <in> the fragility of this flesh. Furthermore, they happily await being conformed to Christ also in the body, when *he will conform the body of our lowness, made like the body of his glory.** May the same Lord Jesus Christ deign to lead us to their society, to whom is every glory with the Father and the Holy Spirit through all ages forever. Amen.

*secundum
animam bene
conformes Christo
*see Gen 1:26

*see 1 Kgs 7:46

*Phil 3:21

Sermon 181

On the Feast of All Saints

1. **I**, *John, saw another angel ascending from the rising of the sun, having the sign of the living God, and he cried with a loud voice to the four angels, to whom it was given to harm the earth and the sea, saying, Harm not the earth and sea and trees*, etc.* It is a great glory, a good success, and a desirable honor to serve the supreme and eternal King: *to serve him is to reign*.* He triumphs everywhere in his saints, and he crowns the chosen whom he predestined for life with eternal happiness. What voice or tongue could sufficiently explain those immutable goods that imitators of Christ happily enjoy with Christ!

2. Certainly all of these—even though some are called patriarchs, some prophets, some apostles, some evangelists, some martyrs, some confessors, some virgins—all are nevertheless counted by one name, because each one is called a saint. Even if they were in different situations according to age and sex, according to the excellence and nature of their works, nevertheless they all had one intention: to live *justly, soberly, and piously in this world*,* so after this life they reign eternally with Christ.

3. The holy men have already attained what they sought, because *a great reward** has been provided for them by the Lord. And who will explain it? There is no person on Earth who could describe it by imagining or speaking. For *what eye has not seen nor ear heard, and has not entered into the heart of humankind*,* God has generously granted to his saints, not

*Rev 7:2-3;
see Rev 1:9

*Pro pace
(CO 2:1110;
CCSL 160A:120)

*see Tit 2:12

*see Ps 18:12

*1 Cor 2:9

367

to those who withdraw from his covenant. All these are from the number of *those who were signed*, indeed, the signed themselves, with whom blessed John deals in the present reading.* Let us attentively look at what these great things might signify.

4. *That* perfect *disciple** who was loved more among the loved, *to whom, a virgin, Christ entrusted his virgin mother while on the cross,** said, *I, John, saw another angel ascending from the rising of the sun, having the sign of the living God.†* Who is this angel? He is that *angel of great counsel* about whom we read, *And his name shall be called the angel of great counsel.** This is the angel sent by God to vanquish the powers of the air,* *whom the Father has sent into the world†* to lead his people from Egypt, lest they further serve Pharaoh *in works of clay and brick.‡* This is the kindly and strong angel about whom the prophet says, *The angel of the Lord encamps around those who fear him.** The angel of the Lord, that is, God's Son, *encamps* himself *around those who fear him,* because *wherever* there are *two or three gathered in* his *name,* he is *in their midst,** according to his promise, keeping them safe from evil and strengthening in good.

5. *John* saw this *angel ascending from the rising of the sun.** The first rising of the sun was according to humanity, when the Savior of the world was born of the Blessed Virgin Mary. For he is the *sun of justice, Christ our God.** This sun lay dead when the Redeemer condescended to die on the cross to save his people.† *The sun was darkened and the stars did not give their light,‡* and all things were wrapped in darkness# *as long as the light of the world* lay hidden *in the heart of the earth.§* But again the sun arose when the light of heaven shone from the ground to the world, when God the Father *raised* his Son from

*see Rev 7:4

*see John 21:7, 20

*Ant and Resp in Ioh (Hesbert 3:3423; 4:7000–7001)
†Rev 7:2; see Rev 1:9

*Isa 9:6 (LXX)
*see Eph 2:2; Eph 6:12
†John 10:36
‡see Exod 1:14; Exod 3:10-12

*Ps 33:8

*see Matt 18:20; Matt 24:28

*Rev 7:2; see Rev 1:9

*see Mal 4:2; see Ant Felix and Nat tua in Nat SM (Hesbert 3:2861, 3852)
†see Matt 1:21
‡see Matt 24:29; see Luke 23:45
#see Matt 27:45; see Job 37:19
§see John 8:12; John 9:5; see Matt 12:40

the tomb *and gave him to be made manifest to witnesses preordained by God,** of whom one was John himself.

*Acts 10:40-41

6. Therefore the blessed *John saw an angel ascending from the rising of the sun*, that is, Christ after his resurrection from the depths of the earth, ascending to the heights of heaven, *having the sign of the living God,** that is, the sign of the holy cross. This sign is the sign of life, because through the cross the author of death was vanquished and conquered. Christ had *the sign of the living God* by healing all the infirm and raising the dead.* For *He is* in fact *eternal life,†* who alone rules and vivifies all, having the power of wounding and healing.‡

*Rev 7:2; see Rev 1:9

*see Matt 4:23; Matt 11:5; see Luke 9:1 †see 1 John 5:20; see John 17:3 ‡see Deut 32:39

7. This angel shouts out *with a loud voice*, because *the voice of the Lord is in power, the voice of the Lord is in magnificence*. He shouts to *the four* bad *angels,** who are far from him in the region of unlikeness and are against him, because they oppose all good as much as they can. It says that he shouts at them, because they are unwilling to listen and obey. For if they were to harm humans as much as they want to, then they would kill every race of people at once and plunge them into death with themselves.

*Rev 7:2; Ps 28:4

8. The four angels to whom the *strong and mighty* angel of the Lord shouts* are four types of malign spirits. Obviously some bad spirits make humans rejoice too much in their well-being and presume on their own strength, according to what the prophet says about some people: *They trust in their own strength and glory in the multitude of their riches.** Others make humans grieve too much about their poverty, so they do not have voluntary but rather forced poverty. Others make those who have not yet obtained many riches *hope in the uncertainty of riches** and desire riches that they do not yet have.

*see Ps 23:8

*Ps 48:7

*see 1 Tim 6:17

Some bad spirits, however, make those who neither have nor love riches fear God's yoke too much, the yoke that is sweet,* and do not let them take up the way of holiness, the way that is narrow and arduous and leads to rest.*

*see Matt 11:29-30

*see Matt 7:14

9. Jesus, that is, the Savior, does not shout to these *four angels* with the noise of a voice; rather, he restrains their assault with the authority of a loving examination, lest they harm *earth, sea*, and *trees** as much as they desire to. The name *earth* designates those who have a sense for earthly things,* that is, the greedy who desire gold and silver, honors, and possessions more than God. The *sea* represents carnal people, those who make God bitter to themselves through illicit desires of the flesh; in the manner of the sea they are driven here and there by the blowing of malign spirits as feelings of the flesh compel them. The name *trees* designates the proud, who have been set aflame by the fire of bad spirits, regularly persecuting God's servants in their habits and life, in will and action, now secretly by setting an ambush, now openly by venting rage.

*see Rev 7:2-3

*see Phil 3:19

10. We must note that it does not say, *Harm not the servants of our God*, but *Harm not the earth, sea, and trees.** Obviously the malign spirits cannot harm God's servants by provoking the greedy, the carnal, and the proud to persecute them; rather they harm the persecutors even more. Obviously retribution will be for evil for those who persecute the just. On the other hand, reward will be for good for the just who suffer *persecution for the sake of justice.** Moreover, *we know that for those who love God, all things work together unto good.**

*Rev 7:3

*see Matt 5:10

*Rom 8:28

11. The occasion for persecuting, however, is put off until God's servants are signed *on their foreheads,** that is, on their souls, the more excellent and

*see Rev 7:3

distinguished part of a person. And by what stamp, if not by the sign of faith and the seal of virtues that the Lord teaches in the gospel? Whoever is signed with these virtues is not hurt by the malign spirits. Still, those who have been signed can be troubled by bad spirits. But if they have been fortified by the sign of faith, if by virtue of humility and compassion, gentleness and justice, peace and patience, then they are not hurt by persecutors, but rather corrected and instructed, so they become *heirs of God, and coheirs with Christ.** ·

*Rom 8:17

12. We have lost our dignity through the disobedience of our first parents. But the obedience of Christ has restored it to us, not on this land that sprouts *thorns and thistles,** in which one works and dies, but in that good and pleasant land to which the prophet aspires, saying, *Let my portion, O Lord, be in the land of the living.** As the Lord describes it in today's gospel,† the humble and *the gentle, the meek,* and *the peacemakers,* and the rest of the faithful *will possess* this *land.** But the proud and the puffed-up, the rebellious and unruly gain no portion *in the land of the living*; they disturb this land in which we sojourn, and they persecute the faithful. No one belonging to a hostile nation of vices can have inheritance *in the land of the living,** where the vigor of virtues is always youthful and flourishing.

*see Gen 3:17-19

*Ps 141:6; see Ps 118:57
†Seq (Matt 5:1-12) in OS
*see Matt 5:3-9; see Ps 36:11

*see Ps 141:6

13. For in that place there will be no disturbance, there where there is supreme peace, and no extravagance where there is supreme purity, and no sadness where there is that joy about which the prophet says, *The expectation of the just is joy.** In that place cannot be avarice where there will be no indigence, no scarcity, but abundance of all goods. And in that place there will be no anger, where there is supreme concord *that surpasses all experience.** In that place

*Prov 10:28

*Phil 4:7

there will be no envy, because there are none of the wicked who envy another's goodness. In that place there will be no vainglory, there where everyone *who glories*, glories *in the Lord.***** And in that place there will be no pride, where there is supreme *charity* that *casts out fear** as well as haughtiness.

*see 1 Cor 1:31; see 2 Cor 10:17

*see 1 John 4:18

14. In that place there will only be beatitude, where God manifests to those who love him that ineffable abundance of his sweetness, about which the admiring prophet proclaims, *O how great is the multitude of your sweetness, O Lord, which you have hidden for those who fear you*!* This beatitude of eternal happiness has not been prepared for all, but for those who love God, that is, for all saints who were found faithful in the Lord's law, obeying the Creator's precepts.

*Ps 30:20

15. Therefore, dearest brothers, as long as we sojourn in this world, we must revere and venerate those true and perfect friends of God, so that just as by their example we are taught to take up the way of salvation, so we may merit to attain eternal life by their prayers and merits. May the all-powerful God deign to bestow this on us, he our helper and rewarder, who lives and reigns through all ages forever. Amen.

Sermon 182

On the Feast of All Saints

1. **L**ove the Lord, all you his saints, for the Lord will require truth, and will repay abundantly those who act proudly.* The exceptional virtue of perfect love* seems to be first, and distinguished among the other virtues. Without it every virtue is either empty or utterly useless. For *faith is dead*,* chastity fruitless, hope ineffective, and every virtue empty and void when charity is neglected. So it says through the apostle, *And if I should have all prophecy and should know all mysteries and all knowledge, and if I should have all faith, so that I could remove mountains, and have not charity, then it profits me nothing. And if I should distribute all my resources to the poor, and if I should deliver my body to be burned, and have not charity, then I am nothing.**

*Ps 30:24;
see Ant in OS
(Hesbert 3:2235)
dilectionis

*Jas 2:17

*1 Cor 13:2-3;
see Luke 6:38

2. If therefore you want the following to profit you—fasting, almsgiving, prayer, chastity, self-control, and the other marks of the virtues that you practice by the work of God—then it is necessary for you to have love, though chaste and spiritual. For just as love* is chaste and spiritual, that which dries up all the blight of sins and cleanses the soul, so reconciling her to the Creator, so love is not chaste [when it is] carnal love that nourishes vices, produces corruption, accumulates sins, and subjects the soul to the devil.

amor

3. Therefore pay careful attention to what you love, lest that cunning *serpent* deceive you under the

373

*see Rev 12:9;
Rev 20:2;
see Gen 3:13;
see 1 Pet 5:8

appearance of virtue, *the ancient adversary* who *deceived* the woman in Paradise.* For just as he was accustomed to kill humans through hatred, so he also knows how to harm humans through love. So diligently consider in whom your love rests. If you love God, and what you love you love in God and on account of God,* then you are saints: you have chaste love, holy and perfect love. To this the prophet, or rather the Holy Spirit speaking in the prophet, invites us: *Love the Lord, all you his saints.*†

*Si Deum
diligitis et quod
diligitis, in Deo
et propter Deum
diligitis
†Ps 30:24

4. The reprobate, the lovers of the world who are not worthy of God's love, are not invited to this love. Loving God only belongs to saints, who do not love the world, who flee carnal desires, who spurn temporal goods on account of God. *Love the Lord, all you his saints,** not only in word, but in word and deed, *for the Lord will require truth.** How does *he require truth*, when he is Truth?* How does he require anything, he who is present everywhere and *knows all things?**

*Ps 30:24
*Ps 30:24
*see John 14:6

*1 John 3:20

*Ps 30:24

5. Are you depending on me to investigate the meaning of *the Lord will require truth?** In fact, all-powerful God will require truth, but not in the way that people do, who do not know it and therefore seek it because what they seek is hidden from them. But having power over all things, knowing all, seeing all, *he will require truth*; that is, he will make manifest true love by bestowing rewards, because he will enrich his true lovers with eternal happiness. In such a way *he will require truth*. Or, in another way, "he will require truth" means that he will have received true love.* Those love God in truth who put nothing before his love.†

*veram dilectio-
nem acceptam
habebit
†RB 4.21

6. The reprobate do not truly love God, because they do not love him for his own sake, but on account of the temporal goods that they receive from him.

And hypocrites do not truly love him, but they are liars, feigning truth, since they are false and vain. One can appropriately apply to them what Scripture says: *They blessed with their mouth and cursed with their heart.** The hypocrites bless God with their mouth when they confess him publicly, praising him with their voice, proclaiming his virtues, *signs, and wonders*, his *mercy and judgment.** In that way they bless God with their mouth, but they curse with their heart, because they do all these things not because of God, but because of vainglory and praise of human beings.* So *the Lord* who *will require truth*,† he who searches *hearts and reins*,‡ *who knows all things before they happen*,# says about them, *Amen, I say to you, they have received their reward*,§ certainly not the eternal one *that is stored up** for the saints unto glory, but an empty and transitory one.

7. Behold what it is, that *God will require truth*:* he will render to each person according to his work.* This is God requiring truth: to give to all *according to the way of their devices.*† *Love the Lord, all you his saints*,* not on account of vainglory, like the hypocrites, not on account of obtaining or increasing or retaining money, like the greedy, and finally not on account of human health* itself, which today begins and tomorrow is no more, but rather on account of that eternal one* for which we hope in heaven, where we will enjoy immutable goods with the saints, which will be ours from God, or, more correctly, which will be God himself for us.

8. If God's saints should do their good [works] for the sake of this bodily health,* then Christ's martyrs would never accomplish the work of confession by sacrificing bodily health. But they deserved help for their tribulation, not regarding vanity *and not desiring the day of humanity*;* because *humanity*

*Ps 61:5

*see John 4:48;
see Ps 100:1

*see Matt 6:2
†see Ps 30:24
‡see Ps 7:10
#see Dan 13:42;
see 1 John 3:20
§Matt 6:2, 5
*see Col 1:5;
see 2 Tim 4:8
*Ps 30:24

*see 1 Sam 26:23;
see Ps 61:13;
see Prov 24:29
†Jer 17:10
*Ps 30:24

*salutem

*salutem

*salutem

*see Jer 17:16

*was made similar to vanity, their days pass away like a shadow.** Spurning the adulation of human beings, they gained consolation from God. They gave *glory to God,** because *in the day of* their *tribulation,** they asked him for help, attributing to God all their patience and fortitude and virtue. They confessed Christ as savior before human beings, so that he might confess them before his Father.**

9. Therefore *we* who *have left all things* on account of God,** stirred by the example of these perfect ones, shall proclaim the glory and virtue of Christ in all our <good works>. For we must not do our good [works] on account of the favors of humans, not for the vainglory of the world, and not at all on account of anything other than the glory of God. The Lord himself, wishing to divert the eyes of his disciples from the concupiscence of vanity,** says, *Take heed that you do not your justice before human beings, to be seen by them.** He admonishes us not to worry about money, saying, *Do not hoard treasures on earth for yourselves.** And in another place, *You cannot serve God and mammon.** He even exhorts us not to worry about necessary food and clothing: *Be not solicitous for your life*, he says, *what you will eat, and not for your body, what you will put on.** Finally, lest we suppose that those who live well do their good on account of these temporal goods, he forbids us to judge, saying, *Judge not, and you will not be judged.** Judgment of secrets must be left to the Lord, who sees what is hidden. But as long as we are enclosed in an earthly body,** we can deceive and be deceived in our judgments. God, *who knows all things,** neither deceives nor is deceived. *True and just are* all *his judgments.*†

10. *Love* him, *all you his saints,*‡ you who are lovers of truth. Render all your goods and all glory

*Ps 143:4

*see Ps 67:35;
see Luke 17:18
*see Ps 49:15;
see Jer 16:19

*see Matt 10:32

*see Matt 19:27

*see Ps 118:37

*Matt 6:1

*Matt 6:19

*Matt 6:24

*Matt 6:25

*Luke 6:37

*cadavere

*see 1 John 3:20;
see Dan 13:42;
see Prov 24:12
†Rev 19:2
‡Ps 30:24

and your virtue to him, because he is your glory, he is your blessedness, he is your whole strength. He alone must be glorified in whom and from whom is all that for which we truly boast. *Love the Lord, all you his saints,** so that you love him in all things and extol him over all things. *Love the Lord* not only with your mouth,* but with your heart and mouth. For God is *the inspector of the heart** and the lover of truth. He does not approve but rather despises phony love.

*Ps 30:24

*ore

*see Prov 24:12

11. For there are those who love God insincerely, about whom we read, *They loved him with their mouth, and with their tongue they lied to him.** The Hebrew people, carnal Israel, loved the Lord with their mouth and lied to him with their tongue when they proclaimed his miracles and wonders and yet worshiped *golden calves,** when they proclaimed him as loving, merciful, kind, and mighty and lied to him with their tongue when their heart withdrew from him,* when they proposed returning to Egypt, barking against Moses, *It was good for us when we sat over the flesh pots.**

*Ps 77:36

*see 1 Kgs 12:28-30

*see Jer 17:5

*see Exod 16:3

12. There are two things that greatly hinder and separate a person from love of the Creator: love of the world and forgetfulness of God's good deeds. Love of the world nourishes carnal attachments, embraces earthly and transitory goods, and rarely contemplates unchanging and eternal goods. Forgetfulness of God's good deeds takes away contemplation of eternal blessedness, brings forth torpor, nourishes weariness, heaps up boldness in committing sin. Forgetfulness is the grave of good deeds. Who will acknowledge the Lord in the grave or in hell?* In that place all things waste away as in death.

*see Ps 6:6

13. *Do not love the world,** lovers of God, but *love the Lord, all you his saints,** *because for those*

*1 John 2:15

*Ps 30:24

*Rom 8:28

who love him *all things work together unto good.**
Call to mind his good deeds at all times, so that you
may always grow in his love. No occupation is more
useful, no concern more agreeable, no thought more
sweet than continual recollection of God's benefac-
tions. These make a soul fervent in love of her
Creator. These compel the soul to be zealous for honorable thoughts and good deeds and join the person
to God.

14. Therefore, let this recollection always grow
strong in our hearts, so that it unites us to God.
Nothing is sweeter, nothing more pleasant, nothing
more useful than to cling to God and obey his precepts. Let us ask the Lord to strengthen us in his love
and make us continually recall his good deeds. Let
us imitate the saints whose glory we proclaim today
so that we may merit to attain their fellowship. May
the Lord Jesus Christ deign to bestow this on us, he
who lives and reigns with the Father and Holy Spirit,
God through all ages forever. Amen.

A Sermon Upon the Translation of
Saint Edward, Confessor

Upon the Translation of
Saint Edward the Confessor[1]

1. **B**rothers, rejoice* and give thanks to God, the bountiful giver of all good things, for a holy day has begun to dawn upon us, a solemn day, the feastday* of Edward, glorious king of the English, your patron, your protector, your defender, the intercessor for your sins, and the founder of your church. This is the day, I declare, of that most holy confessor of Christ, whose whole illustrious life from boyhood to old age shone brightly with virtues and miracles.* In particular it is told that although he was king he did not forsake humility, that in marriage he never violated the chastity he had always maintained, and since neither turtle-dove nor dove* was available for sacrifice he would offer in himself, a living and holy victim, the innocence of humility and the perseverance of chastity. He took a wife indeed of noble blood but nobler character, likewise a virgin outstanding in beauty, greatly skilled in letters, in many arts, and even in crafting precious things from gold and silver. Yet this virgin consecrated to

*see 2 Cor 13:11;
Phil 3:1

*see Exod 12:16

*see Esth 3:13

*Luke 2:24;
see Gen 15:9;
Lev 1:14; 5:11, etc.

[1] This sermon was translated by Tom Licence from the single manuscript in the Peterborough Central Library. It is reprinted by permission from *Cistercian Studies Quarterly*, where it first appeared together in Peter Jackson's article (with critical edition) "*In translacione sancti Edwardi confessoris*: The Lost Sermon by Ælred of Rievaulx Found?" CSQ 40, no. 1 (2005): 45–83. Paragraph numbers have been added in this printing. Jackson argues that Aelred preached the sermon at Westminster Abbey before King Henry II on the October 13, 1163, occasion of that translation.

God undertook to remain all the while in union with the virgin so that each of them is believed to have obtained from God the dotal contract of virginity.

2. Think, brethren, how great is this king of yours, who in the midst of riches, luxuries, and popular applause was neither wounded in his heart by pride nor polluted in his body by incontinence; no, indeed, he preserved the integrity of both unharmed, of his heart through humility, of his body through chastity. Consider therefore what virtue was in this king; how the charm of a noble and beautiful woman, among abundant riches and copious delights, was unable to overcome the constancy of his spirit,* to violate his vow of virginity, or in any way to draw this holy man into the embrace allowed by law, approved by the fathers, advantageous for the age,* and necessary for the succession to the throne. Indeed the king devoted to God elected to forsake his temporal heirs that an inheritance might be his in eternity.

*see Jdt 9:14

*Ps 144:15; 2 Macc 4:32; 14:5

3. What can I say about his humility? Inasmuch as Scripture is my tutor and my own conscience my guide, his life, it seems, is seen truthfully depicted in those words of the gospels where one reads according to Luke that *a dispute arose among Jesus' disciples as to who among them was seen to be greater,* etc.* For since this king was the greater and worthy of precedence he became as a subordinate and an attendant, and in the midst of his servants he was not the one who lies at ease, as it were, but the one who attends.* As a result he deserved, along with the rest of the elect, to hear the Lord say, *I assign to you my kingdom as my father has assigned it to me, that you may eat and drink at my table in my kingdom.* Read the books written about his life by our holy fathers, and it will be found that this king was pious in spirit, often in silence, discreet in speech,

*Luke 22:24

*Luke 22:26-27

*Luke 22:29-30

thoughtful in council, prudent in judgment, of modest countenance, moderate in behavior, gentle in carriage, in gait regular, abandoned always to all works of mercy, and, in short, well-disposed with the entirety of his character to the mold of honest living.

4. It was proof of his great humility that when a poor cripple requested it out of reverence for Saint Peter the lofty king lowered his neck to him and offered himself as a beast of burden to bear the beggar whom he heard had been sent away from him. While he was carried this man was healed, and the more the ulcerous pus flowed over the royal purple the more his returning health straightened the long-crippled sinews and strengthened the members lengthy illness had oppressed. Behold another Elisha! The one revived a dead man thrown onto him by the touch of his holy bones,* while the other healed a cripple set *see 2 Kgs 13:21 upon his back by the medicine of carrying him and Vulg the touch of his holy body alone. Nor is any man advised to say that it is better to restore the dead to life than to heal a cripple, for each, inasmuch as each is great, is wonderful. And as long as God can appear magnificent and wondrous in each it is not ours to inquire which of the two should take precedence, for the same Holy Spirit works all things in all,* giving *1 Cor 12:6 to each as he determines.* He who worked this mir- *1 Cor 12:11 acle in the dead prophet (to show how great in life was he who deserved to obtain so much through God's works after departing his body) also performed a sign in the living king to reveal his great eternal inheritance, who in this miserable life and still oppressed by the monstrous flesh could bring this thing and others like it to pass.

5. A comparable marvel in this blessed king was that he exerted a spirit of prophecy, a gift through which unhesitating testimonies attest that he saw

many things and foresaw many future things in the spirit and in absence. Many things could detain us, but I will say a few words about the drowning of the king of the Danes in Denmark and how the Seven Sleepers in Greece turned over from one side to the other.

6. Now the traditions of our holy fathers (of those who played a part in the stories of the aforesaid king and with revelations attested his honesty by the proven truth of the events) assert that when the king was resting in Westminster palace on the holy day of Easter with his nobles and bishops, he spied the Seven Sleepers on Mount Celion turning over onto the opposite side. It came to light that the strangeness of such a miracle signaled a dire omen, attesting it most truthfully, as the outcome of events later proved beyond doubt.

7. On the holy day of Pentecost moreover, while he stood by the altar of the Holy Trinity in Westminster to hear the solemn service of the Mass, he saw Sven, king of the Danes, his armies prepared and his ships drawn up, hurrying to ransack England. Preparing to climb into his ship from a little boat his foot slipped, he toppled between the two and drowned, and by his death he freed both peoples, that is the Danes and the English, at once from sin and danger. For that nation led their ships back to shore and returned home in peace, while our people, as if Pharaoh had been conquered and our enemies put to flight, passed easy days and an age full of peace from then thereafter in great tranquility under this new Moses.

8. To whom indeed, O great king, O sweetest lord and most cherished father, to whom, I say, will I more truthfully liken you than to that greatest legislator and prince of the Hebrews who, as Scripture says,

was the meekest of all the men who tarried on earth?*   *Num 12:3
Who assuredly protected God's people by law, armed
them with faith, served them with good counsel, fortified them with prudence, with wisdom ruled them,
defended them with arms, raised them up with
prayers, and, as much in times of peace as in times
of war, devoted to God, undertook with paternal
affection to nurture and love them, or more fiercely
to convict and with harsher punishments to chastise
the proud and the rebels? Let us observe that all these
things, whether the life, the behavior, or indeed the
actions and total excellence of Moses most fittingly
converge upon this Moses of ours, upon this our
legislator. For this man appeared as the meekest
among his people,* filled with wisdom and the grace   *Num 12:3
of God, and established a law and dictated justice
for his nation (which he found as uneducated as she
was untamed), according to which matters are settled
and verdicts determined unto this day in the kingdom
of the English.

9. That which he taught with words, moreover,
he fulfilled with actions, and those same things he
advised to be done he demonstrated in his own actions beforehand. The Lord summoned Moses out
of Midian to rule his people,* and this our Moses,   *see Exod 3–4
recalled from Neustria, was put in charge of the English people, as had been foreseen by wonders and
revealed by oracles. One was pursued by Egyptians,
the other by Danes. One freed his people from Pharaoh's tyrannical oppression by divine virtue; the
other, armed with God's grace, shook off from the
necks of his people the fetter of servitude and the
yoke of captivity that the Danes had imposed. One,
after the wicked king had drowned, sang praises to
the Lord with hymns and timbrels for the victory
obtained.* The other announced that perpetual   *see Exod 15:1-21

peace had been delivered unto every border of the
English now that King Sven had been overwhelmed
by the waves, and in order that they should thereafter
exert themselves more earnestly with divine praises
now the enemy had been conquered, he roused them
with a wholesome exhortation. Thus all England
rejoices and exults, over whose whole realm this man
presided, acting at that time more like a father than
a judge, offering mercy instead of censure and, as
much as was permissible without jeopardizing the
peace, leniency rather than punishment.

10. In the remotest confines of the realm he made
peace, rebuking the unruly,* pronouncing justice and
straightening the crooked, doing good and chastising
the errant until tyrannical presumption had no opportunity to contrive evil, presumptuous injustice
lacked the power to harm, and servile discord found
no capacity to torment. All England rejoices, I say,
which this holy king endowed with laws, with customs adorned, tamed at his command, educated by
his sagacity, strengthened by his faith, molded by his
example, raised up by his authority, ornamented with
his sanctity, and, leveling superiors and inferiors to
a certain equality, ordered throughout its realm with
judgment and justice (for justice and judgment prepared his throne).* As a result, in all his works mercy
and truth preceded the king's face;* with these he
calmly tempered the entire business of his realm so
that the profligate would not evade their due punishment of condemnation and devout minds would find
with him rewards befitting their integrity. This
learned and prudent man elected to hold forth in his
own personality that which was appropriate to
whomsoever he met: to the good he displayed in
himself that which they would love, to the perverse
that which they would fear. He preferred to mend

*see 1 Thess 5:14

*Ps 88:15

*Ps 88:15

the tears in our morals than to pile up riches, and to invest in souls, a more demanding sacrifice, than to spend money on material things. Truly it is as the Lord says: *Everyone who has will be given more and will have it in abundance,** and likewise *Seek first the kingdom of God, and all good things will be yours as well.** For since this holy king established divine charity and love in his heart the supernal grace bestowed upon him made him abound in all good things, and since his first concern was to seek and preach the kingdom of God,* worrying not after his own affairs but after those of Jesus Christ, all things better than could be wished for in this life were added to his lot and added in abundance.

*Matt 25:29

*Matt 6:33

*Matt 6:33

11. Almighty God, rich to all who call upon him,* *in whom all the treasures of wisdom and knowledge are hidden,** filled the mind of his saint with such wisdom and glorified his whole realm with such works that it can be truly said of him (as is read of Solomon) that "the glorious king exceeded all the kings of the earth in riches and wisdom, and the whole world desired to see his face that it might hear the wisdom God put into his heart."* For indeed the emperors of the Franks and the Germans and as many kings and princes in the surrounding area as were close enough to hear of this great man, sending messengers and many gifts, humbly beseeched him for his friendship and fraternity, and submitted themselves, their kindred, and their men to him as though to a father and lord, to the extent that he ordained that his will and command be obeyed in all these realms as in his own. Anyone who had acquired any agreement of friendship with King Edward they called blessed, for God was with him, and through him this man prospered in all things he did, and he guided all his works.* The opulence consequently

*Rom 10:12

*Col 2:3

*1 Kgs 10:23-24 Vulg; see 2 Chr 9:22-23

*see Gen 39:23; 39:2

acquired throughout the whole of England under the peace that had been obtained and the sanctity of the king was such as one reads of in the age of the afore-mentioned Solomon: *silver was like stones, and they abounded with much gold.** Rarely would a poor man be seen unless, perchance, if his own wickedness or innate stupidity had driven him into want.

12. And so England rejoices and with all devotion honors the fame of this day which God, for the glo-rification of his saint, illuminated with the solitary celestial stars* and lit up with the glories of everlast-ing renown. The whole world rejoices but especially, brothers, we whom this holy king's esteem elects to be the elite servants of his innermost bed-chamber and deems capable of preserving his holy body, venerating his trophies like so many bridegrooms.* Others have his generosity; we have him. He enriched not only English churches but also many French ones with gold and silver along with estates and diverse possessions. To us however he bequeathed something of greater worth than all, of a price beyond the value of every other precious thing: that is to say, he com-mitted the priceless treasure of his incorrupt body to our sole keeping. For in this monastery that he him-self had constructed in honor of the chief of the holy apostles Peter he chose his burial place, where signs and miracles ceaselessly illuminate the goodness of almighty God, and the magnitude of the virtue of his most holy confessor King Edward is manifested with a clearer light, as he reveals himself who lives and reigns for ever, world without end, Amen.

*see generally, 1 Kgs 10:14-22 Vulg; 2 Chr 9:13-21

*see Wis 50:6

*paranimphos

INDICES

Comprehensive Scripture Index of Aelred's Liturgical Sermons

References are to sermon and paragraph.
SEC = Sermon for Edward the Confessor

Genesis

1:1-2	4.13		155.7; 179.11; 180.18	2:17	39.19; 57.2; 79.3; 86.5; 132.6, 8; 143.10; 170.3; 179.15, 16, 18, 19
1:1	42.9; 66.5; 68.5, 6; 173.5	1:27-29	27.19		
		1:27	28.17; 34.7; 41.22; 67.9, 12; 107.17		
1:2	4.13; 68.5; 74.76; 78.16, 18; 133.12			2:23	75.6
1:2-3	41.17	1:28	49.5	2:24	2.12; 41.10; 50.23; 51.3, 19; 74.11; 165.6
1:3	4.12; 27.12	1:31	77.26; 179.11		
1:4	55.12	2:1-2	70.35	3:1-6	124.15; 125.3
1:5	27.12; 42.9	2:1	27.20	3:1-2	179.18
1:6-7	27.13	2:2	41.13, 22; 53.21; 86.4; 121.5	3:1	54.41; 59.8; 86.3; 122.4; 132.6; 143.10; 145.4; 179.17
1:6	27.14; 42.10				
1:7	41.18	2:6	39.3; 55.19; 69.20		
1:8	42.10, 11			3:2-3	143.10
1:9	27.16; 42.13	2:7	49.6; 86.3; 109.3	3:2	59.28
1:10	66.5	2:8	39.1; 179.1, 11, 12	3:3	57.2; 59.27; 79.3; 88.2; 106.6; 122.4; 132.6; 143.10
1:11-12	42.13; 162.12	2:9	39.19; 40.3; 57.2; 59.7, 24, 7; 79.3; 88.2; 106.6, 7; 168.10; 175.11; 179.1		
1:11	27.16				
1:12	10.5; 39.12; 41.19			3:4-5	49.6; 132.6; 143.10; 179.19
1:14-18	162.13	2:10	39.8; 55.19, 20, 32; 109.7; 168.10	3:4	86.5; 122.4; 125.4; 179.19, 21
1:14-17	48.10				
1:14	55.12	2:11-12 Vulg	39.8	3:5	3.23; 11.14; 27.10; 35.20; 40.3; 49.6; 57.11; 59 n2; 59.8, 29; 61.8; 79.11; 104.5; 116.8; 122.4, 5, 9; 143.11; 179.20
1:16	27.17; 41.20; 71.2	2:13	39.13		
1:20	27.18; 124.17	2:14	39.15, 16		
1:21	41.21; 89.2	2:15	59.25; 179.12		
1:26-27	75.9; 103.1; 109.10; 180.13	2:16-17	59.27, 28; 143.10; 179.11, 12		
1:26	3.4; 34.8; 67.8, 11; 108.6; 150.9;				

51:23	14.16; 47.15; 138.13	59:3	28.11; 95.16	1:7-8	134.12
52:2	78.13; 104.1, 2; 104.4, 5, 7, 9; 154.9	59:7	28.11; 94.14; 96.17	1:7	134.1–4, 6, 14, 16
		60:1	2.9; 4.5, 15, 17, 23	1:8	134.6
52:3	104.5, 8	60:2	4.20, 23	1:10	69.7
52:4	50.13	60:3	4.27; 76.24	1:11	161.9
52:5	110.2	60:4	110.16	1:13	55.4; 76.29
52:10	1.3	60:6	110.19	1:14	179.7
52:14	11.19	60:8	16.4	1:16	130.4
53:2-3	11.21; 26.24; 78.2, 3	60:11	127.8	2:6	56.3
		60:19	74.77	2:20	62.16; 63.12; 74.10
53:4-5	30.6	61:1	48.9; 50.10; 69.19	2:20 Vulg	43.20
53:4	51.6; 63.14; 80.7; 119.5	61:6	28.12; 64.5	2:22 LXX	107.11
		61:10	112.18; 118.27; 169.3; 174.11	2:27	130.4
53:5	80.7			2:35	51.12
53:6	59.1	62:2	96.7	2:36	72.10
53:7	9.13; 45.27; 58.15; 60.11	62:5	74.10	3:1	62.16; 74.10
		62:6	73.11; 130.12; 178.8	3:3	72.13
53:8-9	74.5			3:6	62.12, 16; 74.10
53:8	74.23; 111.2; 176.3	62:11	85.7	3:8	74.10
		62:11 LXX	135.10	3:9	63.12
53:12	32.22; 67.4	63:1	124.10–13, 22, 27, 28, 37, 38	3:14	74.10
54:1	107.2, 3; 124.5			4:10	28.30
54:6	107.2	63:3	12.23; 65.10	5:8	76.5
54:11	63.13	64:1	1.22–24, 27; 50.22; 101.14	6:10	98.4
55:2	74.35			6:11	83 n9
55:6	104.13	64:3	1.27–29, 36	6:14	87.5; 92.4, 6
55:7	80.23; 104.13; 150.2	64:6	178.1	9:1	125.9
		65:2	134.4	9:21	28.10
56:3	177.21	65:15	2.13; 96.7	9:23	71.4
56:10	64.13	65:20	43.9	10:21	64.13
57:1	74.16	66:1	58.5; 140.3	10:24	10.11
57:21	149.1	66:2 LXX	74.24; 101.10; 128.10	11:19	11.31
58:1	101.12; 178.1–5, 7, 8, 13, 14, 16			11:20	147.22
		66:10	29.2, 4	12:10	28.31
58:3	52.22–24	66:12	92.12, 13	13:23	43.16
58:4	52.26, 27	66:23	94.10	14:19	92.7, 10
58:5	53.9; 53.16	66:24	72.19; 107.14; 128.15	15:10	118.2; 148.2
58:6	53.9, 13, 16, 17, 19, 20, 23			15:17	124.26
		67:9	92.14	16:16	175.15
58:7	27.18; 53.23, 24; 74.66; 102.11,12	**Jeremiah**		16:19	182.8
				16:21	132.12
58:11-13	43.5	1:6	49.9	17:5	54.32; 182.11
59:2	22.7; 83.10			17:10	182.7

6:27	87.2; 130.1	**Amos**		2:16		87.10
7:9	9.26	3:6	57.16	3:2		155.5
7:9 Vet Lat	60.19	3:15	90.13	3:6		169.3
7:10	74.3	4:12	101.14; 119.2	3:13		108.9
7:14	110.7	5:14	170.1	3:15		47.33
10:3	53.22	5:15	170.5			
10:11	72.7	6:14	54.36	**Zephaniah**		
10:20	40.6	8:11	64.2; 69.6,	1:12		179.23
12:1	76.11; 87.2		16; 71.9	1:15	85.4, 10, 11
13:5	74.12			1:18		101.2
13:42-45	130.9	**Obadiah**				
13:42	182.6, 9	1:4	45.9	**Haggai**		
13:45-62	135.6			1:6	31.24; 54.38
13:55	86.5	**Jonah**		2:8	1.2; 1.58; 24.44
13:56	171.11	2:1	61.13; 62.20			
13:59	86.5	2:3	125.23	**Zechariah**		
		2:11	61.14; 62.23	1:14		50.14
Hosea		3:4	104.10	3:1		75.49
2:6	116.7, 10–12	3:4-10	105.4	5:7-8	9.7; 53.11;
2:7	74.10; 116.13–14				60.6; 104.3
2:14	168.15	**Micah**		5:7		56.14
2:23-24	50.26	1:3	85.7	5:10-11		53.11
4:2	95.16	2:7	97.11	6:12		110.8
4:6	105.3; 110.6	3:5	74.49	8:19	53.2, 8, 21,
6:3	125.11; 143.3	4:1	28.8		22, 26
7:13	2.10	4:2	27.2	9:9	48.6; 175.1
10:11	178.6	5:2	88.2; 93.5	9:17		50.37
11:4	93.7	5:5-6	92.7	12:10	24.45; 166.9
11:7	86.2	5:5	92.8, 10	13:1	55.20; 119.10
12:1	54.36	5:6	92.8			
12:3	74.33	7:1	63.1	**Malachi**		
13:14	61.13; 62.20;	7:5	74.49	1:11	30.13; 31.7
	108.1, 5; 161.6	7:19	80.7	2:7	50.6; 58.6
				3:1-2		111.1
Joel		**Habakkuk**		3:1	44.21, 22, 24;
1:6	31.25	1:2	7.13		50.6; 69.12; 137.16,
1:17	28.28; 102.9;	1:14 LXX	175.7		17, 19
	103.6; 110.20;	1:15-16	175.8, 12	3:2		111.2
	124.24	1:15	175.7, 13	3:10-11	105.7, 12
2:10	58.1	1:16	175.8	3:10	105.8, 10
2:13	3.12; 105.10;	1:17	175.8, 12	3:11		105.11
	179.23	2:1	32.4; 74.75, 76	3:20		45.43
2:17	28.30	2:3	85.10	4:2	45.13; 62.6;
2:28-30	133.15	2:4	66.10; 121.16, 34		63.12; 73.14;
3:18	93.12	2:6	54.24		74.3; 76.11; 93.12;

Comprehensive Index of Classical, Patristic, and Medieval Citations in Aelred's Sermons

Because the abbreviations used in the various volumes of Aelred's sermons in translation take a variety of forms, this index cites the works by full Latin title, with citations to sermons and paragraphs or notes. It does not include Aelred's own sermons or liturgical references.[1]

Acta Sancti Vincentii
2.7	176.14, 20
2.9, 12	176.14
3.14	176.15

Ambrose
De Paradiso
1.4	39.3
3.12	39.3
3.14	39.9
3.15–16	39.13
3.17	39.15
3.18	39.16

De Virginitate
3.4	124.33

Expositio Euangelii Lucae
6.13	150.3
6.14	150.4
6.17–18	150.11
6.18–21	150.12

Expositio psalmi CXVIII
16.45	179.14

Hymns
"Aeterna rerum conditor,"
vv. 21, 18,
20	136.17

"Veni, redemptor gentium"
	159.7
Hymn 7, v. 1	74.26

Ambrosius Autpertus
S 208.4 (In Assumptione
4 = Ps–Augustine)
	49.1

Thomas Aquinas
Summa Theologica I,
q. 63, a. 2	80 n4

Augustine
De Civitate Dei
1.26	52.3
10.1	42.10; 54 n1
11.5	66.4
11.21	66.4, 5
13.13–15	84 n2

---

[1] For the two indices in this volume, as in all but the first of the translated volumes of Aelred's sermons, we are indebted to Emily Stuckey.

44 69.14
50 2.8, 4.8; 7.14; 15.34; 26.41; 34.10; 45.31, 34, 37; 48.1; 65.5; 71.23; 78.16; 82.3; 97.2; 126.12; 133.17
51 110.19
54 24.40
56 160.4
58 74.73
60 2.14, 15, 17, 18; 13.18; 15.31; 123.12; 126.12
62 1.52; 2.36; 35.14; 38.15; 77.11; 79.13; 118.19; 146.2; 163.9
63 1.17; 4.8; 14.12; 24.21, 43; 26.25; 71.25; 138.9; 153.1; 180.9
64 13.34; 38.12, 14; 57.6; 61.2, 2; 64.9, 11; 65.4 19; 67.21; 75.15; 79.9, 13; 123.20; 145.4; 175.3
65 76.16, 17, 19; 77.15; 151.1; 175.20, 21
66 3.26; 4.3, 10; 58.28; 175.20, 22
67 152.2
68 35.4; 143.3; 144.23; 147.11, 27
69 14.4; 74.73; 138.3; 145.4
70 119.12
71 15.31; 149.14
72 107.12, 17; 152.2, 5
73 8.2; 9.5, 6; 47.20; 54.6; 60.5; 117.2; 152.2; 161.10; 166.6
74 24.21, 44
76 107.8, 17
77 12.16; 54.22; 147.3
78 54.7, 30; 62.6; 63.12; 65.6, 18; 124.5; 143.3
79 3.2
80 9.9; 60.7; 77.15

Epistolae
52:3 20.22
108.10 3.39

In Matthaeum
1 24.13
1.3.13 100.11

Tractatus in Psalmos
5.2 172.9, 10
5.3 172.11
5.4 172.12, 13
5.5 172.16

PsJerome
Breviarium in Psalmos
59 110.13
72 144.15
Epistolae
Ep ad Augustinum (Ep 75.4) 135.13
Ep 9.2 = Pascasius Radbertus, *De Assumptione S. Mariae Virginis* (Ass)
2.10 70.6; 169.14

Passio Sancti Andreae Apostoli 12
  (Acta Apostolorum Apocrypha 2.1)
                175.23
Peter Chrysologus
  Sermon
    143.5   60.10
  Martyrium B Petri
    12   70.6
Pliny
  Naturalis historia
    2.9.6.45   67 n3
    8.18.46   136.13
    8.19.48   136.13
    8.19.49   136.13
    8.19.52   136.13
Proverbia
    2:708, 13614   140.1
    7:460, 35860   146.11
Prudentius
  Peristephanon
    5.189   52.15
Rabanus Maurus
  In III Reg
                69.7
  In Matthaeum
    2.20   175.20
  Rhetorica
    3.2.3   140.3
Rufinus
  Eccl hist
    1.11   145.2
Sedulius
  Paschalis Carmen
    2   153.10; 159.4;
                164.3

Seneca
  Epistulae
    92   96.9
    113   28.12
Sulpicius Severus
  Epistulae
    3.16   101.5
    3.21   173.9
    27.1–2   173.13
  Vita Sancti Martini
                101.5; 173.9,
                13
Terence
  Andria
    1   55.28
Venantius Fortunatus
  "Pange lingua," v. 4
                119.1; 176.5
PsVenantius Fortunatus
  "Quem terra, pontus, sidera"
                57.4
Vergil
  Aeneid
    3.39   79.1
    6.733   118.3
  Georgica
    2.384   145.6
Vitae Patrum
  6. *Verba Seniorum*
    1, 9   147.5
William of Saint-Thierry
  Brevis commentatio in Cantica
    canticorum
    23   150.6, 7